"A solid and well-documented investigation into the Women's Liberation Movement in France: its actions, its components, its relations with previous generations, and its painful internal conflicts. It reveals the very important role played by radical and materialist feminists. It is an effective antidote against the invention of 'French feminism' by some American scholars."

—**Sylvie Chaperon**, professor of contemporary and gender history at the University of Toulouse Jean Jaurès, Laboratory FRAMESPA

"Finally! In Lisa Greenwald's remarkable book on the history of French feminism after World War II, she restores overlooked feminist activists of the 1950s and 1960s to their rightful place."

—**Sarah Fishman**, associate dean for undergraduate studies, College of Liberal Arts and Social Sciences at the University of Houston

"Lisa Greenwald introduces anglophone audiences to the breadth and depth of 'Second Wave' feminism in France. Her bold analysis encompasses much more than theory by restoring to us the complexity of the activist components of the Mouvement de Libération des Femmes."

—**Karen Offen**, senior scholar, Michelle R. Clayman Institute for Gender Research at Stanford University

"'Femininity' and 'womanhood' had long been expressions of women's power and the root of their identity in French society,' writes Lisa Greenwald. Her lively, smart, and thoroughly researched book shows how those terms—and the power arrangements and identities they stood for—were revised, reinterpreted, and repudiated.... The fiftieth anniversary of May '68 will direct new attention to its powerful aftershocks. Feminism was one of those aftershocks, and Greenwald's book will be part of our reappraisal of this historical moment."

—**Judith G. Coffin**, associate professor of history at the University of Texas at Austin

"This is the book you need in order to grasp the complex history of French Second Wave Feminism."

—**Bibia Pavard**, senior lecturer in history, Center for Interdisciplinary Research and Analysis of Media (CAR Paris II

DAUGHTERS OF 1968

DAUGHTERS OF 1968

—

Redefining French Feminism and the Women's Liberation Movement

Lisa Greenwald

University of Nebraska Press | Lincoln and London

Library of Congress Cataloging-in-Publication Data

Names: Greenwald, Lisa (historian), author.

Title: Daughters of 1968: Redefining French feminism and the women's liberation movement / Lisa Greenwald.

Description: Lincoln: University of Nebraska Press, [2018] | Includes bibliographical references and index.

Identifiers: LCCN 2018028387

ISBN 9781496207555 (cloth: alk. paper)

ISBN 9781496217714 (paper: alk. paper)

ISBN 9781496212016 (epub)

ISBN 9781496212023 (mobi)

ISBN 9781496212030 (pdf)

Subjects: LCSH: Feminism—France—History—20th century. | Women's rights—France—History—20th century.

Classification: LCC HQ1613 .G685 2018 | DDC 305.420944/0904—dc23 LC record available at https://lccn.loc.gov/2018028387

Set in Lyon Text by Mikala R. Kolander.

In memory of
B. G.
and
B. F.-G.,
Two mothers
who started it all

To emancipate woman is to refuse to confine her to the relations she bears to man, not to deny them to her; let her have her independent existence and she will continue none the less to exist for him also: mutually recognizing each other as subject, each will yet remain for the other an other. The reciprocity of their relations will not do away with the miracles—desire, possession, love, dream, adventure—worked by the division of human beings into two separate categories; and the words that move us—giving, conquering, uniting—will not lose their meaning. On the contrary, when we abolish the slavery of half of humanity, together with the whole system of hypocrisy that it implies, then the "division" of humanity will reveal its genuine significance and the human couple will find its true form.

Simone de Beauvoir, *The Second Sex*

Many of you asked us who we are. We are women. Women who no longer accept:

› To be destined from birth to give free domestic labor, seven days a week;

› To be educated for this in submissiveness and passivity;

› To be refused any professional or vocational training;

› To be treated like merchandise on the streets; to be insulted when we dare to consider ourselves as people;

› To work for wages that are systematically inferior to those of men, without escaping the tasks of our "sacrosanct role" at home;

› To not even have the right to manage our own bodies and our own lives since the men who rule us impose upon us their laws to perpetuate the species.

We are 27 Million. United, we represent a force capable of radically transforming our situation and imposing the means of our liberation.

Flyer of Mouvement de Libération des Femmes
(Women's Liberation Movement)

CONTENTS

ILLUSTRATIONS

Following page 216

ACKNOWLEDGMENTS

This project has been the work of more than two decades and, as such, has benefited from the help of many—scholars, librarians and archivists, friends, editors, the French government, a multiyear Andrew W. Mellon Foundation Fellowship, historical subjects, and a spouse—only some of whom are mentioned below but to all of whom I owe a large debt. To single out but a few: My first thank-you goes to Sarah Fishman, who never forgot the importance of this project and who pointed me in the right direction, and to my editor Alisa Plant, who embraced the project and has seen it to fruition. As contemporary as this history was when I began, the project would not have been half as rich had it not been for the generous offerings of movement women who ransacked their closets and files for old papers to show me, offered me other contacts, and granted me long interviews.

The following scholars read and commented on this work as it was being developed and went out of their way to do so. For their efforts to help me shape and think through this large project and their sage and detailed critiques, I want to thank Kathryn E. Amdur, Sylvie Chaperon, Judith G. Coffin, Monique Dental, Laura Lee Downs, Judith Ezekiel, Sarah Fishman, Elizabeth Fox-Genovese, Rachel G. Fuchs, Nancy L. Green, Marie-Victoire Louis, Margaret A. Lourie, Judith A. Miller, Claire Moses, Mary E. Odem, Karen M. Offen, Françoise Picq, Keith Reader, Sandrine Sanos, Bonnie G. Smith, and Danielle Voldman. Many friends and family members encouraged me over the years to make this book a reality and helped me in ways large and small, from advising on translations to offering tea and sympathy; but in particular, I want to thank Laurence Bessac, Linda Blaustein, Sophie Boxer, Peter Cariani, Catherine Cruveilher, Ruth Dickens, Antonella Fabri,

Laura Goldin, Vicki Greenwald, Anne-Claire Nguyen Haye, Claudine Jurkovitz, Laurence Lagane, Audrey P. Lavin, Frank Lavin, Maud K. Lavin, Philippe Michaud, Gail Cavat-Negbaur, Michèle Perrin, Anne-Christine Potocka, Agnès Saint-Raymond, Lynn Sharp, Jamie Stanesa, Lucy Tart, Maris Wacs, the late Nori Nke Aka, and my late parents, Beverly and Michael Greenwald.

Finishing this book and teaching full-time has not been an easy task, but it has been wonderful to work with excellent, curious, and passionate students and colleagues at Stuyvesant High School who remind me every day that robust intellectual discourse is not only the purview of universities. Jennifer Suri and Eric Contreras helped me to be both a full-time teacher and a scholar—I could not have done both without their support. James Waller and Martha Ash provided excellent granular editing. Mary V. Dearborn, longtime mentor and friend, encouraged this and many other of my intellectual and professional projects over the decades, for which I am deeply grateful.

Daughters Simone and Eleanor Lavin have always reminded me of the importance of feminism and have demonstrated how these ideas live on through the next generation, molded and changed by the times and also added to in unexpected ways. Last, and most important, I thank my husband, Douglas B. Lavin, former journalist, superb editor, and master of making what seems impossible possible.

INTRODUCTION

Reigniting French Feminism for the Twentieth Century

In the spring of 2011 there was a new sight to be seen in Paris—or, rather, an old sight that had only occasionally been on view for decades: feminists protesting. They came out in record numbers, were interviewed by the press, and held the largest feminist conference in France in more than ten years. In the years preceding this breach of etiquette, France had supposedly been lulled by what the weekly magazine *Le point* referred to as the "harmony between the sexes," which it defined as "a certain style of seduction and of reciprocal listening, of complicity that hardly has been overly concerned with equality."[1] The connection was clear: "seduction" continued to be the way to resolve inequality.

The commotion that had stirred women out of this putative harmony was the arrest in New York City of Socialist presidential hopeful Dominique Strauss-Kahn for sexual assault against a maid in a hotel room—or, rather, the indifferent response of many male French politicians to what was called "the DSK incident." The popular refrain that women were equal members of French society and that they had a more sophisticated rapport with men relative to their Anglo-American peers rang decidedly hollow. Feminist groups in France, which had worked in but mostly out of the limelight since the 1980s, found themselves at the head of a much larger wave of dissatisfaction and protest. Public, political feminism was roaring back.[2]

For a full generation before, the women's movement in France had been seen by a large swath of the population as a quaint politics of the past. The Ministry for Women's Rights, created at the height of Socialist popularity in 1981, had been reduced to an institute for observing parity (or the lack of it) within the public sector. The last militant feminist monthly newspaper in Paris, *Paris féministe*, had folded at the end of 1996 for want of an editorial board and readers (the women's center housing it, on a tiny side street in the Eleventh Arrondissement, hung on with scarcely any visitors). Relatively few women, older or younger, called themselves feminists. Only a small number of the state-run universities had women's studies courses, let alone research institutes, and, for decades, many of the prominent women labeled "feminists" by the press repudiated the term, instead exploring the differences between men and women to bolster female identity. Very few women belonged to feminist organizations, and very few of these organizations had any consistently significant national presence. This is not to say that feminism was dead in France, but rather that it lay dormant as a movement that shaped the national consciousness in a highly public way.[3]

According to the French government, in 2011—the same year that Dominique Strauss-Kahn was pursuing what he called "libertinage"—80 percent of workers without employment contracts in France were women, and women as a whole earned 27 percent less than men. Similarly, less than 20 percent of members of the lower house of Parliament and only 15 percent of executives in large French companies were women.[4] A year later, in May 2012, the new Socialist president, François Hollande, reinstated the Ministry of Women's Rights. Hollande's cabinet also reflected real attention to equality, as 50 percent of its members were female—finally giving substance to the ideal of *parité* batted about ever since a law passed in 2000 had required political parties' local and national candidate lists to contain 50 percent women. By 2012 more women seemed to be talking about women's rights—or was it that more people and mainstream media were listening? The DSK incident gave new visibility to groups that had been around since the 1970s—Osez le féminisme (Dare to be Feminist), La Barbe (The Beard), Paroles de femmes (Women's Words), and Choisir (To Choose).

This response was a significant change from the past. During the decades following the 1970s feminist movement, many women and even some feminists considered the private sphere to be a postfeminist domain. France boasts a highly developed public child-care system that begins after the required sixteen weeks of paid maternity leave and includes after-school programs to allow women (and men) to work full time. Fathers perform more domestic tasks, from taking children to school to grocery shopping, than they did in the 1950s. Nevertheless, caring for children and regular household maintenance are still considered women's work in France. Working women dedicate more hours to weekly household tasks than do men, and parental leave is taken almost entirely by women. Changes from 2000 to 2012 were modest and, in contrast to the protests and foment of the women's movement in the 1970s, women seemed overall to accept the inequity, which is one reason the public protests around the DSK affair were so surprising. French gender etiquette disparages women who make complaints about their men public. And in the decades before 2012, those who pushed for equal opportunity were often met with disapproval from both men and women.[5]

A large portion of French society had turned its back on feminism in the twenty to thirty years since it had achieved so much, including electing a Socialist government sympathetic to many of its demands. And yet feminism was one of the great forces shaping France from 1944 to 1981. It was a social and intellectual revolution that profoundly affected its institutions, politics, social roles, and ideas. Only in 1944, following the Liberation, were women granted the right to vote in France. Until 1965 married women had little legal control of their personal assets, could not open a bank account in their name without permission, could not hold a job without the consent of their husband, and were required by law to live where their husband chose. With the law of July 13, 1965, which reformed the Civil Code's matrimonial statutes, much of this changed. But in 1965 both contraception and abortion remained illegal. With "paternal authority" still in place in the Civil Code, women had no legal control over their children. Moreover, there was no divorce by mutual consent, women had only a short maternity leave of two weeks before and six weeks after birth at half-pay, and women were banned from night work except in particular circumstances. Feminists in the National Assembly, the women's bureaus of trade unions, and political parties worked to overthrow what were decidedly sexist laws and traditions. When feminists took to the streets in the 1970s, they demanded what their less boisterous colleagues had been advocating more quietly: that the French rethink the position of women in every facet of public and private life. Thanks to the women's movement's dogged efforts, many of the constraints listed above had been eliminated by the 1980s.

This book will review the feminist revolution in France from 1944, when women were finally granted the right to vote, to 1981, when the Socialists took power and feminism was explicitly adopted by the government. But the question of the role of women in France goes back to at least the fifteenth century, when *femme de lettres* Christine de Pizan defended women against the then-fashionable idea that the mind of women can learn only a little."[6] Pizan's argument came to be called the *querelle des femmes* (women's quarrel), or the women's cause, and reveals that women's liberation—defined in its broadest sense as freedom from male domination and misogynist insult and the reappropriation of women's natural gifts—has a long history in France. Intellectual women have argued against popular misogynist tradition on their own terms, refuting male authority while recovering a practical and powerful image of womanhood. Feminism, as the historians Laurence Klejman and Florence Rochefort suggest, was born more formally "of the contradiction introduced by the Revolution [of 1789] that proclaimed the equalities of individuals as a universal principle and excluded women from citizenship." The tension between this republican ideology, the civic displacement of women by Napoleonic law in the nineteenth century, and feminist efforts to rectify these injustices is the framework of feminism's political history in France since the Revolution.[7]

The Third Republic, from the end of the Franco-Prussian War in 1871 until France's capitulation to the Nazis in 1940, witnessed a flowering of feminism. Feminist militants became a political and social force on the margins but were insistent enough that they made the "woman question" a problem for society to resolve. For example, feminists fought to open up the court system to women—to be lawyers and jurors and to retain their citizenship status after marrying. These efforts were a back door to suffrage and full citizenship. By the turn of the twentieth century, the *querelle* was one of the most important debates in French society. Savvy feminists like Marguerite Durand put a "feminine" stamp on feminism, showing the French public that it could be pro-family and pro-woman simultaneously, but her message and advocacy was as modern as it was radical.[8]

Throughout most of the Third Republic, anticlerical republicans deliberately stymied women's acceptance as full citizens, refusing to sacrifice what they felt was their tenuous hold on power to women, whom they believed would give their vote to royalists or the Catholic Church. Jules Ferry, a cabinet member during the early years of the Third Republic, argued that the church's control over girls' education divided women from their families and undermined the authority of the father. In part to form a bulwark against female clericalism, new laws, spearheaded by Ferry, established free, secular schools and required boys and girls ages six to thirteen to attend them. Similarly, the (Camille) Sée law of December 21, 1880, allowed for the creation of public high schools for girls, and then a teacher training school for women, but the contest between the church and republicans led both to focus on women's "natural function," thus trapping consideration of women's political role in a bottomless discussion about domesticity and maternity. By 1920, both Christian and secular feminist groups abounded, especially after women had distinguished themselves in the national crisis that was World War I. But the state, committed to repopulation after the devastating losses of the war, promoted a definition of women's rights and obligations in society that emphasized their maternal capacity despite their enlarged public role in the war years. Women's educational achievements and economic participation during the early twentieth century did not lead directly to political enfranchisement. Not until after World War II, when women had, for the second time since 1914, proved that they could be counted on to rally to the defense of the country in crisis, was the issue of women's citizenship finally put to rest.[9]

France's feminist history ranged from outspoken radicalism and violence to periodic phases of compromise and conservatism. Often feminists fought against extraordinary odds and were in the end executed, imprisoned, or deported by their own government—partly because feminism was consistently linked to the boundless French fear of depopulation and to the political Left in France, whose fortunes rose and fell until the late 1970s. In a country buffeted by wars, a fragile Third Republic, and economic crises, gaining acceptance for any feminist demand often required an unremitting battle. Particularly after World War I, legislators and popular male sentiment feared the defeat of republican institutions by an onslaught of enfranchised, clerical-minded (or, alternatively, communist) women.[10] Appeals by feminists were occasionally addressed, but often in a politically charged battle to influence France's female population, often in the cause of population expansion. Generally, as in the case of women's suffrage, they were outright refused.

Even up through the twentieth century, the French government sought to mobilize gender for political purposes. After World War II a relatively tradition-minded state created an abundance of well-received laws that aimed to protect women's double role as mother and worker. At the same time, it passed measures and provided services to defend women's equality in the public and private spheres. Before the Socialists took power in 1981, the most significant institutional changes promoting women's equality—the rewriting of the Matrimonial Regimes of the Napoleonic Code in 1965; legalizing contraception and abortion in 1967 and 1974, respectively; and opening employment and educational opportunities to women—were enacted by socially conservative governments intent on doing their utmost to preserve the French family and, most important, the birth rate. Besides extending suffrage to women, the Fourth Republic's constitution enshrined fair and equal salaries for women, including a clause stating that "men and women have the right to just remuneration according to the quality and the quantity of their work." The law of August 5, 1946, eliminated previous restrictions against women entering court professions, allowing them to serve as judges, jurors, and attorneys. By the end of the 1940s, female registration at universities reached an all-time high (38 percent), and it continued to increase afterward. Many *grandes écoles* (France's elite professional and administrative academies) opened their doors to women, and some women made their way into government and political party leadership. Thus, women were slowly granted many of the same privileges and freedoms as men even as laws safeguarding their female status were simultaneously enacted or maintained.[11]

In the nineteenth and early twentieth centuries, many champions of women's rights were happy to increase women's influence on society by having motherhood accepted as an important social rather than private function. The nineteenth-century feminist, neo-Malthusian, and free-thinker Nelly Roussel, for example, believed in "the doctrine of natural equivalence and social equality of the sexes," but her argument for equality rested on the idea that women should receive a maternity salary so that they could dedicate their lives full-time to the "noble work of motherhood."[12] The tendency to value state support for motherhood significantly diminished with second-wave feminism, which viewed the state's natalist policies as duplicitous attempts to control women for its own purposes. Feminism in France developed with its own advantages and challenges specifically because of this fusion of universal ideals and particular gendered implementation.

This book begins with the Liberation of France in the summer of 1944 because, despite a continuity of attitudes and social policy, the war and its aftermath created a crucial separation from the past. France's dramatic upheaval during World War II, with its shame and ultimate victory and the popular desire to build a new and stronger nation after the Liberation helped France to reconsider gender roles. Advocates of the women's cause argued that their country's reconstruction should include women at its very center. Thus, despite the greater radicalism of the 1970s women's movement, the ideas and social policy that it dramatically rejected were hammered out in the postwar period. Post-1968, second-wave feminism was rooted in post–World War II hardship and economic boom, confusion, and the drive to adapt French society to the demands of the postwar world.

From the Liberation to 1968, the women's cause in France was largely pragmatic and fragmented. There was no centralized political movement. Some Communist and Socialist Party women worked on getting their parties to recognize women's economic equity issues. Researchers analyzed and even criticized women's status, and Simone de Beauvoir published her groundbreaking work *The Second Sex*, but none of these efforts galvanized a political movement. Those feminists who were active during this period adopted a moderate and institutionally based approach to effect change. Both sides of the political spectrum often found agreement on women's issues, and feminists were faced with a united front against their claims to an equal place in society. By the 1950s and 1960s, the numbers of feminists were increasing but, self-identified or not, the vast majority believed they could best achieve social change through patient reform, single-issue campaigns, and, above all, compromise. Advocates for women's rights understood the political climate: no group, Left or Right, had much interest in making women's issues the focus of a political agenda. The Left dismissed feminism as narrowly focused and "bourgeois," and the Right attacked feminists, claiming that they were unnatural women, that their procontraceptive stance was eugenicist, and that they would be the death of France.[13]

In the 1950s and 1960s, the progressive protestant group Jeunes femmes (Young Women) discussed such taboo subjects as psychoanalysis, sex, and birth control at its regular meetings and advocated for Civil Code and contraceptive reform. Its religious affiliation gave it respectability and a degree of cultural distance that allowed it to criticize women's position in the Roman Catholic Church.[14] In addition, the Mouvement français pour le planning familial (French Family Planning Movement), founded in 1956 as Maternité heureuse (Happy Motherhood) and led by Dr. Marie-Andrée Lagroua Weill-Hallé, began publicly to articulate an argument for women's liberation based on the assertion that women were autonomous individuals whose sexual independence had to be respected. The growing visibility of women such as Dr. Lagroua and the sociologist Évelyne Sullerot, who publicly discussed women's position in society, together with studies of "woman's condition" and a smattering of feminist writings, succeeded in significantly influencing social attitudes toward women and sexuality, glamorized the image of women's advocates, and helped build a broader base for feminism. Other individuals played an important role during this time of feminist "quietude": Simone de Beauvoir continued to write indictments of oppressive patriarchal society in novels and essays and lent her name, though infrequently, to specific causes. The journalist, feminist, and pacifist Louise Weiss and the sociologist Andrée Michel, the author of dozens of studies of male-dominated society, built a feminist body of work in the period between the Liberation and the beginning of the organized feminist movement. They functioned as intellectual seedbeds for the more radical feminist movement of the 1970s.

The events of May 1968, with their enormous challenge to the status quo in cultural practices and institutions, triggered another break from the past, and feminism followed suit. When a new generation of women came of age in a now-prosperous and confident country, anger over women's second-class status finally exploded into concerted political action. Women were inspired by the politics of liberation and imagination that characterized the student protests, by collective action, and by the force of burgeoning feminist movements around the world. They initiated their own shakeup, which would have as profound an impact on French society as the May 1968 events. Women's experience at the barricades and in the meeting halls gave birth to a rejuvenated and radicalized feminism that was intensely critical on the one hand and utopian on the other. The utopianism that shaped 1970s feminism both mirrored and contrasted with that of previous generations. Like pre-1968 feminism, it was deeply practical, using quantifiable social change as its measure. It considered feminism a struggle to be won for all women. Yet post-1968 feminism also pushed into previously uncharted ethical territory over the issue of legalizing abortion. It broke with the previous tradition of compromise and working within established power structures, and it challenged the most fundamental ideas about men's and women's relationship to each other. This was its strength as well as its weakness.

After a few years of activism around issues important to many women, the women's movement divided into two largely separate strands, the traces of which remain today. One became second-wave feminism that could best be called materialist: uncompromising in its demand for women's equality and for the reinvention of social roles, ideologies, and institutions, hostile to entrenched political power, and assertive of women's individual subjectivity. The other strand became a postmodern metaphysics of sexuality and the self that distanced itself from feminism and sought to articulate the symbolic interplay of gender and women's consciousness in French society. In its early days, it was less activist than materialist feminism—sometimes antiactivist—and it was "particularist," holding that certain characteristics of masculinity and femininity were distinct and self-determining. *Particularism* refers to definitions of women as essentially different, or particular. The term has been used to describe women in the premodern era, articulating the belief that women had a special biologically and spiritually determined essence. This latter strand, which has been labeled "essentialist" by some scholars and feminists, argued that the relationship between the sexual body and consciousness should be expanded into other realms of knowledge and social organization rather than transcended or changed, as the materialists claimed. Indeed, women's philosophical writing preoccupied with women's voice and consciousness (and indifferent to beauvoirian existentialism) up through the twentieth century was tightly tied to an older tradition of "difference" that had both served and thwarted women's access to power and independence. The other strand of feminism, which burst forth as the activist women's liberation movement in 1968, was in many ways a profound rejection of tradition and an embrace of Beauvoir's prescient materialism. Pieces of these two broad strands have merged in recent decades around the issue of equality of representation, or parity as the French have defined it. French intellectuals and activists have harnessed the linguistic challenges to gender roles not to reduce them to essential understandings but to recalibrate French recognition of male-female power dynamics. Important to note, this position has been arrived at gradually over two generations of activist feminism.[15]

Most of the women who formed the driving force behind the 1970s feminist movement in France had earlier been involved in leftist groups and parties, yet most French women within the women's liberation movement repudiated the traditional French Left and its theoretical canon. The anarchist and virulently antifeminist Pierre-Joseph Proudhon, whose ideas were so influential in socialist movements in the second half of the nineteenth century, had had a lasting influence on leftist party attitudes toward feminist demands. Before World War II and after the Liberation, many leftists had attacked feminism as a distraction from the larger class struggle. They saw it as an independent political movement that challenged their own theory and priorities. Thus, the Socialist and Communist parties channeled their interest in the women's cause by creating women's committees to discuss women's problems and draft proposals often placed under the heading of "women's condition." Their official rhetoric focused on the difficulties women faced that were directly related to capitalist production (thoroughly denying a more basic system of oppression—the private sphere). But what were essentially feminist issues—equal wages and access to jobs and greater admittance to political power, to name a few—were not given priority in the decades before the 1970s among the parties of the Left. Much to their surprise and consternation, it was these parties, as much as the political Right, that feminists chastised in the 1970s.[16]

Like the May 1968 generation, which rejected the traditional Left and redefined questions of power, second-wave feminism sought to reach beyond the claim to material equality toward a reformulation of equality itself. For example, rather than simply demand adequate child care so that mothers could be employed as easily as fathers, feminists insisted that society rethink the accepted definitions of motherhood and that fathers recognize their responsibility to children. Feminists further rejected the simple "insertion" of women into society as it existed, along the lines proposed by government studies of earlier decades. Instead, many feminists envisioned a world in which men and women reframed what it was to be human in egalitarian terms. The post-1968 feminists were willing to place these ideals in a political, not just theoretical, framework, and they sought to incorporate their politics into their daily lives. As the philosopher and novelist Françoise Collin said in an interview, "Feminism is not, for me, an ontology or a metaphysics that would define woman as being, but a political and poetic movement that incites women and each woman to be."[17]

This definition of feminism and its history in France after World War II has not been sufficiently studied in the United States despite its significance to the building of the modern French state. In American universities since the 1980s, French feminism generally has been the purview of literature and philosophy departments and viewed as a postmodern, psychoanalytical, or deconstructionist product—more sophisticated and theoretical than its "pragmatic" American counterpart. By the early 1990s courses on "French feminist theory" abounded, featuring contemporary writers and philosophers such as Hélène Cixous, Luce Irigaray, and Julia Kristeva. But this American analysis was a rarefaction of select ideas without much historical context. To take one small example, the 1997 Texas Tech comparative literature symposium entitled "French Feminism across the Disciplines" stated that the conference would "problematize French feminism as a discourse which cannot be contained by any of the normative disciplinary categories of American academia." American interest in French literary theory and philosophy led some scholars of feminism to focus on just one element of a large political and intellectual movement and to brand it "French feminism." But this portrait left out rich decades of feminist writing and politicking and the background against which these ideas and battles were fought.[18] Women writers who cultivated notions of difference—the *féminitude* writers, as they are sometimes referred to—are only a small part of the "feminist" story post-1968. The feminist novelist Christiane Rochefort, who was one of the first to bring the women's movement political visibility through street protest, clarified this problem when she said in an interview about feminist theory, "We're seeing far too much literary theory being written today, considering that literary theory isn't at all important. The last thing I find important is theory, whether it's literary, philosophical, or psychoanalytical. Most of the time it's just nonsense." French feminists themselves had a more nuanced relationship to "theory" than American scholars have credited them as having (as activists on political parity have robustly demonstrated) and have been active in ways that do not privilege theory at all.[19]

This book was written, at least in part, as a response to this truncated vision of French feminism that continues to hold sway in the United States. A political and intellectual history of the feminist movement in France that flourished in the 1970s, it attempts to clarify the narrative and the place of "French feminism" in France's particular history. The understanding of this vibrant movement has been stunted by a lingering belief that women philosophers and writers were the prime representatives of second-wave French feminism. This is starting to change as American scholars become interested in parity politics, but the generalization still holds true.[20] This ahistorical interpretation has had at least three pernicious effects: First, it has obscured feminism's heterogeneous theoretical composition. It has severed the history of Third Republic (or first-wave) feminism, which was radical and political in a variety of ways, from that of second-wave feminism, which it deems philosophical and discursive rather than material. Last, it has served to decontextualize and depoliticize a complex and highly political movement, its internal conflicts, and its real-life impacts. The loss of political background is all the more misleading given that one theoretically oriented group—Psych-et-Po, self-identified as MLF—spent its first decade repudiating the feminism that focused on concrete political and social change, calling it infantile, beholden to capitalism, and bent on reproducing masculine norms. The idea that French feminism was theoretically dominated appeared farcical to feminists who were dragged into courtrooms by Psych-et-Po and its representatives. Feminism in France, and certainly the French women's liberation movement, have in fact been highly political and committed to action.

Nevertheless, French obsession over theory and ideology did mark the women's movement in France as much as it did French politics in general. This is important for several reasons. First, it created an enormous cultural production—novels, academic journals, newspapers, and films—examining the "woman question" and publicizing debates. Without all this, many women throughout France would not have experienced feminism or participated in the women's movement. Second, the feminist movement of the 1970s, like the Far Left groups from which it emerged, had a penchant for ideological purity—frequently at the expense of political expediency. For example, feminists (and women activists in the Mouvement de libération des femmes [Women's Liberation Movement]) of the 1970s were committed to consensual decision-making, sharing power, and allowing every woman to speak as a matter of uniting theory and practice, but underneath these guiding principles lay an enormous amount of contention. Within the movement as a whole there were frequent rifts and never-resolved arguments about goals, theory, and strategy that undermined feminism's political strength in France. These disputes weakened feminism's political influence, for when feminist ideology moved too far away from the concerns of the majority of French women, the movement lost its base of support.

Beginning the story in 1944, I revisit the political, intellectual, and economic context of France to better situate the theoretical debates, political positions, achievements, and failings of the 1970s women's movement. For what mattered most about feminism in France over the second half of the twentieth century was not philosophy and theory that laid claim to women's issues but the ideas and actions of a fiercely political movement and the material and cultural changes that movement wrought. It is the ideas' relationship to activity in the concrete world that I try to highlight in this book, rather than the intrinsic nature or attractiveness of the ideas themselves, for this book is emphatically a work of history in its focus on the workings of power and in its attention to the political struggles that brought women into the streets and legislatures to create material transformation of society. Thus I discuss gender theory only insofar as it follows a narrative that privileges the ideas of political participants in historical context. Critics as different as Judith Butler, Sherry Turkle, Jane Gallop, and Toril Moi were influential in past decades in bringing the complex ideas of French gender theory to a wider audience not steeped in Continental philosophy. I have made it my task as a historian to focus on ideas of women who participated in political events and influenced socioeconomic developments.[21]

My goal in writing this book was to understand how feminism developed—or reemerged—after the cataclysm of World War II, and in doing so I found surprising parallels as well as disjunctures. I have approached this task by tracing in broad outline the complex theories and practices of the last fifty years as they related to feminism. I examine the crucial national debates, ideologies, laws, and popular attitudes that were affected by feminist pressure or that precipitated change in the feminist movement. I also emphasize what I consider essential to understanding the development of feminism in France: the material context of women's lives. I examine their access to jobs and education and their position in terms of France's laws governing the family, property, and divorce. I look at economic changes and the political machine, seeking to describe why the movement developed as it did, with its ideological emphases, particular political and legal battles, and internecine conflicts, and, finally, what lessons can be learned from French feminism's triumphs and failings before the election of the Socialists in 1981. The answers are to be found both within the movement itself and in France's political and ideological landscape. Beginning the story in the wake of the Liberation, even before the publication of *The Second Sex* in 1949, allows us to see some of the most potent and lasting influences on contemporary feminism.[22]

I hope to expand and refine English-speaking readers' understanding of French feminism: to help them see it as a political movement that strove for change in French society on all levels rather than as an ideological or primarily academic movement. Sometimes that political movement manifested itself in sociological studies and in campaigns to change laws, and it later spilled out onto the street in anger and impatience, but primarily it evolved to address the material concerns of women's lived experience. With this approach, I privilege not just the stories of the feminists "on the barricades" during the 1970s but also the ideas and struggles of feminists of the 1940s through the 1960s. The period between the publication of *The Second Sex* and the birth of the 1970s feminist movement has only in the past fifteen years begun to be seriously examined by scholars of French feminism, but almost all the studies are in French and remain untranslated. On the one hand, I bring the rich and nuanced work of Sylvie Chaperon, Janine Mossuz-Lavau, and Florence Rochefort, among many others, to an English-speaking audience. On the other, I have limited my discussion on the postmodern feminist writers and philosophers of *écriture feminine* who have often dominated English-language scholarship on French feminism—because their writing has already been analyzed at length, and because I believe that they are tangential to the most important arguments to emerge from 1970s feminism in France.

The book will emphasize three important points about 1970s French feminism and its history: First, second-wave feminism of the 1970s sought to rectify women's secondary status in government, education, the professions, and the law and was grounded in a concept of rights that held women to be autonomous individuals as opposed to contingent ones. Beyond renovation, feminism sought to examine, invert, flout, or tear apart the social and cultural trappings of patriarchy and to reinvent—on women's terms—what it meant to be women. As one feminist poster put it: "Abrogation of All Services! Military Service; Reproductive Service; Domestic Service." Second, as universal as the claims of French feminists were, the feminism that developed in France was in many ways singular. This French singularity is to be found in the prominence of the Marxist-Leninist-dominated Left in postwar French politics, in a propensity to seek statist solutions to social problems, in a passion for intellectual debate, in a romance with traditional gender roles, in a longtime obsession over the birthrate, in the legacy of Catholicism's beliefs about social organization and the family as a central organizing structure, and, at the same time, in a fiercely defended ideology of individual liberty that stretches back to the French Revolution. Third, the book also highlights the contradictions among different feminists, some of whom invoked the principle of corporatism to deny feminist demands and others who cultivated a universalist vision of France to bolster them. To complicate matters, certain feminists called on women's specificity to repudiate a feminism that strove to be universal, a key concept in the nation's political ideology since the Revolution of 1789 that envisioned French Enlightenment principles as transcendent. They claimed to be initiating a process of women's true liberation outside patriarchal "universalist" schemas. Others denounced this theory, insisting that any feminism worth its salt was universal. Feminism in France has been described by one feminist activist and theoretician as the "double French exception": to be French was to refuse feminism in the name of French singularity because France was the standard-bearer for universalism, which philosophically could not support feminist singularity.[23]

The nub of the book's argument lies in the convergence of material circumstances and ideology, for feminist theory has always been attached to some sort of activity in the concrete world. It is this relationship, as much as the ideas themselves, that must be accounted for in the intellectual history of French feminism. This book is therefore not a detailed history of all aspects of feminism in France since 1944, nor a chronicle of all the facets of the women's liberation movement of the 1970s and the following decades. Such a comprehensive chronicle would require multiple volumes. Portraits of the 1970s movement itself, more detailed and narrower in scope, have already been written by French scholars and participants in the movement whose perspective was an intimate one from the front lines. And over the course of the past twenty years, French historians have published detailed studies of French social policy directed toward women during the period between the Liberation and the feminist movements. These books—including Sylvie Chaperon's *Les années Beauvoir: 1945-1970* (The Beauvoir years: 1945-1970), Christine Bard's *Les femmes dans la société française au 20ᵉ siècle* (Women in twentieth-century French society), and Janine Mossuz-Lavau's *Les lois de l'amour: Les politiques de la sexualité en France* (The laws of love: Politics and sexuality in France)—go a long way to fill in the missing pieces regarding how second-wave feminism of the 1970s emerged.

These books and other tangential studies in both French and English offer valuable information about the movement, but their historical analysis and context is limited in time-period. My study has sought to carry their work to the next stage: to emphasize the relationship between French feminism, the women's liberation movement, and the historical and intellectual contexts in which they grew. The largest institutional changes in France made after World War II and dedicated to women's equality were enacted by conservative, pronatalist governments, so by the time the Socialists came to power in 1981 a whole series of laws protecting women's interests (but also defending women's rights) had already been put in place. Concurrently, in the postwar period, one of the most influential books of the modern era, *The Second Sex* by Simone de Beauvoir, was published. This book methodically challenged every traditional view of women and society. Such institutional and intellectual realities were extremely important in determining the scope and direction of feminism from the Liberation onward. For this reason, "French feminism" needs to be read in a French context. This book tells stories of the rebirth of feminist theory, legal wrangling, political jockeying, and acrimonious personal battles but, above all, it attempts throughout to analyze the impact of the social and political landscape on women and the way this interaction helped shape feminism into a radical social movement in the 1970s.

Exploring the roots of feminist consciousness since 1945 has forced me to wrestle with definitions. Some women writers and activists called themselves feminists; others did not. Many who shied away from the term believed the old socialist and communist cliché that feminism was reformist and elitist; others considered feminism a dirty word. Indeed, "feminism" in France sometimes still carries with it the specter of the complaining shrew, in part because it is interpreted as rejecting a very basic "femininity" that is said to be tied to women's nature and their relationship to men, although this is also beginning to change. Others rejected the word *feminism* because they saw it connected to the beauvoirian materialism with which they disagreed.[24] Some participants in the women's cause in the 1950s as well as in the 1970s cast aside not only the term *feminism* but also some of its reasoning and objectives, and occasionally they tried to undermine its support and impact. Insofar as is possible, when I refer to "feminists," I am referring to women who used the name and identified with feminism's ideas; when talking about the movement as a whole—including women who marginally participated but perhaps didn't call themselves feminist and women who were fully engaged but repudiated the term—I use the term "women's movement." Far more complicated is the use of the name Mouvement de libération des femmes. For almost ten years this name referred to the diverse movement that sprang out of the May 1968 events (though the name itself was not employed until 1970). Women who were part of the movement used it as a political calling card until such use was imperiled in 1979–1980, when the name was officially registered as an association and it and its symbol (a raised fist inside the female sign) were trademarked by Antoinette Fouque, her colleagues, and her group, Psychanalyse et Politique (Psych-et-Po), creating a crisis within the women's movement about ownership of what had been a collective name. I use the name Mouvement de libération des femmes (MLF) to describe the movement up until the time of its registration, which I discuss in later chapters. In subsequent reference, I distinguish between the broader movement and the "MLF" registered by Fouque and Psych-et-Po by using quotation marks around the latter.

It is hard for non-French readers to appreciate the degree to which the 1970s feminist critique of "femininity" and rejection of the focus on gender and sex was so radical and created such hostility among *women*, and why so many women rejected feminism because of it. "Femininity" and "womanhood" had long been expressions of women's power and the root of their identity in French society. French men and women have prized each other for their mutual admiration and understanding, and they have felt enriched by gender definitions rather than limited by them. It would require another book to unravel the threads of this sexual je ne sais quoi, but, even as a first approximation, it is clear that the French attachment to "femininity" or "womanness" has had a negative impact on the development of feminism as a movement irrespective of the ways it has affected women's status. Historian Sylvie Chaperon remarks that it is difficult to put a label on clearly feminist activity before the mid-1960s that for political and social reasons rejected being so "narrowly" defined. At the same time, feminism loses its meaning when simply equated with "women's activism." Thus, for my purposes, a definition of feminism must be large enough to encompass women who, while not identifying themselves as feminists per se, fought for or identified themselves with causes for the betterment of women. The connecting thread throughout this period of feminist activity was the notion of freedom, albeit articulated in different ways.[25]

A word about scope: I have largely focused on feminist activities in Paris. This is less constraining than it might seem. The feminist movement did grow in the large metropolises of France—Grenoble, Lyon, and Marseilles, for example, and certain feminist activities in those places will be discussed—but the centralization of the French state compels much of its political and cultural life to revolve around Paris. Paris is where most of the movement's biggest players lived and where its most important events took place; it was the center of the national movement. I hope that this study will encourage others, revealing an ever more rich and nuanced account of activism in Paris but also throughout other regions of France, further demonstrating the centrality of the women's liberation movement to late twentieth-century French history.

Much of my primary research was conducted in France during the 1990s. I tried, insofar as was possible, to gather as much material ephemera of what was at that point barely history. There were few monographs on women's issues from the decades before the women's movement, and many unpublished papers from the heady days of the 1970s movement were still in activists' closets. Nevertheless, I profited greatly from the collections at the library of the Musée social, the Bibliothèque Marguerite Durand, and the Bibliothèque de documentation internationale contemporaine, as well as from the ministerial libraries (of education, health, and labor), and libraries of other research centers, such as the Institut national d'études démographiques and the Institut national de la statistique et des études. I made extensive use of the unpublished personal notes, letters, and original pamphlets and manuscripts from the private collections of some of the major contributors to the women's movement. Along the way, I have benefited from the excellent scholarship on the history of feminism by French scholars such as William Guéraiche, Sylvie Chaperon, Françoise Picq, Florence Rochefort, Christine Bard, Bibia Pavard, and Janine Mossuz-Lavau as well as Anglophone scholars such as Jane Jenson, Claire Duchen, Sarah Fishman, Karen M. Offen, Susan K. Foley, Judith G. Coffin, Ursula Tidd, and Amy G. Mazur, to name a few.

While I rely heavily on contemporary written accounts to provide the clearest evidence of events as they occurred, I also interviewed women from the movement (many of whom were public figures during the 1970s, though others were less visible). Many of the interviews proved useful in pointing out sources, straightening out confusion, and providing firsthand accounts of political activism. Though unfailingly inspiring, the interviews also proved puzzling. Specialists in oral history suggest that oral accounts can help to flesh out the historical record, but they warn that such anecdotal evidence can sometimes skew more scientific data. This counsel proved valuable as I began to conduct interviews halfway into my research and unearthed passions and frustrations that a decade or two had hardly dimmed. In the end, the structure and the intent of the book allows me to recount parts of only a few women's stories, using their experiences to draw a vivid portrait of feminists' experience.[26]

I offer a personal anecdote that shaped the timing and future of this publication and that demonstrates the level of contention over some of the subject matter that follows. In the spring of 1996, as a newly minted PhD, who had spent the past decade researching feminism in France, I was invited to present a paper at the Berkshire Conference for Women's History on a panel focused on twentieth-century feminism in France. The paper, "The Power to Own History: Antoinette Fouque, *des femmes*, and the Women's Liberation Movement in France," addressed a divisive issue in the women's movement at the end of the 1970s and focused on political power. It was meant to inspire American scholars to take French feminism's politics more seriously. I was prepared to be critically received by my American colleagues in history, who were used to "French feminism" as a discourse. I was not, however, prepared to find that the attorney for one of my principal subjects had flown over from France, strongly urged me not to present the paper and, when that failed, leafleted the session and denounced my work. This was, for me, a strong reminder of the intensity of the conflict.

I hope to show that the history of the French feminist movement is, to a great extent, the history of French women's claims to the universalism and citizenship already granted to their male counterparts, at least on principle, in 1789. In trying to achieve the equality that many women believed matched their participation in society, they alternatively donned the mantle of pluralism, advancing their contributions as mothers to prove their worth as citizens, or threw it off, claiming absolute equality with men. They struggled to define themselves politically within a world that had adopted universalism as a principle while it largely recognized women's existence as mothers and wives.[27] Until the events of 1968, justice for women was mediated by the collective (the family or the state), which had its own demands on them as individuals. The exceptional women, of whom Simone de Beauvoir with her pioneering work *The Second Sex* is perhaps the best known, led the charge to reconceptualize "woman" in France. But the conflict between women's individual freedom and their public and familial duty was never resolved. It was to reemerge in France's debates over birth control, abortion, and equal opportunity in the 1970s, when a new generation of feminists took the baton from these exceptional women to fight for absolute justice.

1 LIBERATION AND RETHINKING GENDER ROLES

1944-1950

The day will come when we have the right of citizenship. Then, the
social and political contribution of women—those beings of daily
courage, ready to devote themselves, those believers in the embrace
of a mystical nationalism—will be born in their hearts, bringing
with it even nobler actions, and will be, I am certain, the very basis
of our renewal.

Raymonde Machard, *Les françaises* (French women) (1945)

In 1944, in the newly fluid circumstances that followed the Liberation,
the old *querelle* resurfaced again. Disgust with fascism and collaboration and an egalitarian spirit of resistance made traditional attitudes
about women appear tainted by Vichy and cleared a path for a different
approach to social renewal. Women's concerns were not among the most
pressing issues for the French and their new government at the Liberation, and the feminist movement was decades from becoming a political force. Nonetheless, the Liberation period through the early 1950s
was marked by a flurry of writings by a variety of authors on women's
role in a revitalized France and a campaign for concrete action. Most
of these women writers had been active in social movements before
the war and resistance movements during the war, engaging in nontraditional roles. Nevertheless, the arguments they employed echoed
the nineteenth-century tradition of using women and their bodies to
fulfill state goals, albeit with elegant and old-fashioned defenses of

women's status. Women once again came to symbolize resurrection—as they had after World War I and under Vichy—through a combination of personal virtue, domestic guardianship, and fecundity, but this time through France's ultimate victory rather than its humiliation.[1]

Despite its early promise, the postwar period would not change much regarding women's private roles, although their political status changed significantly. The men and women who actively sought to define the new womanhood and the politicians who would implement it largely agreed on a modest plan for women. France was in turmoil for much of 1945 to 1947 and the French people were very hungry. They appeared to want order—gendered and otherwise—and food, not revelation or revolution.[2] Reading forward from the Liberation period gives us a much clearer understanding of French feminism in the 1970s and beyond: We can acknowledge the strength of the arguments in defense of the French patriarchy—how they were deliberately and clearly elaborated during this period, albeit with some modern adjustments, even as Vichy and its nationalist ideology were debunked. Read in the context of Gaullism, with its masculinist posturing and reinvigoration of the republic, this cannot be taken lightly. In contrast, we can see that French ideas of republicanism and women's elaboration of them continued a thread initiated during the French Revolution by playwright and activist Olympe de Gouges, who demanded that revolutionaries make good on their universalist principles of the rights of man by explicitly including women. Many of the female authors discussed in this chapter recalled these principles and challenged the men in charge to honor them; indeed, we can trace the claims made for political parity in the 1990s directly back to these postwar voices. Studying writings by and about women in this period allows us to understand how later feminism rewove a recognition of women's particular identity and capabilities together with demands for women's full participation in the French universalist model. At times, this weaving would look like compromise; at other times, like a contradiction.

My analysis will often highlight a contrast between people who wrote about women (men and women in equal numbers) and people who worked on behalf of women (generally women themselves).

I have examined more than fifty monographs and articles published between 1945 and the early 1950s that were aimed at reelaborating women's special role in a revitalized French society and that represent a cross-section of the debate. Works about gender issues varied. Paul Archambault, an influential Christian Democrat, authored a philosophical treatise called *La famille: Œuvre d'amour* (The family: Work of love and spiritual witness). Pierre Fougeyrollas, researcher at the Centre national de la recherche scientifique (CNRS; National Center for Scientific Research), conducted a detailed survey focused on how women's relationships with their husbands and families had changed.[3] German soldiers still occupied French soil when Raymonde Machard, in *Les françaises: Ce qu'elles valent, ce qu'elles veulent* (French women: Their values and aspirations), cried out against the injustices women had faced in earlier decades. And Odette Philippon's *L'ésclavage de la femme dans le monde contemporain, ou la prostitution sans masque* (The slavery of women in contemporary society, or prostitution unmasked) condemned prostitution in all its disparate forms, including exploitative marriage practices.[4] While these and other works display an array of concerns about women and their past and future roles in society, all rely on conventional and deeply rooted French elaborations of gender, universalism, and republicanism. Some authors, such as Alfred Sauvy and Maryse Choisy, were widely read and discussed by both academic and popular commentators. Others, such as Paul Crouzet and Suzanne Nouvion, were holdouts from a previous era. Taken together, however, they represent a body of work from which we can draw conclusions about popular and academic discourse on women and its connection to French governmental policymaking. One piece of writing in the postwar period did challenge France's most cherished cultural and intellectual assumptions about women, *The Second Sex* by Simone de Beauvoir. But it was a theoretical anomaly, and, while highly influential in the lives of many women who read both volumes when they appeared, this work would not be viewed as a blueprint for action until decades later. Instead, more traditional articulations of womanhood maintained currency and would continue to hold sway throughout the 1970s alongside a more beauvoirian-inspired feminism.

From Ruins to Reconstruction

Much of Europe had been destroyed during World War II. France lost over half a million of its citizens and saw a large chunk of its male workforce shipped off to Germany; those who remained in France subsisted on rations and endured investigations, purges, and vicious reprisals. The Liberation was hard fought, and France endured months of bombardment as the Allies battled against entrenched German positions after the Normandy invasion. The Liberation brought a short few months of celebratory triumph in the spring of 1944, and then France was faced with hunger (official rations fell below 1,000 calories per day for over six months) and some recognition of its participation in the Nazi war machine and its own homegrown fascism. What had France become? This question frightened many and generated debate and scapegoating.[5]

After France's liberation, the French populace enacted vigilante justice against those who collaborated with the enemy. Women who, the argument went, had been seduced by the charms of a strong and dominant occupier were easy targets in many respects. After the war the victors punished "horizontal collaborators" (women who had consorted with the occupiers) as one way to settle political scores and restore moral (and gender) equilibrium. Moreover, women as a group came to symbolize the collective failure and national weakness of France. Some argued that white, Catholic France had been weakened by unfavorable elements within, such as immigrants and Jews, as well as by modern ideas such as contraception, women's employment, and feminist equality, which, the argument went, had weakened the family, the backbone of French society. France's domination by the Nazis was likened to feminine submission, and as early as the summer of 1944 many women were "relieved of their duty" in the Resistance to make way for young men, recently joined, who could rediscover their "manhood" through fighting. Indeed, women's resistance work was rarely referred to as political work but rather as patriotic work. Once the period of "purging" (*épuration*) was over, the government focused on juvenile delinquency—particularly the sexual behavior of girls, which "perverted young women's 'femininity.'" On many levels during the postwar period, the government and social agencies focused attention on girls and women, and much of that focus was on reining in their sexuality and exploitation but also their independence.[6]

Scholars have suggested that the focus on women and girls' sexual behavior to restore moral order and on the active cultivation of French womanhood as the symbol of French resurrection enabled the newly formed government to ignore the far greater moral issue of France's fascist regime under Vichy and its active participation in the extermination of its Jewish population.[7] But this restoration could not mask the weakness of France's entire manufacturing and agricultural sector, its aging infrastructure, and the wartime destruction of property. Much of the writing that focused on improving the "feminine condition" represented women either as a bellwether of France's success at building a modern liberal society or as a means of returning France to an unblemished past.[8] "Familialism," an obsessive focus on the family as the backbone of society and the countervailing force to the general loss of morals and depopulation, was the official doctrine of Vichy. After the war many Vichy bureaucrats who had enacted the policies of the 1920s through the occupation were pardoned and quietly absorbed into the new government. Not only was de Gaulle fully in support of natalist policies, but so were the Christian Democrats, Socialists, Communists, and the unions. Even as France shed some of its sclerotic economic behavior and launched itself into the postwar world with renewed fervor, Vichy's family policies, and thus a large chunk of its social programs and infrastructure, were retained. In the new republic, familialism, together with natalism, triumphed because economic and social expediency were wedded to political legitimacy.[9]

In the post-Liberation context, consciously reviving patriarchal ideas over universal republican values served other purposes: France could repair what many in the government believed had been and continued to be its greatest weakness—*dénatalité*. From the 1850s onward, France's population growth stagnated and stubbornly remained lower than that of all its European rivals. France, exceptionally, suffered from negative growth from the end of the nineteenth century through the 1920s—a unique combination of a low birthrate and the tremendous death toll of World War I. Over a quarter-million French men—the majority in their prime—had died in the course of World War II and the occupation, compounding the large demographic imbalance left by World War I. By 1946 the female population aged fourteen and higher had reached 1,129 for every 1,000 men, causing young, single women particular economic and emotional hardship. Given the loss of such a significant portion of the workforce and France's need to retool and increase production, it seemed quite possible that women would be called upon both to produce children and to take on "nontraditional" roles.[10] These two national requirements would form the crux of the government policy aimed at women from the 1920s onward. With this national obsession over the birthrate, the government focused on women's obligations, not women's rights.

After World War I, pronatalist campaigns, societies to foster hygienic practices for mothers and infants (to reduce mortality), programs to educate girls on aspects of maternity, and medals bestowed on large families were a mainstay of Third Republic state-building. By the 1930s the social security system had been enlarged and family subsidies were linked to the number of children. The Vichy government ratcheted up the pressure in 1941 by making abortion a capital offense. Despite all this, however, the French remained resistant to producing more children through a variety of means, both natural and illegal.[11] After World War II, with Vichy discredited, the French state became more scientific in its approach, subsidizing the creation of demography centers such as the Institut national des études démographique (National Institute of Demographic Studies) and scholarly journals devoted to population study. Even as France entered a thirty-year period of expansive economic growth (often referred to as *les Trente Glorieuses*), many French people in government and industry believed that without a reversal of its population decline, French civilization was doomed. Robert Prigent, the first general commissar of the family and minister of population in the 1940s, insisted that "family" was not a Vichy issue but a French issue. The Fourth Republic agreed. In 1946 the family allowance was 20 percent of base salary for two children, with an additional 30 percent of base salary added for each subsequent child.[12] Men expressed far more concern over the falling birthrate than did women. Men's fear of *dénatalité* and dwindling male authority seemed to drive their critiques of feminism and gender equality.

An institutionalized approach to reviving the patriarchy worked hand in glove with natalism. This was certainly what a number of male postwar authors had in mind when they wrote about women's role in a new France. Regardless of political persuasion, these male authors viewed the small reforms of the Napoleonic Code, the Fourth Republic's constitutional mention of gender equality, the enlargement of workers' rights, and women's increasing activity in the public sphere as evidence that France was headed off the rails. By their lights, the consequences were serious and included the possible dissolution of social hierarchies or even the collapse of France. The philosopher Jean Lacroix said, "To emancipate women and children at the same time as workers—to weaken the power of the father—is at the same time to weaken the power of the master, the priest, and the boss. . . . The death of patriarchy is the end of governance over both state and family."[13] This idea was a cornerstone of the Vichy regime, and it is interesting to note to what extent it was retained after Vichy's destruction. It would reappear in identical form for the next three decades in response to attempts to update the Civil Code and to win the legalization of contraception. Women would be forced to chip slowly away at its arguments to free themselves from its contradictory and suffocating "protection."

Many writers and advocates of the women's cause during this time felt that they were working from scratch, since the Vichy regime had stamped out a once-flourishing feminist movement, which in the first decade of the twentieth century had even managed to establish a state-funded feminist library. Before the war, the Nazi triumph in Germany in 1934 had led a large number of feminist militants to focus on the destruction of fascism rather than on feminism. The Popular Front—a coalition of Socialists and Communists that came to power in France in 1936 and that was theoretically predisposed to progressive legislation—did not accept women's suffrage. Even the Communist Party, officially committed to the equality of women with men, adopted a pronatalist position that celebrated motherhood and women's beauty. France's capitulation to Germany in 1941 largely crushed feminism, or drove it entirely underground, its advocates choosing nationalism and resistance if they were politically active at all. After the war, some of its proponents, for example Cécile Brunschvicg and Andrée Lehmann, attempted to rally the feminist forces, but old age, the granting of women's suffrage, and a general lack of interest in "women's rights" marginalized their efforts.[14]

De Gaulle's April 1944 pledge to extend suffrage to women (a decision hashed out by the Consultative Assembly in Algiers with pressure from the Americans even before France was liberated) set the stage for other policy changes that placed women's new role at the center of French reconstruction. The pledge could be seen as a practical and symbolic gesture of *national* reconciliation allowing all the French (whatever their circumstances or choices during the occupation) to rally around an ideal and forget their political differences.[15] Right and Left approached women's new political participation with different apprehensions and strategies. On the Right, the Mouvement républicain populaire (MRP; the Christian Democrats) believed that women's natural conservatism would swing the vote their way and toward de Gaulle's new party, the Rassemblement du peuple français (RPF; Rally of the French People) and away from the Communists and Socialists. During the previous republic, the idea of women's conservatism had provided one of the most powerful arguments *against* women's suffrage, as republican anticlericals feared the undermining influence of France's Catholic Church. Now, fearing a Communist takeover, they reminded women of their sacred duty to vote. The Left (the French Communists and Socialists) insisted on their respective parties' moral superiority—many in the Resistance had been members—and competed to prove themselves more sensitive to women's desires and better able to respond to their needs.[16] At times political parties seemed torn between the hope that women would be an electoral boon and the fear that women would champion feminine values and theoretically undermine republicanism, but in reality the concern was about male privilege. The Communist Party, for example, was dedicated to retaining the male industrial class as its rank and file and resisted taking up women's causes that might threaten such traditional support.

After some wrangling, the French would compromise by choosing to defend their tradition of family and community while partially accommodating the increased expectations of individual members; by balancing rights with obligations they would preserve an appropriate and useful measure of women's sexual difference while not unreasonably limiting (by men's lights) women's freedoms and ambitions. This was in line with patriarchal governance: women would be lauded and supported but not made equal.

Reassertion of patriarchal power may have appeared all the more important given that France was in a state of submission to the new superpowers at the end of the war. Most of the French viewed America as their savior, but many viewed the Soviet Union sympathetically and were attracted to the Soviet communist program—or to what they knew of it. Despite de Gaulle's bluster, the most powerful resistance network in France (and in Europe generally) had been organized by the Communists, which earned them enormous respect. Political parties recognized this for decades after the Liberation, even as France's ally America exerted pressure on the French government to purge itself of communist influence. By May 1947, for example, Communist ministers were being dismissed from the government, alienating them from direct political power and freeing them to rally their supporters for strikes and protests. The Communists would continue to be influential in union activity while remaining outside the government until the 1970s.[17]

The male authors who tackled the woman question devoted chapters to analyzing history, ostensibly to ground their arguments in French tradition. Linking the decline of men's absolute authority with the end of feudalism, the development of capitalism, and the creation of republics, they then situated women's experience in this broader context and suggested ways that patriarchal structures could be resurrected in an up-to-date fashion. They could agree that some part of the current system was moribund; the question for them was the degree to which the basis of the old system was natural, proper, and useful to contemporary society. Lacroix, for example, performed what he called a "psychoanalysis of the French Revolution," arguing that the Revolution and the creation of a constitution radically changed notions of authority and of prescribed roles in French society. Before 1789 autocratic rule by force, based upon "natural" aggression (what Lacroix referred to as a "law of life"), had formed the basis of social hierarchy and the backbone of the family. Yet, according to Lacroix, the Revolution had ushered in a democratic movement that severed the traditional link between paternalism and paternity in both public and private life. In psychoanalytic terms, it caused the "death of the father."[18] Lacroix proposed to "transcend this imminent fact of hierarchy," relying on patriarchy as a prop to restore the moral and social order.

The social scientists Jean Stoetzel, Marcel Bresard, and Alfred Sauvy, director of the Institut national des études démographiques, agreed with Lacroix. They claimed that from the sixteenth to the eighteenth century, the Enlightenment and burgeoning capitalist production significantly liberated women and children from patriarchal authority. World War II, they said, virtually completed the process. Nevertheless, the authors were optimistic about the future of patriarchy. They saw much potential in the state paternalism that had been seriously embarked upon (they suggested) in 1939 with the Code de la famille, which augmented family subsidies after the birth of a second child, provided loans to young rural couples, required demography to be taught in school, and further penalized abortion. They hoped that these measures, continued into the Fourth Republic but without the taint of fascism, would return France to an updated and irenic patriarchal state. The challenge was to preserve family rights and protections in order to maintain natalist policies while simultaneously creating a strong, unified state and a new "social contract" that would heal the wounds of Vichy and "restore Republican legitimacy."[19]

Even authors on the Right argued in this period that capitalism and individualism had alienated human beings from their labor, from their communities, and from themselves. Some conservative authors believed that their most deleterious effect had been to cut women off from their natural destiny—and men from theirs. Paul Crouzet illustrated the extremes of such an argument in Bachelières ou jeunes filles?

(High school graduates or young ladies?), where he argued that the essential principle of the difference between men and women had been overlooked in the recent past. "There has to be significance in the fact that [a woman's] physical nature is at the same time more fragile and more gracious and displays less force than beauty," Crouzet said. He continued: "It has to be significant that a body's configuration is, as it were, destined less for the burden of work than motherhood's fruition; the fact that a brain has to practice its intellectual activities with a volume usually smaller by one-sixth. There has to be significance, similarly, in the fact that this intellectual activity is usually spontaneously directed less toward speculation and abstraction than toward practical matters; the fact that it applies itself with more conscientious assiduity than originality; the fact that it deploys imagination and sensitivity more often than logic."[20] Male authors were once again reaffirming women's natural inferiority and the necessity for women to take a back seat in government, the economy, and the family.

For conservative male authors, public discussion of women's identity and their role in public and private life was a dangerous development that needed to be checked before the reconstruction of France was firmly underway. Marianne Rauze-Comignan, a Socialist feminist and journalist who wrote her own book on the women's cause, remembers with horror a male director of a political party declaring, "Let there be no feminist demands here. Gather in particular occupations: social aid, summer camp counselors, . . . but not politics, it is not your line of work. Rather, get it into your head that men have taken in hand all political power and that they will never hand it to you *ever*."[21] This position on women would be so elaborated and reasserted in the postwar period that its critique in the 1970s would come as a systemic shock. Even then, pieces of it would be revived in subtler and more sophisticated fashion among a segment of the antifeminist intellectuals through the end of the twentieth century.

Dagmar Herzog has pointed out that over the course of the twentieth century sex—whether in the form of gender identity or expression—grew in importance in terms of politics and state-building. Right-wing male authors of the postwar era feared that contemporary society was erasing essential gender differences including women's subservience and men's dominance. They consistently argued that proper socialization and education were needed to revive femininity and to reestablish patriarchal authority before both withered away. Lacroix stressed that children must be taught that the family is mysterious and sacred. In *Force et faiblesses de la famille* (The strength and weakness of the family), he argued that adults would grow to recognize their full masculine and feminine "virility" (a fusion of mind and body) and perpetuate the institution.[22] Alfred Sauvy and Christian Democrat and philosopher Paul Archambault expressed sympathy for women's second-rate legal and social status but recommended finding a different solution than the universalization of rights and privileges, since a woman's refusal to bear children could result in a "malformation or an unresolved pathology."[23] Crouzet argued that "feminist ideology," equivalent in his mind to the attempt to wash away sexual difference, was a societal dead end. Writing in 1949, Crouzet was advocating the kind of enslavement that Beauvoir criticized the same year. Yet Crouzet genuinely attempted to frame a conception of masculinity and femininity that, while far from the universalist model, would be equally fulfilling for women and healthier for society: "We must state that equal or not to man, the woman is *different from him*. We also quickly add that the education of girls must be considered with respect to the *feminine personality*, with the goal of awakening, developing, and affirming the *feminine vocation*. This simply human vocation, in the natural order, is that of spouse and mother."[24]

For Crouzet and similar thinkers, the world was organized in a natural order more or less consonant with divine creation. Thus, social harmony and productivity would result from men and women's commitment to developing their "natural" selves in single-sex environments. Crouzet elaborated a detailed plan for women's education that would bind women to the natural order, in case instinct was not strong enough to do so. History, philosophy, and literature, Crouzet believed, bore him out. Crouzet proposed sweeping reforms in the *baccalauréat* (high school graduation exam) to create an educational program suited to girls. He argued that a feminine *bac* should not "leave women lacking in science training and create real inferiority" but would include instruction on health, beauty, and motherhood, with a stress on humanities. Its guiding principle, Crouzet said, should "unearth the universal spirit, ... remembering that [women's] orientation is traditionally and fundamentally literary in nature." It was "equality in difference" along the lines of Vichy's educational plan—but with more math.[25] Crouzet's plans did not stop at the *baccalauréat* but went on to suggest, for example, the creation of a chair of family studies that would integrate the care of children and the home into various disciplines and grant advanced degrees. Crouzet justified "feminine education" in many ways: he argued that society was served by the refinement of male and female skills, that women's nature was fulfilled by it, and that this diversity contributed positively to the relationship between the sexes.[26] The possibility that women would refuse to take up the banner of maternal reconstruction frightened Crouzet, who viewed the family as the linchpin of society.

Crouzet's program was supposed to inoculate women against feminism and the independent and "masculine" life that it supposedly encouraged. Nevertheless, he admitted that the necessities of everyday life in a postwar economy forced women to assume uncharacteristic roles. He understood that in war-torn France, the money women earned from their jobs was perforce replacing the material aid women once obtained from a dowry or patrimony even while imperiling both the father's responsibility to his family and the rearing of his children. Forced to compromise because of postwar circumstances, Crouzet defined women's work as less of "a *right* than a *need*." The notion of women's *right* to work, Crouzet argued, is the result of the modern woman's interpretation of her role as a proud free agent desirous of surpassing men. "Women must *be able* to earn a living," Crouzet reasoned, "but ideally they should not have to." A paid women's career, according to Crouzet, was "neither more nor less than a rape of nature and society." Although Crouzet was particularly shrill in his pronouncements, he echoed the sentiments of men like Prigent and Sauvy, who were in a position to make policy. In their view, equality at home and in the workforce brought only confusion, not justice. It would be their vision that shaped the postwar period.[27]

The creation of the Monnet Commission in December 1945 as a first step toward the Common Market brought a 66 percent devaluation of the franc and the reintroduction of bread ration cards only a month after rationing had been suspended. Defenders of the patriarchy could say what they wished about women's employment, but many more women found themselves obligated to seek a job that paid. After 1945 wages gradually rose by 17 percent, but prices rose by 51 percent. Basic supplies remained expensive, forcing many women either to remain in the workforce or to enter it even if their husbands were employed. Census data from 1936 and 1946 show that women's employment rose in the immediate aftermath of the war, particularly in industrial production. By the 1954 census, however, women's employment had fallen, especially for women between the ages of twenty and forty.[28] One early triumph of women's activism within a political party was convincing the main communist union (the Confédération générale du travail, or CGT) to negotiate the suppression of official lower "feminine wages," which was accomplished with the Order of July 30, 1946.[29] Given the CGT's preference for the family wage and its support for natalism, this was no small achievement.

The increased need for paid employment among working-class and even middle-class women did not diminish France's traditional expectations of women. On the contrary, women obliged the natalists—due in part to the return of prisoners of war and the unavailability of birth control—and the birthrate rose by 20.6 percent from 1944 to 1946. Besides repopulation, women were in charge of household duties, which were still labor intensive. Many households throughout France lacked running water, telephones, toilets, and electricity—never mind labor-saving devices—until years after the war. With the continuing decline of domestic labor, women's "double shift," at home and at the factory or office, remained a dominant characteristic of French women's work in the second half of the twentieth century. In response, the state enlarged subsidies to families, maternity benefits, and child care (paid to the male head of the household if possible) to help shoulder the cost of children and to accommodate female employment, despite a lack of data correlating state subsidies to increased reproduction.[30]

Women's Civic Majority: A New Kind of Feminine Republicanism

Universal suffrage served as concrete evidence that the French had liberated themselves from fascist tyranny and rejoined the free world—even though most other laws preserved women's civic minority. Perhaps for this reason, the women's vote (gained later than in most Western European countries) was taken very seriously. Although antisuffrage rhetoric still surfaced in commentaries and in the café (which remained a largely male preserve), it is difficult to find serious texts critical of women's suffrage in the postwar period. Women's suffrage became a shibboleth for women's civic equality, and even the most conservative postwar authors approved its introduction. For example, according to Jesuit priest and novelist Albert Bessières, women could embrace a new kind of "feminine republicanism" that acknowledged women's greater participation in the public world while maintaining their commitment to their home and children.[31]

Naively, female postwar authors also saw universal suffrage as basic proof of equality and of women's liberation. Journalist, novelist, and died-in-the-wool liberal feminist Raymonde Machard was perhaps the most vociferous about women's free exercise of their rights. On the eve of the Liberation she wrote, "Frenchmen of 1944, since, in a new spirit of faith and of social grandeur, you would like to re-gild on the walls of temples, at one time erased or dirtied, the words 'Liberty,' 'Equality,' and 'Fraternity,' this time, give them complete meaning." But she also recognized that suffrage was just the beginning of the work that needed to be done. In a voice consistent with other women writers after the war, Machard appealed to the men in power: "Make us legally and politically your equals as we are your equals in the labor of work and thought, as we are your equals in the responsibilities and sufferings of the war, as we are your equals along the long exodus routes and under the bombardments." She concluded: "Liberate us!"[32]

Machard argued that women's rights had never been included in the basic tenets of the French Republic and needed to be. Her words would find an echo in the action-oriented or pragmatic feminists of the 1960s and 1970s:

> The *Declaration of the Rights of Man* is a synthesis of the principles of '89, which state that the law is the expression of the "general will," from which women had to be excluded since in reality it was not "general" except in name. The word "citizen" signified "man." . . . For nothing has changed since the day when Olympe de Gouges, in front of the Constituent Assembly, made the voice of her oppressed sisters heard, declaring that "the establishment of the law," and an expression of the general will, and "equality for all" must be assured without discrimination, for female citizens as for male citizens or their representatives. [Inequality is a] revolting injustice that today turns to immorality since women's contribution to the commonweal is almost equal to that of men.[33]

Socialist and Communist authors also promoted women's suffrage, but they were often skeptical that women would act responsibly or that they would be able to distinguish between personalities and principles. Cynical about postwar politics and women voters, Henri Calet wrote in the Resistance journal *Combat*, "It seems to me that women still lack a bit of assurance and discretion. The woman next to me [at the polling place] declared to the voting clerk: 'I vote for an honest man.' Great! But I would have liked to know more. How did she plan to go about it?"[34] Women had been schooled for decades to believe that the polity was a male domain, and Vichy had reminded them that their job was to make the babies and take care of the home. Therefore, the few female politicians, including the Socialist Suzanne Collette-Kahn, felt the need to remind women that choosing representatives in an election was not the same as choosing a new hair stylist or dressmaker. If they were afraid to vote they needed only remember that their grandfathers had probably felt similarly in 1848. "Make the effort to educate yourselves," Collette-Kahn admonished. "It is not an impossible task."[35]

Other female authors spoke of suffrage as an intermediate step before the era of true socialism, when capitalism and bourgeois society would be vanquished and women truly emancipated. Suzanne Lacore, former Socialist minister and undersecretary during the Popular Front government, spoke for much of the feminist Left when she said that women's ability to put a voting slip into an urn would not solve the problem of her second-class status. Lacore argued that women were weighed down by the double burden of capitalism and male domination and, with the doctrinal fervor of the French Left after the war, declared that Socialism alone would ensure the total emancipation of human beings, replacing class warfare, exploitation of the work force, and national and international conflict with fraternity, increased productivity, maximum justice, and plentiful material goods.[36] The most strident among the authors on the Left believed that universal suffrage merely papered over women's difficulties, made more serious by the revitalization of capitalism. The Socialist activist Louise Saumoneau warned that women must "immediately raise themselves up to comprehending the vital problems from which they suffer: lack of provisions, the high cost of living, housing, health, . . . whose solution depends on the way in which women fill their civic duties." Communist activist (and wife of Parti communiste français [PCF] general secretary Maurice Thorez) Jeannette Vermeersch reminded her fellow Communists, "Let bourgeois vices not become those of women workers." Presaging some of the feminist conflicts of the next few decades, she wrote, "Women workers have above all salary and household budget problems, and feminist preoccupations concern, above all, the middle class or the bourgeoisie."[37] Suffrage was important but had little effect on women's daily existence, according to Vermeersch. Meanwhile, laws that did govern the scope and structure of women's lives desperately needed reform, and the way to enact them was to vote the PCF into power.

Despite the threats or great expectations, the impact of the "women's vote" proved less clear than most had imagined. For example, in the referendum of October 21, 1945, over the creation of a new republic, the extreme Right was defeated—and the majority center party, the MRP, emerged. Overall the rate of women's abstentions was slightly higher than that of men's, and more women than men were drawn to the Catholic MRP, but the votes they cast were often consistent with those cast by their husbands, families, or communities. So, although the MRP had counted on women's support, it was not entirely clear that the "women's vote" had a particularly discernible effect.[38] A decade after the end of the war, a 1955 study on women's political behavior partly explained the phenomenon. It demonstrated that, practically speaking, women's universe was still the home and that women had limited access to the social spaces of work, unions, political parties, and cafés—and thus limited entrée into the male political and economic world. The authors of the study, Mattei Dogan and Jacques Narbonne, explained that even for women who were employed, their working world was restricted and circumscribed by home and family life. Emphasizing women's relatively narrow employment opportunities and what today we call the glass ceiling, they remarked that, under the circumstances, "One understands that the rich marriage exercises considerable attraction on most women. . . . It is almost the only way (albeit very improbable) to escape an inferior social condition." And they concluded, "Woman is not yet in many cases an autonomous social being, and often she doesn't want to be—this condition can only evolve slowly."[39]

Machard declared that "liberty," "equality," and "brotherhood" must be lived out in the broadest sense. But she did not represent the majority opinion. Most authors, both male and female, argued for a particular role that women alone would fulfill in the new republic rather than a universal notion of citizenship shared between the sexes. They wanted to extend women's "natural" housekeeping abilities to the public sphere and to reinvigorate the active spirit of revolutionary feminine republicanism lost to the bourgeois domesticity of the nineteenth century. According to them, women's civic participation was important because it would engender social renewal. Conservative writers often recycled old suffragist arguments, reasoning that if France expected women to be mothers, it should not stand in the way of their natural authority. In his treatise Le vote des femmes (Women's vote), Bessières suggested that if it were not for women's maternal care, France would be forced to leave children's education to state-run institutions like the youth groups and schools of the Third Reich. And borrowing from a feminist argument he reasoned, "When we take your children for war, shouldn't you have the right, more than anyone, to influence the legislators who decide on war or peace; to influence politics that ... sometimes prepares war and death for your children?"[40]

According to Bessières, France was in desperate need of women's particular influence. He pointed out that the Right traditionally believed that the women's vote would cause division in the home, but argued that "two and a half million women don't argue politics with their husbands because they don't have them, due to the war. Without the vote, they are completely powerless to defend themselves within society at large." By reviewing the Third Republic's antisuffrage position, Bessières was able to attack the failed republicanism of the 1930s and simultaneously point out the extent of postwar France's separation from its political past.[41]

Despite Bessières's impassioned plea for embracing women's full political participation, politics proved to be more cynical. De Gaulle's RPF drew from the same pool of supporters as the MRP—the only party to have actively cultivated women in its party structure. The RPF, as socially conservative as its founder, cultivated women's votes but did not address women's causes or promote women candidates. Although the French Communists had previously fought to defend women's rights as workers and as mothers, their policies toward women became increasingly conservative and natalist as the Cold War set in and Communist cabinet members were ejected from the government in 1947. In a strategy to drum up socially conservative women's votes—and in a significant reversal from its egalitarianism during the Resistance—the PCF began competing with the MRP, the RPF, and Catholic women's organizations to show itself as the defender of motherhood. Even the French Communist Women's Union (Union des femmes françaises, or UFF), which had previously campaigned for a revision of the Civil Code and tied women's paid employment to women's personal liberation, stopped taking these positions after 1947. As the Cold War deepened and France became more entangled in two imperialist wars in

Algeria and Indochina, philosophical debate over women's employment ended.[42]

"Reject That Which Can Divide Us: Search for What Can Unite Us"

The 1946 Constitution established women's fundamental equality to men in France; women were now officially considered full citizens by the government. Under the law, however, married women were still at the mercy of the anachronistic Napoleonic Code, which effectively maintained their legal status as minors. Despite the modest reforms of 1907, which officially allowed married women to dispose of their wages, and of 1938, which granted married women some capacity in civil law, married women could not seek employment, relocate, or keep their finances and business separate without the formal consent of a husband. The constitution's declaration of equality and the slight easing of divorce regulations in the Fourth Republic did not topple France's institutionalized patriarchy. Without deliberate revision of the Civil Code, married women were bound to the dependence required of them by law.[43] As a result, political conservatives like Crouzet, Lacroix, and Sauvy aimed to provide an updated philosophical defense of institutionalized inequality, and the Socialist and Communist parties, by way of countering right-wing dogma, focused their appeals to women concerned with their repressed status under French law.

Examining the discussion around the code—both supportive and critical—lets us see with greater clarity the ways in which the codified law circumscribed behavior, directly affecting women's prospects and consciousness. Women authors of the postwar period called on men to review the logic of their assumptions and urged women to insist that they be taken seriously as citizens.

The Napoleonic Code infantilized women. Its inconsistencies with constitutional principles made it an easy target for criticism. Even conservative writers who still championed separate standards for women could not claim without reservation that this legal system protected or served them. Catholic writers acknowledged the need to update it, and Socialists and Communists included revisions of it in their women's platforms. Propaganda pamphlets for the PCF enumerated the most grievous articles in the code and proposed an amendment to carry out the government's "declaration of equality" in principle. Circumstances after the war underscored the inadequacy of the code's claim to protect women. Commentators noted that marriage, if it had ever represented a guarantee of material security for middle-class women, could hardly be expected to constitute one now. Female postwar authors cited dramatic examples of how it trapped honest women. Marianne Rauze-Comignan, for example, argued that men seduced women to marry them and then, when their wives became pregnant, abandoned them by taking them to court for adultery. Men could carry on adulterous relationships without penalty (as long as they did not bring the other woman into their household) or at the worst received a few months of prison without salary or a fine. "Such is the law of man," Rauze-Comignan protested, in *Pour la paix universelle* (For universal peace), "governed or inspired by the Rights of Man."[44] Insisting that the French needed to undertake a collective reassessment of male and female roles and see it enshrined in law, Rauze-Comignan prescribed individual betterment combined with the reinforcement of morality and civic discipline. According to her, the role of feminine republicans would be essential to such an enterprise.

If we take Rauze-Comignan's commentary at face value, it might appear that men were uninterested in improving themselves; regardless, many women authors believed women could collectively assure concrete change. Some urged that feminine republicanism be cast as the "feminine will" to be collective and independent of male authority, despite sociological studies that downplayed the prospect of women's political cohesion.[45] Another version of this feminine consciousness— euphemistically referred to as "women's particular mission"—provided idealized accounts of women's public service or suggested ways women could help make the world a better place. It would be inaccurate to label this call to unite "feminism," since most of the authors would have denied this label. Nevertheless, the postwar 1940s were witness to a renewed sense among women advocates that women had to speak up for themselves and for each other if they were to be heard at all and that it was women alone who could best articulate the problems and desires of their sisters. Indeed, some women writers believed that women's solidarity would come about through their new self-awareness. "Reject that which can divide us. Search for what can unite us, . . . [and] together we can save the world," the newspaper *Femmes françaises* (published by the newly founded in 1945 Communist-aligned UFF) trumpeted in support of a women's antiwar campaign. It called upon French women, as "Friends of Peace," to use their influence to build a new world, as did Catholic intellectual and writer (and wife of Paul) Pauline Archambault's 1955 *La femme entre deux mondes* (Woman between two worlds):

> If all women of the world wanted to lend their hand
> lend a hand in the hamlet, in their neighborhood, in
> the commune
> to give a hand to the country;
> to lend a hand past the frontiers;
> to lend a hand all around the world;
> to lend a hand without care to language, to color of skin, to
>   physical characteristics, without care to social class and
>   lifestyle . . . this hand which, from centuries and centuries,
>   has only cradled the child, prepared the soup, received
>   men's kiss . . . what weight would be on the side of
>   universal peace![46]

Female authors, more publicly self-reflective than their male counterparts, admitted that women would have to become more conscious of themselves and the world around them for any collective movement to take place. Maryse Choisy, a psychiatrist, progressive Catholic, and author of over twenty-five novels, books of poetry, and psychiatric studies, coauthored along with fifteen of her contemporaries a collection entitled *Conscience de la féminité* (Awareness of femininity). She spoke for all the contributors when she suggested that women would become more intelligent if they and society as a whole would "denounce the sophisms that imprison them" and strive to develop their intellect to its greatest capacity. Condemning the pretense of equality that the idea of universalism created, and presaging the essentialist women-centered theory of the 1970s, she suggested that the twentieth century had evolved into the most sexist century, in which "masculine imperialism had invaded women's minds."[47] Suzanne Nouvion, a leftist sociologist with similar essentialist leanings who also contributed to *Conscience*, agreed that women had to rid themselves of this masculine "imperialism," and she suggested that the future of France's happiness lay in women rediscovering the true female self:

> Currently we are at an impasse—a serious gap existing between a female body becoming "socially" adult and a personal consciousness remaining childish. Women have been publicly acknowledged in the outside world of civic and work life, ... but they have had to do it by thinking and acting in ways which are not their own. Feminism has been a useful step, ... but as with all things human, it has had its deficiencies, and now it must be completed by another effort: that of a *knowledge* of women, no longer only by what she can *do* but by what she *is*.[48]

Similarly, in the same collection Jacqueline Martin, a former member of the Protestant Resistance, remembered that while suffrage was essential, "equality is not identification, nor is it rivalry. Women have specific aptitudes and a feminine value, ... and prejudice must be eliminated against them."[49]

Rather than dispensing with gender roles to redefine themselves or embracing French universalism, these women authors insisted that they must incorporate the female principle into their culture. Nouvion, a founder of the French Girl Scouts, explained in her article "Femininity and Autonomy of Judgment" that to be female was not to be "undifferentiated magma," nor was it to be the "eternal feminine," which she saw as a caricature of women's intelligence and being. Femininity had as much value in human society as masculinity, and women's femininity, Nouvion believed, had the power to unify the masculine mind and the feminine soul. Thus, for example, women could simplify the "discursive verbiage of male intelligence" (she wrote that talkativeness, often associated with women, was against their nature) and could enlarge human understanding by the application of their intuition to the domain of scientific research. Challenging the traditional view of women as shallow, Nouvion argued in the long tradition of the *querelle* that while men often only hear and respond to the surface of things, women could deepen human understanding by "resurrecting a past belief in contemplation that this epoch has lost."[50] Female authors across the political spectrum believed that as much as women should aspire to positions of authority, to higher education, and to traditionally male professions, they should, like missionaries, bring their femininity with them to enlighten the dark and mismanaged male world and reinvigorate republican France. The core of these ideas would thread its way through women's discourse defending their sex up through the development of second-wave feminism.

Refashioning Womanhood for Contemporary Times

The Pétainists had had their revenge on feminism, sending women back home, and the Liberation forced women out again and allowed feminism the potential of a revival. Regardless, the past decade had been exhausting, producing a psychological fatigue in the aftermath of the war and a desire to "return to normalcy." Pauline Archambault called it "feminine malaise, masculine malaise, general malaise." Jacqueline Daubigny, a high school teacher and the author of a pessimistic report entitled "Anguish of the Contemporary Woman," believed French young women felt suspended. She described them as not only reluctant to commit themselves to lives as independent women but also very uncertain about the future. In these instances, the idea of marriage—"justification of existence and bearer of happiness"—was very seductive. Reflecting on this study, Archambault lamented that girls were brought up to view sex as something that created a "condition of physical and mental balance" and love as providing "real contact with the world and promotion to adulthood," when really women would be better served if they focused on career options.[51]

A group of progressive Catholics tried to split the difference between patriarchal resurrection and republican egalitarianism, and in many ways their voices exemplify the temper of the time. Catholic authors pressured the French state to reimagine itself, fusing Catholic and "familialist" doctrine with "republicanism."[52] Explicitly Catholic and Protestant participation in the Resistance had raised the ideological profile of the Christian Left during the postwar period, thereby providing a political alternative to Communism. Founded by progressive Christians, the MRP was represented in almost all the governments during the Fourth Republic and provided France with three prime ministers. But Catholic influence was more complex than this, as the Catholic philosopher Emmanuel Mounier's post-war writings illustrate. Mounier tried to forge an accommodation between radical individualism and state authoritarianism and to disentangle Christianity from the moral stain of Vichy. Mounier's and Jean Lacroix's philosophy of personalism, a kind of Catholic antiscientific accommodation with modernity that they developed in the 1920s and 1930s, grew in popularity after the war in part because it offered an antidote to the horrors of the scientific rationality of World War II. Personalism was an amalgam of humanism and compassionate Catholicism, of forward-thinking republicanism and old-fashioned paternalistic traditionalism that resonated with many French intellectuals at the time.[53]

According to Mounier, everyone, including women, had "natural" rights that could not be denied them, but these rights rested on concomitant duties to society and responsibility to others. What exactly these duties and responsibilities were lay at the crux of the debate, but the popularity of personalism demonstrates that, to a large extent, the debate over the "self" revolved around models of "difference" and of "nature," even though intellectuals wanted to expand the meaning of the terms. The parameters of the debate had been elaborated in the nineteenth century by Ernest Legouvé in *Histoire morale des femmes* (The moral history of women); the book, popular among feminists when it was published, and throughout the nineteenth century, emphasized the difference between the sexes while arguing for the separate but equal authority of both. Such mutual respect, Legouvé suggested, would raise the status of women while at the same time creating more harmony in the family and society. His catchphrase "equality in difference" was echoed by a large majority of postwar writers, both male and female. Thus, while these authors championed an enlarged role for women in France and greater respect for women's individual integrity, they clung to the notion that the world was ordered in terms of complementary and naturally different functions and that social harmony and personal fulfillment would be achieved only by embracing them.[54]

Authors of the postwar period agreed that women were profoundly different from men and therefore needed to occupy different civic spaces and play different social roles, but women authors tended to agree that women faced substantial barriers to what we might now call "self-actualization" or "having it all." Women argued that they played a larger role in society than was commonly recognized, and they contested the retrograde notions of womanhood prescribed by the former Vichy regime. These authors argued that women were strong and could take on the traditional burdens of men. "One seventh of the French female population must support itself alone and must assume moral direction and sustenance of the home," Andrée Lehmann, president of the Ligue française pour le droit des femmes (French League of Women's Rights), reminded her readers.[55]

Female authors of all political persuasions were likely to cheer the decline of patriarchy and to shy away from the same vulgar determinism shown so vividly by Crouzet. On the Right, authors such as Pauline Archambault bemoaned the increasing separation (economically and psychologically) of the individual from the household. And Jeanne Picard, a Catholic leftist, condemned any work that "made it impossible or difficult for a woman to realize her human and Christian vocation and which hindered her blossoming."[56] Women writers on the Left and Center viewed the death of patriarchy as a new beginning. In the preface of her book *Pour la paix universelle* (For universal peace), entitled "An Era Opens," Rauze-Comignan remarked, "If it is true that the enslavement of the feminine sex has been determined historically by the institution of property rights; that it has been maintained by the need for muscular force at the service of (industrial and agricultural) production, then we are in the era of great industry, of great motorized culture, the era of the mechanical supplanting the muscular."[57] These writers were aware that men's fear that their superior physical capacities were becoming increasingly irrelevant to production and sustenance underlay men's warning against femininity's decline, while women's "natural functions" remained as vital as ever to contemporary society. They wanted to establish new norms before routine and tradition forced women back into their prior status. They believed that beneath a badly trodden national morale lay a tantalizing freedom that, despite all the hardships it imposed, had to be fought for and won before inertia and social conservatism settled over the Fourth Republic.

Simone de Beauvoir wrote *The Second Sex* in the context of the government's effort to restore order and tradition and in an intellectual landscape that was overwhelmingly male dominated and socially conservative—so much so that it is unsurprising that the second volume (focusing on women's sexuality) was vilified by the Communists and attacked by both leftist writer Albert Camus and right-wing Catholic writer François Mauriac.[58] Although her work shared in the phenomenological tradition of Edmund Husserl and Maurice Merleau-Ponty, Beauvoir's fundamental thesis—that women are made, not born, and that "femininity" is a social construct developed and maintained to the detriment of women and the advantage of men—shook up her intellectual milieu and reverberated beyond France. Beauvoir radicalized phenomenology, arguing that women were objects in the act of becoming rather than subjects like men. She further argued that neither biological difference nor recent history could justify men's domination of women and culture. As an existentialist who asserted that the individual person is a free and responsible agent who determines his or her own actions, she replaced the concepts of "nature" and "destiny"—commonly seen in other writing about women—with free will. Thus, she theorized that the present was largely shaped by individual choice, with destiny and nature playing little part. Beauvoir drew a direct link between male patriarchalism, French colonialism, and racism—an analogy that was at once trenchant and scandalous. The fundamental nature of her arguments was different from that of any of the other writers concerned with women's subjugation, and her erudition was unequaled.[59]

Beauvoir's thesis can be divided into three principal arguments: First, men have dominated society since the beginning of civilization. In so doing, they have placed their existence and subjective experience at the center of culture and have constrained women to assume a peripheral role, the position of "other." Women have never existed for themselves, she insisted; they have always conceived of themselves in relation to men. Second, she marshaled broad research in psychology, anthropology, sociology, history, and biology to prove that femininity is not intrinsic to being female, although it can be both a tool and a trap. Third, she argued that women's reproductive function constitutes a perpetual handicap. Women alone suffer the pain, inconvenience, and hazards of child-bearing, and this often causes them to experience their own bodies as alien. In a country without reliable birth control and where abortion was illegal (though frequently used as contraception, despite the danger), all this was indisputably true. Beauvoir's arguments would serve as a basis for the feminist critique of France's natalist policies in the 1960s and 1970s. Both at the time of *The Second Sex*'s publication and a generation later, Beauvoir's descriptions of motherhood and childbirth as intrinsically alienating to woman-as-existential-subject would be fiercely embraced and fiercely contested.[60]

Beauvoir's arguments attacked all of France's ideological sacred cows, both popular and intellectual, and by the end of the 1960s were influencing radical feminists both in France and abroad. Her critique of Freudian psychoanalysis while privileging women's lived experiences and the material circumstances of their lives, her rejection of essentialism (a reductive binding of woman's identity to her sex) in the formation of women's identity, and her theoretical formulation of "the other" (on which much of poststructuralist semiotics is based) mark her as one of the most important thinkers of the twentieth century.[61] When she was writing *The Second Sex* in the late 1940s, however, hers was a singular voice, in direct conflict with the Crouzets and Archambaults of her day. While Pauline Archambault described women as torn between a natural desire for motherhood and an unspecified social activism, Beauvoir was unconcerned with the physical and sexual differences between women and men. Rather, she was interested in the social elements of male-dominated institutions and culture that suppressed equality between men and women. She accepted basic differences between the two sexes *despite* her criticism of "naturalist" reasoning, a point that is sometimes ignored or misunderstood.[62]

Beauvoir's analysis of women's condition irritated her critics, but they wholeheartedly objected to her solutions for its transformation. Rejecting the liberal social-contract idea of the republican Right, she preferred the Marxist model of history as shaped by material factors and class struggle. Legal equality was important, but it was not enough according to Beauvoir, who wrote that "woman today is divided between the past and the future. Without economic, moral, social, and cultural change, the new woman will never appear. . . . She will not succeed without a collective evolution." Beauvoir believed that the path to women's liberation was blocked by exploitative capitalism (which thrives on the unpaid labor of women in the home) and that only through socialism could women reach equality with men in the public and private sphere. Like other French leftists after the war, she staked her hope on the Communist Party, which, in fact, gave only lip service to women's equality. The work's two volumes were bestsellers following their publication in June and November of 1949, but Beauvoir was attacked from both Left and Right. (The Catholic Church put *The Second Sex* on its index of forbidden literature soon after it was published.) Beauvoir notes in her autobiography, *Force of Circumstance*, that she and the book were criticized with a "particular French meanness," attributing this to men's fear of women's economic competition. By sexually excoriating her and, by extension, independent women in general, Beauvoir suggested, men could assert a false sense of superiority. But despite Beauvoir's rhetorical power, the interest taken in her ideas, and a few women authors who shared her undeclared feminism, the voice of the immediate postwar feminist generation did not belong to her. While *The Second Sex* was avidly read by many women, Beauvoir's radical individualism exceeded the prevailing standard for popular acceptance, as were her solutions for a real destruction of the patriarchy and the triumph of gender equality. It was left to more centrist theorists and politicians to fashion a concept of womanhood that was both comfortable and serviceable to France's national ambitions.[63]

Rather than follow Beauvoir's lead, other women authors wrestled with the contradictions inherent in what historians call a particularist model for women, one premised on a premodern idea of women's singularity rather than on their existence as people and individuals socially interchangeable with men.[64] Jacqueline Martin was piqued that the French language required that the masculine take priority over the feminine. It is "an abuse of sorts to employ the term 'man' in the neuter sense," she proclaimed, while reminding readers of the work of Hubertine Auclert and Olympe de Gouges, who fought for equal rights during "heroic times." In the end, however, Martin, like Nouvion and other female authors of the postwar period, eagerly engaged in theories of physiological difference to exalt femininity and women's influence on society.[65] Martin conjured up the nightmare of a world in which women's nature no longer contributed to their competence and social value: "It would be regrettable," she said, "if men, under the pretext of equality, saw in women 'a comrade,' expecting them to have the same tastes, dragging them to violent sports or excessive jaunts, obliging them to work in rude professions." Thus, Martin reasoned that when educating children, boys and girls should have the same right *to instruction* but not the right to the *same* instruction. Women should be helped to blossom with respect to their specific qualities.[66] Arguing that "equality is not similitude," she clearly was unable to reconcile her instincts of fairness with her belief in the necessity of gender differences. Pauline Archambault, in her essay in *Conscience de la féminité*, tried another tack—to give back to women the security of their past, help them face the future, and even propel them to initiate social change: "The woman of today who declares she is not a feminist . . . either refuses the modest effort of imagination necessary to compare her lot with that of generations before, or underestimates the gift of God, and misunderstands the grandeur of this human evolution of which the feminine evolution is but one aspect. She refuses to associate herself in her small part with the effort of poor humanity searching, haltingly, in stages, on a road paved with difficulty, to make its way to a superior level of conscience and being."[67]

By certain standards, Archambault continued, women had lost things in the new world of egalitarianism and universalism—their mystery and their ignorance of realities (identified as innocence), as well as some of their self-respect—by entering into competition with men. Despite these changes, Archambault was confident that women would embrace the future as "women." She reminded her male readers (whom she knew played the *dénatalité* card to deny women the means to independence) that "the cradles will not be empty just because we are creating young intellectual women with modern educations!"[68] For Archambault believed, as did most of her intellectual cohort, that if given the freedom, women would cultivate their own internal principles and constraints, which would serve society better than maintaining women as dependent minors.

Men believed that their vision of the natural order did not subjugate women; rather, it enhanced women's status in society. But they were torn between denunciation and reconciliation. Pauline Archambault criticized Crouzet's *Bachelières ou jeunes filles?* for being inadequate when she said that "red flags go up whenever I hear of different programs for men and women or 'feminine humanities.' This can only have the eventual effect of discounting women."[69] But instead of repudiating such talk, Archambault comforted those, like Crouzet, who were afraid that women's suffrage and their vision of greater equality would permanently destabilize the relation between the sexes, reminding them that love would always bind men and women together as partners. She took care to distance herself from the implications of erasing gender differences, adding that she did not share the "unconditional fervor of Madame Simone de Beauvoir." Convinced that a social framework elaborated on particularist notions based on "natural law" of gender differences would revitalize France, these thinkers viewed the advance of individualism as detrimental to society as a whole.[70]

From the perspective of these women authors, whatever their politics, it was necessary to look forward, not back, for a model of responsible and productive female citizenship in postwar France. They speculated about the future, weaving their visions out of an elaborate mélange of a large universalist spirit laden with patriotism and strongly particularist principles. Evoking traditional solidarity and cooperation between women acting in a community, they tried to dodge the conservative assault on women's rights while claiming a degree of autonomy for themselves. These apparently contradictory approaches would resonate for decades to come. The radical feminists of the 1970s rebelled against this earlier generation of feminists. But many other women during the 1970s spoke of women's liberation but deliberately rejected the term *feminist* for its universalist implications. Well beyond the scope of the feminist movement proper, social programs and various government policies interwove individualism (abortion rights) with communalism (support for mothers), thus forming a strange compromise that the movement would adopt after the Socialist Party's victory in France in the 1980s.[71]

Nouvion and her colleagues knew that history had no buried blueprint to guide them in their search for a just society or to help women build a new female identity. Their vision of the future was not one in which, as Beauvoir put it, "through their natural differentiation men and women unequivocally affirm their brotherhood."[72] Ultimately, these women fell back on "nature" as one element that was theirs alone and that continued to renew itself. To draw from the depths of their "womanness" meant to tap into an unadulterated and overwhelmingly powerful source, strong enough to shake the "masculinist" foundation to its roots. Womanness was a space in which women would rediscover some lost protean self that, through its particularity and difference from men, would enable women to carve out a special space in French society. But these women authors of the postwar period were not separatists. They wanted as much of the pie as their male contemporaries, though perhaps not the same slices. And they saw like-minded men as their best allies in the struggle to achieve their goals. At once pragmatists and idealists, they interwove their pleas for a more woman-centered society or for the ushering in of world peace with concrete demands for legal changes and financial support for families.[73] Almost all these women authors have passed, like their male cohorts, into complete obscurity. Yet their richly illustrated critiques and analyses of France's male-dominated society of the 1940s, their clarion call to French women, and their visions of a world in which sexual difference played an active role, survived into the following decades. The conflicts they articulated and their effort to contest the remains of patriarchal institutions and ideology would reappear in the fight for women's liberation in the 1970s. In the aftermath of the war, women had asked to be absorbed into their society as full citizens *and* as women. This feminism—which was not then labeled as such—wove a particularist vision that dignified women's roles in French society as equal and complementary to men's while demanding women's full participation in the French universalist model. Both threads of this argument would continue to be articulated throughout the twentieth century. Thirty years later, and closer to their goal, women would demand a more absolute equality, based primarily on individual rights rather than on special roles in a corporatist society. This new generation of women, born out of the Liberation's emphasis on fecundity and family and raised under a revamped Civil Code and a more equal educational system, would insist that they be recognized as full citizens.

2 REFORM AND CONSENSUS

Feminism in the 1950s and 1960s

In a society where women's work appears increasingly necessary, it remains impossible to relegate her to an inherited passivity. Women have measured the breadth of their possibilities, their worth, their usefulness, their role—not only at the heart of the family, but in the life of this nation.

Pierrette Sartin, *La promotion des femmes*
(The promotion of women) (1964)

Few historians of twentieth-century feminism in France have focused on the years between the Liberation and the events of May 1968 but rather on the rich decades of the Third Republic, on Simone de Beauvoir and her book *The Second Sex* (published at the end of the 1940s), and on the theoretical debates about women from the 1970s onward. But recently a new generation of scholars has begun to unearth a quiet activism that, although it didn't make many headlines, nonetheless resulted in significant material changes for women in the two arenas where their lives were specifically affected because of their gender: the Civil Code and laws governing access to reproductive freedom. A closer look at activism by women across the political spectrum and at women's intellectual production of the 1950s and 1960s allows us to better understand the roots of second-wave feminism that later emerged from the events of 1968.[1]

Most of the women who worked on equity issues in the pre-1968 years, and who by current standards would be called feminist, chose not to refer to themselves as such. This contributed to their former neglect by scholars.[2] Other pioneering women who were active in the 1960s but not uncomfortable using the term, such as Colette Audry, Évelyne Sullerot, and Yvette Roudy, claimed to have been deeply influenced by Beauvoir's *The Second Sex* yet did not try to articulate an independent feminist politics. In fact, the number of female parliamentarians declined in the years following the Liberation. A powerful combination of women's desire to "return to normalcy" and the popular model of woman as housewife and mother (embraced by political parties both in and out of power) made the notion of women and politics seem nonsensical.[3]

In the 1950s and 1960s, activists focused on rectifying blatant inequalities, pushing for married women to be able to maintain their own bank accounts, to have authority over their children, and to use contraceptives.[4] This period stands out as a time of moderate pragmatism on both a material and a theoretical level. Pragmatists understood that there was a limit to what the public would entertain in terms of social change and agreed to push for basic fairness: that women should be granted the same opportunities and freedoms that men enjoyed. Interested in addressing the vast majority of women whose largest concerns included finding a profession and balancing their familial and employment responsibilities, pragmatic feminism was also willing to compromise—to be satisfied with moderate success rather than principled failure.[5] Feminists renewed pressure on the government to review the *régimes matrimoniaux* (matrimonial property laws) of the Civil Code and to overturn legislation barring the sale of contraceptives. And in the full swing of economic and social recovery, they attacked practices that "protected" women, such as part-time employment, which a decade earlier had seemed like a realistic compromise but now smacked of discrimination. As this chapter will show, a variety of factors—from improvements in girls' education to advancing technology—would work together to modernize the country and, with it, to expand the parameters of women's public and private lives. Feminists of the 1970s would borrow from the research of the 1960s feminists but would be critical of reformist approaches, declaring that the promise of suffrage had been a hollow victory. Regardless, the few women with political and institutional power before 1968 made an enormous impact, pushing through reproductive-rights reforms and reforms to the Civil Code, which overturned centuries of married women's status as minors and of state policy to prevent depopulation. Although exceptional, these politicians also form part of the feminist story in this period.

Persistent Injustice

By the end of the 1940s a majority of working women were being funneled into low-wage, dead-end jobs and the postwar "guarantees" of equal pay for equal work still allowed for a 10 percent discrepancy in salaries. For the most part, women were restricted to traditionally "feminine" occupations, and social expectations at home and in the economy served to mitigate any equality established on paper.[6] Women's political gains also slipped away in the war's aftermath. After the fall of the Fourth Republic and the construction of the Fifth in 1958, elections shortly after returned only 1.7 percent of women deputies to the National Assembly, down from 6 percent in 1946. A 1955 study of women's political participation in the ten years since they were allowed to cast ballots showed that speeches by female deputies in the National Assembly primarily addressed public health, family questions, and children's education; there were almost none on foreign affairs, agriculture, or national defense.[7]

Women's wages remained lower than men's, contributing to women's poverty and lack of independence. And among the working and lower-middle classes, it was not uncommon for the husband or wife to work a second shift at a "black market" job. "We only live to sleep, eat a little, and above all to work," reported one working woman.[8] Women's employment had remained relatively stable following the Liberation despite a drop after the 1940s, which was due partly to the reabsorption of war prisoners and ex-soldiers into the workforce and partly to women's own desire to return to "normalcy."[9] Indeed, a national survey found over 70 percent of men and women believed that it was better for women to devote themselves to the home. But given that approximately 40 percent of married women were employed, beliefs did not square with reality. The French were conscious of the flagrant contradictions in their societal expectations for women but accepted them as a phenomenon of modern life.[10]

These contradictions grew during the 1950s and 1960s as the structure of employment changed, while girls' education and training remained stagnant, affecting both women's labor patterns and their salaries. Positions for working-class women in traditional trades and businesses were narrowing as large manufacturers and retailers replaced small workshops and corner stores, and from the postwar period onward women moved from the agricultural and industrial workforce into the "tertiary" service sector, which expanded from 16.4 percent in 1954 to 25.8 percent in 1968. Hourly wages for women and men showed only a 6.8 percentage point difference by 1972 (after yet another law guaranteeing equal salaries, this time without any differential), but after all employment benefits were calculated, yearly salaries differed by between 20 and 35 percent. The growth of semiskilled tertiary-sector female jobs added to the already low rate of women's salaries overall: jobs in the "pink collar ghettos," where most women either elected or were encouraged to work, paid less than similarly skilled jobs for men.[11] Women faced the worst discrimination in management and the professions. In 1954 women constituted 2,000 out of the 115,000 engineers in France, but only 60 percent were employed and they were frequently denied opportunities and advancement.[12]

By 1961 three-quarters of the workforce was employed for more than forty hours per week and half for more than forty-five. It is no wonder that given women's "double day" of full-time employment and care of the children and household, absenteeism and part-time work were more common among women than men of parenting age. Indeed, "legalized absenteeism" in the form of paid maternity leave (mandated by the government) accounted for only a small percentage of all worker absenteeism, yet it was considered an important justification for lower wages and promotions. The state increased maternity leave from eight weeks in 1945 to fourteen weeks in 1966 as part of a pronatalist policy. And with the employment protections for full-time workers, women continued to be employed by companies as a stopgap labor force that could allow companies growth flexibility. Part-time work was praised as a way to allow women to juggle work and family as well as to discourage them from climbing the job ladder, becoming a permanent fixture during and after France's period of postwar growth.[13]

Women's second-class status in the French economy was worsened by living conditions that were not adequately addressed until well into the 1970s. Many French urban dwellers lived in poorly constructed, outdated, and crumbling residential buildings. Before the war, housing had been scarce and much of it inadequate. The destruction during the war of approximately 1.5 million homes seriously exacerbated the problem, and in 1945 planners expected it would take thirty years to bring buildings up to standard in sufficient number; and indeed the housing problem persisted well into the 1950s and 1960s. A small sampling of twenty-five working-class families in the Paris region in 1958 found that nine were without running water, seven without gas, and two without electricity. Only one family had central heating. Conditions such as these, combined with the difficulty in finding adequate child care or housekeeping (or the inability to afford them) and a tendency to downplay the importance of women's careers, made holding down a full-time job particularly taxing for the average woman.[14] By 1954 the government began implementing an updated plan for housing and regional development, and construction for working- and middle-class homes, particularly in the suburbs, began in earnest. With new housing and a housing subsidy intended to ease the stress on the working class, the government felt better able to pursue its family-centered natalist policy.[15] The program of allowances for children, motherhood, and housing reestablished by the law of August 22, 1946, served as the basis for a social security program that would grow in the following decades.[16] The system of family allowances was revamped, partly because of the significant influence of the Left in France after the war and because of the conservative government's efforts to restore domestic stability and high birthrates. Disbursement of such funds aided families and directly shaped women's and men's social roles.

The government's direct financial involvement in the French family necessarily forced it to take notice of the way the family functioned.

Because the work of women was central to the family, the government researched women's status and, at times, intervened to improve it. Government studies and debates, principally emanating from the Ministry of Labor and its subsidiary groups, made the continuing discussion of "women's insertion" in society more public and acceptable. This was helpful to both women and the economy as the number of single mothers grew by 20 percent between 1962 and 1975 and divorces increased by 8 percent. The state made its intervention palatable because it targeted children for support rather than adults indirectly through the Single Salary Allocation, which incentivized women to stay home but did not force them to do so.[17]

Women made perhaps the most headway in education. Greater access to education helped women prepare to compete in the job market and helped convince them that they were no longer required to submit silently to a second-class status. In middle and high schools, girls accounted for just 40 percent of the student population after the war, but that number rose to 50 percent by 1960. They followed a program almost equivalent to that for boys, and by 1957 almost half of France's high-school girls passed the *baccalauréat*, up from just one-fourth in 1938. Women's attendance at universities nearly trebled, from 53,789 in 1954–1955 to 148,709 in 1965–1966, and their attendance at the exclusive teacher-training schools, the *écoles normales supérieures*, also increased. Women used their education to further their employment opportunities, however constrained. In 1938 France counted 104 women faculty members in its universities—triple the number of 1924. By 1956 the number had nearly tripled again, to 280 women faculty members, 170 of them in science. Teaching high school (which required a far more rigorous training and licensing than in the United States) continued to attract young women at the top of their class, and by 1964 female high-school teachers outnumbered their male colleagues by a ratio of approximately three to two.[18]

Although women had more educational opportunities than before the war, there was a bias against taking women seriously as candidates for intellectual pursuits or training them for specialized careers. Madeleine Guilbert has noted that just when women finally gained a foothold in higher education, largely in the humanities and social sciences (where 60 to 80 percent of students were female), these subjects lost status. Meanwhile mathematics—where female students represented only 20 percent of the total student body—grew in prestige. Out of 15,000 students in preparatory classes for the *grandes écoles* (the consortium of elite French professional schools) in 1957, fewer than 22 percent (or 3,350) were women, and even up through the 1970s women never constituted more than a third. Moreover, women students' choice of subject matter decreased their eligibility for plum jobs. Those who were most dependent on full employment were less likely to seek out educations that would prepare them for professions in which there was little female precedence and scant guarantee of success.[19]

In this new French society of equality in principle but disparity in fact, one of women's key failures was participation in politics. A national survey showed that for the April 1953 municipal elections, female abstention exceeded 30 percent in some areas, and over 50 percent of women polled expressed disinterest in politics altogether.[20] The causes of women's political marginalization were complex, and a number of researchers sought to understand them. One study of the 1946 and 1951 legislative elections by the political scientists and sociologists Jacques Narbonne and Mattei Dogan suggested that women's continuing legal subordination to men in marriage, their relatively poor integration into the workforce, their continuing religious attachment, and a life centered in and around the home afforded them less political education. Traditional antifeminist prejudices also worked against women becoming full-fledged members of the polity and full participants in party politics (a push toward elective office). Until this situation changed, the authors predicted, married women would remain political shadows of their husbands and would tend to lean toward the right of the political spectrum. Dogan and Narbonne shied away from criticizing the social roles responsible for women's political immaturity, but the feminist sociologists Andrée Michel and Geneviève Texier did not. Women's lack of political involvement, they argued, did not come from women's natural proclivity toward religion (or what they called women's pseudo-antifeminism) but rather from their early socialization and from the narrow field of opportunities available to them. Other studies showed that women *were* interested in politics but were deliberately excluded from the party machines. Thus, according to Michel, it was no surprise that Dogan and Narbonne found younger single women to be the most active and most politically outspoken: in addition to their superior education, they had yet to be bent to the cultural demands of motherhood and the psychological constraints of married life. Later studies would elaborate Dogan and Narbonne's findings and confirm their argument, referring to the "masculinization of power within the French state" by the end of the 1950s. The decision makers in France during *les Trente Glorieuses* remained, with almost no exceptions, men. Educational reforms had allowed women what had been the exclusive possession of men, but as long as France celebrated women's "feminine" traits, employers (including the government) would only allow them certain options.[21]

The "Shocking Backwardness" of Civil Law: Reform of the Civil Code

In the 1950s and 1960s women fought two large feminist battles, exposing to public scrutiny the second-class status of women in France and establishing a vocabulary of women's rights. The issues—equality in the marriage contract and the legalization of contraception—formed the basis for a two-pronged attack on French society and institutions. The 1965 Civil Code reform of the matrimonial property laws, which took a large step toward granting married women full equality under the law, was the beginning of a process that continued throughout the 1970s and 1980s. The 1967 Neuwirth law (named after its sponsor, the Gaullist politician Lucien Neuwirth), which legalized contraceptive methods such as the Pill and the diaphragm, also gave official recognition to the idea that women should not be used as pawns in larger collective objectives such as natalism. The effort to update the Napoleonic Code would be a centerpiece of feminist activity over the next few decades, and purging the code of its Bonapartist stamp would be one of the greatest achievements of French institutional reform. Begun in 1945, much of this work would continue into the 1970s and

1980s thanks in part to the constitutional provision of equal rights in law incorporated into both constitutions.

Before the 1965 reform, the husband, as the head of the household (*chef de famille*), had the right to decide whether his wife worked, where his children went to school, and where the family lived. He also had the right to manage his wife's assets. For all practical purposes, women remained minors in marriage. A small code reform of 1907 established women's "reserved assets," which theoretically allowed women to control their earnings, and another reform in 1938 endowed married women with civil capacity, permitting them, for example, to sign contracts or bear witness. But any independent action was still subject to the husband's approval. It was a legal loophole that was gapingly large and constructed to preserve the sanctity of the male-headed family as the foundation of French society. Before the 1965 reforms it was possible for a couple either to sign a prenuptial agreement (or marriage contract) stipulating a woman's control over certain property or to adopt the *régime dotal* (dowry regime), which stipulated that a woman's dowry be returned to her after the termination of a marriage, but only a small number of women had the resources to necessitate such arrangements. Even in the case of a dowry regime marriage, dowered property could be managed by the husband and moveable property could by default become communal. At any rate, most women were married under the standard marriage contract without a dowry, giving the husband control of the wife's assets and community property as well as his own.[22]

A closer look at the legislative fight to reform the Napoleonic Code, of which the Civil Code was a part, reveals the fissures in French society during this time. The efforts of female deputies and, indeed, of paternalistic male deputies to address the Civil Code's shortcomings placed them at the center of a debate over the very nature of women as individuals and their relationship to the family and then to society. The Civil Code's modifications—in 1965 and then the more radical changes of the 1970s and 1980s—marked France's gradual abandonment of particularism and embrace of the universalism that would establish the same legal framework for both married women and men.

From the moment that the Parliament resumed normal activities after the Liberation, the new government reestablished a Commission to Reform the Napoleonic Code, which was specifically charged with updating the laws governing married women. In the context of the independence women gained during wartime and the new government's recognition of their equal status as working and voting members of society, the existing Civil Code seemed terribly out of date. Raymonde Machard put it tersely when she wrote, "Here is the spirit and the letter of the law: the minor spouse; the incapable spouse; the slave spouse; the crucified mother . . . and we are in 1944!"[23] As early as 1950, bills were introduced in the Chamber of Deputies, notably by Deputy and Minister of Public Health and Population Germaine Poinso-Chapuis, of the Christian Democratic Party (MRP), to give women more autonomy in marriage. Poinso-Chapuis had been successful after the war in making brothels and pimping illegal (in the name of women's citizenship) by sponsoring the law of April 13, 1946, called "Marthe Richard" for the city councilor—and former prostitute—who wrote it. But pressure groups such as the Catholic Church, bankers, and notaries, as well as assorted conservatives, managed to derail any serious discussion of liberalizing marriage codes or reproductive rights right after the war and for a decade after.[24]

Conservatives continued to stymie reform until 1963. For almost fifteen years they argued, much as they had after the war, that to marry meant to enter a community of interests that was larger than the sum of its parts. It was an argument fundamental to the corporatism of traditional France. Sanctioning women's independence, conservatives feared, would tear apart this inviolate coupling. The marriage community ultimately needed one voice, and as men were "undoubtedly" heads of households, that voice was naturally theirs. Of course, this had been one of the arguments used to prevent women's suffrage—which did not seem to destabilize the family—but in 1959, when the Reform Commission submitted a bill to the Parliament suggesting that the law be changed to allow married women to have some ownership over movable goods (e.g., cash, stocks, valuables), thereby increasing the average woman's control over her assets, it was shot down in the

Senate. At the time, married women could only control immovable goods, and only a small percentage of French women inherited land. The proposed reform was modest, since the bill merely reflected the economy's evolution away from land ownership and toward financial transactions. During the bill's brief discussion, the jurist and decorated resistance hero Henri Mazeaud said that such meddling reforms meant "a regime of community reduced to zero." It did not help that no women sat on the commission or that only a third of the senators participated in a debate they considered unworthy of their time.[25]

After the bill's initial defeat, it and the Reform Commission's large study of the Civil Code on which it was based languished for a few years, but in 1963 an event occurred that forced the conservatives' hands. A national study of public opinion requested by the minister of justice, Jean Foyer, demonstrated that although there was much public support for maintaining a regime of community, there was an overwhelming consensus for legally establishing equality between spouses and, in particular, for allowing women to handle their own finances. Pierre Marcilhacy, president of a second legal reform commission formed after the 1963 survey, revised the postwar Reform Commission's report. He pointed out that the current laws demanded of women "servitude to marital authority" and that "on the social level, economic expansion, the enlargement of the urban population, and the division of tasks imposed by the constraints and sufferings of two world wars have brought women to play a larger role each day in the running of their homes as well as in public affairs." Trying to balance justice with the prevailing views on womanhood and the family, jurists and politicians strove for compromise, but new ideals of fairness left little room for it. By the end of the debate, the Parliament would exceed its original plan, transforming even parts of the Civil Code that had been left standing by the Reform Commission and the government to reflect a more radical vision of equality than the conservatives had expected.[26]

Parliamentary debates on the reform of matrimonial property laws began inauspiciously in June 1965 and revealed a dedication to perceived fairness mixed with a lingering embrace of tradition. The debate was scheduled for the weekend, when the assembly rarely met. Yet

as Communist Deputy Jeannette Prin said, "This project that interests women equally interests the large majority of French families."
She was applauded by her Communist colleagues and the deputies
from the Rassemblement démocratique révolutionnaire (RDR; Revolutionary Democratic Rally), but the president of the assembly made
no apologies for its scheduling.[27]

Abandoning an initial pose of indifference, the National Assembly
and Senate began to debate the legislation passionately. Minister of
Justice Foyer presented the project of reform: "Ladies and gentlemen,
the assembly will crown a productive session of sweeping reforms by
changes of the utmost importance in the domain of private law, that
of matrimonial property law."[28] And Secretary of State Jean de Broglie
used a similar tone when he addressed the Senate at the start of the
debate: "In calling women today to participate in the direction of the
home and the administration of their own goods, the bill brings the
reform of the marriage settlement to its logical conclusion; men's and
women's new sharing of their life's work."[29] Foyer insisted that the goal
of the reforms was to create more equality between the spouses, but he
established from the outset that there must be a balance between the
spouses' individual independence and the requirements of family life.
Since both spouses were living under one roof and were collectively
supporting the family, their relationship required a cooperative effort.
The updated code would honor such an arrangement, Foyer explained,
allowing each spouse to administer and dispose of his or her goods
while at the same time preserving the communal status of marriage.[30]

The debate over the husband's status as head of the family demonstrated the fault lines in the argument over patriarchal authority. During
a discussion of Article 213 of the Civil Code, deputies Jacqueline Thome-
Patenôtre and Jeannette Prin (a Radical Socialist and a Communist,
respectively) and Marie-Claude Vaillant-Couturier (a Communist and
the vice president of the Union of French Women) all suggested separate amendments to change the language "the husband is head of
the family." They were supported by protesters from French wom-
en's groups who gathered outside Parliament.[31] These female deputies argued for using language such as "the direction of the family is

assured by a common accord of the two spouses" or "the spouses exercise jointly the direction of the family." But their proposals were met with patronizing commentary. Henri Collette, the Gaullist speaker of the assembly, reacted to the "primordial problem" of women's equality by suggesting that France had informally established "a rather strong matriarchy in which the husband does not act before consulting his wife." He assured his fellow deputies that the codirection of the family existed in fact if not in law. Foyer added that "the term 'head of the family,' attributed to the husband by the current Article 213 of the Civil Code, is certainly not contrary to the idea of equality between the spouses. . . . Marriage always exists as a 'division of labor' demanded by the nature of things."[32]

Since the deputies and senators in Parliament wanted to revise the Civil Code to reflect contemporary standards but were committed to keeping the family firmly intact as a male-headed institution, they found themselves drawn into a deep philosophical morass. The mostly male Parliament was willing to grant wives independence on a practical level—for example, giving them authority over their own personal property—but not to bestow on them absolute equality in principle. Indeed, many in Parliament hoped that the new freedom granted to wives by these reforms would serve mainly to allow them to run the home better than before. The title "head of the family," which Collette called "more honorific than real," and which was maintained in the final version of the reform, was a significant stance against the encroachment on male authority.[33] This issue is illustrated in a June 26 exchange concerning the elimination of the husband's authority over the choice of residence (Article 215):

> Mme. Thome-Patenôtre: There is no reason why both spouses should not choose their residence together.
> President: What is the advice of the commission?
> Speaker of the Assembly (Collette): The commission has rejected both amendments because as Mme. Prin herself has said, spouses will choose their residences together, which happens in real life.

Mme. Prin: So why not say it?

Speaker: It is evident that it is done; it isn't necessary to confirm it with a law. Moreover, we don't see who could decide the matter. . . . Conforming to the intention adopted from the beginning of this debate to leave to the husband the power of head of the family, . . . it is close to the only power that he will keep.[34]

Evidently, the conservative majority was unwilling to take reform to its logical conclusion. The outcome of the bill demonstrated that as long as "harmony reigned in the household," wives would be allowed to have greater individual autonomy, but if a bill promoting equality threatened conventional ideas of family unity, the government would consider itself morally obligated to censure it.[35] Adhering to the state-supported vision of familialism, many senators argued that the first object of the new law would have to be the protection of the family. Only after this institution was secured could the government begin providing for wives' equality in law as it was increasingly being lived out in fact. Despite this weighty contradiction, the representatives who debated the bill maintained their optimism. As Jean de Broglie concluded:

In the final analysis, the bill that is submitted to you introduces in our law a rejuvenated philosophy of marriage and the family. It cautiously returns to a matter that is at the base of life, but the bill is bent upon making . . . a definitively stronger and harmonious family unit. It constitutes in every way a necessary step toward the evolution of our society. *(Applause from center right and right benches.)*[36]

This reform never fully resolved the legal bind that it created, although the new matrimonial property laws would stand as a bulwark against men's abuse of power in marriage. A husband was now required to consult his wife before making significant financial decisions and could be held accountable in a court of law. In a profound change for French society, wives were guaranteed the right to open and control bank accounts in their own names, to exercise a profession independently, and to freely dispose of their own goods without their husband's consent. Moreover, both spouses were declared equally responsible for the welfare of the household and children.[37] But in the decision to retain the husband as the head of household, the government fell back on the belief that the needs of the community were more important than the rights of women. This idea was enough to justify maintaining husbands in a position of authority relative to wives. Female parliamentarians and their supporters from both the Left and the Right were disappointed. "Today, the countries that remain socially and economically backward are precisely those where women have not yet joined men on the road to equality," Deputy Odette Launay remarked. In the end, however, they voted for the reform despite its weaknesses, and in doing so they set in motion a series of amendments that would call into question much of what Foyer, Collette, and the other public officers of the war generation had worked to preserve. As Thome-Patenôtre acknowledged, the new Civil Code reform "constitutes a future hope for a more complete modernization of matrimonial property law."[38]

Depopulation or Civilization:
Dénatalité and Contraception

For centuries French women, both married and single, had actively sought to limit their pregnancies through primitive contraceptive methods available to them and, when that failed, through abortion. By the 1960s, however, the contradiction between France's posture of a nation reborn, free from backward habits, and the secretive, unhygienic, and dangerous methods women were forced to employ to prevent or terminate pregnancy overwhelmed a lingering popular sentiment disapproving of contraception. Women activists' triumph over the national obsession with pronatalism as key to women's equalized social status became the crucible in which active, political feminism erupted.[39] Some women activists during the 1960s insisted that women should have absolute control over their fertility; other women were more circumspect. But in this time of emerging feminism and tenacious paternalism, women activists were largely united in pushing for these changes with enough political delicacy to get laws passed. Embedded in the debate over contraceptive access was the taboo notion that sex existed for pleasure as well as reproduction.[40] Frank discussions about legalizing birth control paved the way for more open discussions of sexual matters within the women's liberation movement.

De Gaulle's famous counsel directly aimed at women—that France needed thousands of babies—was only one in a long string of demands on women to reproduce voiced by a sequence of leaders after the war, but laws to ensure this began decades before. The law of July 13, 1920, penalized women who aborted and the abortionist, as well as outlawed any antinatalist propaganda, punishable by up to three years' imprisonment. Any discussion of birth control methods other than the church-approved temperature method (renowned for its inadequacy) was strictly forbidden. The law met with significant popular disapproval, and juries that tried abortion cases frequently acquitted the accused. The government did not give up, however, and three years later, the law of March 27, 1923, completed the prohibition against abortion, punishing anyone helping or trying to help a woman procure an abortion with up to five years' imprisonment and a fine of up to 7.2 million old francs. Penalties for members of the medical establishment were even more severe. The French birthrate, however, stubbornly refused to climb high enough to repair the losses of the previous half-century.[41]

On the eve of World War II, in a belated attempt to shore up defenses at home, the government promulgated a set of new laws, the Family Code of July 29, 1939. Intended to reinforce the family, increase the birthrate, and invigorate public morality, Chapter 3 of the Family Code, entitled "Protection of the Race," stiffened abortion penalties and made the crime easier to prosecute.[42] Ostensibly intended to protect the family, the law could easily imprison a mother who had had a miscarriage or was trying to limit her number of children. After the armistice with Germany in 1940, the Vichy government extended its efforts to wipe out abortion and to prevent the underpopulation that Marshal Pétain had expressly blamed for France's defeat. By February 15, 1942, abortion became a crime against society (against the French "race") and thus was considered an act of sabotage or treason and carried the death penalty. Some women were condemned to hard labor, and a convicted abortionist was executed. After the Liberation, the laws passed during the Vichy regime were annulled, but the 1920 and 1939 laws remained on the books, now subsumed under Articles L647, L648, and L649 of the Public Health Code. Article 317 of the Penal Code called abortion a *délit d'intention* (offense of criminal intent), punishable by fines and imprisonment. France's concern over the birthrate needs to be seen in the context of growing immigration from its overseas colonies and (after 1962) the return of one million French nationals to France after its defeat in the Algerian War of Independence. Recent scholarship has pointed to the French obsession not just with population loss but with virility and France's place in the world, alongside simple xenophobia and racism. There was no conclusive proof that stricter laws stemmed the tide of abortions; it was clear, however, that they added fear and shame to the procedure and increased the number of infections, maimings, and deaths. Until the revitalization of the economy in the 1960s, it seemed that France staked its main hope for renewal on the reproductive capacities of its women.[43]

After World War II and before contraception and abortion were legalized in 1967 and 1974, respectively, these practices were only allowed in very specific circumstances. Before 1967, birth control pills could be legally prescribed only to women with serious medical problems that contraindicated pregnancy, and abortion was permitted only when a woman's life was threatened. Three doctors had to certify this in front of a tribunal, and a copy of their decision had to be sent to the president of the Department Council of the Order of Physicians.[44] Sexual practices in France were loosening during this time, and increasing numbers of French citizens were ignoring church precepts banning contraception and premarital sex. Yet religious leaders exerted influence on policymakers, creating a powerful firewall between common practice and policy reform. It is important to note that during this time condoms were sold over the counter in pharmacies for the prevention of venereal disease, but, extraordinary as it may seem from a contemporary perspective, they were considered so socially unacceptable and "unnatural" as to go unmentioned in discussions of contraception. It was also sometimes possible for women to acquire other forms of birth control, such as spermicidal chemicals and pessaries, but the withdrawal method and illegal abortion remained the most commonly practiced birth-control methods.[45]

In 1947 a young gynecologist, Marie-Andrée Lagroua Weill-Hallé, witnessed the criminal trials of women who had desperately sought abortions and, around the same time, saw the success of family planning clinics in the United States. She became convinced that birth control should be made available to French women, particularly after she saw some of the horrors the French medical establishment inflicted. Doctors sometimes chose to perform curettages without anesthesia after botched abortions as a way of punishing women for what they saw as the crime of refusing motherhood. "For the first time," Dr. Lagroua recalled after she witnessed this practice, "I was scandalized in the name of moral principles." She was not alone. Belgian doctor Jenny Leclercq's pioneering book, *Le contrôle des naissances et le malaise conjugal* (Birth control and marital malaise), published in 1947, also argued for the legalization of contraception on practical as well as ethical grounds, but her book remained an intellectual curiosity rather than an impetus to reform.[46]

After studying French legislation in detail, and with the support of her husband, who was an influential pediatrician, Dr. Lagroua in 1953 published an article in *La semaine des hôpitaux de Paris* (Paris hospitals weekly) arguing that the 1920 law should be abolished. Faced with older male colleagues who were, overall, as disinterested in birth control methods as they were ignorant of them, she did more to scandalize the medical community than to create much interest in reform. Two years later, when a couple was tried and convicted for abandoning their fourth child while the twenty-five-year-old woman was pregnant for the fifth time in five years, Dr. Lagroua broached the subject again.[47] In a speech to the Academy of Moral and Political Science in March 1955, she denounced the dangers of the 1920 law for the health of both the family and women:

If we have recalled this particularly painful drama before your illustrious company, it is because today it is not an isolated case. Each day, young households confront similar problems. Because they experience conditions, with which each of you are familiar, exhaust their health, or because of moral or economic difficulties of all types, they see the stability of their home compromised by an undesired birth at the wrong time. It is precisely because it is first and foremost a human problem to resolve that we appeal to you. Until now in France birth control has collided with doctrinal opposition; defensible perhaps . . . for the followers of certain dogmas, but unjustifiable nevertheless, in a country that believes it leaves individuals free to follow their conscience.[48]

Her speech prompted a few articles and letters by prominent journalists and demographers, but not enough to create a national discussion even after it was the subject of the first International Congress of Medical Ethics, where Dr. Lagroua argued for the secularization of family planning. Important public figures, including conservative politicians, the clergy, and the National Council of Physicians, remained intransigent in their opposition. Some doctors were already arguing that the legalization of birth control would help lower the high abortion rate—but they were not in the majority. Then, in 1956, one male journalist, Jacques Derogy, shocked the forces of tradition, both Left and Right. Prefaced by Dr. Lagroua, Derogy's *Des enfants malgré nous* (Children in spite of us) was an explicit and unapologetic discussion of contraception and abortion that challenged the state's position on both ethical and practical grounds, instigating a sea change in French attitudes on birth control.[49] Derogy argued for the legalization of both contraception and abortion, basing his arguments on the fact that illegal abortion was increasingly becoming a national scourge. For every live birth, he wrote, there was one abortion. This translated into about eight hundred thousand abortions a year in France, a majority of them performed by unskilled practitioners or by the pregnant women themselves. If we are to believe Derogy, approximately thirty-five thousand women died per year from abortion or related complications.

The government and medical community had recognized the problem, however quietly, but it would take the general public's outrage to force laws to change.[50]

Derogy was a member of the Communist Party and therefore suggested that poor social conditions were a major cause of the high abortion rate (and that abortions would not be necessary if those conditions were improved). Yet he showed that the data ran counter to his ideological premise: most women who sought abortion were not from the bottom rungs of the socioeconomic ladder. For example, two studies performed in Lyon and Paris hospitals concluded that 85 percent and 62 percent, respectively, of women receiving care after an abortion were middle-class and married. (Other studies performed in the 1960s supported Derogy's observation, which ran contrary to all the received communist wisdom: birth control was not a right-wing capitalist plot.) Derogy wrote that the attempt to control fertility artificially had existed throughout the history of civilization and that abortion, when performed in hygienic conditions by trained personnel, was relatively safe and did not leave women sterile or incapacitated. Moreover, he asserted that women of all classes, married and single, had a variety of reasons for not wanting to have children and that they were quite willing to seek out abortions—even illegal ones—to avoid becoming mothers.[51]

Derogy was influential, but many others—philosophers, scientists, and social critics—had entrenched opinions about reproductive rights. Alfred Sauvy, director of the National Institute of Demographic Studies and one of the most vocal and influential anticontraception and antiabortion voices in the country, supported the thesis that abortion essentially stemmed from society's failures. But he argued that women's desires were driven by societal expectations, not individual aspirations, and that the solution lay in the paternalist state, which should offer more support to women and their families—a policy that the government had been pursuing with gusto but with limited success. Sauvy also believed that if France were to allow birth control to improve the "quality of children's lives," as the "neo-Malthusians" argued, it would find that only intelligent families would use it; those he judged stupid would continue to reproduce, resulting in the decline of French civilization.

In the 1960s, in an atmosphere of loosening cultural norms (declining church attendance, a greater incidence of premarital sex, and the growth of an independent youth culture), Derogy's arguments ultimately held sway. But initially *Des enfants malgré nous* was largely met by shock or indifference. The reason lies not just in Derogy's support for abortion but also in his challenge to the collectivist and patriarchal social order—which both conservatives and Communists supported. By suggesting that women as individuals ought to be able to control their reproduction, Derogy angered representatives of both sides of the political spectrum and encouraged the nascent feminism of the time by articulating a women's liberation that began with women's bodies. In a voice reminiscent of postwar utopianism, Derogy concluded, "If tomorrow the legislature replaced the prohibition against birth control education with more humane and efficacious arrangements, it could mean the end of biological servitude for the women of our country, a step toward their liberation, and the promise of a more satisfying love."[52]

In 1956 Dr. Lagroua, along with sociologist Évelyne Sullerot, amassed a large group of supporters, some socially prominent, and formed the organization Maternité heureuse (Happy Motherhood). Its goal was to legalize contraception and make it widely accessible, permitting women to choose when and if to have children. As Sullerot wrote in a letter to Dr. Lagroua, "I am not outrageously feminist, but I find that in this country where women are considered adults, and where women have been given the right to vote, it should be principally up to women to state their views on what most concerns them." Dr. Lagroua had said elsewhere that "those who would turn a family planning organization into a feminist organization make a big mistake." As will become clear, Dr. Lagroua believed that the narrowest approach to winning this essential legal and medical change would have the largest impact. Given the fact that feminism had largely disappeared from the public scene in the wake of the "return to normalcy" of the 1950s, this tactic served her purposes. By January 1963, Happy Motherhood had changed its name to the Mouvement français pour le planning familial (MFPF; French Family Planning Movement) and had sixteen thousand supporters on its rosters. Its governing board included a number of professional women—Sullerot, the journalist Andrée Marty-Capgras, and Solange de La Baume from *La revue de Paris*—as well as doctors and professors.[53]

Happy Motherhood was a cautious but politically astute beginning. The group limited its goals to the legalization of contraception, understanding that reference to abortion would thwart any chances of reform. Given that much of the anti-birth-control lobby admonished women for refusing motherhood, Dr. Lagroua used Happy Motherhood to stress family planning over women's right to sexual independence, arguing that family planning did not mean limiting conception or promoting one politics over another: "Let no one say that the goal of our association is the limitation of births," an official statement said. "We want consensual motherhood in the best conditions." Many feminists of the 1960s approved of this tactic. Even Simone de Beauvoir, whose views on motherhood were more ambivalent, insisted in her introduction to Dr. Lagroua's book *Le planning familial* that "in preventing men and women from planning their lives, we make it impossible for them to organize correctly the entirety of their existence. . . . Today, in all domains, man refuses to abandon himself to caprice or chance; he organizes, he rationalizes, he takes his destiny in his hands; why submit to fate where the life of the family is concerned?"[54]

Thus Dr. Lagroua's argument was socially conservative, understanding that the government viewed population growth as one of its most sacred responsibilities, and she needed to create a public understanding of contraception that would respond to these concerns.[55] Supporters of family planning began to suggest that pronatalism might be defeating the state's goals of protecting society. Dr. André Berge, an MFPF supporter, addressed the state's position directly: "If the state has, without a doubt, the right to substitute itself for individual conscience in the face of social peril, it appears evident that it overreaches these rights when it intervenes in a domain like this one . . . by so much more that one is tempted to ask oneself if the law doesn't end up thus creating a social danger."[56]

By 1960 Dr. Lagroua and the family planning movement were successfully making contraception, and women's condition in general, the subject of popular debate to an extent unheard of since the Liberation. Popular magazines as well as scholarly journals discussed public opinion, moral positions, and medical findings. The debate began to shift from family planning toward individual rights, even if granting women control of their bodies came at the possible expense of the country as a whole. In October 1960 the television show *Face à face* featured a public debate on the subject after a sensational advertising blitz. Viewers witnessed poignant testimony from couples whose lives had been dramatically altered because birth control was unavailable. The show claimed that a majority of viewers polled were dissatisfied with the 1920 law and wanted contraception and information about it. As Andrée Michel noted in the journal *Les temps modernes* (founded by Beauvoir and Jean-Paul Sartre), viewers cited personal and health reasons for legalizing birth control: the desire to prevent unwanted births and the birth of children with severe medical problems, as well as women's right to choose if and when to have children for their own physical and psychological health. "In contrast," Michel noted, "the notion of 'family planning,' in other words trying to control births for the welfare of the family itself, never mind the state, was anathema to the viewers. Individual freedom held more sway than the rights of the family, regardless of the attitudes of the elites."

Similar sentiment was reflected in the statements of women tried between January 1956 and March 1957 for having aborted (most had been "caught" in the hospital where they had gone after botched self-abortions). A little more than a third of these women (37.8 percent) cited economic reasons such as insufficient funds or inadequate housing, while almost the same number (36.2 percent) cited personal reasons independent of family or economic status. The rest were women who had been recently divorced or separated or who had medical problems.[57] Another survey on women who underwent abortions showed that over three-quarters of those surveyed said that men were not prepared to be fathers and refused to take up the responsibilities of fatherhood. An unwanted pregnancy often left women to "take care of their problem" alone; in reality, family planning was more euphemistic than real. In her book *La grand peur d'aimer* (The great fear of love), prefaced by Beauvoir and published in 1960, Dr. Lagroua asserted that women had a variety of personal reasons for not wanting to carry a fetus to term. Often, "happy motherhood" was no motherhood at all, a reality the government found difficult to avoid.[58] Knowing that most of the public was behind them, proponents of contraception continually hammered away at the idea that pronatalists wrongly conflated family planning with the limitation of births.

Meanwhile, "family planning centers" were being opened rather brazenly in various parts of the country. Dr. Henri Fabre, a Trotskyist obstetrician-gynecologist, opened the first family planning center in Grenoble on June 10, 1961, illegally dispensing advice and contraceptive devices either imported or concocted in the back room. (The office would remain a major center of women's activism into the 1970s.) Six months later, in January 1962, a consultation center for students was opened at the Mutuelle générale de l'éducation nationale (MGEN; General Mutual of National Education), supported by Dr. Lagroua and an appeals-court lawyer, Anne-Marie Dourlen-Roullier. By 1966 eighty-five centers were operating in France. The reaction in the non-Catholic press was positive, and the authorities seemed to keep their distance, through a form of "don't ask don't tell." MFPF activists insisted that the 1920 law actually did not punish the fabrication or use of contraception, only the active dissemination of contraceptive products or information about contraception, and that only if used for the purpose of propaganda. MFPF's stated goal was educational—for the *regulation* of conception—so they argued they were safe from prosecution. Yet such arguments would not have prevented the state from taking serious action if it had chosen to. Popular acceptance doubtless played a role in preventing this.[59]

Le livre noir de l'avortement (The black book of abortion), published in 1962, galvanized public opinion in much the same way as Derogy's *Des enfants malgré nous* had six years earlier. Written by Marcelle Auclair—a novelist and a co-founder of and frequent columnist for the women's magazine *Marie-Claire*—the book is a shockingly direct account of the abortion issue and was the first public statement in defense of abortion rights by a mainstream cultural icon. *Le livre noir* presented heart-wrenching testimony from women and men—young and old, married and single, and from all walks of life—describing their problems in avoiding conception, the difficulties of being forced to add another child to their family, and the pain, humiliation, and frequent medical complications of illegal abortions. Auclair argued persuasively that abortion was an entrenched social phenomenon and that popular sentiment demanded that it be legalized along with birth control. The book had enough of an impact that it was followed by Anne-Marie Dourlen-Roullier's demographic study *La verité sur l'avortement* (The truth about abortion) in 1963 and then by the French Protestant church broaching the subject with its congregants in Francine Dumas's 1964 article in the Protestant magazine *Réforme*, "L'avortement: Il faut en parler" (Abortion: It has to be discussed).[60]

Some advocates expanded the discussion around contraception to further a national reflection on sexual morality. For example, Catherine Valabrègue, a sociologist and co-founder of the family planning movement, noted, "We can deplore premarital sex, but why is sex 'moral' only when there is risk or fear involved? One would think that contraceptives would have the effect of moralizing—providing a more correct estimation of reality." To practice family planning, Valabrègue continued, "is not just to learn contraceptive techniques, it implies a plainly responsible manner of living, therefore, plainly moral." Other writers, influenced by modern psychology and sex research, argued that sex was not only a social reality but a biological need that had to be fulfilled for the equilibrium of the individual and the couple. They claimed that many health dangers (frustration, accidents at work, nervous illness) resulted from a lack of sexual activity.[61] This change in strategy would frustrate Dr. Lagroua and lead to her resignation in 1967 from the MFPF and the radicalization of the family planning movement from 1968 onward.

The gap between popular support for birth control's legalization and the stance of some of the most powerful institutions in France began to widen, with many on the Left and in the medical establishment avoiding taking a clear stand. Nevertheless, at a colloquium organized at the Paris Faculty of Medicine in November 1963, participants agreed that contraception in whatever form was a necessary aspect of contemporary civilization. The law of 1920, they concluded, contributed to fear and neurosis surrounding sex rather than nurturing a sense of responsibility. The colloquium's participants created a standing commission to study contraception as a public health measure and to create services that would offer information to those who sought it.[62] An influential segment of the medical profession had come around to supporting contraception and dismissed the notion that it was immoral, which led the way for other large French institutions to follow suit.

At the time, the Socialist and Communist parties were hostile to birth control, but began to change their positions in part because the support of female constituents could lead to important electoral gains. As late as 1961 the Socialists had compared abortion and contraception to castration and sterilization, referring to them as the "dehumanization of man." Communists had referred to family-planning supporters as "neo-Malthusians" who wanted to deny workers what they were owed by capitalists and to "turn away the laborious masses from the struggle for social progress and peace." The abolition of capitalism and the dawn of real socialism, the Communists believed, would herald the abolition of women's oppression and the need for abortion, since its root causes would be gone. Truly "happy motherhood," the Communists said, meant bringing children into the world without the fear of starvation or homelessness.[63]

But the PCF ultimately decided not to alienate its female members (and potential voters) at the expense of its ideals. By January 1965, during the party's annual Week of Marxist Thought, Jean-Marie Legay, professor at the Faculty of Sciences in Lyon, stated unequivocally that "no viable solution for the liberation of women can avoid birth control, that this is a necessary condition for this liberation."[64] And Jeannette Vermeersch revealed the party's new position in *L'humanité*: "Family planning is a fact in France; the average number of children per family is a little over two. . . . We struggle together for the right to liberate motherhood."[65] The Section française de l'internationale ouvrière (SFIO; to be renamed Parti socialiste in 1969) also revamped its position on the law of 1920 to encourage family planning for the health and welfare of couples and their children, and François Mitterrand, during his presidential campaign in 1965, declared himself in favor of abrogating the 1920 law. By 1967 the Left had shifted course from its original aim of repopulating France through supporting the working-class family to a commitment to the specific needs of its female constituents. In doing so, the Left stumbled into an alliance with the "feminists" it had once denounced.[66]

By the mid-1960s momentum for legislative action grew as the reticence of both the Left and the Right diminished. Finally, the Ministry of Social Affairs gave a green light to contraceptives by welcoming the registration of legislative bills for legalization. By 1965 Parliament had enacted sweeping reforms in married women's rights. In 1966, with the number of illegal family planning centers becoming a national embarrassment, the Socialists, the Communists, the Federation of the Democratic Left, and the Union des démocrates pour la République (UDR)—led by its secretary-general, Lucien Neuwirth—all proposed bills to legalize contraception. The Parliament chose to debate the proposals of Neuwirth and Jacqueline Thome-Patenôtre (a Socialist), and the Neuwirth bill became law on December 28, 1967, though not without serious opposition from the far Right.[67]

The debate in the assembly and Senate over contraception hinged on the question of where collective responsibility ended and personal freedom began and tried to determine nothing less than the degree of equality women should possess in French society. Arguments for and against the legalization of contraception ran from the practical and, some might say, cynical to sweeping propositions that attempted to embrace larger moral positions. Once again, natalist concerns were paramount, and much energy was spent determining the birthrate needed for a vital population, over and above any moral issues that contraception might impose. The debate over legalizing contraception tested the validity of France's social policies against its principles of equality. After all, natalists could claim that the birthrate had risen slightly in 1930, a decade after the implementation of the 1920 law outlawing contraception and increasing child welfare benefits. And since World War II there had been a substantial increase in the average number of births annually: from 667,000 in the 1930s to 849,000 in the period from 1965 to 1974.[68] Prohibiting contraceptives seemed to be working.

The natalists stood their ground during the entire debate, arguing passionately against contraception based on health and morality and spent hours discussing the medical and physical repercussions of various devices and chemicals. This, to a great extent, is why the bill took more than six months to become law. Significant parts of it were defeated because of concern over health risks. Marcel Guislain, a doctor and senator, who was convinced that the state should repress contraception and regulate morality in general, stated that "the maintenance of foreign bodies in the uterus . . . provokes permanent irritation of the organ. . . . How many cases of endometriosis, salpingitis, pelvic inflammations, and infections do these objects cause?" His colleague Jacques Henriet vigorously supported Guislain and claimed that hormones and chemicals behave "like an angry bull in a china shop" when they are introduced in a woman's natural cycle.[69]

Officially, birth control remained primarily an issue of national security rather than one of child welfare or of the viability of the fetus; most of the arguments presented reinforced this argument, and much of the debate was taken up defending or rebutting it. Natalists such as Alfred Sauvy warned that the legalization of birth control would imperil France's birthrate while failing to address the broader social problems of inadequate housing and resources that often drove couples to limit their family size. Derogy and supporters of contraception countered that in other countries such as the United States, where contraception was legal, the birthrate had increased. But ultimately the debate over family planning was so heated because it centered on the question of women's independence. If women were actively procuring contraception to remain relatively free of risk while sexually active, that meant they were consciously pursuing sexual satisfaction. The positive image of the powerful woman existed in traditional French culture, but strictly as a mother within the family. The idea that women might be able to control their fecundity and thereby devote themselves to the public sphere while still engaging in sexual activity led to the unsettling possibility that women might neglect their "true" responsibilities to their children, their husbands, and their homes. Nevertheless, with the threat of women's growing power and equality looming, legislators swallowed hard and voted to permit contraception. The report on contraception by the High Commission on Population and Family put it more poetically: "The situation of women in society has been profoundly transformed; they are no longer our last colony."[70]

Contraception became legal with the passing of the Neuwirth law on December 28, 1967. It was a rather modest bill, although radical in its break with France's long-standing demographic obsession. Created to remain in effect for five years pending reevaluation, it authorized the import and manufacture of contraceptives for sale exclusively in pharmacies and only with a prescription. The Ministry of Social Affairs would oversee the distribution of contraceptives. Minors under twenty-one were required to obtain parental consent for certain contraceptives on the ministry's list, and all contraceptives were prohibited for those under eighteen except with written consent of a parent or guardian. All antinatalist advertising remained strictly prohibited under pain of imprisonment. Commercial advertisement was restricted to medical and pharmaceutical publications, and purchases of contraceptives were not reimbursed by Social Security. The law provided that the family planning centers, established to educate the public on contraceptive techniques and strategies, be forbidden from providing contraception itself.

Because of the number of restrictions contained in the law, it appeared that the government erected every impediment to prevent their use. One source claims that even by 1968, only 3 percent of French women of childbearing age took oral contraceptives as compared to 16.95 percent in the United States and 8.13 percent in Britain. Another estimate puts birth control usage made available by legalization at 10 percent.[71] It was not until the fight to legalize abortion, when the demand for reproductive freedom was significantly enlarged, that the 1967 law was expanded and liberalized. The law—and the strategies for passing it—did not satisfy contraception advocates or detractors. Many proponents found the notion of "happy motherhood" beside the point and had lobbied to make contraception available without a prescription and for it to be paid for by Social Security.[72] Even so, the 1967 law undeniably granted women more personal freedom and opened the way to a full-fledged attack on the state's regulation of women's lives in the decades to come.

The Women's Cause: From Compromise to Challenge

Challenges to French law over women's civic majority and reproductive control led women to develop a language of rights and a taste for challenging the status quo. Between the time when Beauvoir wrote *The Second Sex* and the events of 1968, the gap between feminist theory and feminist activism slowly began to close. During this period, sociologists and historians intensified their scrutiny of women's status in male-dominated France, highlighting the injustices women suffered. A few still pondered the deeper questions of women's identity, subscribing to essentialist visions of womanhood even as they fought to defend women against prejudice and abuse. But the most original feminist work to emerge during this period focused on women's lived experience rather than on their "true self." These writings reflected feminists' deeper thinking about women's condition in society and their increasingly sophisticated gender analysis long before it was popularized in the 1970s. Some of the works were narrowly focused, but all tried to use scientific methods to study the condition of women and to demonstrate concretely the discrimination they faced, implying that such knowledge would serve immediate and practical purposes. The Left, both within and outside political parties, served as the political vanguard for these changes, although ironically both the Communist Party and the Socialist Party would receive a sound rebuke for their backwardness in these studies and in the wake of the May 1968 protests.[73]

Madeleine Guilbert's *Les fonctions des femmes dans l'industrie* (The functions of women in industry) is one of the better known of these studies and remains well regarded by historians.[74] Guilbert charted a modest course of research: to understand men's and women's professional roles, claiming their distribution was central to any study of women's employment. She chose to examine only the industrial sector, where the majority of women worked (except for those in agriculture) and where she claimed the historical differences between men's and women's jobs were greatest and among the least well understood.[75] Guilbert's findings detailed the intense prejudice women experienced in the job market, and her description of this prejudice was itself an argument for reform. Comparing women's industrial work to that of North Africans employed in France (a group that French society overlooked), she reported that women were confined to industrial jobs that ranked lowest in terms of skill, responsibility, and pay. Despite constitutional promises of equal salaries, she found that even women with the same titles as men systematically received lower salaries. Such conclusions, drawn from hard data, were damning.

Other broad national and international studies provided ammunition for the next generation of feminists. Marie-José and Paul-Henri Chombart de Lauwe's study *La femme dans la société: Son image dans différents milieux sociaux* (Woman in society: Her image in different social milieus) exemplifies this sort of work. Published in 1963, its arguments are reflected in the legislation of the late 1960s. Like Guilbert's study, it was rigorous, incorporating the research of many other scholars and using clearly demarcated samples and statistical data. The authors postulated that the malaise that feminists at the time of the Liberation had noticed—and that women continued to experience—was due to a twentieth-century phenomenon: the gap between women's aspirations and persistent traditional images of women's role. Thus, women were held back not by inexperience but by prejudice. The Chombarts concluded their study by noting that although opinions varied widely, the most common image of women had evolved to include an acceptance of basic equality with men and that young middle-class women were most likely to take this idea seriously.[76]

These young middle-class women were caught up in the tension between French capitalism, which seemed to cooperate with the state's traditional expectations of women, and a new generation's embrace of the rising individualism of postwar Europe. Many middle-class women objected more and more vigorously to their continued second-class status, pursuing their independence more aggressively after reconstruction was well under way, but they did so with a certain amount of uneasiness. Françoise Giroud, one of France's most prominent female journalists, recorded this phenomenon in *La nouvelle vague* (The new wave). A popular survey more than a scientific study, it nevertheless considered the effect of social influences on women's experience. "Young women," Giroud observed, "define themselves more in relation to their personal situation within society than in relation to their milieu, to their social class, and to particular problems of that class."[77]

Women researchers and activists of this time were keenly aware of contradictions between the new possibilities for individual freedom and material parity and the old myths, laws, and policies that kept women from claiming their fair share. France had recently championed women as self-sufficient Resistance fighters, but during the 1950s and 1960s, the popular idea that romantic love fulfilled women completely suffused popular women's magazines such as *Elle, Marie-Claire,* and *Marie-France.* And so did the Janus face of this image—that of the enfant terrible, a young woman who smashed social convention with her unbridled sexuality. "Without confusing myths and prejudices," Michel and Texier wrote, "it can nevertheless be stated that the majority of myths relative to women carry with them 'a lesson of contempt' that is diffused by the mass media every day to millions of listeners and readers."[78]

Michel and Texier pointedly addressed the negative consequences of women's socialization in their work *La condition de la française d'aujourd'hui* (The condition of the French woman today). Published under the auspices of Colette Audry at Éditions Gonthier's Collection Femme in 1964, before the marriage codes were changed or contraception legalized, the two-volume work was considered by many 1970s feminists as the *Second Sex* of the 1960s.[79] Like Beauvoir, whose writing had influenced them, they analyzed both attitudes and concrete experience, and like Beauvoir they suggested that any true "transformation of formal rights into real rights" would only occur through profound social change. They went further than Beauvoir, however, in describing the pragmatic changes that would have to take place, and their list reflects their generation's greater acknowledgment of the complex ways in which French society maintained women's secondary status. Real rights, the authors concluded, reside[d] in the socialization of domestic work, the creation of a whole network of collective services (child care, playgrounds, camps, kitchens, inexpensive ready-made meals, etc.) that capitalism has refused women in order to obey the law of maximum profit. Real rather than formal emancipation implies that the development of production not be impeded by the barriers individual interest sets up, but attains a level able to permanently (as opposed to episodically) furnish employment for women. . . . It also demands that . . . democracy cease to be elitist (composed of business owners, bankers, notaries, and priests, etc., who have reigned until now) to include all people (men and women).[80]

Women scholars and activists of the 1950s and 1960s also began to be more critical of political parties' auxiliary groups and instead turned toward each other in solidarity. Françoise Marzellier, former Resistance fighter, pilot, and journalist, commented from experience that while men from the Right might be attached to a past "golden age" of female servitude, men on the Left shamelessly adhered to the same social conservatism; Andrée Michel said that it was the "ambiguity of leftist men" in France that inhibited women's equality.[81] Either way, as the feminist Claire Salomon-Bayet lamented, "Fifteen years after the fundamental book *The Second Sex*, a systematic essay demystifying the feminine problem, are we not in the height of restoration . . . of old myths and the creation of new ones?" Frequently referencing Beauvoir, if only obliquely, these women argued that both culture and politics needed to be changed.[82] "We never ask what is man?" Ménie Grégoire, advice columnist, radio host, and prolific author on women's condition, wrote in 1965. "Masculinity has a fixed value, is a permanent model. . . . To be woman, what is that?" Grégoire continued, "The 'profession' of womanhood has experienced a profound revolution. To become an adult, women today must invent their own models, pushing aside old ones." Similarly, Salomon-Bayet explained, "It is a wonder never to see in the press geared specifically to men a survey on what is man. Question, doubt, . . . and definition seem to be confined to women only in the press specifically geared to them. If man appears, he is to be the criterion by which to gauge woman."[83] Concurrent with their experience, social scientists began to combine analyses of class and gender that would be taken up by 1970s feminists. From Michel and Texier's multilayered materialist analysis to journalist Françoise Giroud's commentary, they agreed that "Together, [women] constitute a class that can be called 'the proletariat of man.'"[84]

The pre-1968 generation of feminists, who struggled to defend French women against prejudice and abuse at the hands of the state and individual men, also called on women to meet the challenges that male-dominated society posed. They encouraged women to shake off their lack of interest in politics, their timidity at work and school, and, generally, the inferior role to which French society had traditionally assigned them. Michèle Aumont's essay "Jeune fille, lève-toi!" (Young woman, arise!) encouraged women to "abandon the part of themselves that was puerile" and to "look in the face destiny, the world, and . . . the life which awaits them." They also defended feminism.[85] As Marzellier reasoned: "It has been acceptable to make fun of the suffragists at the end of last century. They nevertheless defended their dignity as women with the only means that they had during that epoch, and some of them paid with their lives. Women, as women, have a role to play in society as important as that of men. Technical progress permits them to deliver themselves from obscure work linked to their functions as spouses and mothers, while remaining spouses and mothers worthy of that name."[86] Marzellier distanced herself from "aggressive feminism" (whatever that conjured up for her), but she nonetheless clearly voiced a popular desire to reinvigorate feminism to remedy women's unequal position in society.

Much of what we would term feminist criticism during this period would be expanded in the early years of the feminist movement of the 1970s. Indeed, questioning accepted standards to produce new meaning in society would become one of the cornerstones of later feminism. The majority of pre-1968 feminists launched this criticism by taking up Beauvoir's call to universal principles. "What men want, women want," wrote long-time feminist author Françoise d'Eaubonne, "and not 'man' in the sense of the word *male* but the human being without distinction to sex."[87] These feminists believed, however, that they could achieve their goals through patient negotiation rather than revolt. Even the most outspoken feminist activists and thinkers of the period before the 1970s were well integrated into the political or intellectual worlds of their time, many maintaining relatively conventional lives with spouses and children. In other words, they did not inhabit the world of 1970s radical feminists, who tended to be young, unmarried, and often committed to separatism, at least in politics if not in private life. Three doyennes of modern feminism—Simone de Beauvoir, Colette Audry, and Andrée Michel—all worked within established institutions. Audry was an author and editor as well as an outspoken feminist who founded the Bureau de defense des peuples colonisés (Office of the Defense of Colonized Peoples) in 1939. She spoke out against French imperialism during the postwar years, spurring the Socialist Party to reform its platform and organization regarding women's rights (one of the reasons for its victory in the 1981 elections). Michel, a member of the Algerian National Liberation Front underground in the 1950s, received an *aggregation* (advanced diploma) in philosophy, moved on to study psychology and sociology, and became an expert in family and social relations. Her work remains to this day a standard for feminist scholarship within the respected Centre national pour la recherche scientifique (National Center for Scientific Research). Even Beauvoir, who was perhaps the most flamboyantly unconventional of the three and who went on in the 1970s to work with militant feminist groups, never denied the value of collaboration with men and constantly returned to the material concerns of the average woman. Her brusque manner and eccentric lifestyle notwithstanding, she was known for her lack of snobbery and her interest in the problems of housewives as well as professionals.[88] To summarize the vantage point of almost all of these women of the 1950s and 1960s: they focused on expanding "liberty" to many groups denied it for various reasons—defending colonized peoples from French imperialism, attacking discriminatory laws and institutions and the attitudes behind them, and helping French women obtain access to good jobs and child care.[89]

Women's status and experience in the years following 1960 shifted, and with this shift came a concomitant change in feminist perception and analysis. In 1960, when Audry published "Ten Years after *The Second Sex*" in *La nef*, the journal of contemporary politics and culture, she insisted that women's situation had improved superficially—in dress, mores, and some attitudes—but not profoundly. "To be woman," Audry quoted Beauvoir as saying, "is a certain way of living a situation." Considering these changes, women seemed to be making progress. But Audry cautioned against confusing the trappings of independence with the real thing. To achieve true liberation, Audry wrote, women would need to transform society on a more basic level.[90] At the end of the decade, *La nef* published another issue devoted entirely to the condition of women: by 1969 women had gained access to contraception and had greater control over their assets, wages, and children, and they were increasingly incorporated into the workplace as employees and as salaried professionals. Even working-class women had found some relief from daily domestic drudgery with the eventually widespread installation of water and gas lines as well as with new appliances such as washing machines and vacuum cleaners that eased the double day. And family support services for housing and child care were also in place. With basic needs taken care of, the few self-identifying feminists read Beauvoir's book and saw that the myths that bound them to their second-class status as a sex remained in force. As feminists and as polemicists, they considered these impediments more significant than women's achievements over the past twenty years. In hindsight, however, we can see how much women had actually gained since the Liberation and how the feminist boldness of the 1950s and 1960s, combined with pragmatism, broke down barriers and established a feminist protocol that would champion women's independence and integrity.[91] The epoch of men's particularist world, with its avowed special roles for men and women, were drawing to a close. By the next decade, using the analytical tools this generation of women had developed, feminists would grab hold of this burgeoning individualism and would demand changes to French society in a way never foreseen before the May 1968 events.

3 THE MAY EVENTS AND THE BIRTH OF SECOND-WAVE FEMINISM

1968–1970

> In this growing revolution of women, we have begun to regroup. We
> alone can know our oppression, it's up to us to take charge of our
> liberation. . . . Until now we've been separated, each of us shut up
> in our own family. WE MUST BREAK this isolation. We must talk
> together, sharing our experiences. Together, all of us women will set
> the agenda of this Movement.
>
> MLF, Fifteenth Arrondissement (flyer)

During the spring of 1968, women began to find a fresh new language
to articulate their grievances and a politics that forced France to pay
attention. May 1968 revolutionaries talked about liberation from a culture that they claimed was rigid and obsessed with consumerism, and
yet in the end they were satisfied with leaving the domestic side of *la
patrie* (the motherland) well intact. The women who became active
through their experience in the 1968 movement sought a different kind
of liberation: to expand the terms in which human relations were discussed and to transform the private as well as the public world. This
movement went on to initiate fundamental changes in human relations and in the way France conceived of its citizens.

By 1970 activist women were bursting upon the scene with protests, agitprop, and a torrent of writing. The reform-oriented wom-
en's groups and scholarly voices that had dominated the pre-1968
discussion were drowned out by a chorus of women publicly denounc-

ing the same society that these earlier activists had been willing to work within. Women active in the Socialist and Communist parties turned on their male comrades, accusing them of failing to live up to their ideals and of promoting bankrupt ideas of social revolution. Beauvoir had been correct, feminists declared: women's bodies were a locus of patriarchal power and, in a capitalist society, of consumerism as well. In many ways the women's movement had a far deeper and longer impact than the May 1968 events themselves, and viewing the events through a feminist prism changes our understanding of this dramatic period in the history of France.[1] How activist feminism burst out of the May revolt and coalesced into groups, conferences, huge marches, and a popular climate of women's liberation is the subject of this chapter.

In the 1960s French society remained strikingly resistant to change: the "old boys' network" maintained itself, and politics and industry were structured around distant centers of authority whose decisions were not allowed to be questioned and which tolerated various managerial abuses. French attachment to traditional ways clashed with economic development and with young people who felt they had been betrayed by empty promises of success as a reward for good behavior. In fact, demographics were key to a protest movement that occurred internationally in countries affected by the post–World War II baby boom. By 1958 one-third of France was under twenty years old. This growth in the youthful population, combined with a housing crisis that was hitting its peak in 1967–1968, led to greater-than-normal social pressures. Alfred Sauvy had warned that France needed to open its society or there would be trouble, arguing repeatedly that a large population of young people would provide salutary benefits to France's moral and demographic burdens only if France accommodated them. Indeed, historians have argued that France's focus on youth and "renovation" while ignoring its discrimination and social sclerosis provided the generational levers for the May events.[2] Additional population pressure was caused by a steady increase in the number of African migrant workers and their families from France's colonies, and then, beginning in the 1950s, by more than one million *rapatriés* (white French citizens who had fled the colonies during and after the Algerian War) who expected compensation for their losses abroad.[3]

By 1968 France's conflict between economic expansion and its political and social traditions came to a head. The new French economy increasingly absorbed the working class and the petite bourgeoisie into what economic historians call the "broad middle stratum," which had more social homogeneity and greater social expectations. This homogeneity enabled the political movement to cross social and class boundaries. For a brief few months, social barriers between workers and the largely middle-class students broke down, with workers engaging in wildcat strikes in response to student protests and students showing up at the factories in solidarity with the striking workers. The strikes of May 1968 did force the government to capitulate to the unions and its workers; the Grenelle Accords negotiated between the government and the unions in late May mitigated some of the worst effects of the French industrial structure. Workers gained an immediate increase in the minimum wage, and unions were promised more authority in resolving labor issues.[4] But the traditional worker was changing: before the 1960s, the typical worker was a skilled man and a (white) French national. Economic changes that developed rapidly over the course of the 1960s caused structural changes in the workforce with the growth of the female-dominated tertiary sector and the development of an immigration program. Women had been underrepresented in union power politics, and immigrants (European, Algerian, and African) had not been represented at all. May 1968 gave voice to the frustrations of these politically marginalized groups. Beyond labor politics, however, the great legacy of May 1968 was to privilege the private and cultural domains of society and to repudiate the notion that to be truly revolutionary one had to be a striking worker or a leftist party member— what Keith Reader called "dethroning economism from its place at the center of left-wing thought."[5]

May 1968 also ushered in a radicalized individualism (voiced twenty years before by the existentialists) that expanded definitions of gender and led to a reexamination of the self in society. Behind the May revolutionaries' demand for *autogestion* (economic and political self-governance—one of the watchwords of the strikers) was a refusal to march in step either with the government or with traditional revolutionary movements.[6] For the next decade—at least until abortion was legalized—this individualism would become the benchmark against which women would measure their status and their progress in society. This was also the moment when discourses about women made a break with the essentialist underpinnings that had been so prevalent in prior decades, rejecting identification with "women's nature." During the roughly ten-year-long window from the late 1960s to the late 1970s, the ideas of Simone de Beauvoir—so anomalous thirty years earlier—came into currency, and feminists demanded a change in French society that would enable them to operate as autonomous individuals.

May 1968 was broader than just "dethroning economism" within France. Its political and ideological roots had been planted in the generational scrutiny of the prior generations' war activity (and a desire to compensate for its failures) and anticolonialist activism that culminated in France's admission of defeat in the Indochina and Algerian wars and its subsequent struggle to adjust to its postcolonial status. France had boasted a significant antiwar movement, particularly popular among the French Left (Beauvoir, Sartre, and Camus among them). Younger radicals were influenced by the American civil rights and antiwar movements. (Daniel Cohen-Bendit, for example, attended the memorial service for the murdered civil rights workers Andrew Goodman and Michael Schwerner in 1964.) In this larger context, anti-imperialist ideology would be wielded first against the French authorities and further still by 1970 against a new oppressor—men.[7]

The events of the spring of 1968 were dramatic but short-lived. Paris roiled with nights of street violence, police crackdowns, and thousands of workers striking in solidarity but ended a month later with fresh elections that solidified de Gaulle's party's power and the government's reassertion of authority. They left their psychological mark, however, by providing space to examine "power"—who had it and who didn't. They also opened up social and philosophical expectations of what it meant to be French. Jacques Sauvageot, one of the student leaders of the rebellion said, "I believe that all myths should be abolished, as they distort reality. That's why we want our challenging power to be permanent." The young men leading this revolution would soon experience that very principle unleashed by women in the private sphere, which they had largely considered irrelevant to politics.[8] By 1968 a new generation of women had access to birth control and had more economic and legal rights than their mothers had enjoyed. They had a long way to go, however, before achieving parity (as their successors would call it) with men.

Feminists of the generation of 1968 did not repudiate the previous generation's advances but rather rejected its compromises and reform agenda. The 1970s feminist theorist and activist Christine Delphy recalled that although she knew women were getting a raw deal before 1968, no one had spoken about it in political terms. "I was prepared to live a life of unhappiness," Delphy remembered, "knowing that I was right but that I was fifty years ahead of my time." Fortunately, Delphy said, "I was only three years ahead of time. History caught up with me."[9] The events of May 1968 transformed feminism's definition and image, catapulting women's demands to the top of the political agenda in France.

Women's changing economic circumstances added power to the surge of post-1968 feminism. Female employment rates began declining after the war and continued to do so until 1962, after which they rose rapidly. By the mid-1960s French industry had intensified its efficiency efforts, contributing to growing worker resentment, which burst into full-scale conflict during the 1968 strikes. Yet when the last poster demanding *autogestion* had been torn down and business went back to usual, most new jobs created in the industrial and service sectors went to women. Traditional female employment shifted from textiles and shoes to electronics, food, and chemicals, with concomitant low pay. By the early 1970s women represented almost 40 percent of all wage workers in many branches of the workforce.[10]

The May events ushered in a more uncompromising brand of feminism, one identified with women who fought for their cause without asking permission from party leadership or any men in charge. And this brought forth what came to be known as "radical feminism," a politics formed from a sex-based materialist analysis that enjoined women to ban together as a "proletariat" intent on overthrowing patriarchal society. Radical feminists found the political struggle itself uplifting. According to one flyer, women were now able "to express themselves and to be heard for the first time without reticence. . . . [The women's liberation movement] permitted certain groups to affirm themselves and to leave their isolation, for others to constitute themselves: many dispersed feminists finally could meet and thus rationalize and radicalize their revolt."[11] Ultimately, the 1970s women's movement would use an amalgam of radical agitprop and the calculated strategies of 1950s and 1960s feminists to win reproductive rights that influenced the degree of support for the movement.

The May events were a catalyst in bringing disparate women together to build a feminist movement, but focusing only on them obscures the movement's slower, embryonic development. Economic pressures were enlarging the pool of frustration. In addition, by the mid-1960s some women were gathering in small groups to examine their position in society and their identity as women. To be clear, most women in consciousness-raising groups were university students—or former students, academics, or professionals of some kind. And they were French by birth. Immigration by North and sub-Saharan Africans from France's overseas possessions began apace in the 1950s and 1960s thanks to civil war, French demographic decline, and loosening immigration policies to fill labor shortages in the burgeoning domestic economy. But the immigrant population was largely male and unintegrated in French society. This began to change with the reunification of families and border closings by the end of the 1970s, but women from North and sub-Saharan Africa largely missed the feminist decade in France, and even activist male immigrants operated only on the margins of the French cultural scene until the 1980s. Those who were active largely focused on bringing the plight of women in their own countries to an international audience.[12]

The core of the women's movement remained French and middle class, with higher-than-average levels of schooling. Members of groups such as Psychanalyse et Politique (Psychoanalysis and Politics, or Psych-et-Po), the Mouvement démocratique féminin (MDF; Democratic Women's Movement), and Féminin-masculin-avenir (FMA; Feminine-Masculine-Future), which would later become Feminisme-marxisme-action, addressed different aspects of women's experience and promoted different theories on women's oppression. The work of these organizations was crucial to the rapid development of the movement, not because of any political power that they wielded but because they furnished proficiently crafted ammunition for the spontaneous ebullience of the MLF. From early on, however, they introduced the large ideological conflicts that would plague the movement: separatism, rejection of class solidarity, incompatible attitudes toward "womanhood," and for some, the repudiation of feminism itself. Feminists never resolved their differences, but by 1970 a new kind of radicalized feminism—with a materialist critique of the private and public spheres and a willingness to engage in political battles without compromise—emerged as the defining voice of the 1970s women's movement. Activist groups such as FMA and the Féministes révolutionnaires (Revolutionary Feminists) as well as other advocacy organizations, such as feminist attorney Gisèle Halimi's group Choisir (To Choose), elevated the debate over women's place in society to new levels and enacted even more change.

The MDF, the FMA, and the Origins of Second-Wave Feminism

Two small groups already functioning when the street fighting began in May 1968 would become very important to the evolution of second-wave French feminism. The MDF and its daughter group, FMA, produced a synthesis of revolutionary theory and dynamic activism. Perhaps most important, they opened the field of political action and political critique to include personal relations between the sexes, a position that would mark contemporary French feminism for the next two decades. Officially founded in 1963, MDF was run entirely by women and addressed only women's concerns.[13] Many of its members were professionals and intellectuals who had experience asserting themselves and articulating their ideas. These women included prominent

Socialists Marie-Thérèse Eyquem, Colette Audry, and Yvette Roudy; sociologists Andrée Michel, Madeleine Guilbert, and Évelyne Sullerot; and attorney Gisèle Halimi. The women of MDF had come of age in a world of greater opportunity and had carved out niches of power that their suffragist predecessors could never have imagined. Since most MDF members were employed, they met in the evenings, a distinct change from their nineteenth-century counterparts, who organized lectures and meetings during the day.

MDF was not an outwardly militant group, although it produced the most revolutionary feminist arguments of the time. It analyzed the position of women in society, encouraged women to achieve, and pressured influential lawmakers. MDF defined itself as a "nonpartisan group that defends democracy, freedom of thought and expression, fights against all causes and manifestations of violence, for rights of women workers, for the civic education of women, . . . the defense of public school and the democratization of teaching." One of its core goals was ending the French occupation of Algeria. Yet MDF, more than other groups, was conscious of itself as explicitly feminist and was willing to demand equal rights for women in the press as well as in Parliament. As MDF explained: "In the world women play a role as human beings and as women. Of the first, they are not always entirely conscious. The second poses specific and unresolved problems replete with consequences for their own happiness and for the lives of their children. We intend to enlighten and to help women on both fronts. Not with well-rehearsed and passionately delivered slogans, but by examining the facts and by studying possible and desirable remedies in the name of reason and justice."[14]

MDF published a mimeographed newsletter, *La femme du XXeme siècle* (Woman of the twentieth century), which had a readership of about two thousand. The group's regular lecture series drew the most prominent women in France. At one lecture held in June 1963, Eyquem, together with Dr. Lagroua, and Dr. Aaron Brunetère (an internationally recognized physician), presented an evening entitled "Where Are We with Family Planning in France?" And early in 1964, Ménie Grégoire spoke on the controversial issue of part-time work. The deputy Jeannette Thome-Patenôtre and the attorney Marcelle Kraemer-Bach lectured on the reform of marriage law when that debate was in its earliest stages.[15]

In the early 1960s MDF was focused on intellectual debates held at small dinners in the style of *cercles républicains*, as Eyquem called them, but by the late 1960s moved toward larger gatherings that tried to appeal to working women and professionals. The power behind MDF began shifting from Eyquem, who resigned as president in 1971, and toward the rising star among the reorganized Socialists, Yvette Roudy, who increasingly tried to use the MDF to broker feminist demands within the party. MDF became more of a political pressure group, meeting frequently at the National Assembly and tying its actions to the parliamentary calendar.

In the political climate of 1968, MDF was largely dismissed as "reformist." Internal struggles over its place in the movement weakened its influence, and it dissolved quietly in the political ferment of the early 1970s.[16] Yet during its lifetime, MDF brought once-marginalized issues into public debate; it helped some feminists join the ranks of the Socialist Party; and it encouraged the formation of at least one other group, Féminin-masculin-avenir (Feminine-masculine-future). FMA was one of a few tiny yet influential groups of the early movement. It was founded in 1967 by several younger militants, notably Anne Zelensky and Jacqueline Feldman-Hogasen, whom Michel had encouraged to join MDF; its core members also included Christine Delphy, Emmanuelle de Lesseps, Charlie Tcherkawsky, and Roger Rebes. FMA members—students who saw themselves as unaffiliated leftists and part of a younger, more rebellious generation—viewed MDF's nonpartisan stance as insufficiently radical. FMA saw itself as a think tank convening to study "the evolution of masculine and feminine roles in modern society." According to an early group statement: "FMA claims kinship with *an authentic socialism*, for only a politics based on a long-term perspective can guarantee a proper education to children, and satisfying work to men or women. FMA, conscious of the very serious problems that weigh on humanity, refuses to subordinate indefinitely the solution to the individual relations between men and women. On the contrary, FMA sees the effective equality between the sexes as a decisive factor for the process of liberation."[17]

FMA's story illustrates the birth and development of what historians have called second-wave feminism. FMA began as part of the New Left. Its early ideology and strategy were not entirely clear, but its members wanted to fuse class and gender analysis with personal liberation. In marked contrast to reformists of the prior decade, FMA initially set out to demonstrate that "women's problems" would not be solved by the bourgeois notion of "progress," which members declared was pure fantasy. Technical progress, they claimed, no longer was a motor liberating men and women. The group did concede that automation "abolishes the distinction between 'feminine' and 'masculine' work" and that "the progress of medicine increasingly unburdens women of their biological destiny, which has for so long been confined in its only role of genetrix." But masculine and feminine norms extended, they said, "far beyond the underlying biological reality. They prevent the individual from blossoming according to his or her profound impulses, the couple from understanding each other, and the collectivity from profiting better from its diversity." FMA's engagement in the "battle against the oppressive role of men, sacrosanct monogamy, and the taboos against the sexual pleasure of women in general" separated the group from its feminist mothers. FMA members wanted to remedy what they saw as the relatively narrow legalistic or institutional approach to women's problems pursued by many pragmatic feminists of the 1950s. And FMA also wanted to analyze the cultural and psychological aspects of women's oppression the way Betty Friedan had done for American women in her 1963 book *The Feminine Mystique*.[18] FMA's studies led its members to take more radical political positions. They pushed for sexual freedom (ending taboos against "female sexual pleasure, adolescent masturbation, and homosexuality" and opposing prescribed monogamy), destruction of all structures of authority ("capitalism, religion, bourgeois morality, and the autocratic modern family"), an increase in the number of local child-care facilities, wider access to contraception, and abortion legalization. Its broad "platform" expressed the politics of imagination that characterized May 1968.[19]

More than any other group, FMA played midwife to the nascent women's liberation movement in France: "We are, as far as we know, the only feminist revolutionary group constituted," Zelensky had written before 1970, "but other small groups must exist that may not be at the stage of action yet." After decades in which women on the Left struggled to improve women's condition while distancing themselves from the feminist label, members of FMA adopted it as a badge of honor. "Our starting point is feminist," they stated up front. "This word has bad press but this is why we are feminists: we are interested in the place of women in society because we are women."[20] Because FMA embraced feminism as its theoretical construct, it reframed "women's issues" for the 1970s movement. FMA rejected the definition the Left had long given feminism—a bourgeois reformist movement bent on giving the wives of capitalists equal political power. Instead, they repositioned it to the extreme Left by recasting Marxist theory to describe the oppression of women by men throughout history and in contemporary society. Their criticism was no longer limited to the institutions (education, industry, and the law) that held women back; rather, it was leveled at men personally and at the patriarchal system in its entirety. Delphy later expounded on the connection between sex and class oppression in her article "L'ennemi principal" (The main enemy), writing under the pseudonym Dupont (a common name). In this piece, she argued that patriarchy and men were the principal enemy, not capitalism, which only facilitated oppression. Delphy's article generated much debate and discussion even among her supporters, such as Zelensky and Rochefort. It was critical to much foundational intellectual work on women, women's historians have shown.[21]

FMA's members summarily rejected the postwar solution articulated by feminists such as Beauvoir—that socialism offered the best possibility for changing women's condition. The key problem for women, FMA said, was not what revolutionaries called the "empty human relations of bourgeois society." Rather, FMA wanted trenchant gender analysis and a political program that spoke to the concrete reality and contradictions of women's lives, such as the "double day" or a male-defined view of sexual liberation. In 1971 Beauvoir explained why she became involved in the women's movement:

> I said I wasn't a feminist because I thought that the solution to women's problems must depend on the socialist evolution of society. By feminist, I meant fighting for specifically women's demands independent of the class struggle. Today my definition is the same, but I have come to realize that we must fight for an improvement in women's actual situation before achieving the socialism we hope for. Besides this, I realized that even in the socialist countries, women's equality has not been won. So, it is necessary for women to fight for their rights."[22]

This idea that women would first fight for their own cause because otherwise their cause would always be made a lower priority was a hallmark of this feminist period. Likewise, the concomitant ideology of "sorority," or sisterhood (fighting together for each other), became embedded in the women's movement and ultimately inscribed in the broader context of sexual liberation.[23]

FMA was ready to provide both by combining Beauvoir's revolutionary critique of gender relations with political activism. From its inception, FMA refused to sacrifice its own goals for the revolution and instead proposed that women recognize themselves as a class oppressed by the ruling class of men. "We refuse to subordinate the solution of the women's problem to that of workers or students' movements," their early tracts stated. "We refuse to wait for the victory of the proletarian revolution, as we are frequently enjoined to do, before we focus on the problem of the alienation of women."[24] FMA's seditious appropriation of "critical Marxism," a formulation of the New Left, allowed it to use Marxist theory while denouncing Marxists, their personality cults, and their party organizations. Delphy, who joined the group around the time of the May protests after meeting Feldman-Hogasen at CNRS, formulated much of FMA's critical Marxist theory and changed its name to Féminisme-marxisme-action. FMA honed its analysis to argue that the specific relation of the sexes was defined by the relations of social production and thus that women must be fully employed in order to liberate themselves. It denounced part-time work as a scheme that benefited capitalism and the state at the expense of women's economic independence and their emancipation. FMA took Engels's analysis of women's roles to its Marxist conclusion: that there had to be a fundamental social revolution in which women would take control of their lives and, in so doing, overthrow patriarchy.[25]

The women members of FMA were some of the first to translate their grievances into a publicly articulated feminism during the May events: "The permanent struggle cannot accept that any subject is taboo," said one document listing thirty theses on "Sexuality. Couple. Family." "If our revolution must generate new human relationships, it is only through a critique of prior arguments and all that exists . . . that it can do it." Sexuality had already been a topic of discussion after the publication of the first Kinsey report in 1947, and Beauvoir had critically addressed it through a feminist lens in *The Second Sex*.[26] But this kind of thorough "challenge to the system" had been missing in much of the rhetoric generated by women activists since the Liberation. This new generation of feminists argued that "the reference to an 'eternal nature,' defined within society, is the reactionary ideology used to justify a society based on male domination . . . and always corresponds to Simone de Beauvoir's analysis."[27]

A good thirty years younger than Beauvoir, the 1968 generation was instantly struck by the cogency of her theory and moved by her seemingly exhaustive knowledge of a variety of intellectual disciplines. Encouraged by American feminists, who had also adopted Beauvoir's analysis (*The Second Sex* had been translated into English in 1952), FMA members and other early self-identified feminists sought out Beauvoir. Testifying to the rise to prominence of feminist politics and ideas, she was placed on a pedestal at the same time that the old-guard intellectuals were being denounced for their naïveté. (Sartre, for example, was heckled at the Sorbonne during a speech he made in May 1968.) Beauvoir was sympathetic to the antagonistic position of FMA and other feminists toward the French Left, as she explained during an interview: "Even at the heart of these movements [of May 1968], which in principle are made to liberate everyone [including] youth and women, women become inferior. . . . I don't say all but a certain number of male leftists are hostile to women's liberation." The years after May 1968 were as much of a turning point for Beauvoir as they were for feminism. She was by Sartre's side during May 1968, but she did not speak up for women; she had been a writer all her life, not an activist. Young feminists from a new generation gave Beauvoir's ideas new relevancy and gave Beauvoir a new "activist" voice.[28]

Beauvoir's problematizing of the female body as a site of sociopolitical intervention resonated within the larger women's movement. Contrary to the belief that she had disappeared into her novels and memoirs after the publication of *The Second Sex*, Beauvoir had been applying her analysis to concrete endeavors, sometimes writing short commentaries in *Les temps modernes* and at other times adding analytical and feminist heft to feminist polemics by writing introductions to works like those by Dr. Lagroua and Gisèle Halimi. Nevertheless, she had kept a relatively low feminist profile. The development of the women's movement at the end of the 1960s, Yvette Roudy later remarked, "would not have had such power had it not been for the clear, historical, and analytical reflections of Simone de Beauvoir." At a time when Sartre's health and popularity were declining and his relationship with Beauvoir was strained, she welcomed the attention of feminists, who considered her their spiritual mother.[29]

FMA was also radicalized by the American feminist movement, which had been organizing itself since 1967. Feminism in the United States was at least five years ahead of the French movement. French women who spent time in the United States in the 1960s and American and British feminists who traveled to France at the end of the decade and into the 1970s brought Anglo-American feminism's ideas and spirit with them. American feminists' own disavowal of the Left in the late 1960s, after they had been shabbily treated in the civil rights movement, lent legitimacy to French feminists' rejection of their old leftist comrades.[30] Thus, by 1968, when FMA officially coalesced, Betty Friedan had already founded the National Organization for Women. New York Radical Women had formed a year earlier, in 1967, with members Shulamith Firestone, Ros Baxandall, and Robin Morgan. In 1968 the group published the tract *Notes from the First Year*, which made its way into the hands of some French women. By 1970 Robin Morgan had compiled *Sisterhood Is Powerful*, a collection of early writings from the women's liberation movement in the United States, and Shulamith Firestone and Kate Millett had published their famous critiques of the patriarchy, *The Dialectic of Sex* and *Sexual Politics*.[31]

In France, mainstream news coverage of the feminist movement was kept to a bare minimum. In 1969 *Le Monde* briefly reported that Friedan had been invited to France by MDF and FMA to spearhead a campaign to eliminate the practice of mentioning gender in help-wanted ads, a crusade that Friedan had begun in the United States. A year later, *Le nouvel observateur* published another article, "A Revolt of American Women: Against 'Male Chauvinism,'" laced with the patronizing commentary that "thousands of American 'women warriors' have begun the revolution." FMA was optimistic, however: "We are happy to state that for the first time in the French press *Le nouvel observateur* published an article on the feminist revolt in the United States. The American papers have already given good coverage to this event: *Time* and *Life* magazines have devoted long reports to the subject in January 1969."[32] Whatever their connections to the American feminists, many early groups felt that they had come to feminism on their own rather than adopting an ideology imported from the United States. As FMA members commented: "Our group was born before May '68. . . . We learned of American feminist politicians only a year ago, because the press didn't speak of it before that, and because these feminist movements haven't been around for a long time. We have discovered that their positions are very similar to ours. This coincidence has brought us to believe that the situation in the entire western world, and not only in the USA, is favorable to a renewal of feminist combat."[33]

The May Events and the Feminist Attack on the Left

The French feminist rejection of the Left was sweeping and forceful. Echoing the May 1968 general insurrection, in which students and workers accused the major parties on the Left of "Stalinism," women rebelled against the patronizing authority of the men at the barricades and the double standard for men and women. The May events shaped new attitudes toward individuals, social participation, and even the human body, challenging France's proud national myths. Feminists joined in the challenges and pushed for political analysis and change. The various feminist groups would remain politically marginal, but feminism itself was able to chip away at a conservative culture and help inaugurate a new era of socialist politics. The feminism of the 1970s revolutionized the way French society approached the "woman question." No longer would the discussion revolve around "the insertion of woman" into society; rather, it would explore and challenge the definition of what women were and what they could do. To fight against the status quo, *soixante-huitards* ('68ers) had created a practice of improvisation, theater, and individual action, and the women's movement drew upon this practice in its own demonstrations.

Much of the movement's power came from a generation of young, rebellious women committing what many viewed as outrageous acts. Their rhetoric underlined the stark contradiction between the greater freedom and opportunity women supposedly enjoyed and the eclipsed reality they actually faced. Many of these young women were high-school students and progressive-minded female instructors who had arrived at the vanguard of women's professional success by way of France's teacher-training schools. A leaflet distributed around a high school questioned:

> When will our liberation happen? You are not allowed to go out at night, have sex, and choose certain professions. But you are directed to do your homework, clean your room, and help your mother (dishes, errands, household cleaning). Do you have the impression you are living?
>
> You get married: you will be the maid for your husband in the kitchen as in the bed; you will have kids; you will abandon work in order to take care of them as you should. Or you will reconcile your professional life to your home life. That means 90 hours of work each week minimum.[34]

These young women gave voice to a sentiment widely felt but unexpressed by middle-class women in their teens and twenties. The women most drawn to women's liberation groups in the 1970s were urban and educated, generally from upwardly mobile families. They were frustrated by their limited professional options, by the hostility they endured from leftist men, and by a sense that the contradictions between their ideals and their lives were becoming untenable.[35] It was these women's recognition of what sociologist Margret Maruani calls "social specificity" (as opposed to "natural differences") that made feminism so popular and gave it its polemical force. Women began to view their oppression as having no natural justification; rather, they saw their continued second-class status in the private sphere as directly responsible for discrimination against them in the public sphere. A pamphlet entitled "This Isn't Called Work!" listed seventeen jobs that women did daily—preparing meals, washing up, shopping, cleaning, ironing, and so on—and continued:

> They tell us that we don't earn a living; that we are just fed and housed and so we should say thank you. If we work outside, it's all that [domestic work] in addition to eight hours of work a day and then rushing in the metro to try to shop before the stores close. Us = 110 hours; them = 48 hours of work per week. And they tell us that we earn pin money!!! Yes, this is love; yes, this is the family. Change them! Love should not be slavery.[36]

Working-class women, who had less education and who started working at a younger age, suffered similar frustrations. Their protests also revealed traditional gender prejudices against women acting in a public capacity—their occupation of factories, for example, was seen as creating sites of debauchery rather than as serious political action. Socialist and Communist propaganda associated feminism with bourgeois frippery, but working-class women's feminism was key to changing the social and political landscape of France.[37] In the late sixties the main Communist union, the CGT, did not question the socioeconomic role of women's part-time work, which satisfied the interests of men and families as well as many women. The CGT's women's magazine, *Antoinette*, did cautiously criticize part-time employment in its September 1969 issue: "It might seem like a good solution to balancing domestic work and balancing a budget, but it is a superficial solution. The pay is low, there are no benefits, no unionizing, and little security." But until 1972, when Chantal Rogerat took over as editor, *Antoinette* shied away from attacking men's refusal to equally share domestic tasks and childrearing, which made women view part-time work as the only realistic alternative.[38] Shared frustration with these compromises fostered political collaboration between working women and female university students in the heady days of 1968.

The May revolutionaries' denunciation of traditional politics and parties challenged the traditional forms of revolutionary expression and created a political space for women to voice their ideas. After the May events, the Left, including Far Left Maoist and Trotskyist groups, endured savage mockery at the hands of revolutionary women.[39] Feminists were angered by Gaullist paternalism and by their leftist comrades, who had spoken so eloquently of human liberation. In a flyer from one of the earliest MLF meetings this anger was on display:

> Who cooks when you speak of revolution? Who takes care of the kids when you go to your political meetings? Who types the memos while they [*sic*] direct and organize the future? Who takes notes when they have the microphone? Who always sees these initiatives co-opted at the level of speech and of action? It's us, always us. This sexual, economic, and political oppression is one of the pillars of the capitalist system. It's these pillars that oppress us. It's these that we attack. You tell us: "There will always be time to approach that later." Later: after the revolution; but which revolution, made by whom? Now is the time. A party of people. Power to all people.[40]

Many women who had been at the barricades during the nights of street fighting, who had participated in the factory strikes, or who had in other ways worked with male revolutionaries were nevertheless denied access to important meetings where strategy was discussed. Instead they found themselves required to serve coffee and to take care of the children of busy rebelling fathers while the men formulated policy and held forth on Engels's theory of women's oppression.[41] With all the discussion of personal liberation, with all the denunciations of capitalist oppression and the mediocrity of bourgeois society, most men remained entirely uncritical of their own sexism. The historian Danièle Voldman's description of her political coming of age illustrates this disconnect: In the late 1960s she and about twenty friends labored over many works of political philosophy in order to determine their own politics; they ultimately decided to join the *Bordiguistes*, a small splinter Communist group, which they believed shared their principles: "The experience was very bizarre, for this group was composed of old Italian antifascists for whom women had little place in a political meeting. And there we were, women who were barely twenty years old who wanted to make the revolution. It went *very* badly. We weren't allowed to open our mouths and anyway we didn't dare!"[42]

As Voldman recounts, she and her friends were "doubly shocked" by the problem of male-female relationships during the protests because "in our *Bordiguiste* group things went badly, at the Sorbonne things went badly because women were the ones asked to distribute the tracts and not to write them, and because we didn't dare to try to speak in public." Delphy felt the animosity toward women's rights that permeated popular culture and expressed itself in politics. She spent her adolescence sensitized to the different treatment of men and women but found no means of expressing it. She remembered "always having feminist reactions" and her father saying to her, "'Don't be a feminist!' as if feminist was a four-letter word."[43] It was not until she graduated from college that she decided she *was* a feminist and began to articulate what that meant. Years later, after working with civil rights groups in the United States, she returned to France with a clearer analysis of women's subordination but still with little sense that it was possible to take action: "In 1965, I would talk with my best friend about relationships between men and women and the way women were treated, but there was only one person whom I could talk to because I felt that if I said that [women are like African Americans in that they are politically oppressed] to anyone else they would think that I was crazy." In a similar vein, Anne Zelensky and Jacqueline Feldman remember watching the events unfold and the posters go up around the Sorbonne and remarking that nothing they saw was about women.[44] Once women recognized the hostility of their male compatriots and their own lack of self-confidence in public arenas, they found themselves drawn together as political allies. The sense of female solidarity was crucial to the development of a reconstructed feminist consciousness and to the formation of a movement, however loosely constructed. "We had all sensed the same things despite our different experiences," the collective authors of *Le livre de l'oppression des femmes* (The book of women's oppression) wrote in the early 1970s. "We have broken the silence, we have spoken, [and] we have recognized each of us crushed by the same oppression." Women's solidarity led to the mutual recognition that they all had believed either that they were crazy or that others would think they were. From such recognition, they moved to denunciation. "What woman doesn't have things to say?" asked a flyer announcing the Days of Denunciation of Crimes Against Women: "Come! Participate! Testify! Dare!" Another leaflet from the same event read, "What crimes? Legal crimes, daily crimes, invisible crimes. . . . The fundamental crime is that half of the world is enslaved by the other because of their sex."[45]

A spokesman for the student revolutionaries of May 1968 claimed that politics was about how people lived and not just about parliamentary games. Yet the feminists saw themselves as the only ones who seriously adopted this argument and incorporated it into a broad and sophisticated theory. When a 24-hour "child-care center" was created at the Sorbonne during the early days of its occupation and then at the University of Nanterre, it was seen as a symbolic victory representing a world where public and private were no longer starkly separated by gender or location. During the May protests, certain circles agreed on principle that adequate child care constituted a cornerstone of women's economic and social equality, and yet, practically speaking, child care was low priority and left to the women to figure out. The 1970 study *The Decisive Importance of Day Care: Its Value Today*, published by the Center for Marxist Study and Research, shows that the French Communists and others on the Left did in fact argue for adequate child care and a state-sponsored solution. But on a personal level, the push for better state child care seemed to take men off the hook as far as reproductive labor was concerned. The subject was treated with even less interest by revolutionaries of the New Left, with their full-scale rebellion against the government, than by the Communists, who argued that working women needed special support to perform the dual function of workers and mothers. Indeed, in 1970 there were only 579 *crèches* (nurseries) in France, with 24,027 beds—hardly enough to accommodate the children of the baby-boom generation.[46] Average working women's difficulty in obtaining child care was in practical terms a private affair. For revolutionary women who reasonably questioned what, if anything, the May events had achieved for them, the idea that "the personal is political" served as a theoretical springboard from which to take action.

If the personal served as a starting point for politics, the success of women's liberation could be measured by women's personal autonomy in society. A decade earlier, the measure of women's progress had been legal access to contraception or ridding France of the legally established patriarchy bequeathed by Napoleon. Another gauge during the postwar period had been state support for children and child care. By the 1970s, however, feminists from a growing number of groups were publicly asserting women's right to equal sexual pleasure and to equal power in male-female relationships, as well as demanding economic and political justice. Feminists wanted radical equality—equality based on a single, nongendered standard in personal life as well as in public. Politicizing the personal was a powerful tool for addressing the power imbalances and oppression that women faced in patriarchal society and that had always been considered outside the realm of public debate or politics. But, as would later become evident, personalizing politics could fragment political movements with smaller and more closely identified groups defining a politics of their own, as was the case with lesbian separatism (to be discussed later in the book).[47]

Delphy, who wrote many of the tracts for FMA, was particularly sensitized to the gulf separating men's political theories from the way they led their private lives. In the mid-1960s, when she participated in and closely scrutinized the civil rights movement in the United States, she witnessed female social activists in organizations such as the Students for a Democratic Society and the Student Nonviolent Coordinating Committee rebel against movements in which they had once passionately believed. As she wrote a few years later, "Revolutionaries from Marx to Mao have been excellent in their principles and material, they have denounced women's oppression and have been determined to combat it . . . but in general the 'woman question' has been left to women." Delphy argued that men had not been able or willing to combine principles and practice. "Malcolm X experienced the humiliation of racism only to convert to Islam, a religion that subjugates women; Che Guevara barely ever saw his wife and children, believing that women should take care of the home while men went out to defend it; and Sartre, who, despite his statements about Beauvoir's independence, carried on with women in a typically sexist way."[48]

When women began meeting in small groups to talk about the sexism they were experiencing, they very soon ejected the men who attended in solidarity. These women argued that they needed physical and psychological freedom from men in order to analyze their own oppression and that their separate bonding for a political aim was vital. They rejected men's "help" to combat women's definition as passive and incompetent. Their separatist position was not misandrist or clubbish; it was a political position that enabled women to analyze their situation together, free of male judgment, and was the closest thing they had to a unifying strategy. While MDF had maintained a women-only policy in the 1960s, FMA initially opened its doors to men. FMA members argued that women's problems were in fact larger social problems and therefore had to be solved by both men and women. The honeymoon period with male revolutionaries was brief, however. Although the months following the May protests saw a thinning of the ranks of committed militants, the women of FMA asked the remaining men in the group to leave, explaining that they were an obstruction to the development of a feminist consciousness. A bulletin entitled "Why FMA," written soon after the protests, demonstrates the return to female solidarity in the face of a hostile male world:

The history of the servitude and liberation of oppressed groups shows that nothing is ever given by the oppressor, but that each crumb of freedom has to be snatched from him. . . . Women have been the rank and file of all revolutions; they have also been the dupes because they have fought the revolutions of others, as the proletariat has fought the revolutions of the bourgeoisie for more than a century. It has only been when women have decided to demand something for themselves and to claim it themselves, rather than having it given to them, that they have obtained the most elementary freedoms.[49]

Their old male comrades by and large ridiculed their decision. At one of the first large women-only meetings, held at Vincennes in 1970 with any women interested in women's liberation, some of the men who were asked to leave refused. For a while they shouted at the women, yelling, "Power lies at the tip of the phallus!" and calling the women *mal-baisées* ("badly [or not] fucked"), implying that if the women were sexually satisfied they would not be angry at men.[50]

Thanks in part to Friedrich Engels, young leftist men had experience critiquing the family and the role of women. During the student uprising at the Sorbonne (which lasted from nine in the morning to midnight), male students attacked the traditional family as the site of bourgeois mediocrity and perversion, arguing that young children should be separated from their mothers to prevent the next generation from being corrupted. Feminists appreciated the attack on traditional family structure but not by their derisive male contemporaries.[51] As one woman pointed out: "It became evident that separatism was the only way . . . to discover women, shared feelings, a community of analysis, of hearing. The women's movement allowed women to go beyond internal rivalries, to create a new solidarity, a new common identity. Each woman felt herself reinforced by collective power in her private life and her relationships."[52]

Most of the feminists who were active during and after the protests shared this mistrust of male revolutionaries and of leftists in general. Zelensky wrote that even though it seemed that a mixed-gender movement would be desirable, "the logic of the movement and of the liberation of women needs it to be separatist now. First of all, for the obvious reason that speaking in a mixed group is much more difficult if not impossible for women, since habit reproduces itself: man speaks, the woman is crushed. It is indispensable that women finally be able to take account of the effect that they could make, foolish or not." When men are around, Zelensky explained, they demand that women justify what they are doing, and women need to stop feeling the need to justify themselves to men. Feldman-Hogasen wrote to Delphy, "Our discussions with the Trotskyist guys have made me realize to what extent they were not behind us, and dragged us down; and I must point out that the [American feminists] refuse to allow men on the editorial board of any journal." Feminist self-reliance developed hand in glove with the early feminist recognition that men did not necessarily have women's best interests in mind.[53]

Sexuality and Feminism

The 1970s feminists politicized sexuality to an unprecedented degree. They believed that free love and a redefinition of sexuality were revolutionary strategies to free women from their oppression in the family and even within the French economy. This attention to sexuality functioned, in part, as a trope for a more radical form of individualism in which individual pleasure and self-actualization took precedence over social mores or responsibilities. "Sexuality seems to us the privileged point of impact to unmask the real relationship between man and woman," an FMA internal memo stated. Where women's sexuality had once been officially contained within the family, women now freely expressed it outside of marriage.[54]

The demand for sexual freedom was very concrete: for example, a group of high-school students petitioned their school to change its rules governing social behavior between the sexes; when one of their teachers was brought up on charges for discussing the same petition in class, two thousand students staged a walkout. It was also symbolic. Expressing sexual freedom, whether homosexual or heterosexual—particularly women expressing sexual freedom outside of marriage—represented a refusal to remain within the corporatist order of old France.[55]

Although sexual freedom was sought by some women participants in the May revolt, there was a problem: in the context of double standards and male attitudes toward women as sexual objects, sexual freedom could be just another way to serve men at the expense of women. (One of the male mantras during the occupation of the Sorbonne, which feminists came to see as fundamentally sexist rather than liberating, was said to have been "You have to fuck at least once a night to be a good revolutionary"). One of their abiding contributions was to make sexuality and the family primary focuses of the Left while redefining sexual standards. No longer would they accept the dominant image of the good girl, saving herself for the right husband so she could be simply a wife and mother, while at the same time putting on lipstick and playing the vamp.[56]

FMA used women's sexual freedom as the yardstick for judging patriarchal oppression. This would culminate in the popular campaign for abortion rights. FMA championed women's sexual liberation on the grounds that it liberated women as persons, gave them a sense of their own autonomy and power, and put them on equal footing with men in the private sphere, which had always eluded social revolution. "Girls live under the double standard," an FMA tract read. "If a girl has many sexual partners, she is called promiscuous and she is sent to a juvenile delinquent specialist. If it's a boy who does it, it's considered normal." Indeed, the French treated sexuality with a combination of freedom and repression.[57] Exploration of sexuality was certainly in fashion in the late 1960s. Popular magazines and books increasingly treated sexual issues openly and with more fanfare than they had received before. Nevertheless, abortion was still illegal, women under eighteen years of age could not use birth control without parental permission, and it was still all too easy for a young woman to "catch a bad reputation."

FMA's position was understandable given its members' disgust with leftist men's pursuit of sexual freedom at women's expense. After all, the wave of student protests that culminated during May 1968 had begun in part over the fight—largely waged by men—for freer access to women's dormitories. Daniel Cohn-Bendit describes how, after students began a sex-education campaign on campus, clashes between the administration and a group of students "culminated in male students forcibly entering the women's hostels, and after this many of the petty restrictions surrounding these bastions of French purity and chastity were repealed."[58] By the winter of 1968, men had freer access to women, but many women did not experience this as real liberation.

Men had long taken advantage of the double standard accepted in French society. France was still a country in which the "straying" of married men was accepted as a matter of course. Unequal penalties for adultery in criminal law were not removed until the divorce reform law of July 11, 1975.[59] FMA addressed itself to two separate but often entangled issues governing French sexual relations. The first, and best articulated, was that sexuality as understood and practiced in 1968 favored men's desires and encouraged female passivity. Much of the new interest in sexuality, FMA members were quick to point out, came from a predominantly masculine perspective, which called for women's erotic submission to men's power. They declared that "pornography and puritanism were two poles of the same collective neurosis of French society," and they demanded "honest, open sexual education." As Delphy wrote, "The problem is not resolved and will never be until society creates women capable of taking their destiny in their hands in all domains." For example, Gabrielle Russier was a high-school teacher who committed suicide after her affair with a seventeen-year-old male student was discovered and she was charged with seducing a minor. FMA started a letter-writing campaign to the editors of Le Monde and Le parisien during the "affaire Russier," alleging that society could only accept the outward expression of male desire.[60]

FMA's other interest in sexuality, however, involved its desire to transform sexual behavior itself. They asserted that current sexual practices were fundamentally dominated by men's expectations, and they sought to explore an alternative female-driven sexuality that, besides empowering women in heterosexual relationships, would allow them to fully explore relations between women. This second interest in sexuality would lead many feminists, including FMA members, to embrace lesbianism and sometimes to repudiate sexual relations—or any relations—

with men, illustrating the fluid nature of gender definitions and sexual practice, a hallmark of the early movement.[61] FMA records show that in the autumn of 1969 (around the time of the first feminist meetings at Vincennes), FMA members Emmanuelle de Lesseps and Anne Zelensky formed a commission on sexuality—one dedicated to understanding sex in society and the possibilities for change, particularly in the French context. They read and reported on sexology studies and conducted surveys of their fellow students' sexuality.[62] The commission's goal was to "make a critical examination of the reigning, phallic ideology."

FMA's archives reveal a continuing commitment to rigorous feminist analysis and enjoyment of intellectual debate, even though they had little faith that their small group could achieve much in the way of social change. An early tract stated, "We don't pretend to furnish ... a definitive analysis, since this analysis must evolve in relation with a praxis. We limit ourselves to opening a debate, to underline its importance for the future of the socialist movement, for men as for women, and to invite those who are interested in this to follow with us."[63] The scope of their investigations was far-reaching. For example, a paper entitled "Differentiated Education, or The Soldier and the Doll" criticized France's conservative educational system. In papers like "Sexual Revolution or Bourgeois Eroticism?" and "Sexual Revolution: Speech or Action?" the group argued that feminism is dangerous to bourgeois society because it calls society's most fundamental institutions into question. Even when the already-small group was reduced to four active members, FMA continued to organize debates, correspond with out-of-town feminists, and send a steady stream of letters to the editors of major French publications. FMA writings from this period display an intellectual originality and richness, but the group was losing its raison d'être and soon disbanded. Women no longer needed a small, protected think tank in which to experiment with outrageous feminist ideas. Political activism and the theoretical avant-garde were finally running apace. FMA had played midwife to the now-exploding women's liberation movement.[64]

Libération des Femmes: Année Zéro

In May 1970 an independent leftist rag founded in the wake of the May events, *L'idiot international*, featured an illustration titled "Combat for the Liberation of Women" and showed a woman wearing a revolutionary cap and shouting. *L'idiot*, an "underground" university paper with a following in the hundreds of thousands, had invited Monique Wittig, her sister Gilles, and two Americans living in France, Marcia Rothenberg and Margaret Stephenson, to write a piece on the women's liberation group that they had been organizing since the spring of 1968. Part policy statement, part invective, and part historical survey, the short article pointedly addressed the Far Left—the men with whom they had marched in the streets—as much as it attempted to summarize the movement's ideas. Criticizing Freud, Shakespeare, Marx, and other "great thinkers," the authors asserted their intellectual authority and positioned themselves as challengers of a historical tradition of patriarchy on the Left as well as the Right. For the next decade, the old *querelle* would receive more critical attention than it had for decades. Some of the *querelle*'s contributors, such as the *fémininitude* writers, would fashion a politics around its discursive expression. But others, such as the radical and Marxist feminists, would fuse theory with fierce activism. This difference in strategy and interest led the two sides to disagreement, misunderstandings, and then to acrimony.[65]

"We [women], from time immemorial, have lived as a people colonized among a people, so well domesticated that we have forgotten that this situation of dependence should not be taken for granted," the authors of "Combat" wrote. Indeed, the feminists of 1968 criticized their male comrades' perpetuation of the same colonialist relations at home that they denounced abroad. By arguing that women were a colonized people dominated by men of all classes, feminists demanded that women's oppression be treated as its own political phenomenon. This materialist theory had been honed by feminists such as Colette Audry, Andrée Michel, and members of FMA, and it eventually received widespread feminist support.[66]

After their appearance in *L'idiot*, feminists began searching actively for other publication venues. Zelensky and Feldman-Hogasen approached Maspero Press in the summer of 1970 about publishing a book on feminism, sexuality, and revolution. Maspero offered instead to turn over a special issue of its review *Partisans* to their group. In her memoirs, Zelensky describes her excitement at seeing the double issue emblazoned with the title "Libération des femmes: Année zéro" (Women's liberation: Year zero). She was thrilled to bring feminism to a wider audience: "Finally, evidence, reflections, accounts of what we *really* lived and thought. . . . All my years of solitary revolt, of research, had not been in vain, they had brought me to this result." The issue included short articles by French as well as American feminists, who used pseudonyms or first names to cast off their old patriarchal identity and bourgeois individualism. Roxanne Dunbar wrote an article on caste and class; Anne Koedt's widely quoted article "The Myth of the Vaginal Orgasm" (originally published in *Notes from the First Year*) denounced Freud's theories regarding women's dependent sexuality and declared men unnecessary for women's fulfillment. Kathie Sarachild laid out a program for inspiring a feminist consciousness.[67]

The success of "Libération des femmes: Année zéro" spurred this feminist collective to publish more. This time, *L'idiot* gave over an entire issue to feminists, publishing what they would call *Le torchon brûle* (The dishtowel burns), the first of six times between 1971 and 1973.[68] But by December 1971 the members of the small editorial group had decided that they wanted their own publication. They felt that having complete control over speech—owning their ideas and the means of expressing them—signified control of their own movement. "To publish our theses even without having a political direction," Feldman-Hogasen wrote in a letter to Delphy, "is very important. Even if a specialist bastard contradicts what we say in a review like *Partisans*, directed toward a leftist public, there will be readers who immediately will be touched by our arguments." A group of approximately sixteen women took on the task of collecting articles and finding a printer independent of *Partisans*.[69] Their editorial policy reflected the ideals of the movement: beyond discouraging articles concerning the intimate details of the movement, they decided not to censor themselves or each other. Women had been censored for too long.

The conflicts and the successes of producing *Le torchon brûle* reflected many of the difficulties and triumphs of French feminism in the 1970s. Although editorial and production meetings were as disorganized as the movement itself, they were also filled with overflowing energy, enthusiasm for a common project, and the conviction that the women involved were driving change. Some of the most committed and financially experienced members of the group wanted to talk about expenditures, while others refused to take an interest in such mundane and capitalist details. The printer needed to be paid, but few women were interested in actually buying or selling the newspapers, and money from sales often did not end up in the coffers of the editorial group. To be concerned about money was seen by some as a "bourgeois" affair. Controversy arose because the editorial group worked on *Le torchon brûle* during the day. (Most of these women were on student schedules, and few women who were otherwise busy during the day expressed interest.) At some point the editorial group was accused of elitism by women who believed it represented an educated and privileged few who did not need to work. The tension between intellectuals and workers, which had been temporarily smoothed over during the strikes and protests of May 1968, returned to the movement's politics early on and would become fractured, preventing a unified movement.[70]

The experience of publishing *Le torchon brûle* exhausted some and exhilarated others. Despite the confusion and disagreement, the final product proved that women had much to say about themselves and their situation in France. Indeed, the words seemed to tumble out in a frantic rush untempered by calls to be reasonable or to support party strategy. Personal confessions, cartoons, manifestos, and reports filled *Le torchon brûle*'s pages. "What do they want?" asked an article entitled "Why an Autonomous Movement of Women?"

We want all women to say: *We*. We don't want to be separated any more, each one in her family; our division is maintained to keep us in a situation of economic, social, and moral inferiority.

We want economic independence . . . child care that is open 24 hours a day . . . domestic work collectivized . . . the freedom to have or not to have children . . . not to be continually harassed on the street. . . .

For all these reasons we have regrouped in a women's liberation movement. We are 27 million. United we represent a force capable of radically changing our situation.[71]

May 1968's embrace of liberation and challenge to the social mores of French society allowed feminist ideas to grow. "Feminism caused a tremendous break in France's social codes," argued the philosopher Michèle Le Dœuff. "In traditional French culture a woman must always hide her sadness or her problems and must always present a smiling face to the world. To say '*no*, all is *not* well,' was a terrible cultural rupture in a country that was most resistant [to challenging social norms]."[72] This "no" amounted to social treason, a refusal of women to sacrifice themselves for their families and for France. Women activists understood that although male protesters struck out against "social norms," considering them the "the smoke and mirrors of bourgeois culture," the men were more likely to be focused on women's sexual liberation than women's social liberation.[73] The rejection of long agreed-upon social behavior seemed threatening to many French men particularly because these women were not banding together (as they had for centuries) to assert traditional rights and privileges; rather, they were joining in a revolt against French society—or at least social and sexual norms. Sexual expression would remain a focal point of the movement because it challenged social mores and was so fundamental to women's physical autonomy. It also served as rich theoretical terrain for those who contemplated a nonpatriarchal world in which sex and sexual difference would be shaped differently.

4 NEW FEMINIST THEORY AND FEMINIST PRACTICE

The Early 1970s

We rise, women slaves
And break our shackles
Stand up!

Women enslaved, humiliated,
Bought, sold, raped
In every house,
Women, in every house,
Relegated outside of the world.

Women, alone in our grief
Ignored one after the other
Women, they have divided us
And from our sisters, separated.

Women, we recognize ourselves
We speak amongst ourselves, see ourselves
Women, together they oppress us
Together we rebel.

Women, this is the time of anger
Our time has arrived
Women, we know our force
We realize we are millions.

"Hymn of the Women's Movement"

Amid the sweeping changes in philosophy and history, feminists took to the streets to shock France out of centuries-old habits. By 1970 feminists had adopted staged protests as a political tool useful for publicity since magazine editors seemed to enjoy assigning stories about them, and they provided an outlet for aggrieved activists. The movement gained public recognition and was dubbed the *Mouvement de libération des femmes* when, on August 26, 1970, a date meant to coincide with the "Women's Strike for Equality" in the United States, a group of women who would be at the core of the 1970s feminist movement tried to lay a wreath at the Tomb of the Unknown Soldier at the Arc de Triomphe to honor his even lesser-known wife.[1] They carried banners with slogans including "One man out of every two is a woman" in addition to a large wreath. They were prevented from laying the wreath and were escorted (and carried) into the police station under the arc by local police while groups of tourists and passersby gawked in uncomfortable amusement.[2]

Feminist activism worked. The government and the mass media increasingly spoke of women's place in society as a subject worthy of public debate. The Arc de Triomphe group, which grew as other interested women joined, continued to protest: "Métro-Butt-Pinchers, we've had enough!" one mimeographed flyer proclaimed. It continued: "We, women, we have had enough of men profiting from rush-hour crowds in order to rub themselves against us, to put their hands on our backsides.... They should go jerk off by themselves! We are not the 'dolls of love'; we are not the 'objects' of love. We are *human beings*."[3] Feminist flyers attacked sexist billboards and advertisements with their own rueful slogans, such as "I am the dog-woman DIM [lingerie brand] that is spread out on the posters. I am the center of advertising. I am the consumer consumed. I am the turkey that gets stuffed nonstop with publicity slogans.... I don't recognize myself in this image nor in the inverse image of the erased woman-wife-virtuous homemaker."[4]

Three months after the march at the Arc de Triomphe, several public figures joined forces with *Elle* magazine to resurrect and update the 1929–1931 États généraux de la femme (Estates-General of Women, its name taken from the original ancien régime governing body).[5] *Elle* attracted intellectuals, doctors, lawyers, journalists, and a wide range of prominent politicians to the conference, which was held, appropriately, at Versailles. Prime Minister Jacques Chaban-Delmas attended, along with the minister of education, the minister of employment and population, members of the Académie française, various deputies and senators, and the Socialist Party leader François Mitterrand. Also attending were women active in promoting feminist causes: Dr. Marie-Andrée Lagroua Weill-Hallé; the prominent Socialist and feminist Évelyne Sullerot; the up-and-coming Socialist Party member (and soon to be minister of women's rights), Yvette Roudy; the longtime advocate of women's causes, Louise Weiss; the president of the Communist women's union, Marie-Claude Vaillant-Couturier; and other equally prominent women. The aim of the conference was to highlight the successful development of the "modern woman" while acknowledging that there was still work to be done. Its organizers declared that they wanted to "view women's place in present and future society . . . their aspirations, their hopes, their demands, their difficulties, and the solutions that they propose."[6]

Elle's Estates-General was designed to be a big show, with important men and women in fashion rubbing elbows with important political leaders, and all of it receiving positive coverage in the press. As the daily *France soir* declared in a headline: "The Estates-General of Women: Arriving at Equality while Bypassing the Battle of the Sexes."[7] *Elle* helped prepare for the conference by launching a survey to drive interest and illustrate the condition of the newly equal and liberated woman. Divided into sections such as "Love," "The Couple," and "Marriage," the questionnaire asked, for example, whether women could have many "great love affairs" and whether it was excusable for a man to cheat on his wife. The "Civil Status" section and the section on "Cultural Life, Information, and Politics" asked more abstract questions, such as whether women believed divorce was now easier to obtain and whether women were more cultivated than men. One of the final questions directly addressed feminists: "One often speaks of the 'liberation of women.' Do you feel that woman today is a prisoner? (Yes or No)."[8]

A small amount of feminist activism had succeeded in draw-ing attention to women's concerns in France, but feminists did not accept the way those concerns were bandied about by mainstream politicians and the media. Thus, *Elle*'s grand gesture toward "fem-inism" was ripe for a feminist disruption. Some of these core femi-nist activists of the early years had acquired passes to the opening reception, where they handed out their own spoof questionnaires and grabbed a microphone. "Men exploit us to the core!" their voices boomed as conference guests politely sipped their drinks. "Women, take what is your right and don't wait for them to give it to you!" Their questionnaire, a parody of *Elle*'s, has gone down in the annals of the movement's history as one of feminist activists' more clever stunts. Questions included these: "In your opinion how should women be treated: equally, better, worse, or differently?" "Can a woman who submits to a hysterectomy write a symphony?" And "Do you think that women's need for autonomy is: a glandular hypertrophy, a vital need, man's prerogative, or a sign of frigidity?"[9] The statement the women read at the microphone before they were removed from the premises is less well known but marks a turning point for French feminism—the moment when women reappropri-ated the "women's cause":

We denounce the campaign of the Women's Estates-General launched by the magazine *Elle*, which assumes the right to rep-resent all women in a questionnaire that professes to take over their rebellion. It tries to co-opt all attempts at women's soli-darity and to defuse the inevitable collective revolt of women.

This campaign lets women believe that their advice is asked for: it offers women insignificant choices that are supposed to be seen as essential when the essential choices have been made for them. Their fundamental oppression remains: love, marriage, the couple, femininity, maternal instinct, domestic service, eco-nomic dependence, etc. aren't questioned. They try to force on us the idea that these notions belong to "women's eternal nature," [an idea] that we violently contest.

Woman doesn't exist. It is a creation of the patriarchy (the economic, political, social, sexual, cultural domination of man) destined to crush women.[10]

To a certain extent it might have seemed that these women were
caught up in the radicalism of their times. The writings of what would
be called poststructuralists—from Michel Foucault, to Gilles Deleuze,
to Jacques Derrida (to name a few)—provided a conceptual framework
to criticize the symbolic order of things; the Front homosexuel d'action révolutionnaire (FHAR), led by Guy Hocquenghem, maintained
a sustained critique of homophobia. Broader still was the assault on
France's sacred image of itself as the victim of World War II, thanks in
part to Marcel Ophüls 1969 film *The Sorrow and the Pity* and American
historian Robert Paxton's revelations about Vichy and French collaboration. The two failed colonial projects of Indochina and Algeria also
shook French understanding of its importance on the world stage. But
it was more than this.[11]

These women were a product of the post-1968 philosophy and
world outlook as well as the May 1968 events themselves, the sexual
revolution, and the egalitarian reformed curriculum. They were the
university-educated women whom the dignitaries were ostensibly celebrating, and these women thumbed their noses at such pretension.
What might have seemed a great contribution to the women's cause
a decade or two earlier looked to a new, more radical generation like
an anachronistic and self-congratulatory party that made important
people, including established women activists, look foolish. As Delphy, a participant in this agitprop, jotted down at a planning meeting,
"For anyone who doesn't make a profession of their 'femininity' or
who hasn't succumbed to a pathological attack of passivity, this survey is infuriating, humiliating, and degrading."[12]

Delphy had good reason for such contempt. Prime Minister Chaban-
Delmas's opening speech on "equality but not identity" considered it
"contrary to nature, stupid, aberrant and disastrous" to confound the
two. "How can we possibly envision a feminine career," he intoned, "in
any domain, in any echelon, identical to a masculine career?" Women

had the responsibility of motherhood, he said, and had different faculties and different ways of developing their full potential. As with its namesake, the Estates-General of 1789, which rapidly disintegrated into the French Revolution because of its lack of real power or representation, this 1970s conference seemed bankrupt to a more radical generation.[13]

The young feminists' disruption of the *Elle* conference touched off a debate in the popular press that gave this new, radical feminism visibility and established new grounds for speaking of the woman's cause and assessing women's status. For the next decade, even feminists working within institutions would be able to more effectively weave a radical agenda into compromise-oriented strategies. No longer were activist feminists in France concerned only with equality, suffrage, and broadening economic opportunity. The new feminists wanted to transform society on every level.

"We Are 27 Million"

During the first year or two of the movement, women participating in the MLF held general assemblies and debates at public forums such as the École des Beaux-Arts, the Mutualité, and the École normale supérieure, rue d'Ulm. At some of these meetings, feminists discussed and edited texts awaiting publication, such as *Le torchon brûle*, or fabricated assorted banners and pamphlets. At others, they read aloud a doctor's professional secrets for performing a safe abortion or discussed a comprehensive strategy for ethical and social revolution. But often there was no particular agenda at the meetings, and women came simply to revel in the jumble of people, cigarette smoke, and ideas. As the philosopher Michèle Le Dœuff recalled about those heady years: "This is my most vivid and most precious memory from those years: having gradually learned, with other women, to put a name to what was hurting me, through the discovery that I was not the only one being hurt. This enabled the rather lost woman I still was to face up to things."[14]

The women who coalesced around a shared feminist vision understood that they were building a larger political movement while undergoing their own internal transformation. One flyer from the early years reminded women that their struggle was revolutionary on two levels—individual and collective—they emphasized that "women united were a force capable of radically transforming our situation and imposing the means of our liberation." Another flyer stated, "We Are 27 Million . . . up until now we have been separated, each woman enclosed in our family. We need to break this isolation, speak with each other, and share our experiences."[15]

The MLF was not entirely disorganized, however. Even during its first year, it was evolving into a loose umbrella organization for groups with specific ideologies and agendas. But rather than coalescing in a more cohesive form—as, for example, American feminists did with the National Organization for Women—most activist French feminists argued that such action would "confine the movement to the same schemas from which it had escaped." Instead, they created small, insular groups of like-minded women, which became known as *tendances*, or factions. Mimicking a common pattern in French radical politics, feminists often chose isolation over compromise and centralization. Some feminists, notably Anne Zelensky, saw the danger in factions— "Those who are stigmatized as the bad ones are ignored"—but she understood their origins: "It's the fear of losing our revolutionary identity that really gets us . . . the fear of indulging in the desire for relations based more on identification and narcissistic reassurance than relations of difference, of transformation." The political scientist Françoise Picq cautions against describing the MLF as composed of three factions—the "Class Struggle," "Radical Feminists," and "Psychanalyse-et-Politique"—arguing that this analysis is reductionist and hides the diversity of the movement; indeed, the majority of women who rallied to legalize abortion during the 1970s did not belong to these factions. Nevertheless, factions monopolized the heart of the movement, forming its principal dividing lines, and by 1974 had virtually taken it over.[16]

The first large division within the movement occurred as early as 1971. The disagreement centered on whether or not women constituted a class in themselves and even whether traditional class distinctions mattered. The *lutte de classe* ("class struggle" or Marxist feminist) faction, as it would come to be known, could not accept the argument that gender should take precedence over class in either theory or organization. Many participants came from groups such as the Maoist Vive la révolution (The Revolution Lives), la Gauche prolétarienne (The Proletarian Left), and the Trotskyist Ligue communiste révolutionnaire (LCR; Revolutionary Communist League) and were wary of speaking about male oppression outside the context of class relations. One of their first manifestos, which appeared in the second *Le torchon brûle*, railed against oppressive models—the mother and the whore—that confined women, but they tended to speak of women's oppression in the context of a larger system that oppressed both women and men rather than as a phenomenon of systematic and one-sided repression that crossed social and geographical boundaries.[17]

The Cercle Élisabeth Dimitriev (named after the founder of the Union des femmes of the Paris Commune of 1871) was one of the Marxist feminist groups formed in 1971. Founded by women who had disappointedly left Trotskyist groups and now sought feminist solidarity, it made a formal declaration of autonomy from the MLF in the spring of 1972. This proclamation, "Out of the Shadows," declared that the Cercle Dimitriev would not separate the oppression of women by the capitalist system from the struggle for women's liberation; for the group's members, gender and class were not interchangeable categories. Equally important, the group stated that it would not abide "the lack of coordination," discipline, and commitment that characterized the movement, particularly in the early years. Because the MLF functioned so loosely, the cercle believed it could not become a mass movement.[18]

The members of the Cercle Dimitriev also had little patience for the MLF's attention to theory, which overcomplicated the decision-making process and, in their view, seemed inaccessible to many women. They perceived MLF participants' tendency toward self-reflection and talk as self-involvement. As a Cercle Dimitriev pamphlet bluntly put it, "We've had it up to here with the 'femino-sexual revolution' or 'How to make a revolution while masturbating!'" According to the cercle, the MLF, "shut in its petit bourgeois nature, . . . doesn't go toward the working class except to bamboozle it, to find in it the false reflection of its own problems."[19]

The group suggested various ways to tighten the movement to achieve specific goals, attain a larger membership, and hew more closely to the needs and ideals of the average woman. It proposed the development of neighborhood and university committees with regular representatives and set meeting schedules; the creation of a committee to liaise with the provinces; the regular publication of a journal by and about women; and making the general assemblies places for discussion and information, not just "meeting places" (an allusion to the free-for-all atmosphere that prevailed at the general meetings). They even suggested that the movement collect dues to ensure its continued existence.[20] Some of these proposals were implemented in the campaign to legalize abortion, but given many feminists' rejection of traditional politics, it proved impossible for the movement as a whole to adopt the degree of organization that the Cercle Dimitriev was suggesting.[21] Moreover, as was true of participants in the May 1968 events, many of those involved with the MLF participated only tangentially and could not be counted on to make firm commitments of time or money.

The demand for greater organization by the Cercle Dimitriev and other Marxist feminists was further complicated by efforts to recruit more women to the larger cause of socialist revolution. This often involved infiltration: some Marxist women would camouflage their primary affiliations to gain other women's interest and confidence and then dominate the MLF's meetings and agenda, sparking outrage and accusations of betrayal. Eventually some of these women, like Françoise Picq, committed themselves wholly to the MLF, while others returned to their original political affiliations. But feminists went so far as to put traitors on trial and to publicly excommunicate them. In a few cases, the accused confessed, apologized and "converted"; most were summarily jettisoned.[22] Nevertheless, this ongoing effort at cooptation alienated potentially interested feminists from the MLF and certainly distracted attention from broader goals.

The greatest challenge to the Cercle Dimitriev and its supporters, however, came from radical feminism. One of the most influential and long-lasting of radical feminist groups, the Féministes révolutionnaires (initially composed of Giles and Monique Wittig, Rochefort, Stephenson, Delphy, and filmmaker Micha Garrigue), challenged the Marxist feminists in practice as well as in theory, in part because they knew their theory so well. Initially calling themselves Les petites margue-rites (The Little Daisies) after a 1966 avant-garde Czech film about two young, mischief-making women, they soon decided to give their group a name that communicated the seriousness of their purpose. In their *Le torchon brûle* manifesto, the Revolutionary Feminists juxtaposed a class-identified feminism with a new categorical approach: "*Feminists* means: For women and with all women. . . . We know . . . that 'woman' was our first identity before 'proletarian' or 'bourgeois.' Moreover, we feel that even in their different class identities, women have one point in common: a man. Why *Revolutionary*? Revolutionary for us means radical. We take charge of our revolution . . . not to ameliorate condi-tions of subjugation, but to completely overhaul them."[23]

The Revolutionary Feminists compared sexual oppression to racial discrimination and saw the development of feminism as analogous to the progress of the civil rights movement in the United States, in part because one of their most articulate spokeswomen, Christine Delphy, had been a participant. After completing university in France, Delphy had traveled to the United States with a fellowship from the Eleanor Roosevelt Foundation for Human Rights to work for the Urban League in Washington DC, arriving at the height of the civil rights movement. There she started seriously thinking about racism and its historical and philosophical roots. Delphy viewed the growing black separatist movement with interest: African Americans, she observed, were dou-bly exploited, as proletarians and as a racial minority, and after hav-ing fought in the civil rights movement alongside whites, had come to understand the necessity of separating themselves and forging their own identity free from the influence and definition of their oppressors. As she lobbied and engaged in community-building on behalf of Afri-can Americans, Delphy experienced blatant sexism (sometimes from men with whom she was working) and ultimately concluded that she would only fight for "her" people—for women.[24] In Delphy's view, women had to band together with the understanding that overturn-ing the patriarchy was their primary goal. One of the Revolutionary

Feminists' early flyers explained: "Today's society needs the exploitation and the slavery of women. . . . For this and other reasons, we have begun to regroup. We alone can know our oppression; it's up to us to take charge of our liberation. We have until now been separated, each enclosed in our family. This isolation *must be broken*. We must speak among ourselves, share our experiences. It is the totality of women that will give these objectives to the Movement."[25]

Delphy's contribution to feminist theory has been extraordinarily significant, although only since the beginning of the twenty-first century has she begun to be widely recognized for it. Her trenchant analysis of patriarchy and her deep humanism have manifested themselves in a large body of work that addresses sexism, racism, homophobia, and what would come to be called identity politics (exclusive political alliances around identity such as gender or sexuality). Among her contributions was the materialist analysis of the invisibility of domestic work and the family that she elaborated in her essay "The Main Enemy." Moreover, her experience with the racism of 1960s America threw France's own problems with racial and immigrant minorities into relief.[26]

While the Cercle Dimitriev wanted to shape the feminist movement into an organized revolutionary party, radical feminists wanted to brashly challenge the expectations of French society. Radical feminists created open conferences on feminism, such as the Days of Denunciation of Crimes against Women, held at the Mutualité in May 1972, as well as protests on Mother's Day: "Today, television, newspapers, and radios all repeat to us that we are their little queens. Where does Mother's Day come from? From Pétain, the little friend of Hitler, who established a day to the glory of mothers of the fatherland, *whose duty it is to make babies*. It is a question of celebrating mothers only, for in our society only women who have children represent something. And again, not just any mother! She must be married too. Single mothers don't receive anything except scorn and hassle!"[27] In a related action, five women—Monelle Quaglio, Alice Schwarzer, Marie-José Duval, Emmanuelle Curchod, and Françoise d'Eaubonne—staged a demonstration in the Chamber of Deputies during the discussion of the Neuwirth law in the autumn of 1974.They entered the gallery during the debate and shouted epithets and hurled flyers onto the heads of President Valéry Giscard d'Estaing and the deputies. They were quickly ejected but were joined by hundreds of other women descending from the Pont de la Concorde to the National Assembly.[28]

To overturn the patriarchal order, radical feminists declared that the most fundamental aspects of society had to be called into question and all relations of oppression had to be destroyed. Part of their success would lie in "promoting the capacities of each woman to take charge of herself, to think for herself, to take initiatives, to be creative, at the same time refusing to integrate into society."[29] But it was not so easy to find militant women prepared to follow the radical feminist challenge to its utmost—that is, entirely excluding men from the movement and repudiating any social convention deemed sexist. As Feldman-Hogasen noted, "At the last meeting I attended (at Monique's [Wittig's] place on abortion) I was convinced that there were nevertheless more ideas and enthusiasm than the actual number of militants. Growth is therefore very important."[30]

Despite their relatively small numbers, radical feminists had a broad influence on the development of 1970s feminism in France. To a great extent, radical feminists set the terms of the debate, pushing ideas (and feminists themselves) further and further. Moreover, with the radical feminists taking the lead in demanding the most extreme changes on behalf of women, parties of the Left—traditionally recalcitrant on feminist issues—found themselves forced to take at least a moderate position in defending women's rights. The adoption of progressive feminist platforms by the PCF and by the revamped Parti socialiste (PS) would have long-range political consequences for France, helping to bring the Socialists and the feminist positions they adopted to power in the presidential elections of 1981 and thereby putting the demands of their feminist constituency at the center of their commitment to reform.[31]

Besides the class struggle and radical feminists, another group would lay claim to the *querelle* and cause tremendous tension among all factions who spoke in the name of women's liberation. This group, calling itself Psych-et-Po, emerged from the literary and psychoanalytic academic milieu of the 1960s. Although small, it had an extraordinarily divisive effect on the entire movement. Indeed, the radical and Marxist feminists found they had more in common when faced with this third faction. Initially the group preferred quiet study and discussion to demonstration, which set it apart from the others. It emphasized psychological and emotional change on an individual level rather than political and institutional revolution. Radical feminists also believed that women needed to shed the thought patterns of the patriarchy, but for Psych-et-Po, transformation of consciousness was not simply the means to a greater end but the end in itself. Especially during its first years, it eschewed political involvement, although it did eventually choose to participate in the effort to legalize abortion. Beyond Psych-et-Po's theoretical and structural differences from other feminist groups, it eventually claimed to be the original—and only legitimate—voice of women's liberation. Understanding how this happened shines a light on the strategic and cultural challenges feminism experienced in France. But it also highlights the current gaps in American scholarship on French feminism, which has tended to examine theory in the abstract, divorced from its impact on policy or the people who espoused it.[32]

Antoinette Fouque and Psych-et-Po

Antoinette Fouque, the undisputed leader of Psych-et-Po, dates its founding to a study group focused on psychoanalysis at the University of Vincennes even before the outbreak of the May 1968 protests. At the time the group included Josiane Chanel and Monique Wittig, who soon abandoned Fouque and her project to join up with more action-oriented feminists. The group originally came to be called "groupe psychanalyse," although Fouque claims its members repudiated the moniker. Another member of the group, "Yvette," remembers its original name as "groupe Beaumarchais" (after their meeting place on the Boulevard Beaumarchais) or simply "groupe d'Antoinette." Its objective was to "articulate psychoanalysis and the political discourse of historical materialism."[33] The origin of this interest was Fouque's relationship with her mentor, Jacques Lacan, whose Écrits she edited for publication. Fouque had been writing a doctoral thesis under the direction of Roland Barthes when she met Lacan in October 1968. She underwent analysis with him from January 1969 to 1974 and was one of his staunchest supporters. Fouque increasingly tied her own self-discovery and liberation to a larger project, that of spreading this self-discovery to large numbers of women.[34]

Fouque eventually broke with Lacan over what she considered his phallocentrism, and she developed her own idea of the genital construction of human consciousness—that the libido was sexualized. "There are two sexes," Fouque argued: "Humanity is neither man nor woman; it is the guarantee of the species, which is the guarantor of the universality of the human genus. . . . In refusing to sexualize the condition of citizen of the Republic, law by unconscious reference to monotheist dogma neurotically denies reality, recovering it with a veil of ignorance, rather than facing it by analytical work and philosophical presuppositions, in other words, a work of democratization."[35] Upon this principle, Fouque developed her own understanding of the origin and workings of patriarchal oppression and a strategy for breaking it. While she accepted Lacan's Freudian argument that it is through the acquisition of language at the resolution of the Oedipus complex that the child enters society, she understood society to be imprinted by the "law of the father." For the child to accept this coming of age, Fouque argued, the child is compelled to reject the mother, both practically and symbolically. Thus, according to Fouque's analysis, both girls and boys grow up accepting the phallocentric world, in which the feminine is outside of the principal "libidinal economy." She referred to this paradigm as the "foreclosure of women's body." Women would have to realize their symbolic homosexuality to free themselves from patriarchal domination. They would also need to rediscover the power and essence of the other libidinal economy—the feminine.[36] This would require a profound separation, not only from any physical dependence on men but also from "masculine" thinking; will to power, organization, language—all masculine attributes as defined by Fouque—would have to be challenged and overcome.[37]

Fouque considered writing to be at the crossroads of identity formation, and this belief informed her projects. She considered herself a child of the Left and of the May events, and she wanted to elaborate a materialist politics, but one that was rooted in psychoanalysis and manifested in the written word. Within such a schema, reproduction and production grew to encompass creativity, language, culture, and desire. Tying reproduction to self-recreation and allowing women the space to shape their own production would enable them to exist on different terms, without need for or reference to masculinity. Fouque was fascinated by women writers who she felt were already engaged in this process—Wittig, Hélène Cixous, Luce Irigaray—and her notion of the relationship of the body to writing parallels many of their ideas. Fouque would never stray far from this position. When eventually she took on political causes— such as freeing political prisoners like Eva Forest (a Spanish resister of Franco's dictatorship) and Jiang Qing (Mao Zedong's wife and a member of the Gang of Four during China's Cultural Revolution) or supporting the Socialists in the 1980 elections—it was almost always in the context of publishing their writings (she opened a publishing house in 1972) or publishing her ideas in her newspaper, *des femmes en mouvements* (women in movement/s). Later, *des femmes en mouvements* became *des femmes en mouvements—hebdo* (women in movement/s-weekly) and reached a circulation of about 150,000. It continued publishing (with regional editions) until 1982, when its publishers claimed to have been forced out of business or "repressed" by the government.[38]

For all of her insistence on the essential importance of writing oneself into existence, Fouque, who died in 2014, left only a small legacy of her own writing. In 1992 Fouque received a doctorate in political science from the Université de Paris VIII for her thesis, which was a four-volume collection of transposed flyers from the movement, short essays, and transcripts of interviews and discussions called "Une expérience du mouvement des femmes en France 1968–1991 de la libération à la democratization" ("An experience of the women's movement in France from liberation to democratization, 1968–1991"). (Hélène Cixous, chair of the Department of Women's Studies and a published author through *Éditions des femmes*, presided over her defense).[39] The collection is not a work of scholarship nor of one individual. None of the essays reproduced in it is more than a few pages long, and it is unclear which pieces she herself wrote since many were taken from anonymous publications. Footnotes are likewise nonexistent. Included in one volume is a "Chronologie-femmes: 1968-1991" which states that Antoinette Fouque founded the MLF. (As will be discussed later, she founded and registered the association called MLF but did not found the movement—a point her dissertation does not make clear.)

Fouque's working-class heritage and alignment with early gay rights activists, as well as her interest in psychoanalysis, brought her to reject what she perceived as superficial feminism. Feminist demands for "equality" and "recognition" seemed to her a refusal to break fully from patriarchal standards. She did not want to position herself in opposition to male authority but to place herself beyond it. Thus, she argued that feminism represented "the last historic form of the patriarchy" and that she and her group were "postfeminists." Fouque accused feminists of reductionism, and she contrasted "feminism" with her praxis of "women's liberation," which "refused identification with a masculine model." Fouque strenuously opposed the beauvoirian and feminist maxim *On ne naît pas femme, on le devient* (One is not born a woman, but becomes one). For Fouque, symbolic function was inscribed in the body, hence it was not just history and society that defined womanhood.[40] The Psych-et-Po text published by *Libération* in 1974 claimed that "feminism is not women's struggle; women's struggle advances by a struggle *against* feminism" (my emphasis) and, even more dramatically, "Feminism is an adversary of the Women's Liberation Movement, of all liberation movements, and of all anti-imperialist movements." The history of modern feminism, Fouque declared, represented a continuous attempt on the part of some ambitious women to grab a fairer share of power in a male-dominated society. It was therefore trapped in an unwinnable—and fundamentally conservative—struggle: the fight to gain access to the male libidinal economy to which it would never be allowed entry.[41] In contrast, Fouque was quoted as saying, "Our women's struggle is a thought, a practice in movement that refuses to be named, to be enclosed, to be fossilized; a process of transformation, a continuing production of understanding by, on, for women in view of the taking of power by all the oppressed forces."[42] Her assertions make it difficult to place Psych-et-Po on the political spectrum or to analyze it as a political faction in relation to other groups. This is particularly true because, despite the group's initial renunciation of politics, it had changed course by the 1980 elections and actively campaigned for the Socialists, even marching in the streets in support of them.

Consistent with her belief in an inward-looking liberation, Fouque challenged the general feminist line on male domination and women's subordination. This became evident in the early meetings at Vincennes. Radical individualist feminism of the beauvoirian sort accepted that men had subjugated women into the position of "being" while men occupied the transcendent realm of "becoming." Most feminists agreed that they wanted to combat this status of the "other" and claim their own subjectivity, but Fouque argued that these feminists were male-identified—that they wanted to be people exactly like men or that they demanded equality but not a transformation of what constituted that equality. More fundamentally, she saw them as defining their consciousness and their subjectivity in relation to men, which she considered antirevolutionary: "Individualistic feminism seemed to me to be saying: 'The same model for everyone, and everyone for herself.' As for us, ours was the utopia of 'each according to her own uniqueness, together.'"[43]

As subsequent women's historians and theorists have argued, Fouque's strategy of reviving a "woman's nature" grounded in sexual difference put her close to the nineteenth- and early-twentieth-century "bourgeois feminists" she derided. For centuries both Anglo-Saxon and European women activists had based their demands for liberation on their special attributes as women and mothers. Universalist feminism was a largely post–World War II development, particularly in France, and one that remained undeveloped until the 1970s. The appellation "feminist" had previously been attributed to those advocating women's legal emancipation. One need only glance at the nineteenth-century Civil Code to recognize that women's demands for economic independence, legal rights over children and their own bodies, equal opportunity for education, and suffrage were, in their time, as radical and transformative as Fouque's claim on women's liberation.[44]

Fouque's view of male domination and women's liberation seems relatively clear, but her method of carving out ideological and political space in the women's liberation movement led her into a tangle of contradictions. Initially, Fouque claimed that she and her friends wanted to study, to understand their relationship to themselves and each other, rather than parading and demanding media attention. Fouque was admittedly plagued by an undisclosed and advancing illness that left her partially paralyzed and that made mundane tasks such as getting to a meeting a physical challenge.[45] But she was also as inspired by the May events as others and desired to act. She criticized the Arc de Triomphe protest as a superficial celebrity media event, although her subsequent actions reveal an equal desire for media attention. If protesting publicly intrinsically meant collusion with the patriarchy, then what constituted an independent politics?

To create a politics that was in the public eye while maintaining her ideological distance would mean adopting contradictory stances and claiming them as a coherent whole. For example, Fouque argued for the importance to women's liberation of writing and speaking but professed to have more concern with issues of class and material conditions than "bourgeois feminists."[46] Fouque carried on what sometimes amounted to a double life—elaborating her ideological themes on the one hand while pursuing her political ambitions on the other. In the 1980s and 1990s, for example, she spoke of the necessity of existing and working outside the phallic order, while at the same time she successfully campaigned for a seat in the European Parliament, founded a relatively pragmatically oriented group entitled Alliance des femmes pour la démocratisation (Alliance of Women for Democracy) as well as Club Parité 2000 (pressing for equal representation in Parliament), and accepted the honor of being named a Commander of the Order of the Legion of Honor by the French state in 2008.[47]

Françoise Picq, who has written one of the best analyses of Fouque and her activities, has noted that Fouque formulated a praxis that maintained the classic opposition between "reform and integration [and] revolution and subversion," with Fouque claiming to stand staunchly alone on the side of the latter.[48] But this theoretical opposition drew hostility from many women, who saw Fouque creating an abstraction out of very real oppression. As an anti-Psych-et-Po chant put it:

When I hear about independence erotic
I respond with a silence analytic
Psychepo [sic] is annoying and tragic
They have a discourse esoteric
Which women find hermetic
Lacking in dimension historic.[49]

This debate aside, the whole MLF, as loosely constituted as it was, was revolutionary because it rejected the old practices of integration and individual promotion, which remained de rigueur in other political movements. But it also offered more than this: its challenge to the political, social, and ideological status quo was significant and would spark real change. In the world of leftist French politics at the time, "reformist" was just about the worst slur one could utter, and Fouque used it to sabotage any hope of finding a broad feminist middle ground that would appeal to all the women of whom she spoke. For the women's liberation movement, the fear of reformism served as a strong brake for change that involved compromise.

Fouque's largest contradictions, however, lay in the realm of her relations with others. The subjective nature of claims made about her, however, make interpretation difficult. From certain accounts, it seems that the boundary between her political and social activities and her professional work as a psychoanalyst was blurred. Some followers have recounted that women in the Psych-et-Po group underwent a kind of collective analysis as well as sometimes seeing Fouque individually. She seemed to remain the undisputed leader of the group, holding evening meetings, described as "open" or "fluid," at which she would arrive hours late but then take her place at the front of the room. Some women described the experience as transformational, revolutionizing their thinking. Houda Aumont, an analysand of Lacan's and member of Psych-et-Po in 1972, recounts:

For a while I had the illusion we were experiencing a collective analysis. We treated machismo, masculinity, pederasty, and rarely femininity, because we thought that it was a trap set for us by man. We spent our time analyzing each other and critiquing ourselves under the leadership of Antoinette Fouque, our great priestess. There were daily meetings that often lasted into the early morning with the idea of helping a spontaneous voice to emerge. These meetings were real tortures, but I kept a warm memory of celebrations between women where there was a warm ambience and a kind of jubilation.[50]

Nevertheless, many women quit the group not because of Fouque's theory, to which they remained attracted, but because of its cult-like practices or because belonging to Psych-et-Po proved impractical for any woman with family or friends outside the hermetic group.[51]

Other women had a more negative experience. For example, *Libération* reporter Martine Storti related the "interrogation" and tongue-lashing she received at a Psych-et-Po encounter group in 1975. She reported that she had been forced to justify her presence at the meeting as if she were standing before a tribunal. "Each word spoken, each phrase, was used against me," she wrote. She described the sense of culpability that the group worked to instill in her: "Guilt for not having paid the price of my desire to be there, guilt for working at *Libé* [the newspaper *Libération*], guilt for not having been (part of) the only group that had the correct line." Storti continued, "I use religious language because I perceived not a group, but a sect, dominated by the speech of one woman alone, always the same, who questioned, condemned, represented the law and the father, assured of her power and of the submission of others." Indeed, Storti remarked that among the one hundred or so women at the meeting, the vast majority remained silent during her grilling.[52]

Other women experienced similar behavior. In June 1977 one of Fouque's former adherents, Nadja Ringart, accused Fouque of unethical behavior. In "La naissance d'une secte" (The birth of a sect), which *Libération* published on a full page, Ringart recounted the practices engaged in by Psych-et-Po under Fouque's direction: "We were witness to a stupefying metamorphosis, women of different languages and behavior transformed themselves, day after day, into parrots, obstinately repeating the speech of the master. One woman alone thought, spoke." Ringart recalled that the indignation expressed by a new arrival at seeing such a spectacle was met with a censorious and yet deliberately puzzling challenge: "Hey you, from where do you speak?" Such censure and the silence of the rest of the group were "prodigiously effective to shut the trap of this newcomer," she wrote. "From that day forward, thirty women of the group went from meeting to meeting, angrily barking a 'from where do you speak?' at the smallest attempt at discussion."[53]

The most dramatic example of popular dissent over Fouque's dealings with her associates involved her relationship with the Schlumberger heiress Sylvina Boissonnas, who was Fouque's staunch supporter. In the late 1960s and early 1970s Boissonnas had been commonly regarded as "the bank" for various leftist groups and projects (the Zanzibar film group was perhaps the best known), but her philanthropy did not have a particular focus. When Boissonnas met Fouque, she was immediately attracted to her as someone who understood the psychology behind the frustration and anger felt by many early MLF participants. Psychoanalysis fascinated her; she felt that it enabled her finally to understand some of her own motivations and frustrations. In Fouque she found a sympathetic ear and a wise woman who cared. Fouque's idea of creating a woman's publishing company inspired Boissonnas, and she helped Fouque's dream become a reality. Many feminists acknowledged that such a benefactor provided institutional capacity, although there were some who disparaged the source of the financing. And, beyond ideological differences, many feminists disliked Fouque's bourgeois lifestyle (she lived in a large private townhouse in the fashionable Seventh Arrondissement), believing that she appropriated Boissonnas's money for her personal use. Rumors about this greatly affected many feminists' view of Fouque.[54]

During the 1970s Psych-et-Po distanced itself from other groups in the movement. The group declared itself open to all women and spoke in the name of all women (as did many others). And, like other groups, it maintained certain subtle or not-so-subtle rites of passage that were deliberately exclusive. But Psych-et-Po's reliance on psycho-analytic language and the belief that Fouque was, in Aumont's words, "a high priestess" appeared controlling to many women in the movement. Moreover, by the end of the decade, Psych-et-Po increasingly proclaimed itself the sole representative of the movement for women's liberation (discussed in subsequent chapters); this was interpreted as direct aggression toward other groups and clashed with Fouque's message of radical egalitarianism.[55]

"One Is Not Born a Lesbian": Sexuality, Lesbian Politics, and Women's Liberation

Sex as a challenge to social norms and a territory of liberation was key to the gay political culture that burst forth out of the May events. The growth of lesbian political culture through this experience pushed feminism in directions that were both constructive and destructive to the movement as a whole. Formed in the tumult of protests, the Front homosexuel d'action révolutionnaire (Homosexual Front of Revolutionary Action) was an eclectic and ebullient group of men and women who began to meet and exchange experiences, share in the joy of being "out," and strategize about rectifying legal and social discrimination. It was in the 1970s women's movement that lesbians formed a public social movement for the first time. Much of the medical community and the public continued to view homosexuality as deviant and women's homosexuality in particular as outside the realm of normalcy (or as a titillating sensual excess not to be taken seriously). Over much of the twentieth century, this proved advantageous, as lesbianism remained unspoken of and thus vaguely tolerated. Until the publication of The Second Sex in 1949, lesbian desire had been considered something innate, driven by internal forces. Beauvoir, who devoted an entire chapter to "The Lesbian"—and who was subsequently criticized for her canned descriptions and generalizations despite her own lesbian relationships—nevertheless shined light on the phenomenon, suggesting that lesbian relations could also be a personal choice made either instead of or alongside heterosexual relations. It was not until the second-wave feminist movement of the 1970s that lesbianism was given public legitimacy as a viable alternative to heterosexuality and a political position.[56]

The gay liberation movement in France dates its beginning to March 10, 1971. On that day a popular talk-radio show, *Allô Ménie*, hosted by the psychologist Ménie Grégoire broadcast a live program in the concert hall Salle Pleyel on the topic of homosexuality. In keeping with the usual format, Grégoire had gathered a panel of "experts," who included a priest, a psychiatrist, one of the few openly gay journalists in France, and André Baudry, the head of Arcadie, which for more than a decade before the May events had been the only organized gay (or "homophile," as he called it) group in France. As was typical, Grégoire posed questions to stimulate a discussion among the panelists, which was followed by a period of call-in questions and questions from the audience. This time, however, something surprising happened. In the middle of the broadcast, a few lesbian and gay audience members jumped up, shouting, "Stop talking about your suffering!" and "Down with the heterocops!" About thirty protesters then stormed the stage, overturning tables and chairs, assaulting the panelists (except for the journalist, Pierre Hahn, who had invited them), and shouting "We want liberty for us and for you!" from the podium microphone before the broadcast was suspended. Interestingly, the majority of these "commandos" were lesbians, including Anne-Marie Fauret, Marie-Jo Bonnet, Françoise d'Eaubonne, Cathy Bernheim, Monique Wittig, Christine Delphy, and Margaret Stephenson. They had already become politically active through the feminist movement and some had met at Arcadie—before being ejected for talking politics at a "nonpartisan cultural organization." The publicity generated by Grégoire's talk show led them to formalize their group, and Front homosexuel d'action révolutionnaire (Homosexual Front for Revolutionary Action [FHAR]) was founded later in the spring of 1971. A mixed gay and lesbian group, FHAR focused on sexual liberation, solidarity, and visibility. It published its goals in a series of articles and statements in a special edition of the Maoist newspaper *Tout!* One of its most provocative manifestos, for both its sexual explicitness and its racial overtones, declared, "We are more than 343 sluts [referencing the famous abortion petition of 1971, which will be discussed in chapter 5]. We have been buggered by Arabs. We're proud of it and we'll do it again." Soon, hundreds were attending FHAR meetings, held in the same auditorium of the École des Beaux-Arts on the rue Bonaparte that had been hosting MLF meetings since 1968. Members of both organizations interacted, and FHAR joined the MLF in its first public march in the streets of Paris on November 20, 1971. The women's movement had transformed the discourse around homosexuality.[57]

The women's and gay liberation movements had somewhat parallel trajectories. They shared a new, muscular rhetoric, imprinted with Marxist concepts of class consciousness and a World War II–inflected vocabulary that referred to "occupation," "resistance," and "collaboration."[58] At first, gay women met in groups within both MLF and FHAR, but they shifted their allegiance toward the former fairly quickly. As FHAR built up steam, lesbians who were also feminists felt increasingly alienated from the organization, seeing that its priorities were being shaped by men. By the summer of 1971, some of the lesbians most attuned to these power dynamics founded the Gouines rouges (Red Dykes), named, Christine Delphy later remembered, after an epithet once thrown at her when she was handing out copies of *Le torchon brûle*. At the same time, lesbians who were participating in MLF activities felt bound together by the sheer excitement of being around other smart, politically aware women like themselves—what Delphy has referred to as a kind of homoeroticism. Yes! these women were saying. We feminists are all lesbians. We claim the insult.

The idea (and catchphrase) "One is not born a lesbian, one becomes one" emerged within the shifting politics at the center of the MLF. The counterculture of the 1970s, from which radical feminism emerged, valorized modes of living freely that made it possible to multiply and exchange experiences in communities both ephemeral and enduring. This produced a flurry of experimenting that led sometimes to disenchantment and sometimes to a broadening of sexual and emotional existence. It helped women to imagine an alternate lifestyle and an existence beyond the realm of patriarchal relations. Stigma had become a brand.[59]

The lesbian feminist cause received another boost during the gathering at the union assembly hall, the Mutualité, the following year, during the "Days of Denunciation of Crimes Against Women" (May 13-14, 1972). There, Marie-Jo Bonnet, Cathy Bernheim, Christine Delphy, Catherine Deudon, and Monique Wittig went up on stage (accompanied by Bonnet's guitar for some courage and levity) and read an affirmation of their lesbianism that was interwoven with feminism. They called on all women who felt the way they did to join them: "Women who reject the roles of wife and mother: the time has come for us to speak from the depths of silence." The song they composed articulated the intensity of their desire to rid themselves of guilt, self-hatred, and the feeling that they had to live a lie in heterosexual France:

> We are dykes, lesbians, depraved and foul
> We love other women
> We will break our chains
> No more cowering in the corner
> Let us love each other in broad daylight.

Cathy Bernheim remembers feeling extraordinary freedom and sisterhood at that moment, which solidified her commitment. Witnesses remember it as a moment of powerful solidarity that was as intensely personal as it was political. There was now a real political movement, perhaps the first in France, that directly opposed "familialism."[60]

It is simplistic to view the gay liberation movement in France from the May events through the early 1980s as having been primarily about breaking taboos and gaining social acceptance (and legal protections) for homosexuality. If the gay liberation movement was as much a political movement as a sexual one, then the lesbian movement was more so. First fearing that making a declaration of homosexuality would undermine the legitimacy of feminism in the public eye, but then embracing it as part of women's liberation, lesbian feminists became intensely political by the mid-1970s, establishing new political norms for gay women and changing the conversation around sex. As Bonnet remembers, "the boys" were very focused on "fucking," which in many ways seemed the same old focus for French men. Lesbian women by and large split with FHAR until later in the century, when they rejoined gay men to advocate for solutions to the AIDS epidemic and to combat homophobia. Then, the mixing of genders again became the norm, particularly among students.[61]

Reinventing Feminism: Women's Liberation

For decades sexuality and the physiological nature of women was a shared discourse of the Left and Right: France needed to give women protection in order to bolster their roles as mother and wife. Women in the MLF boldly repositioned the issue as one of individualism or identity rather than of family or natalism, which provided feminist entry into domains ranging from reproductive control to the manifestation of women's personhood. With Fouque speaking of women's libidinal economy and the radical feminists declaring themselves fed up with men in society and in the bedroom, movement women changed the debate over women's position in society and allowed them to reject French state protectionism and to claim the independence granted to men. In doing so, however, they placed motherhood and what were considered traditional roles for women in a nebulous position. Undeniably, many women in France were or would become mothers and therefore would create, to a greater or lesser extent, the very roles that feminists had hoped to eradicate. Feminism was a movement of the avant-garde and, as such, was not constructed to fit comfortably into familiar expectations. But to be a viable movement, it had to reckon with the majority of women who would form heterosexual partnerships and have children. Married women did participate in the MLF, but they felt the double sting of living within a sexist society and of being treated as traitors by some of their contemporaries. As one frustrated woman stated, "We refuse to consider ourselves reformists, irredeemably alienated, or in a compromised situation because it is a real situation. Each woman becomes conscious of her oppression at a different time in her individual history. [Even] if our husband isn't a ruthless tyrant who rapes us every evening—making us into the oppressed type gathered in open arms by the MLF—our situation is economically and emotionally complex (even before taking account of the rights of our children) and doesn't allow for a simple solution."[62]

Feminists' demand for safe and legal abortion and then for protection against sexual assault became the logical rallying points for a movement that increasingly embraced the idea that control of one's body was the starting point of personal liberation. Because of France's history of supporting families, motherhood and traditional causes such as adequate maternity leave and child care would not be political priorities for second-wave French feminists; indeed, they would be rejected outright by the radical feminists.[63] Viewing feminist priorities in the context of France's social policy since World War I, it seems clear that government subsidies aimed at supporting children within families were to some degree responsible for feminists' focus on sexual and cultural battles such as abortion and male domination. But it was also why many working-class and professional French women who were politically engaged steered clear of feminism as a politics of extremes.[64]

Women's liberation groups consciously refused to engage in the traditional operations of a political organization. Elected offices, rules of order, taking minutes, and so on were scorned as the property of the same men who had so disillusioned feminists during the May events. As Nadja Ringart, a *soixante-huitarde* and subsequently a feminist put it, "I couldn't help but be there [at the revolutionary meetings], but I spoke words that weren't my own. Theory didn't interest me. I wanted us to speak normally in the leaflets, but I didn't dare demand that. . . . I had the family spirit and I believed in the revolution, but organizational hierarchies were grotesque, the little war repulsed me."[65] The hallmark of this post-1968 feminism remained autonomy: autonomy of women's bodies and freedom from organizations and formal structure.

The reinvention of feminism also occurred at the crossroads between pure theory and practical reality—between wanting to push France beyond its comfort zone and risking alienating broad popular support. This became a central challenge within the women's liberation movement. Feminism was ephemeral and disorganized and only became part of mainstream French politics when it was absorbed into and reformed by the major parties in the late 1970s. Aside from its practical dimensions, the 1970–1979 campaign to legalize abortion unified the disparate theories and practices of the different feminist factions while at the same time offering a symbolic reconciliation between reform and revolution.

The Mouvement de libération des femmes, from its official beginning in 1970 to the end of the decade, designated all the feminist groups—self-identified or not, organized or transient—who fought for women's liberation. The goals that the movement accomplished were many and the impact that feminism had on institutions was considerable. But many reasons—among them sectarian politics, lack of cooperation, and working-class fear of "bourgeois political agendas"—caused a significant portion of French women to avoid participating in the MLF and to disavow the "feminist" label, blunting the popularity of the movement and enabling the forces of conservatism to reassert themselves where actual laws had not yet been changed. The movement was rich in ideas and energy, but its contentiousness diminished its public impact, and its internal disputes, power struggles, and endless debates over correct theory and practice hampered coalition-building—a necessity in the hostile political climate feminism faced.[66]

5 THE MOUVEMENT DE LIBÉRATION DES FEMMES AND THE FIGHT FOR REPRODUCTIVE FREEDOM

1970–1979

I signed because . . .
I signed because I have lost too much blood
And because on top of that you want me to keep quiet.
All that is finished. Now we speak. Mister
Legislator, look at all the blood on your hands
And you don't even realize it, you carry on like this.
But we're going to rub your nose in
the law that says "all are equal under the law."
And then the law selectively touches only one
Group. And then you take on your moralist airs.
Cheater.
You codify my physiological functions.
You describe in detail what passes in the interior
of my uterus. You put it all in the "Official Law Journal."
What indecency!
And yet you demand modesty from me.
It is thus that you win my silence, which suits you well.
Hypocrite!
But the silence is broken.
We are giving you the finger. And the whole world will see your real face.
How horrible!

A signatory, "Manifesto of the 343," *Le nouvel observateur*, April 5, 1971

Between the summer of 1970, when the MLF first made its entrance onto France's political stage, and 1979, when much of it exploded into an angry war of accusation, betrayal, sabotage, and greed, the women's movement managed to permanently transform public debate on women. It unified effectively to change the abortion law even while fragmenting into splinter groups. It was a time of legislative success and of political contention. The MLF's vibrancy changed politics as usual and made room for a much greater acknowledgment of women's equality with men. It was so successful that by mid-decade many moderates as well as conservatives had integrated its ideas into new programs for reform and had acquiesced, to a certain extent, to a revised model of womanhood. Within less than ten years, this volatile and disorganized movement managed to achieve the passage of laws liberalizing access to contraception and legalizing abortion, created equality provisions in education, increased the attention to discrimination against women in politics and the workplace, and broadened women's economic prospects.

France remained male dominated and women still faced sex discrimination. But the MLF indisputably changed the structure and attitudes of French society. "The principal success of feminism," the writer and publisher Françoise Collin wrote in 1992, "was to have created new and direct relationships between women, sometimes harmonious and also sometimes conflictual, but which have made them speak and think in their name, and made them take charge of their own lives whether or not they are intellectuals or feminists."[1] The movement came to symbolize the battle between women and men as well as a battle between the old guard and the new, and, as in the case of abortion, between republicans infused with a revived egalitarianism and the clericals and natalists who had dominated politics for the previous hundred years.

Many feminist groups—large and small, organized and spontaneous—sprang up and dissolved in the 1970s; only the most influential will be considered here. Many feminists sought to defy categories, but they nonetheless operated on a spectrum from militancy to reformism. Adding to this spectrum were the members of the Psych-et-Po group who advocated a transformation of society loosely along gendered lines but who decried the term *feminist*. In many ways radical feminism set the theoretical tone for the MLF in the 1970s, but other feminists—Françoise Giroud and Yvette Roudy, working within government; Gisèle Halimi of Choisir; and Anne Zelensky, Annie Sugier, and Simone de Beauvoir of the Ligue du droits des femmes (League of Women's Rights)—were willing to engage the establishment. They took feminism away from the autonomous and antiestablishment experiment of the late 1960s and the early 1970s, moving it toward a more integrationist pragmatism by the end of the decade.[2] Reform from inside did not necessarily mean capitulation, as Choisir and the Ligue demonstrate. These groups represented an interesting amalgam of radical demands and political expediency that over the decades became a lasting force in contemporary politics. Four years of intensive advocacy and celebration of women's solidarity that led to that achievement were also what some called *les années noires* (the black years)—a period of fruitful activism and intellectual production that also was a time of weakened political power due to internal disputes and disorganization.[3]

"I Will Have a Baby When I Want, If I Want"

The 1970s women's liberation movement in France explored a broad range of subjects and disagreed about many of them. Yet despite the cacophony of voices and lack of any set agenda, feminists managed to unite around one issue that gave the movement its political force: women's right to sexual freedom and their legal right to control their bodies. It was one of the central issues to emerge from the May 1968 protests, and in the movement's first years this demand for corporeal independence was the essence of women's liberation as the new generation defined it—not as a crusade to ameliorate women's subordinate position but a revolt to break entirely free of it and to transform society in the bargain. As Gisèle Halimi explained during an international colloquium on abortion and contraception: "For those who believe in God and for those who do not, to give life is the freedom of freedoms on which all others depend. A physically alienated human being cannot become adult and therefore responsible. To achieve equality in work, to exist completely in the political, social, and cultural life of the body politic requires for women a preexisting condition: to be one's own master. All struggles for women's liberation are in vain if women remain in a state of powerlessness in their own bodies."[4]

This position was not merely philosophical. Two decades before, Beauvoir had starkly laid out the alienation women felt from their bodies as they tried to live both with their sexual desire and with the nagging terror of pregnancy, especially when sex was considered an indecent subject for public discussion. The MLF's abortion legalization campaign struck a chord in women from many social strata who were struggling to make ends meet, who sought economic betterment, or who wanted more personal independence. More women than ever were employed, and they found themselves trying to maintain the delicate balance between work and family life, knowing that an unwanted pregnancy would throw their already difficult world into disarray. These women joined in the rhetoric of individualism and liberation voiced by the movement, but their sentiments had much to do with their own future and their relationship to their families.[5] As an early recapitulation of prolegalization arguments stated, "The interdiction of abortion is but one of the material oppressions that constrain women and force them to live exclusively as wives and mothers. Most women are not able to control their pregnancies or the conditions in which their children are raised." Or, put in a less academic way:

Who should decide how many children we have?
The pope who has never had them?
The president who has whatever it takes to raise them?
The doctor who has more respect for the life of a fetus than for the life of a woman?
The husband who goes "couchie-cou" when he comes home in the evening?
We, who carry them and who are the ones currently obligated to raise them?
Legal and Free Abortion![6]

The fight over abortion began at almost the moment that the MLF became a recognizable political entity in the autumn of 1970. The following spring, women from early groups such as the Marxist Cercle Élisabeth Dimitriev, the lesbian Polymorphe perverse, and Psychet-Po held meetings in large auditoriums (for example, at the École des Beaux-Arts), where they strategized about how to gain the legalization of abortion.[7] Lesbian feminists joined with heterosexual women on the principle that a woman's control of her own body was a basic right. The campaign for legalization demonstrates that the MLF could be supremely effective when it channeled its resources toward a concrete goal even when many in positions of power in France were against it. Feminist efforts dovetailed with larger changes, led by the burgeoning middle-class baby boomers rather than the elites. Over the course of the 1970s, a growing number of French citizens from all classes as well as government officials would either support women's right to choose or not stand in its way—all of them caught up in the new culture of personal freedom that the May 1968 events and a more individualist consumer society had ushered in.[8] Feminists shaped popular opinion concerning women's best interests and redefined the contours of the debate, moving it well beyond what the politicians intended.

French governments had for centuries kept abortion illegal on moral grounds, although they had increasingly shifted their arguments toward the problem of France's low birthrate, with which they remained obsessed well into the twentieth century. The law of July 31, 1920, reaffirming the criminality of abortion and any "antinatalist propaganda" became the cornerstone upon which subsequent legislation was based despite poor public support.[9] The 1967 Neuwirth law, which legalized—in the narrowest way—the production and distribution of contraception, passed by a relatively small margin despite public consensus in favor of birth control with abortion purposely left out of that debate and the 1920 law remaining on the books. The result was that contraception was largely only available to middle-class women in big cities who had doctors willing to prescribe it. Even by 1978, with the Neuwirth law liberalized and abortion legal, an INED study of three thousand women aged twenty to forty-five found that only 37 percent were effectively using a method of contraception. Reproductive rights pamphlets argued that this was because women were raised in a culture of sexual repression where the only acceptable women's role was that of mother. Because of the limited availability of birth control, French women underwent (by the best estimate) hundreds of thousands of abortions a year, most of them performed abroad or illegally in France under unsafe conditions.[10]

From the first year of the movement on, many women concluded that only heavy public pressure would sway the government to legalize abortion. As a way to build media attention, feminists canvassed for interested celebrities and quickly recruited Simone de Beauvoir and the actress Delphine Seyrig to their cause. The *groupe avortement* (abortion group) soon produced one of the most famous and effective actions of the MLF: the "Manifeste de le 343" (Manifesto of the 343) printed in *Le nouvel observateur* in April 1971. The full-page advertisement listed 343 signatories and proclaimed: "One million women undergo abortions each year in France. They have them in dangerous conditions because they are condemned to secrecy, whereas this is one of the simplest operations when performed under medical supervision. Silence reigns over all these millions of women. I claim I am one of them. I claim I have aborted. Not only do we demand unrestricted access to contraception, we demand legal abortion."[11]

Other papers picked up the story. Women who signed the statement knew they were admitting having broken the law and risking prosecution, but they believed that the government would not have the courage to indict all of them, especially when the list of *salopes* ("sluts," as their detractors called them) included Catherine Deneuve, Marguerite Duras, Françoise Fabian, and Simone de Beauvoir. "The cover [of that issue] had the effect of a bomb," Françoise Picq recalled. "Abortion, as taboo a subject as it was, suddenly was on everyone's lips." The following months produced long conversations in the letters to the editor pages of many newspapers and magazines.[12] Activists rapidly formed the Mouvement pour la liberté de l'avortement (MLA; Movement for the Freedom to Abort) to cash in on the spontaneous popular support and prepare for a legal defense of the signatories. The right to abort is "an elementary freedom," MLA declared, although the need for abortion signaled the failure of contraception and pointed to the oppressed state of women. By the end of April 1971, a public opinion poll for *Le nouvel observateur* registered 55 percent in favor of women's right to terminate a pregnancy. Perhaps more important, 87 percent of the people surveyed declared that the decision to abort was a private rather than a societal one.[13]

The Manifesto of the 343 was the first salvo in a long campaign to force the legislature into passing a bill legalizing abortion, or *l'interruption volontaire de la grossesse* (IVG; voluntary interruption of pregnancy). A month later, in May, 252 doctors signed a similar manifesto in *Le nouvel observateur*, declaring their aversion to the current ban and asserting the individual's right to decide on the morality of abortion. Deputies started floating abortion legislation that they believed would satisfy both religious and natalist concerns. Radical Party deputy Henri Caillavet proposed that only women with more than three children and all single women younger than twenty-one be allowed to abort. The PCF proposed new legislation legalizing abortion for "therapeutic and social reasons" to be performed in hospitals and covered by Social Security. And in February 1973, 330 doctors signed a statement that, following their conscience, they had performed abortions despite the ban; no prosecutions followed.[14] By then, those 330 doctors seemed the least of the government's problem.

More dramatic but in the same vein, the Mouvement pour la liberté de l'avortement et la contraception (MLAC; Movement for Contraceptive and Abortion Freedom), a militant coalition founded in 1973 by different reproductive rights organizations, declared that it was performing and would continue to perform abortions for women who were in need. It proclaimed that individual liberty did not exist without the free disposition of one's body. Equally illegal, the film *Histoires d'A (Stories of A)*, which demonstrated the Karman aspiration abortion method, was shown widely around France. Other than the seizure of the film during a public screening on the orders of Minister of Cultural Affairs Maurice Druon, the government did relatively little to crack down on illegal abortions, information about abortion, or abortion-rights protesters.[15]

At the time of the Manifesto of the 343, however, it had not been clear that the government would be so lax. Taking every precaution, women from the MLF, the MFPF, and the MLA formed Choisir (To Choose) in July 1971 for the possible legal defense of the signatories. Led deliberately and cautiously by Tunisian-French lawyer Gisèle Halimi, Choisir was not always popular with militant feminists, some of whom felt that Halimi wanted to control the campaign. But there is no question that Choisir under Halimi's leadership became an extremely useful tool for influencing public opinion and for extinguishing much of the antiabortion forces' fire in the courts and the legislature.[16] Halimi had already made a name for herself defending Algerian nationalist militants during the Algerian War in the late 1950s and early 1960s, in particular a young Algerian nationalist, Djamila Boupacha, who had been raped and tortured while in police custody. While condemning Boupacha's incarceration and torture, Halimi used legal arguments to get Boupacha a fair trial. This ability to work the levers of power was Halimi's trademark and made her one of the most brilliant and successful feminists of twentieth-century France. Halimi's subsequent book about the trial, introduced by Beauvoir, demonstrated her keen understanding of politics and of how women's bodies and sexuality could be used for larger political aims.[17] Beauvoir had been against the French prosecution of the Algerian War, which had been her primary reason for involving herself in the case, and Halimi's book, published in 1962, transformed Beauvoir into an engaged intellectual and placed Boupacha's sexual torture at the center of public debate about the Algerian conflict, forcing the French to think about their treatment of Algerians and specifically of Algerian women.[18]

The MLF played tough, protesting at the Conseil de l'ordre des médecins (Council of the Order of Doctors), interrupting debate in the National Assembly, and organizing demonstrations much like those mounted by the suffragists of the nineteenth and early twentieth centuries. Women who had found themselves pregnant too many times and who had headed to Switzerland or shared chartered buses to the Netherlands to have abortions or who submitted to back-street abortions in France marched together in demonstrations and wrote letters to legislators. Their common slogan, "Class abortion: Switzerland for the rich, the courts for the others," called on the French people's basic sense of fairness and dignity. Their claims went beyond practical considerations, calling male domination and the whole organization of society into question: "We don't exist as humans, we are only roles: object-woman, wife-woman, mother-woman, whore-woman, child-woman ..., always dominated by the role of the virile-man."[19]

While the MLF took to the streets, Halimi calmly argued the courts into a corner and published thoughtful pieces criticizing the existing law. She argued that women deserved equal freedom and equal rights to physical autonomy under French law. Slavery was outlawed, she reasoned, so why were women forced to bear children if they did not want to? Would the courts be willing to mete out punishment against women who chose abortion (and their accomplices) in any situation? Were politicians willing to defend the law against Halimi's arguments? They would need to be quite persuasive to counter her challenges to their "intellectual honesty" in the face of legislation that was, as she said, "directly inspired by the imperatives of a Judeo-Christian civilization but against the great principle of secularism affirmed by our constitution."[20]

The chance to discover whether the courts would cease enforcing antiabortion law came in December 1972, during a celebrated trial held in the Parisian suburb of Bobigny. It was the case of a minor, Marie-Claire Chevalier, who was accused of having had an abortion because she ended up hospitalized after complications. The abortionist and her accomplices (including Marie-Claire's mother) were also inculpated. Marie-Claire declared that she had been raped by a boy from her high school and that he had refused to take responsibility for the pregnancy. Her mother could not afford the payment demanded by a doctor willing to perform a medically sound abortion, and so, after various inquiries, she found an abortionist through her fellow workers at the RATP, the Paris transit authority. Once accused, Mme. Chevalier remembered reading Halimi's book on Boupacha in the RATP union library and sought her out. "Since that lawyer defended that tortured Algerian woman, maybe she would accept to defend us," Halimi remembers Mme. Chevalier telling her. Halimi countered, "All right, if you want a great public trial." Certainly, Marie-Claire and her mother were excellent defendants, and it seemed probable that the judge would grant clemency to both (the sexual encounter that resulted in Marie-Claire's pregnancy had been her first, and both of the "moral inquiries" issued by the judge gave mother and daughter high marks). It was the extraordinary testimony from celebrities and scientists, however, that most affected the judge and the numerous people who followed the trial.[21]

Supporters rallying outside the court were so raucous that the judge kept yelling, "Shut the windows! Shut the doors!" Inside, Halimi argued that the antiabortion laws were contrary both to popular consensus regarding women's freedom and to the latest scientific evidence. Yes, abortion was nothing to take lightly, but had to be a legal medical procedure to protect women's health. This argument was personal for Halimi, who remembered her own experience of an illegal abortion, performed without anesthesia, when she was a young lawyer. (The doctor had told her, "This will teach you not to do this again!") To bolster her arguments, Halimi arranged for testimony from celebrities such as the comic actress Delphine Seyrig; from the feminist intellectuals Christiane Rochefort and Simone de Beauvoir; from Jacques Monod and François Jacob, Nobel Prize winners for physiology and medicine; and from the historian of science and morals Jean Rostand. To the judge, Seyrig stated simply that she had "aborted several times" (she had also given birth) and that "it was a deeply personal choice" not based on abstract morality. She added that she freely aided any woman who came to her for help in getting an abortion.[22] Monod spent some time theorizing on when the fetus could be considered a living being, but he ultimately concluded that early abortion did not pose a moral dilemma. He also added some concrete reality to the rumor that the current law was a dead letter: "It has become relatively public knowledge, in any case, in many hospitals, that excellent doctors [perform abortions] for no remuneration but because their conscience as doctor and as citizen moves them to."[23]

Marie-Claire was acquitted. Her mother, who swore to the judge that she would do anything in her power to keep her daughter from falling into the same trap of single motherhood to which she had succumbed, received a small fine in a separate trial. The other intermediaries were let off, although the abortionist was given a one-year prison term. Overall, the trial was considered a victory for the prochoice cause and another step toward legalization.

A few months later, large protests followed the arrest of a doctor accused of performing illegal abortions in the offices of Choisir and the MLAC. Dr. Annie Ferrey-Martin, along with her husband and sister-in-law, was arrested on May 8, 1973, in a raid on the MLAC's Grenoble offices, which since the 1960s had been a principal center of reproductive-rights advocacy. A wave of petitions, marches, letters, and sympathetic articles made the case too dramatic to litigate. In Grenoble, a protest march in support of Ferrey-Martin on May 11 was attended by approximately ten thousand people. The public knew there were plenty of doctors performing abortions in France and charging thousands of francs for the procedure. Ferrey-Martin, a fragile-looking gamine of a woman in the press photos, had been doing them for free.[24]

This obvious inequity was more than the government could publicly ignore. On the same day as the protest, the minister of public health and social security, Michel Poniatowski, announced to the National Assembly that the law of 1920 would be revised. Over the following weeks, Prime Minister Pierre Messmer and Minister of Justice Jean Taittinger worked on a bill to present to the Parliament. Eight groups, among them the parties of the Left as well as Choisir, Laissez-les-vivre (Let-Them-Live—an antilegalization group), and the Ligue des droits de l'homme (League of the Rights of Man), filed their own proposals. The government finally accepted the bill of Lucien Neuwirth—the same UDR deputy who had written the law legalizing contraception in 1967—but it could not assemble a majority to pass it. Not until after the death of President Georges Pompidou, the election of a new government, and another year of political pressure did the Parliament decide to support the reform. Ironically, the bill that eventually passed was much more liberal than the one rejected in 1973.[25]

In the meantime the MLF, the MLAC, and Choisir kept up their assault. Choisir promoted its slogan, "My liberty: contraception; my choice: to give life; my ultimate recourse: abortion." Choisir decided to foster the belief that the acceptance of abortion was a fait accompli and that legalizing abortion would do no more than allow the procedure to be regulated and performed competently under medically safe conditions. Media coverage was positive; the press published an ongoing stream of letters of protest from various groups, articles by proponents, and statistics on the estimated number of abortions in France. *Le Monde* reported, for example, that in 1966 there had been thirty abortions for every one hundred live births and that the number had risen as high as forty by 1973. The newspaper also speculated that approximately fifty thousand abortions had been performed outside of France on French women in 1972 alone.[26]

Giscard d'Estaing did not support 1970s French feminism (and feminists did not support him, rallying instead to François Mitterrand in the presidential elections of 1974), but perhaps because polls were showing the contest to be the closest in modern French history (with a 1.6 percent margin separating Giscard d'Estaing from Mitterrand in the run-up to the election) he had declared that the ban on abortion must be lifted. Once elected (without a margin of female support), he pushed the legislature to pass a bill reforming abortion law—sometimes at his reputation's peril.[27] Although Giscard took the initiative to liberalize abortion law, the Right still controlled the Senate and the National Assembly in the 1970s, so the Left proved indispensable to Giscard's reformist platform, tipping the political balance. The same parties of the Left that had deplored the legalization of artificial contraception in the early 1960s now argued that women had to be free to choose. In the words of Communist senator André Aubry: "The woman who believes she cannot continue her pregnancy should be allowed to end it and at the same time preserve her health, her psychological balance, and her dignity; that she may cease to feel ashamed and guilty since it is the fault of the capitalist system, incapable of giving women the moral and material means to be a mother each time she desires to be."[28] The newly revived Socialist Party, led by Mitterrand, campaigned actively for the women's vote on a program that included the legalization of abortion. And the historically socially conservative Communist Party followed the Socialists' lead.[29] Legislation to legalize abortion had been proposed by both the Socialists and the Communists as early as 1965, when they reversed their long-held natalist principles and decided to join the fight to legalize contraception. But their earlier proposals had put the decision to terminate a pregnancy in the hands of the courts or doctors and had allowed abortion only in specific cases, such as rape or incest, if a woman's mental or physical health was in danger, if the woman was single and under age twenty or without resources, or if the fetus was found to be malformed. These bills had been rejected in the legislature, some without debate, and the PCF was able to remain publicly uncommitted—for example, denying Halimi's request for aid in defending Mme. Chevalier's daughter.[30] But now the Communists did an abrupt turnabout, arguing with the Socialists that free access to abortion was the only way to eliminate blatant class discrimination. By framing the issue as one of discrimination against the underprivileged rather than of equal rights, Communists were arguing for fairness in a brutal capitalist world rather than for women's independence. As Communist deputy Gisèle Moreau argued in a speech to the National Assembly: "Society must be liberated from the law of profit and from the domination that industry and finance exercise on every aspect of life. [Industry and finance] take advantage of women's inequality, siphoning off national resources for their own gain instead of constructing collective mechanisms necessary for the promotion of social policy. For reasons of principle and economics, they prevent a large dissemination of the means for couples to control their fertility."[31]

Despite some leftist politicians' support, Giscard's government also needed the women's movement to galvanize the public since many parliamentarians on the Left were unwilling to risk their reputations on legislation they believed was not widely supported. The MLF forced their hand, but it did so by taking the debate to an entirely different level. It should be women alone who determined whether or not to terminate a pregnancy. Having made the issue so public that everyone felt they needed to have an opinion, the largely feminist coalition of organizations supporting abortion's legalization declared that "political parties should clearly announce their positions on the issue before the elections," and the parties of the Left wasted no time in doing so.[32]

For the MLF, legal abortion was just one part of a larger campaign to broaden sexual freedom. The movement believed that such a strategy, coupled with the increase of individualist sentiment among the public, would give women a significant measure of freedom on many fronts. While artificial contraceptives had become legal in France in 1967, it remained illegal (except in limited circumstances) to provide information about how they worked or their effectiveness. Thus, advocates for abortion's legalization launched a three-pronged campaign: to legalize abortion, to increase the use of contraception, and to educate the general population about human sexuality. Feminists believed that if abortion were legalized, the government would be more interested in actively promoting birth control to keep the number of abortions low. Moreover, allowing women to control their own fertility would take decision-making power away from the state and from men in general. "The law prohibiting abortion is an essential piece of the system that society has put in place to oppress women," Beauvoir wrote. "When woman has obtained—thanks to the diffusion of contraception and freedom of abortion—a command of her body that is no longer poisoned by fear or remorse, she will be available for other struggles. She will understand that she must fight to change her own status and the society that imposes it." Women would be free to become more than "slaves of the home"—economically independent, politically engaged, and able to meet men on equal ground in the public sphere.[33] Also, many in the MLF concurred that a sexual revolution was healthy for France. In her preface to a book entitled *Demain la société sexualisée* (The sexualized society of tomorrow), MFPF president Simone Iff wrote of the "need to speak no longer of sexual education, but of a sexualized education." Her working principle, and that of many MFPF activists, was "to accept the psychosexual development of the child to realize its possibilities in an adult sexuality filled with pleasure." The MFPF's impact on the mentality of the French cannot be measured exactly, but in one year alone the group held 3,339 forums involving 80,358 participants.[34]

Beyond expressing the need to reduce clandestine abortions and the desire to promote sexual liberalism, the fight to legalize abortion embodied a radical individualism that rejected French cultural norms of natalism and familialism, insisting that women be recognized, physically and legally, as people in their own right. The legalization of abortion symbolized the ascent of the May 1968 ideal of personal freedom wrapped within the idiom of sexuality. The thoroughly individualist stance of the women's movement—"I will have a baby if I want to. . . . No moral pressure, institution, or other imperative will force me"—came close to replacing any other collective morality.[35]

Two Separate Moral Universes?

The debates leading up to the vote on abortion provide a window onto France's changing attitudes toward women and female politicians' growing boldness on "women's issues." For the most part, the debates divided along two major lines of argument: one hewed to the ethical and the other to the pragmatic, with proponents of each embracing the other as they tried to fashion a new ethics that included women's autonomy. The traditional moral argument against killing a fetus or the danger presented by France's dwindling population were largely drowned out by a new element that had barely ever been discussed previously—the moral ideal of women's unconditional sovereignty over their own lives and bodies. Legislators were in effect debating whether "natural rights" extended to reproduction. Their tortured reasoning demonstrates France's difficulty in accepting women's right (in Beauvoir's words) to reject the immanence always assigned to them and to embrace women's equal potential for transcendence. But it also reflected an equally strong businesslike tendency where issues of public health and hygiene were concerned. More young, unmarried women than ever were having sex, and, despite formidable risks (evidenced by the statistics on illegal abortion), they were refusing to accept the notion that sex must be tied directly to procreation or marriage. In the view of many, society was changing, and it seemed increasingly clear that the government had a responsibility to make way for this change and to leave decisions regarding a large number of ethical questions to individuals.

The French populace seemed to be recognizing that France needed to update its moral strictures, but this did not mean that France would question its core values of corporatism, which stretched back to the

Middle Ages. Adherence to a group (party, church, locality) still served as a pillar of society; familialism, with its assumption of a heterosexual marriage with children, formed another pillar, as did traditional gender definitions. Scholars of sexuality in France have pointed to the strong influence of "hegemonic heterosexuality" in popular culture and social policy. As the gay liberation movement was only just then coalescing, nonheterosexuality was considered deviant and outside of expected norms. The fluid definitions of gender by theorists such as Irigaray and Fouque did not resonate among the French populace or policy makers. France remained resolutely heterosexual and was content merely to challenge the confines of what heterosexuality would mean in social terms.[36]

Fear of a declining population—particularly of native-born French—continued to shape the debates. The natalists argued that a vital population was evidence of a self-confident country "animated by a great national élan" (and they weren't referring to North African immigrants, who tended to have large families). Feminists countered that only a country filled with children who were wanted could ever be considered vital.[37] The concept of women being used for breeding purposes led feminists to shun a package of social supports for pregnant women because it aimed, in part, to deter potential aborters (and therefore to generate more pregnancies). As welcome as it was to the majority of French women, such legislation was too charged with natalist sentiment and undermined the basic premise that women, not the state, should control childbearing. Many feminists were sure that the government wanted to maintain women in a state of subordination, especially in light of the IVG bill, which was deliberately cast as promaternity.[38]

The MLF did not participate in the parliamentary debates, and only one legislator, Communist deputy Hélène Constans, lashed out at her opponents for their hypocritical paternalism couched in high moral sentiment, but her speech was neither addressed nor referred to for the rest of the debate. She pointed out the irony of her colleagues' championing "respect for life" while showing little interest in the "genocides committed in Vietnam, ... the deadly repression in Chile and Spain, or tortures perpetrated in Algeria." Constans observed, "Life, for women, for mothers, and for parents is a whole of concrete and daily facts and not some sort of metaphysical or moral entity on which one can lecture in the abstract."[39] On this last point many legislators had to agree; they had already begun to consider the moral difficulty of continuing to ban abortion given France's limited capacity to care for the children resulting from unwanted pregnancies.

During the parliamentary debates, some deputies drew analogies between abortion and euthanasia or Nazi crematoria—a direct insult to Simone Veil, the Jewish minister of health, who herself had been interned in Bergen-Belsen and who had lost many family members in the Holocaust.[40] But Veil sidestepped these provocations and, when introducing the IVG bill, chastised the "almost exclusively male assembly," asking, "How many are there who have taken the trouble to help these women in their distress? How many are those who have overcome their feelings about what they see as a fault and have shown single young mothers the understanding and moral support they so badly needed?" The politicians' "general morality," Veil conveyed, was often a shibboleth for challenging women's right to control their sexual lives, a right that members of Parliament never directly addressed. Between the pragmatic and the ethical lay the question of whether the state would maintain control over people's decisions or whether individuals would be allowed to make their own moral and practical choices. During her presentation, Veil said directly that she refused "to enter into scientific and philosophical discussions about a problem that the commission's interviews have demonstrated to be insoluble." The bill to be passed was a health measure that most male legislators had put off enacting, and their anxiety was evident. As Jacques Henriet (senator and former surgeon) commented during the bill's discussion: "The project submitted to us, which can be placed in the context of evolving morals and reducing the tension surrounding sexuality . . . threatens to change in a profound and disturbing fashion the life of French women and men as much in the present as in an already heavy and uncertain future."[41]

Hard-nosed realism, however, finally pushed the legislature into passing the bill for many of the same reasons given by Choisir and the MFPF. They accepted that the then-current law was only enforceable in the most heartless way since it was the average woman without connections and resources who suffered most from the ban. Thus, moderates and the government could agree that the ban placed the country in a state of moral, political, and social disorder and that it was "vain to hope that, however rigorous the law, ... women could be deterred from voluntarily interrupting their pregnancies especially when they find better facilities in many neighboring countries."[42] The Senate finally concluded: "To maintain the current law is, in fact, to tolerate this situation. To abrogate the law without proposing another is equivalent to letting anarchy rule. Between two extreme solutions, the bill authorizes abortion but controls it. It is realistic, it preserves women's health as much as possible, it is humane, and it gives new sense to penal measures that we intend to maintain with vigor."[43]

It was Veil herself who finally managed to patch together an acceptable bill permitting voluntary pregnancy interruption and to force its passage on November 29, 1974. It suspended (pending reevaluation in five years) Article 317 of the Penal Code, which punished the procurement of, aid to, or performance of any sort of abortion with fines and imprisonment. It legalized abortion performed during the first fourteen weeks of pregnancy providing the woman had visited a state-approved counseling center and was apprised of all facilities and services available to her if she did not terminate the pregnancy. (The fourteen-week restriction did not apply if a fetus was discovered to be gravely deformed or if the procedure was necessary to preserve the mother's life.) Before undergoing the procedure, women were required to wait at least one week after the date of their initial request and at least two days after the consultation with a social worker. To prevent profiteering from the operation, the law required that abortions be performed by doctors and in facilities where abortions did not exceed 25 percent of all obstetrical and surgical procedures. The government also tried to avoid the embarrassment of France's becoming an abortion center for other countries where the operation was still illegal by requiring proof of three months' residence to qualify for an abortion.[44]

The Veil law, albeit restrictive, was stamped with a realism that had grown in currency since the reforms of the Civil Code and that sought a middle ground between opposing sides. Veil concluded: "History tells us that the great debates that have at times divided the French later appear as a necessary step in the creation of a new social consensus, adapted to the tradition of tolerance and moderation of our country." Women throughout the MLF celebrated the passage of the Veil law even while objecting to the law's lack of acknowledgement of the principle of women's autonomy. Nevertheless, although the law demanded that to have an abortion a woman would have to be in a "condition [which] places her in a situation of distress," it did allow the woman herself to determine that she was in that condition; authority rested with her and not with her doctors or counselors.[45] This did not mean, however, that the government would not try to sway such a personal decision. The final draft of the bill began: "The law guarantees the respect of every human being from the commencement of life. There shall be no derogation of this principle except in cases of necessity and under the conditions laid down by this law." By stating its commitment to "respect for life" in a general sense, the government implicitly acknowledged its respect for the individual woman's life along with that of the fetus, as well as its commitment to education, demography, and family. As the MLAC had hoped, the government, having legalized abortion, now felt morally compelled to accept the role of birth-control educator.[46]

The bill and the legalization movement in general were both met with vociferous opposition from a number of legislators, some quite prominent, as well as some academicians, clergy, and average citizens. During 1973, as the original bill was being discussed, more than ten thousand doctors signed a protest, and, in one survey, only 36 percent of doctors claimed that they would perform abortions, as opposed to 46 percent who declared they would not. This resistance, along with church opposition led by the organization Laissez-les-vivre, challenged the constitutionality of the law. The opponents managed to stall its implementation until January 1975 pending a hearing by the Constitutional Council, which eventually decided in the law's favor. Yet in the end, the bill passed the National Assembly with a vote of 284 to 189, with all the deputies on the Left voting yes, and, even more surprisingly, it sailed through the more traditionally conservative Senate.[47]

In addition to the appointment of the first Jewish woman minister of health (Simone Veil), the year 1974 brought the legalization of abortion, the reimbursement of contraception by Social Security, and the creation of the Secrétariat d'etat à la condition féminine (Secretary of State for the Female Condition). It is true that the 1967 Neuwirth law and the 1974 Veil law were both restrictive and that neither had passed without a fight. But traditional French morality was clearly loosening, and France was in a state of some political and cultural flux, as evidenced by the publication in both *La croix* (the newspaper of many observant Catholics and political conservatives) and *Le Monde* of many articles speaking favorably of some kind of abortion reform.[48] The MLF and abortion reform groups were able to use such shifts to their advantage in much the same way as women activists in the immediate postwar period had raised demands for reform at a time of social upheaval and questioning.

Les Années Noires: 1974–1980

Despite the political and legislative successes of 1974, Annie Sugier called it "the first black year" in her memoirs of the movement.[49] Others agreed. At first glance, it seems impossible that those closest to the movement—some of its very founders—could be so disaffected after four years of achievements. But the movement faltered in the mid-1970s. The increasing radicalism of many core MLF members coincided with a recession in France. While these women (including the very vocal and organized members of the MLAC) were urging a socially conservative population to explore their sexuality and challenge gender norms, the increasingly powerful Socialist Party was telling women that, if elected, it would promote their employment and educational opportunities and renew its support of family life—an attractive proposition for middle- and working-class French women. In this atmosphere, and with ongoing internal dissensions, the political cohesion the MLF had created in its first years began to dissolve.

The "black years" had a host of causes. At the same time that the Veil law passed and Giscard created the secrétariat, the political climate for feminism looked particularly bleak to many women in the MLF.

The abortion campaign was essentially over, at least for the present, and with its conclusion, women lost a central rallying point that had brought a diverse group of women together. Christine Delphy said that legal successes created a sense of achievement, with everyone heaving a sigh of relief when only an inch had been won. The government and the legislature had played their trump card by taking decisive steps in the direction of women's liberation and by showing concern, albeit limited, for the status and condition of women in general, and so the discussion surrounding women's autonomy was said to be over. In 1976, for example, when some feminists tried to perform abortions outside the medical and legal requirements outlined in the Veil law, the government swiftly charged six women with illegal abortion and the illegal practice of medicine. Feminists' arguments to "demedicalize" abortion to allow women to keep their autonomy fell on deaf ears.[50]

Giscard's inauguration of the secrétariat in 1974 served to steer attention away from feminist radicalism to a more compromising version of the women's cause.[51] Its first director, the journalist and cofounder of *L'Express* magazine, Françoise Giroud, pushed through many cabinet-approved decrees to equalize women's opportunities in work, education, and the law, such as an interdiction against firing or not hiring pregnant women and an extension of Social Security to stay-at-home mothers. Giroud also proposed adding a ban on sexism to the antiracism law of 1972, which eventually was passed (although not during her tenure), and she commissioned studies to examine the gap between male and female salaries and the continuing low rate of participation of women in politics.[52] Feminists argued that the secrétariat was a vastly underfunded and politically marginalized position, and, indeed, Giscard found reason to eliminate it two years later. The laws of July 4 and 11, 1975, banning sex discrimination in employment and firing without a "legitimate motive," for example, proved easy to evade. And the secrétariat had a tiny staff and no budget of its own, so it had to work for change through other ministries. Even so, Giroud was no patsy for Giscard. She had made no secret of her support for Mitterrand in the 1974 election and had embarrassed Giscard himself during the campaign by asking him in an interview if he knew the price of a métro ticket (the elitist and cossetted Giscard did not). She was shocked when he tapped her for the position and initially declined it, fearing the loss of her journalistic independence. Finally, however, she decided that she could use institutionalized power to get things done rather than just writing about them. Despite feminist criticism, Giroud insisted that the secrétariat's work was materially beneficial, believed her time in office was fruitful, and that she was supported by most French women and encouraged by Giscard.[53]

Giroud was certainly interested in women's progress, but as a member of the older generation she also believed in conciliation rather than dissent. As strongly as she felt about the need to equalize women's opportunities, she opposed a feminism that, as she put it, "wanted to cut off men's heads." In a voice characteristic of an earlier generation, she said, "Women are not angels, but they know—better than men—the vanity of the baubles of power and of its appearances. And perhaps because they give life, they know better its price." In a more audacious vein, she condemned women's lack of political representation. She also argued that the right to birth control and employment must be considered essential.[54] In creating the secrétariat and placing an avowed moderate at its head, Giscard understood that he was extending a hand to French women while effectively keeping his distance from feminism. But from Giroud's perspective (and that of other moderates of that era), the secrétariat's activities were "all that the French could swallow at the time."[55]

Many in the women's movement agreed that women needed to participate more fully in France's political and economic life. But Giroud was still referring to women's "insertion" into society, while movement women were speaking of liberating women from society and redefining its boundaries. Thus, the moderates' position moved certain very vocal segments of the MLF further away from being able to negotiate with the government. To the tune of a traditional folk song, they chanted:

Men don't know what to do any more
To make us march in line
Look at how they liberate us
That's all we needed!

They take up our cause in the forums
They prepare for us little reforms
Three steps forward, three steps back
Three steps to one side, three to the other.[56]

Groups in the MLF had difficulty relating to established loci of power. The MLF staged a large demonstration on March 8, 1975, International Woman's Day (organized around the UN-sponsored International Year of the Woman), not to celebrate its recent victories but to protest the "multinational takeover of women's struggle." Psych-et-Po's newspaper, *Le quotidien des femmes* (The Women's Daily), published a special edition entitled "Against the International Year of the Woman." It declared that the occasion was "officially and unofficially a counter-revolutionary operation; a coalition of all the authorities that aim to paralyze and condemn to death the movement, immobilized in order to be exploited, assassinated if it refuses to be raped." And a group of Marxist feminists distributed a flyer showing a woman being gagged by the United Nations and by Françoise Giroud. "Neither the UN nor Giroud will speak for us! Together we construct the Mouvement de libération des femmes," it announced. Psych-et-Po's derision for the secrétariat was echoed by women active throughout the MLF when they said that the "function of the secrétariat creates a deadlock on feminist desire. With the pretext of newness, attitudes that are in fact reformist or even reactionary aren't questioned."[57]

Demonstrations like this gave the appearance of a united movement, and indeed, it was united over certain issues. But, increasingly, two very different responses to constructing a viable movement emerged and sometimes battled for the public's ear: official feminist organizations versus independent political or cultural "actions." Two sizable feminist projects in the second half of the 1970s reveal that the movement was in serious disagreement over the best means of attaining women's liberation: on the one hand, the creation of the Ligue du droit des femmes—a legal and institutional approach for creating the conditions for women's freedom and equality—and, on the other, the launching of a Mother's Day march down the Champs d'Elysées in 1972, dressed as little girls and chanting "Women in the street, not in the kitchen!" and "No children to chain, no chain for children!"[58] This was just one apparent schism because there was some crossover in participation. Other fissures went deeper, calling into question, as for example Antoinette Fouque did, the very essence of feminist demands and the project of political action itself. This fracturing was perhaps inevitable, given the newness of the movement and the diversity of the participants, but it would prove destructive.[59] Personality conflicts and questions of power and authority, which became increasingly significant as the decade wore on, set the movement back.

Another explanation for the black years resides in the conflict within the family planning movement and its relationship to the MLF and French society. The MFPF had been the engine of the family planning movement since the 1960s. Its origins were humanist and reformist, and its primary goal was legalizing contraception. But after the Neuwirth law passed in 1967, the MFPF, rather than dissolving, grew more radical and demanding. In principle, the law provided women access to many forms of contraception. In practice, however, it fell far short of this. Many doctors refused to learn about new contraceptive methods and to offer them to patients, and few minors asked their parents for the permission, required by law, to access birth control. With most women remaining relatively ignorant of contraceptive methods or how to get hold of them, back-alley abortions—which MFPF activists had hoped would greatly decrease as a result of contraception's legalization—continued unabated. It became clear that the law was working in the way its most conservative supporters—and detractors—had hoped. It had suspended public debate by making it *possible* for women to obtain birth control but not probable that they would.[60]

The May 1968 events had a profound effect on the MFPF. The calls for rebellion against the old cultural order—for greater personal independence, sexual liberation, and free expression—resonated within the ranks of the family planning movement. May 1968 inspired many members to relinquish their commitment to a relatively low-profile professional organization and to turn to militancy. The increasing visibility of the MLF also had its effects. The more militant members of

MFPF began to accuse their own organization of the same sexism that contributed to restrictions against contraception and the ban against abortion. They pointed out that while the organization had been created and was staffed largely by women (who had to submit to very rigorous training), the "notables" were male doctors who dominated positions of power within the organization.[61] The MFPF's official position on abortion had always been somewhat ambiguous. The group had declared itself against abortion in principle as a way to justify legalizing contraception. But when pressed, it declared itself for the freedom of women to choose. By early 1973, however—after the Manifesto of the 343, the Bobigny trial, and petitions by doctors—a new, militant majority within the MFPF gained control and aligned with the MLF. The MFPF members brought with them a concrete sense of women's oppression in French society, having worked with many women desperate for ways to limit or terminate their pregnancies. Together with militants from the women's movement, the family planning movement (including the MFPF and the Groupe-information-santé [Health Information Group]) and various leftist parties and syndicates, they created the MLAC in the spring of 1973.[62]

The goals of the MLAC, freed from the strictures of the MFPF, broadened to include a complete abrogation of all restrictions in the Neuwirth law (to ease access to free contraception) as well as the repeal of the natalist antipropaganda law of 1920 and articles in the Napoleonic Code criminalizing abortion. Philosophically, the MLAC went far beyond the attitude of the original family planning groups: it was against the constraint of free sexual expression but also against the sex trade, prostitution, and the male-dominated sexual order of French society. "The weight of traditional ideology," the MLAC's charter stated, "the systematic repression of all real efforts at liberalization, and the refusal to bring to bear all scientific progress are the most evident signs of the oppression that society exercises on the sexuality of women and of men, especially those among the popular classes, which have neither the means nor the information necessary for their liberation." More controversially, the group argued that dispensing contraceptive information and devices should not be the exclusive domain of specialists and that abortion not require a doctor in a hospital.[63]

The MLAC's objectives were ambitious and potentially unrealistic, but this umbrella organization had a certain amount of clout: members of the MFPF, for example, brought with them the weight of a national and respected organization, and the Groupe-information-santé was composed almost entirely of well-established doctors, many of whom were associated with universities. Yet at the same time MLAC was beset by troubles that reached a boiling point after the initial abortion law was passed. Its larger goals of a fundamental transformation of sexuality and unrestricted contraception and abortion seemed further away than ever, and, more destructively, rivalries among groups within the organization all but paralyzed it. MLF militants, for example, rejected MLAC pragmatism and what they saw as its lack of interest in the deeper issues involved in reproductive freedom. Many MLAC-affiliated doctors viewed abortion less as an ideological battle than as a procedure whose risks had to be weighed against its benefits.[64] And, on the whole, the family planning movement was avant-garde and thus somewhat at odds with the very people it attempted to serve. While its different factions debated and in some instances fought among themselves over the precise nature of the problem and how to solve it, the general population viewed the issue in different terms. The French people in general were unwilling to accept either an excoriation of the patriarchy or the demedicalization of reproductive-health procedures. While the family planning movement remained influential throughout the 1970s, its goals were thwarted by a widespread apathy regarding its most strident demands.

Strengthening criminal penalties for rape would be another rallying point for 1970s feminists, but this topic was considered more "strident" and was therefore less popular. Taking on the cultural attitudes toward rape struck at the heart of many French men's sacrosanct view of heterosexual norms. Thus, rape appeared as a "women's issue"—not as a family or societal issue. Women seemed to be "carrying on" again, as when they marched in the street to "take back the night." The trial of three French men accused of raping two young Belgian women outside of Aix-en-Provence in 1974 was a case in point. Entered into the arguments for the defense was evidence that "the girls" enjoyed the experience and that they were looking for it (on the basis that they had been camping and were lesbians, which suggested a libertine attitude toward sex). Once again, Gisèle Halimi took up the defense of the women, hoping to raise awareness, but she had to cut through a thicket of assumptions (expressed and implicit) about "sexual need," masculine fun, and what was normal for men.[65]

Activists were challenged by their own disagreements over a cohesive strategy on rape and by a backlash against feminists, who were accused of a new moralism and of policing sexuality. Three public events helped show the need to address sexual assault on women. First, the International Tribunal of Crimes against Women, held in Brussels in March 1976, put both rape and female genital mutilation at the top of its agenda. It articulated a clear position at variance with popular norms. As a flyer said: "Rape is not a made-up story; rape is not the law of nature; rape is not an accident; rape is not desire or pleasure." Second, at the same time, Susan Brownmiller's book *Against Our Will* came out in French translation. Third, in the late spring of 1976, another mass women-only meeting was called at the Mutualité on the topic of rape, during which women testified about experiences and strategized about solutions. A throng of men hovered outside, hurling epithets and jeering, and it became clear that such criticisms came from men on both the political Left and the Right.[66]

The law of December 23, 1980, ushered in a new era in terms of how the courts addressed sexual assault. It said that "any act of sexual penetration, of any nature, committed by one person on another by violence, constraint, threat, or surprise, is rape," enshrining in the law books the concept that rape is a legal, not just a moral, transgression. When a woman says no, Halimi said at the Marseilles trial of the Aix-en-Provence rapists in 1978, you have to understand once and for all that it means no, not yes. With that trial ending in convictions and substantial prison terms for all three of the accused, and with the eventual passage of the antirape law, the woman's movement could have celebrated another triumph. But the celebration was muted by an ambivalence about using the powers of the state for feminist ends, as well as by an intense backlash against feminist "repression" displayed in the pages of *Libération* and the leftist journal *Tout!* Old allies such as Guy Hocquenghem, a spokesman for the early gay liberation movement, were chastising women for cloaking themselves with the bourgeois power that they had once claimed to despise. Although lesbians were completely committed to criminalizing rape, militant gay men like Hocquenghem preferred to fight against "bourgeois justice," believing that sexual violence was overestimated, especially where women were concerned. Cathy Bernheim cogently argued that the "antimoralism" born of 1968 expressed men's desires for no morals at all—or limitless desire—which would take the form of sexual violence when it chose.[67]

Giving close attention to sexuality was possible while France was growing economically and was relatively stable politically. But France's poor economic performance during the second half of the 1970s did not encourage interest in economic and social parity or in promoting concepts such as women's autonomy. During what was the worst economic crisis since the 1940s, many men and women were most concerned with keeping their jobs and maintaining their standard of living, and French society became less tolerant of feminist battle cries.[68] By 1976 the economic crisis had hit women particularly hard. According to the CGT, 75 percent of working women earned less than 2,500 francs per month (a figure toward the bottom of the pay scale), and 40 percent of employed women lived alone, adding to their financial insecurity. Women also made up 53 percent of all the unemployed. Perhaps an enormously popular women's movement would have had the political influence necessary to demand higher salaries and more promotions, but the MLF was too marginal and disunited to attract the kind of support needed to sustain a strike or to twist the government's arm. The latter half of the 1970s proved to be a very different time than the events of 1968 had seemed to forecast. That "collective adventure" gave way to a fierce individualism that the raucous protests had masked.[69]

Also, once legalized abortion was secured in 1975, a certain disaffection set in—not just among those at the margins of the MLF's cause but also among some at its very center. Being a revolutionary was tiring. It meant never being able to sit back and enjoy successes, no matter how large, but always to be pushing on.[70] Mobilizing women required tremendous energy and creativity. Feminists had chosen to launch a spontaneous movement rather than to slowly build a political party to direct institutional change toward their more radical politics. In choosing the former option—denying the legitimacy of politics as usual—the women's movement politically and culturally shook up a country that had long refused to recognize its sexism. But this choice also hampered the movement, preventing it from devoting more of its raw energy toward concrete accomplishments. As we have seen, feminist activists did accomplish concrete changes—to the Civil and Criminal codes, as well as to cultural expectations—in the second half of the 1970s. At the same time, however, the Socialist Party had begun mobilizing a young, independent, and frustrated electorate around women's rights, among other issues. Along with Giscard and the Right, the Socialist Party increasingly played its feminist hand, successfully appealing to women and diverting public attention from the MLF.

6 TAKEOVER? FEMINISTS IN AND OUT OF PARTY POLITICS

The Late 1970s

> Never before have women been as much in demand as during this electoral period. It is both a recognition of the massive mobilizations of women in recent years against the most scandalous aspects of their oppression (abortion, rape, domestic abuse, right to employment) . . . and an electoral channeling tactic that aims to make the aspirations expressed by women themselves into propaganda themes, perfectly integrated with the various organization strategies of the system.
>
> **Édito**, *Cahiers du féminisme* (Editorial, Feminist notebooks), March 1976

Many militants in the MLF were frustrated that their transformative ideals of liberation were diluted into campaign rhetoric of women's parity and "inclusion" in society. Political parties observed that feminism struck a chord among many women in France, and they wanted to appeal to this electorate. But it bothered many militants that certain politically influential women—for example, Yvette Roudy of the Socialist Party—were willing to work within party organizations to bring about moderate change. Core MLF members' concern over the movement's co-optation expressed itself in two separate ways: some were obsessed with maintaining the movement's independence from outside political influences, while Marxist and Socialist feminists mounted a concerted effort to correct their parties' shortcomings. Integrationist or independent, both these strands developed and published their ideas. Their differing goals would form the strategic fault lines of the movement over the next decades and would shape beliefs about what kinds of transformations were necessary for the project of women's liberation to succeed.

After women received the right to vote in 1944, political parties assumed that women constituted a voting bloc, but surveys and sociological studies indicated that women tended to share the same politics as their families. Women's growing role in the job market and their economic independence during the second half of the 1960s began to change this familiar pattern, and the 1968 events intensified the trend. In the presidential elections of 1969, the electoral gender gap in which men voted for the Left and women for the Right narrowed to 10 percentage points, and in 1974, to 7 percentage points, the change being most evident among women under thirty-four.[1] The gap between the "conservative nature" of French women and the "progressive nature" of French men narrowed, and political leaders began to change their general opinion of women, no longer seeing them as traditional voters interested in family issues but rather as progressives concerned with their rights. Political observers even began speculating that women might actually bring the Left to victory.[2] This change in voting patterns during the 1970s led political parties to consider that feminism was certainly affecting women's attitudes and would have to be reckoned with. Socialist and Communist Party rhetoric aimed at women grew more progressive, declaring that "the freedom to dispose of one's body is an inalienable right," and women acknowledged the parties' efforts by increasingly leaning left politically.[3]

The Communist Party, which in France during the 1940s and 1950s was closely allied with the Soviet Union, had agreed with the Center-Right over issues concerning natalism and relations between men and women. During the 1940s and 1950s, the government remained dominated by the Center-Right, which made anticommunism a policy pillar, and the Left took on the role of gadfly, organizing industrial actions. Party rhetoric had changed noticeably since the postwar period, when PCF secretary-general Maurice Thorez had spouted the Soviet-influenced notion of women as necessary, but subordinate, workers. Moreover, the creation of the "Third Force," an alliance of parties of the moderate Left and Right to counter both Communism and Gaullism, further distanced the PCF from mainstream political power. By the 1970s, however, with the Gaullist decade over, things had changed. While the PCF still courted male industrial workers more energetically than any other group, it grew increasingly interested in hedging its bets and underwent, over a period of a few years, what amounted to a small internal revolution.[4]

In 1975, inspired by the International Year of the Woman, the party devoted its Week of Marxist Thinking to "Women Today and Tomorrow." And at a special assembly in December 1977, five thousand women turned out to hear Communist leader Georges Marchais speak about the party's dedication to solving women's problems. By the 1970s the PCF was publishing reports such as *For Women: A Happy, Free, and Responsible Life of Equality*.[5] It advocated improved working conditions (a reduced workweek, longer holidays, and better working environments), greater maternity and retirement rights and benefits, the improvement of women's legal status, and broadening of the state's responsibility toward children. It also added more women to its lists of candidates and publicized its support of a woman's right to choose. Meanwhile, the LCR, the main Trotskyist group, experienced a similar awakening. In 1974 its congress adopted a policy that "permitted" women to unite together to discuss the "problem of their role and their place in the organization and to reject collectively all the manifestations of phallocracy." In 1977 the LCR magazine *Politique hebdo* (Policy weekly) recounted that "the 'woman question' took a considerable place in the congress. No militant could ignore it anymore."[6]

But it was the Socialist Party, with its focus on democracy and social justice under the leadership of François Mitterrand, that pursued the women's vote most aggressively. "The whole Left, and particularly myself," Mitterrand wrote to a leading feminist Socialist, "are conscious that there will never be a free and just society without the emancipation of women and the recognition of their rights and liberties, and without their total integration at the centers of decision and action." Mitterrand knew that it was the Left that had passed the Veil law and that the law was roundly supported. He also had the solid endorsement of feminists such as Roudy and Audry, who were committed to both democratic socialism and feminism and who believed the two could coexist. The presence of feminists within the Socialist Party was key to a more progressive agenda, with their support of the liberalization of the Veil law, greater distribution of contraception, and wider implementation of sex education, as well as women's equality.[7]

Many of the most militant women in the movement—from the radical feminists to the Psych-et-Po group—believed they had much to fear from the Socialist Party's adoption of "women's liberation." As Delphy wrote in 1977: "We have some good friends among men. We flee them like the plague and they try to force our interests. Who could fail to recognize in this the marks of true friendship . . . ? They want to substitute themselves for us; they actually speak instead of us; they approve of women's liberation, and even of the participation of women in this project, so long as liberation and women follow and certainly do not precede them; they want to impose on us their conception of women's liberation."[8]

It is unclear just how many women voted for the Socialist Party in 1981 specifically because of its feminist rhetoric, but 49 percent of them did vote Socialist, up from 39 percent in 1965. Yet the militant feminists believed the Socialists were cynically manipulating feminist rhetoric for their own ends. This led women in the movement to reject mainstream politics and develop a theory about action outside established institutions. The Left was denounced by MLF militants for what seemed like obvious political pandering. Psych-et-Po's famous poster of 1973, "We Are Women/We Do Not Vote," explained: "In a capitalist, imperialist, patriarchal state, to vote is to reinforce the existing power. . . . We won't lend our voice to those who have power over us."[9]

The PCF and the PS, which historically had accorded women an important role in "the revolution," nonetheless always managed to separate the "personal" from the "political." As a result, the relationship between feminists in leftist parties and trade unions and their male cohorts was tense throughout the 1970s. Leadership positions for women on the local and national levels were scant, and women were largely absent from the bargaining table. The idea that the capitalist system alone was responsible for women's oppression remained intact among the parties of the Left, and male party members seemed loath to perform any kind of feminist examination of their own behavior.[10] Thus Communist and Socialist feminists found themselves in a quandary, trying to maintain the integrity of their ideals even while making compromises so that some of their ideas might be put into action. In 1978 grumbling by feminist militants exploded into full-blown confrontation when the Communist daily *L'humanité* (Humanity) refused to publish an open letter from party women that was critical of the PCF. Finally published in *Le Monde* and entitled "The Communist Party Stripped Naked by Women," the letter claimed that the traditional male-female relationship, founded upon the patriarchal system inherent in "the dominant ideology, has never been called into question."[11] Some female members left the party over this confrontation and began publishing their own newspaper, *Elles voient rouge* (Women see red), in May 1979. Similarly, women from the LCR complained during the preparation for the LCR congress in 1978 that "there has been very little stress upon revolutionary Marxist tasks in the struggle against women's oppression." They demanded that feminism be recognized as enriching the politics of their program and that "women's work" not be considered only a "sector" of the organization. They subsequently began publishing their own review, *Cahiers du féminisme* (Feminist notebooks).[12]

That same year, the Socialist Party faced similar dissent when a group of about 150 of its women militants—some of them longtime party members—declared that they would form a separate wing of the party, which they called Courant III (the Third Way). They intended this wing to transform theory and practice in the party by combining socialism with a rigorous feminist analysis. Dismissing earlier "women's commissions" that focused specifically on women's "special problems" while promoting existing party doctrine, these Socialist women produced a formal proposal within the party hierarchy, held a conference, and seemed determined to make sure their group became an official party wing alongside of those led by Mitterrand and Pierre Mauroy. This was the only way they saw of acquiring political power to change laws and institutions. Their proposal was viewed as nothing less than a betrayal and defection by most party activists, who claimed they were trying to create a feminist ghetto. Courant III, it seemed, had put the party to the test but failed to bring about the desired result. Many party women who considered themselves feminists viewed Courant III as a hostile effort by disgruntled feminists to stymie otherwise conciliatory relations between the party leadership and them. Even party members who were sympathetic or quietly supportive saw Courant III's stance as politically futile, believing that an explicit feminist agenda could undermine support at the national legislative elections of March 1978 and the presidential campaign in 1981.[13]

Dissatisfied feminist militants in both the PCF and the PS had similar complaints and similar ambivalence when it came to calling their respective parties to task. They believed that their parties only paid lip service to feminism. They argued that the workers' movement would never win unless it mobilized women and integrated their struggles into its strategy. Until such time, it could certainly never be called a "global political project," as Socialists had been wont to call socialism for the previous hundred years. They pointed out, moreover, that women constituted a paltry 1.6 percent of PS senators and 1.8 percent of PS deputies. With women making up 50 percent of the "working class" and 54 percent of the unemployed, the PS would have to look long and hard at its policy, recruitment, and promotion. It is no wonder that in the 1990s original members of Courant III, such as Françoise Gaspard, went on to form the network Demain la parité (Parity Tomorrow) in an attempt to rectify these imbalances in political and professional domains.[14]

Party women knew that criticism could be hazardous to their already tenuous careers. But beyond such professional trepidation, Marxist and Socialist feminists were committed to bringing the Left to power, and, with both Giscard and Chirac running for president, they knew the entire Left had to pull together to win. Was it worth fighting over principles if the larger goal of putting a sympathetic Left in power failed? Many in the PS abandoned their original commitment to Courant III (renamed Courant G), implying that, at least for the present, they would choose socialism over explicit feminism in France. Even the most radical of Marxist feminists found themselves under fire from other feminists, who called them collaborators: "Autonomy has always appeared as the minimal condition for the existence of any movement of women's liberation," one internal document of the early feminists commented.[15] Autonomy was a gamble, however, because it meant not just rejecting power but being shut out of it.

Radicalism within the Established Order

The MLF gave birth to a few feminist groups that tried to honor its radical principles and work efficiently within the political arena. Gisèle Halimi's Choisir—a legal advocacy group turned political watchdog—became perhaps the most influential and long lasting. Other groups with smaller footprints, such as the Parti féministe and the Ligue du droits des femmes, managed to exert some political pressure and gain respect among feminists and the Left, yet despite these groups' best efforts to recruit members and to create a viable agenda, none managed to secure a broad following.

The Ligue and Choisir shared many characteristics with the National Organization for Women in the United States, but the French political context can help explain why they did not attain similar fame and influence even though their institutional impact was enormous over the long term. Both the Ligue and Choisir were founded with the intention of defending women on an institutional level. They considered women's control over their own bodies essential to their full citizenship, but they extended that commitment to include the institutionalization of broader educational opportunities, the establishment of parity in male and female representation within the government and political parties, and the tightening of laws against rape and sexual harassment. Although their positions on abortion, women's place in society, and the relationship between men and women bore the stamp of the MLF and of the uncompromising feminist politics of the 1970s, they nevertheless followed in a long, pragmatic tradition of women's groups that fought discrimination in education, the professions, and the law.[16]

Materialist in philosophy, the Ligue had no doubt that legal and institutional reform would play a major role in transforming women's place in French society. Thus it protested against maternity leave (as opposed to a more egalitarian parental leave), arguing that maternity leave imprisoned women in their traditional role. By 1975 the Ligue had presented the Secrétariat d'état à la condition féminine with legislative proposals defining sexist practices in society, tightening penalties for rape, and making domestic violence a crime, which would allow women to bring charges against their abusive partners and obtain protection from them. They rallied against a protective quota for men in certain professions and contested the national census categories of "head of household" and "spouse" as contrary to the reformed Civil Code, which declared that the spouses equally and together "assure the moral and material direction of the family." Additionally, in an open letter to the government, they protested two bills designed to protect women workers from jobs considered hazardous to women particularly, arguing that the bills simultaneously created a women's ghetto in the service sector and inequality in the home.[17]

From its inception, however, the Ligue suffered from a lack of broad support among women in the MLF. Some women in the Ligue who wanted to concentrate their efforts on a grassroots level left the group as early as 1975 to escape the "elitism" and "terrorism" they found among certain women there. They created the Groupe de liaison et d'information femmes enfants (GLIFE; Liaison Group for Women, Mothers, and Children). GLIFE sponsored a variety of activities—film screenings, yoga and music classes, activities for children, and assemblies of women's unions—all held in a large meeting room near Les Halles in Paris. It published a newsletter, *L'information des femmes* (Women's information), which served as a notice board for events and groups of interest to women and feminists and, to a lesser extent, as a forum for feminist analysis. GLIFE's project was ambitious, and although it wanted to embrace all women in the movement, it was not widely supported. Even its newsletter was challenged by feminists who claimed that all feminist factions were not represented on its editorial committee. The founders themselves complained that feminist groups in France would form for a few months and then break up when "they realized what a big task they had to accomplish." GLIFE overextended itself as an umbrella organization and disappeared in December 1976. Similarly, the Ligue drew fewer adherents and its influence petered out in the 1980s, especially following the death of Beauvoir in 1986.[18]

The contrast between the commitment of a few and the disinterest of many is illustrated by the story of the first battered women's shelter in France. In the wake of the 1974 Aix-en-Provence rapes and the subsequent trial in Marseilles, some women from the Ligue decided to create SOS-Femmes-Alternative (SOS-Women's-Alternative), a legal advocacy and emotional support organization for rape victims and battered women. SOS petitioned the government for funds to build rape crisis and battered women's centers and went so far as to occupy Françoise Giroud's office with a small group of women who refused to return home to their batterers, demanding a safe haven. Giroud found them one.[19] Their occupation of Giroud's office was only one action in a long series designed to break the taboo against publicly confronting the problem of violence against women. Then, in February 1976, SOS occupied the abandoned former maternity hospital Château de Plessis-Robinson to demand the creation of a permanent refuge for battered women. The government eventually came up with money to build a center; named Flora Tristan and opened in March 1978, it was financed by the state and organized and run by SOS. After the center opened—and underscoring the antifeminist sentiment against which feminists battled—the leftist journalist Jean Cau was inspired to write "humorous" articles satirizing feminist efforts. Some women occupied the offices of *Paris Match*, where the articles appeared, and eventually sued Cau for defamation and won. But the fact that such articles were published in a popular magazine illustrates the hostility toward feminists that only a few women were willing to publicly oppose.[20]

Other feminists decided to impose feminism itself, rather than just its ideas and programs, on political life. In the first few years of the 1970s, some women formed a group called the Front féministe, which lived a short, bright life in an uneasy relationship with political parties and women's commissions. Designed to present a direct political challenge to standard "patriarchal" parties, it changed its name to Parti féministe in 1974. The Parti féministe aimed to foster a wide range of challenges to the political system. "We have no allegiance to any party or movement. We are women like you and we say to you: feminism can be nothing without you, feminism is you!" claimed an early leaflet from the group. But by 1975, a dozen or so women broke from the Parti féministe, declaring that "a political party isn't defined only by collective demands or by vague humanitarian aspirations, but by a political ideology which is its own," and they created the Parti féministe unifié (PFU). Suzanne Blaise and Jane Pelletier (both of whom were associated with the Socialist Party) drew up a platform for the PFU, together with many concrete proposals.[21] PFU members wanted to be engaged with institutional politics, and they wanted to be unified in doing so, yet it seems that their attempts to eliminate dissent within their own organization failed.

The PFU's powerful critique of both capitalism and patriarchy seemed a potential magnet for a broad spectrum of 1968-generation feminists, but it too hobbled itself by an insistence on "autonomy" and "the refusal of all external political interference." The party called all aspects of society—from mentalities to economic structures—into question and rejected private capitalism (masquerading as liberalism) and state capitalism ("socialism"). Initially, the PFU declared itself against separatism: "Feminism is the common cause of women and men." But within the PFU's first six months, members eliminated this principle and came to see separatism as their only hope for breaking old patterns of socialization, politics, and ideology. The PFU was designed, they argued, "not to be a party of women, but a feminist party, demanding not only equal rights between men and women, but autonomy and the political identity of the women's liberation movement."[22] Both its politics and its structure were intended to be imbued with materialist feminist philosophy. It would refuse the typical hierarchy of most political parties by maintaining relatively autonomous small neighborhood and interest groups, which would choose to support each other on certain key issues. For the PFU as for the Ligue, with whom Blaise felt a close affinity, the fundamental question was not whether power should be refused but what kind of power was needed. "The PFU," as Blaise described it, "wanted neither masculine nor feminine power [but] the socialization of economic and political power. In other words, that each man and woman have an effective share of power and that "self-determination" replace a more frequently debatable representation."[23]

Perhaps because the PFU's thoroughly radical ideas were served up in a more standard political medium, the group was derided by some and considered a threat by others. An anomaly among feminist groups in the 1970s, it was treated as such not just by feminists but also by formal political institutions to the point of absurdity. For example, the PFU was refused membership in a union meeting of women's associations on the occasion of the 1975 Year of the Woman principally because it was a political party, even though feminists from established political parties were allowed to attend on the grounds that they were feminists or belonged to women's associations. During the 1978 election campaigns, the PFU joined with radical feminists to encourage women to protest the political system by not voting. They accused the parties of perpetuating women's oppression. Neither the Right nor the Left, they claimed, gave sufficient attention to women's issues or fought against the patriarchal family, which they believed was at the root of women's oppression. Feminism was not something that could be contained in a nugget of party doctrine, they argued, but was "the foundation of our conception of politics."[24]

By the autumn of 1976, the PFU had gained a swell of support from both grassroots activists as well as prominent women in academia, scientific research, and law. It inspired women in countries as diverse as Ireland, Israel, and Spain to establish their own PFUs and held its first Féministe internationale at Montreuil in May 1977, uniting the PFUs of Belgium and France with other Spanish and German feminist collectives. The PFU's French founders believed that the organization's flexibility, combined with tough feminist theory, would make it a powerful political force, but it didn't seem to do so. Even Blaise, who had no illusions about the "natural sorority" of women, grew so disenchanted with the "imbecile controversies," manipulation, and "bad faith" that in 1977 she left the party she had helped create. In her resignation letter, she spoke of some participants' lack of respect for decisions made by others and criticized the organization for demanding a great investment of militants' time and energy without a "minimum of democratic guarantees." Her complaints about how the party was run were, at bottom, similar to the complaints of others who tried to organize activists during the black years. "A minimum of cohesion and continuity seems to me indispensable for a liberation movement that wants to organize itself," she wrote.[25]

The Movement and Its Diversity:
Writing Feminism into History

The black years might have been politically disappointing, but they were intellectually rich. The personal and political discord and entrenchment that followed the jubilant early 1970s bred, among other things, considerable intellectual production. Feminist literature as well as energetic political activism flourished. This section will examine prominent women writers of the day in the social and political context of the MLF. Liliane Kandel, in her study of the French feminist press, noted a "veritable explosion" of journals, bulletins, and newspapers of all kinds beginning in 1974–1975 and continuing at a rapid pace until 1978. In fact, the increase in feminist newspapers and magazines paralleled a loss in readership of the traditional "feminine press"—a 30 percent drop from 1966 to 1976—which threw the industry into a small crisis. By 1978–1979, approximately 150,000 readers purchased feminist journals—a small but robust following of feminist ideas of both independent activists and committed feminists within national political parties.[26]

The causes of this burgeoning journalistic expression were many. First, and most simply, printing technology continued to improve and to become less expensive, making it possible to print text and pictures relatively cheaply and rapidly. Second, many core participants in the movement were either students or in some way connected to the university; writing and reading were how they interacted with the world. At first, printing their own work was the easiest way to disseminate and share their ideas (without the distorting filter of the mass media); later it became a way to solidify those ideas. The proliferation of feminist journals during the second half of the 1970s reflected both a broadening of the feminist mission and a turning inward on the part of independent MLF militants. Having a "journal of one's own" meant that a group could publicly advance its ideas without having to share space with women of opposing views. Feminists believed that the mainstream media had depicted them as hysterical harpies and castrators and distorted their ideas and principles, and different feminist factions wanted their own outlets.[27] It was a time of breadth of French feminist theory, much of it entirely different from the ideas—more familiar to the foreign reader—of Julia Kristeva, Luce Irigaray, and Hélène Cixous.

The profusion of theoretical writings and informational news also provides a clear record of the movement's development along several separate lines. As the 1970s continued, radical feminist theory deepened its critique of French society in the pages of *Questions féministes* (*QF*; Feminist issues), and certain factions embraced a separatist position. Similarly, Marxist feminists, long accommodating of party exigencies, grew less so in journals such as *Mignonnes, allons voir sous la rose* ... (Cuties, let's look under the rose), *Elles voient rouges* (They see red), and others.[28] Against these voices, which were predominantly materialist and focused on social change, emerged another that is hard to categorize but that centered on the search for and discovery of a specific female identity. This disparate body of work has consistently linked ideas, the realm of the symbolic, and women's liberation together. Among certain authors, the act of writing itself was frequently described as political and essential to women's self-realization. I refer to this category of expression as "feminine writing," a direct translation of *écriture féminine*, although the unitary name obscures significant disagreements among these writers. In these academic discussions of women or feminine writing, feminism is often mentioned in the depoliticized abstract. Kristeva, for example, once referred interchangeably—within two paragraphs—to "the women's movement" and "feminine studies."[29]

In contrast, *Questions féministes*, one of the principal journals of materialist as well as radical feminism, was at the forefront of the crusade against feminine writing, which it deemed essentialist. *QF* was run by a small, closely knit editorial collective, with Simone de Beauvoir as its figurehead director of publications. Some members of the collective had worked together since the MLF's beginning.[30] They did not conceive of the journal as a free-for-all forum like *Le torchon brûle*; rather, they envisioned it developing a "feminist science" that could be honed "to describe and unmask [women's] oppression." The journal was founded on the materialist theory, articulated by Christine Delphy during the first years of the movement, that women constituted an oppressed social class in and of themselves and that their struggle for liberation was not secondary to the struggle against capitalism. It directly linked a theory of women's oppression to a political schema aimed at overturning the current social hierarchy. This challenge to Marxist class analysis and strategy, with its elaborate examination of reproductive labor and patriarchal ideology, was nevertheless significantly materialist. It stood in opposition to feminist identity politics and the concomitant growing feminist interest in "naturalist ideology"—what American historians have sometimes called "cultural feminism." "Our oppression doesn't reside in the fact of 'not being woman enough,'" the review argued, "but, on the contrary, in that of being too much. We are prevented from existing as independent individuals on the pretext that we are 'women' [and therefore] 'different.'"[31]

The QF collective in effect turned Marx on his side, arguing that the real class conflict was between the sexes, regardless of social class. In the 1940s Beauvoir had observed that throughout history and across societies, women's function as reproducers was linked to their oppression. The radical feminists, particularly those in the QF collective, built and expanded on her analysis and took it a step further. If marriage and childbearing in male-dominated society placed women in a position where their labor (both reproductive and productive) was in men's service, then marriage and childbearing were tantamount to slavery—or, to use a term coined by Colette Guillaumin, "sexage."[32] QF attempted to undermine theory espoused by "feminine writing" writers by demonstrating the political implications of their ideas. In its first issue, for example, Monique Plaza criticized the "body speak" represented by Hélène Cixous, Annie Leclerc, and, in particular, Luce Irigaray. "What I metaphorically call the 'patriarchal lock-up,'" she concluded, "is an ideological arrangement that intervenes after the emergence of feminism, in other words, after the recognition of women's oppression by the social system. It consists of invalidating this discovery, in channeling women's research within a perspective that conceals and maintains the patriarchy."[33]

The QF collective refused to make theoretical distinctions, present within feminist discourse at the time, between patriarchally conditioned femininity (characterized as passive and submissive) and female nature (defined as nurturing, open, and egalitarian). For QF, "woman" and "femininity" were social constructs designed to impede women and bind them to serving men. Women who claimed these definitions— even as they proposed to redefine them as part of their liberation— obscured this social reality. Women's oppression by the patriarchal social system had clear material consequences. The QF editors did not deny that women could take pleasure in their bodies, in nurturing, or in child rearing, but they argued that there was no direct relationship between body and consciousness and that to articulate such a relationship constrained women rather than liberated them. Any relationship that existed between the two was strongly mediated by various social pressures, and to tease them apart was impossible.

Moreover, as the collective pointed out, there was an inherent contradiction in the emphasis on naturalism: if nature could justify the existence of a feminine "essence," then social functions would simply be considered the same as natural functions and would lead back to all the speculative prejudices of the patriarchy. "Women's liberation" in the essentialist sense—to delve into discovering "womanness"—was a trap.[34] Thus they argued that "more than women, we are individuals." The link with Beauvoir's existentialist reading of women's position in society was clear: "Until now, only the masculine had the right to be neuter (nongendered), to be general. We want access to the neuter, to the general. Sex is not our destiny. . . . We cannot criticize women for wanting to be considered as valuable as men. . . . In a society where men and women share the same values, "same" necessarily means antiphallocratic, and antihierarchical."[35] QF continued to hammer away at this point, which its editors believed was key to the feminist movement's survival and to feminism's integrity. Guillaumin's article on "difference" in *QF*'s September 1979 issue argued that, far from being "natural," difference between men and women was the social expression of women's subordination to men. Women's reduced mobility, their restrictive clothes, and their passivity were actually functions inscribed onto their bodies to make them internalize submissiveness, availability, and service.[36]

Radical feminism also found its way into other important feminist journals—principally *La revue d'en face* (The review from across) and *Les cahiers du GRIF* (The GRIF notebooks) issued by the Groupe de recherche et d'information féministes (Group for Feminist Information and Research), both of which tried to integrate radical feminist tenets into what they considered a more inclusive feminism. The editorial committee of the *Revue* claimed membership in a variety of groups, from the Cercle Dimitriev (on the Marxist Left) to the Féministes révolutionnaires (Radical Feminists) and even neighborhood women's groups. The *Revue*'s editorial statement encouraged all feminists to participate in the publication, and, indeed, it tried to cater to a broad range of feminist interests beyond criticism, cultural or otherwise. Similarly, *Les cahiers du GRIF* attempted to bridge the hostile waters separating the radicals, Marxists, and essentialists.

Both journals took as a starting point Beauvoir's argument that gender was socially constructed and that male domination was historical and cross-cultural. The *Revue* was particularly concerned with navigating its own theoretical course around what it considered the economic determinism of French Marxism and the predominantly materialist concerns of radical feminism. So while the contributors challenged economic and social structures, they also stressed the role that ideology and culture played in women's subjugation. At the same time, however, they disputed naturalist ideas and writings, which fetishized language. "Language may be functional without its constituting a barrier to the expression of what remains unknown," the editors wrote, implicating, in their criticism, intellectuals who tried to transform the act of writing into a political act. Contributing writers to the *Revue*, like their counterparts at *QF*, resisted the dichotomization of character traits that attributed feelings and bodies to women and analysis and minds to men. Thus when Évelyne Sullerot's *Le fait féminin* (The feminine reality), a mammoth collection of multidisciplinary articles about women (largely focused on women's biology and psychology), appeared in 1978, the *Revue* robustly criticized it.[37] The editors devoted many pages to uncovering the ways in which discrimination functioned in the workplace and to examining women's complex and often oppressive situation at home: "In France, women accomplish daily 91 million hours of domestic work, which is colossal relative to the 118 million hours that represent the work of both men and women together. Even more troubling, women, whether or not they are also employed, don't spend less than 4 hours per day on domestic work and the care of children (no man, even on Sunday, even including household repairs, performs more than 2)."[38]

Les cahiers du GRIF, perhaps more than any other feminist journal of the epoch, was noted for its openness to different feminist arguments and to women's studies in general. Its first issue, in 1973, included the article "Féminitude et féminisme"(Femininitude and feminism), criticizing the former, but its fifth issue contained a very positive review of Psych-et-Po and Éditions *des femmes*, Antoinette Fouque's publishing house. That issue also included an article by Luce Irigaray. On other occasions, *Cahiers* published interviews with Julia Kristeva, an attack on the Catholic Church and its policies regarding women, and an article on the relationship between writing and revolution. Contrary to other radical feminist groups, GRIF also tolerated the presence of the few men who showed up at its meetings and seminars.[39] GRIF seemed to view women's liberation from a more holistic perspective, believing that different methods and theories of achieving liberation only added to the movement's richness.

Marxist feminists from the PCF and the LCR (as well as some nonaligned militants) also worked out their revolutionary theory and criticized their respective political parties in the pages of various journals. For example, *Elles voient rouges*, the journal of PCF feminists, argued that the "belated interest of political parties in the woman 'question' contains drawbacks: false analyses, manipulation, and takeover."[40] Likewise, *Les cahiers du féminisme* (The feminist notebooks), an extension of the defunct feminist journal *Les pétroleuses* (referencing women supporters of the French commune), edited by members of the LCR, wanted to be "a militant tool in the service of women's struggles ... rather than a theoretical review." In committing themselves to a feminism that embraced the fundamental principles of Marxism while taking Marxist theory, leftist parties, and leftist men to task for their evident sexism, its editors broke from a long tradition of capitulation to a larger party agenda and the longstanding silence on women's issues by such party women as Louise Saumoneau and Jeannette Vermeersch. At the same time, *Cahiers* criticized Psych-et-Po and Éditions *des femmes* as the epitome of bourgeois elitism for imputing ultimate value to writing careers, which only the smallest percentage of women had access to. These journals wanted to be "a place for debate and exchange of experiences" because they recognized the organizational torpor of the movement and the need for common ground between feminists and other women.[41]

Although largely ignored by party chiefs, the journals did manage to touch some raw nerves. *Mignonnes, allons voir sous la rose ...* did not exercise great influence within the Socialist Party but turned out to be a nice little thorn in its side. Its authors mercilessly mocked the two Socialist Party presidential candidates, François Mitterrand and Michel Rocard. They analyzed the development of legislation relating to women and commented on the activities of other feminist groups such as Choisir and the Ligue. Some readers suggested that its editors stop their nonsense and start toeing the line: "Why do you always attack the PS since feminism is inseparable from socialism?" one man wrote to them. But by offering a feminist critique of party ideology instead of propaganda designed to attract women to the party, *Mignonnes* provided a theoretical standard that party members were increasingly hard-pressed to ignore. In *Mignonnes*'s second issue, in 1979, the editors published an article about party men's lack of commitment to feminist principles, entitling it "On the Art of Accompanying the Women on the Street without Really Walking Down It, or PPS (Parti papa socialiste [Socialist Party daddy]) and the Women's March of October 6." In another issue, which focused on the coming presidential elections,

Mignonnes noted dryly: "When men of the Right oppress women it's to be expected since they are reactionaries; when men of the Left oppress women, it's not their fault—poor things—they are weighted down by old ideas."[42]

The genre of feminine writing that became recognized as "French feminism" by American scholars in the 1980s and 1990s emerged during this period. The social upheaval at the end of the 1960s, which was enlarged by the feminist movement, highlighted the contradiction between the complex reality of women's lives and the uncomplicated "superwoman" so lauded by the mainstream women's magazines in the 1970s. How could women articulate an integral sense of self amid this cacophony of voices? Psychoanalysis was considered a potent tool for such a project, but, within the French academy, Lacan exerted an "overweening phallocracy" over the discipline. It is no wonder that women writers, philosophers, and psychoanalysts sought their own ontology—steeped in France's rich intellectual traditions but reshaping them at the same time.[43] It is also no wonder that some women who had participated in the political activism of the movement were increasingly drawn to this more introspective kind of social criticism and to intellectual venues that were not dominated by men.

"Feminine writing," as well as works of psychoanalysis and philosophy written by women, flourished in the latter part of the 1970s. Theorists as different as Luce Irigaray, Michèle Montrelay, Chantal Chawaf, and Julia Kristeva, among others, shared a general interest in the relationship between language, consciousness, the body, and feminine identity. Women novelists and playwrights such as Hélène Cixous, Monique Wittig, Annie Leclerc, and even Marguerite Duras fused their revived interest in the women's cause with deconstructed language and utopian visions of women's liberation. In different ways, all of them took advantage of a period when sexuality—and women's sexuality—was being openly discussed. Cixous's early works *Le prénom de dieu* (The first name of God), *Dedans* (Within), and *Les commencements* (The beginnings) spoke of a woman's painful voyage out of the prison of her father's house and its narrow psychological boundaries into a new space, both dangerous and inviting. The writing in these early novels is stark and poetic, bearing witness to an author engaged in a process of self-discovery.[44]

Monique Wittig's *Les guérillères* (The women warriors) was one of the first major works of what could loosely be defined as feminist fiction; Wittig herself was a radical feminist and on the QF editorial board until 1981. *Les guérillères*, published in 1969, was a narrative of women's innate, powerful beauty, of women's triumph over the patriarchal world, and of the author's own power to rewrite myth and history. A sample passage: "The women say that they expose their genitals so that the sun may be reflected therein as a mirror. They say that they retain its brilliance. They say that the pubic hair is like a spider's web that captures the rays. They are seen running with great strides. . . . The glare they shed when they stand still and turn to face one makes the eye turn elsewhere unable to stand the sight."[45] In Wittig's fictional island-world, Rose Red arouses Snow White into angry protest, women's bared breasts represent their power rather than their submission, and it is said that "the summer day is brilliant, but more brilliant still is the fate of the young girl." It is a place where "the young girl in the house of her mother is like a seed in fertile ground. The woman under the roof of her husband is like a chained dog."[46]

Les guérillères became one of the literary mainstays of women's liberation during the 1970s and a decade later was being called one of the "immortal" texts of the women's liberation movement. At least one critic has named Wittig a "women's writer," arguing that she bent language to express a new feminine identity and locus of power. But this evaluation is in many ways misplaced, as it stems from (mostly) foreign critics' habit of lumping together the work of all French "feminist" novelists under the label *écriture féminine* (feminine writing), a label coined by Cixous in her essay "Le rire de la méduse" (The laugh of the medusa). Such critics considered Wittig's work to be part of the trend toward inscribing women in history through the written word—a kind of writing that avoids the standard masculine voice believed to perpetuate women's alienation. This challenge to traditional constructs is certainly present in Wittig's language and story, with its fractured narrative interspersed with illustrations of circles and lists of women's names and

its lack of conventional novelistic practices such as character development. But Wittig had begun with a solid grounding in Marxist theory
and saw women as a class because of their sex, not a caste because of
their gender, and she rejected the idea that she was a "woman writer."[47]

Hélène Cixous, a major contributor to the genre of "feminine writing," came into her own as a writer in the 1970s with the publication of
numerous novels, plays, and critical essays. In these works, she honed
her theory of feminine language and its relationship to identity and
women's bodies, arguing that the masculine and feminine were free-
floating signifiers to be applied to either sex. Cixous emphasized that
the feminine is therefore not fixed and should be understood as an
archetype and not as a prescription for women.[48] Yet her discussion
of femininity slips between archetypal theory and concrete referent.
Radical and Marxist feminists opposed her work in part because it is
never entirely clear whether she is writing about women as flesh-and-
blood individuals or "woman" as a construct. She argued that "woman
must write herself: write about women and bring women to writing from
which they have been driven away as violently as from their bodies."
Cixous has said she is more interested in the act of writing itself than
in theorizing about writing and language, considering herself more a
novelist, poet, and playwright than a theorist. She called upon women to
reject theories that prevent them from experiencing the power of their
own bodies, but kept her distance from the movement's activism and
remained a staunch supporter of Antoinette Fouque and her projects.[49]

Luce Irigaray also has been classified with the feminine writing
authors even though she is a psychoanalyst and has attempted to
construct a scientific description of women's repression. She was so
categorized because she argues that, on an unconscious level, bodies circumscribe consciousness. Her work as a psychoanalyst in the
1960s and her doctoral thesis, *Speculum de l'autre femme* (Speculum of
the other woman), published in 1974, caused a stir among colleagues
and students alike. Irigaray's unorthodox and critical approach was
disturbing enough that Lacan forced her from his department at Vincennes. *Spéculum* and its complementary 1977 text, *Ce sexe qui n'en
est pas un* (The sex which is not one), argued that women do not in

fact have a sex, being deprived of subjecthood in a phallocratic world. Whereas the radical feminists claimed that the socially constructed categories of sex needed to be brought down, since only women (not men) were marked and therefore prevented from being universal subjects, Irigaray argued that the neuter was impossible since it was always inscribed as masculine. She reproved radical feminists for uncritically embracing a humanist notion of universalism.[50] Women's role as prescribed by masculine "spécula(riza)tion," she argued, has little to do with women's own desire. In order for women to realize themselves, they would have to embrace their bodies and the knowledge contained therein.

Irigaray and Cixous shared a certain intellectual common ground in their mistrust of individualism and their embrace of the body as a way to uncover the independent desire of women and, thus, to change society. Interviewed in 1988 about her work, Irigaray said, "I am implying that the female body should not remain the object of male discourse and various male arts, but that it should become central to the process of a female subjectivity experiencing and defining it or herself."[51]

Irigaray's philosophical position on the question of essentialism has proved hard to pin down. While she repudiates the term, the philosopher Michèle LeDœuff has argued that in her search for a repressed female voice, Irigaray reduces women's voices and experience to a kind of hegemony of powerful women. Moreover, for Irigaray, to hear a repressed female voice is automatically to hear a patriarchally created voice. More recently, Amy Mazur has written that Irigaray "made fundamental contributions to rethinking core ideas about politics and democracy that represent different currents of western feminist thought." The duality of this debate over the meaning of "woman's voice" has yet to be resolved but, beyond this question, Irigaray always maintained that women must struggle for concrete gains and against discrimination; she also participated in the demonstrations and protests of the women's movement in the 1970s.[52]

Of these writers, philosopher and linguist Julia Kristeva—considered one of France's great contemporary intellectuals—was the most distant from the women's movement, although she has more recently acknowledged the formative influence *The Second Sex* had on her sense of self and purpose. What distinguished Kristeva, according to literary critics, was her attempt to move away from questions of feminine identity, avoiding the trap of essentialism, by merging discourse on femininity into a theory of marginality and subversion.[53] Kristeva nonetheless remained an outsider to the feminist movement in the 1970s and into the 1980s. She rarely wrote of feminism as an actual political movement with active members, and when she did it was as an observer. In her article "Les temps des femmes" (Women's time), for example, Kristeva reduced the past hundred years of the feminist movement by distinguishing between a "first wave" of egalitarian feminists who demanded equal rights with men "in linear time" and a second generation of post-1968 feminists who emphasized women's difference and their desire to remain outside linear time. The distinction, narrowly described as it was, served her speculative argument that a third generation was required—was in fact beginning to emerge—to harmonize both past generations into one that embraced motherhood. But while elements of her theory have general historical parallels, and while her proposal that feminism would have to reconcile itself to motherhood was apt, her analysis of "generations" is ahistorical. In a *Tel quel* (As is) editorial she contrasted the "sulkiness and isolation" of a certain type of feminism with the real female innovation that she postulated would come from the link between maternity and creation.[54]

Regardless of their philosophical and literary contributions, these writers remained marginal to the political heart of the women's liberation movement, although some of them gained increasing visibility within the university, and the press at times found them appealing.[55] Their celebratory or highly symbolic language engaged an older, unbroken discourse about women—who they were and what their relationship to the world was and should be—that had occupied French intellectuals for centuries. Their work was part of a proud French tradition of intellectual discourse and was that much easier for the public and the media to digest than the work of the radicals since lines were drawn and demands were made within the confines of symbolic language, not laws and political power.

It is important to note that while French intellectuals spoke of language, desire, and signs (with gender and sexuality as one focus), materialist feminism, speaking in concrete terms about women's position in society, became the lingua franca within the MLF. Even the moderate *F Magazine* (*F* for *femme* or woman), which was edited by feminist journalists Claude Servan-Schreiber and Benoîte Groult and which competed with the glossy fashion magazines, explicitly avoided articles about women's innate femininity. When it was launched in January 1978 its first issue sold four hundred thousand copies and was considered a great success. Covering topics including menopause and sexual harassment at work and featuring interviews with female politicians and stories of feminist campaigns, the magazine outwardly recognized that, as Servan-Schreiber wrote in the first editorial, "An increasing number of women now see themselves, other women, and men in a new light.... Why portray women as creatures born to seduce, cook, and consume?" *F Magazine* survived for four years with approximately two hundred thousand loyal readers, only to be supplanted in the early 1980s by more traditional fashion magazines, which declared that women's struggle was over and that they were heralding the new epoch of reconciliation among femininity, feminism, and the "new woman."[56]

The failure of *F Magazine* points to the prominence of essentialist visions in France, and it also explains why radical and Marxist feminists spent considerable intellectual energy disproving the claims of feminine writing even though its proponents remained more or less aloof from the debate. Materialist feminists felt they had much to fear from the liaison between traditional cultural depictions of women and updated naturalist visions of femininity or womanhood said to represent women's true liberation whether or not they were presented by glossy magazines or by "féminitude" writers. Because of the politics that such ideas historically implied—denying women freedoms and opportunities because of their sex, and emphasizing women's difference from and inferiority to men in order to keep them in a subjugated position—radical and Marxist feminists saw these essentialist women writers as the bane of the movement. Because of this enormous theoretical divide, women from these opposing sides would have less and less to do with each other, and almost no dialogue between them emerged.[57]

"I Myself Am the Material of My Struggles"

Antoinette Fouque's work also belongs to the category of "women's writing," but Fouque is a case apart for a few reasons, among them that she has only a very small body of writing that is definitely attributable to her, that she functioned more as a publisher than as a writer, and that she was intensely engaged in the debate over the term *feminism*.[58] Fouque and Psych-et-Po took part in the publishing ferment of the second half of the 1970s; her comment in an interview—"my 'historical' ambition as woman: I myself am the material of my struggles,"—defined both her personal and professional activities.[59] By early 1975 her group had launched the first attempt to publish a daily newspaper of the women's liberation movement. *Quotidien des femmes* survived for two years but never managed to make the leap to daily publication. The difficulties it encountered taught its publishers how much money and work such a venture required, but, difficulties notwithstanding, the *Quotidien* did give Psych-et-Po space to develop its positions. It tried to adopt the broadest possible interest in women and their movements for liberation, printing at least as many articles on women's struggles around the world as on those in France. The sentence "This edition was composed, written, fabricated by colonized, menaced, imprisoned, struggling women in all countries" was emblazoned under the masthead of many issues of the *Quotidien*. "In South Vietnam, Women Chase the Rapists from the Land," was the cover story of issue number 3, while numbers 5, 6, 7, and 9 published protests against Franco's repression of political dissenters in Spain—in particular Eva Forrest, whose prison journal and letters of appreciation to her women supporters the *Quotidien* quoted at length. The *Quotidien* was a different kind of journal, published regularly (although not daily as the title implied) and printed on glossy paper with large print runs. It was Psych-et-Po's mouthpiece and an important place to lay out its ideology of antifeminism which, for a while, was Fouque and Psych-et-Po's calling card—it stood out from the cacophony of voices and attracted media attention.[60]

The connection between Fouque's business and her politics was close and brought more attention to women's issues while garnering more visibility and sales for the publishing house. It blurred the line separating it from its readers by speaking about the collective process of creating the newspaper and its liberating potential, and it blurred lines between Fouque's own personal journey and public writing with her claim that she was the "material of her struggles."[61] "Women's relation to writing is the most fundamental problem of the women's struggle," Fouque commented. "Women—people without writing—absent from history, have entered in the struggle. We are in a tactical, political, and historical need to publish as a matter of priority, and exclusively women's texts." Writing women into history (discursively) and into themselves (symbolically) were twin objectives of the *Quotidien*. "I was as greedy to read as to eat food that would never fill me, ... but I still read insatiably," confessed a writer who said she had always felt forced to identify with the masculine and thus always felt psychologically displaced. Work with a women's publishing company, she said, helped her fuse her love of the written word to a new love of self.[62]

Fouque's process for creating a revolution of the symbolic was accompanied by a kind of euphemistic homosexual practice that would give birth to a new woman. This required the rejection of "the name of the father" (the law) and the embrace of the mother's body. Woven into many of the *Quotidien* articles was a belief in women's homosexuality and a belief that homosexuality was suppressed. Sometimes the suppression was described in purely symbolic terms but at other times as directly caused by male power. An unsigned article by "a woman ... an analyst" (but later claimed by Fouque in her doctoral thesis) challenged the phallic domination of the libido and thus the definition of women in misogynist terms. At the same time, it inveighed against women's real (rather than symbolic) homosexuality: "Attached to the demands of identity and of individuality, lesbianism, in line with Socialist feminism, marches willingly in the clichés of 'unisex,' turned over, seen-unseen, forward-backwards, upside-down, always the same. Specular, narcissistic lesbianism to me seems a counter cross-dressing, an intensification of inversion."[63]

The *Quotidien* also discussed women's experience in real terms to place their concerns at the center of social discourse. One article, for example, discussed women's unemployment and working women's efforts to combat it. Another article described giving birth in contemporary male-dominated society and railed against doctors (and nurses) who remained insensitive to women's pain, who ignored women's bodies, and who saw women merely as "genitals laid bare." The child born in this atmosphere of "silence, noninformation, sadism, and sterilization" was "already the private property of the Institution and of the State," the article concluded. This was as angry and critical an article as could be found in the *Quotidien*. Between the mid-1970s and the early 1980s, Fouque and most of the articles seemed to avoid expressing anger against flesh-and-blood men and relegated their criticism to symbolic patriarchal oppression.[64]

Fouque's publishing business grew during the second half of the 1970s. A few years after she founded Éditions *des femmes*, she created several other series: *du côté des petites filles* (On the side of little girls), *des femmes presse* (Women's press), *des femmes filment* (Women's film), and *des femmes du* MLF *éditent* (Women of the MLF publish). Her substantial financial resources enabled her to publish more books at low prices and to put out a much slicker-looking magazine than those of other groups working on shoestring budgets. Many of *des femmes'* editions sold well, giving their authors exposure and allowing more women to read books written by and about women.[65] The successor to *Quotidien*, called *des femmes en mouvements* (Women in movements), mainly contained information about women's activities and successes around the world. The magazine was filled with joyous photos of women gathered together, talking, walking, or reading, often out of doors. Its articles often described women's oppression at the hands of male institutions, repressive regimes, and the law, although sometimes without the precise political discussion of concrete issues found in other journals. The response to such oppression in the pages *des femmes en mouvements* was an elaborate exaltation of womanhood divorced from an attachment to children and male partners.[66]

Women's Identity and Separatism: Empowerment or Alienation?

As the 1970s continued, it became clear that feminism or the woman's cause was headed in multiple directions. Dispersion was as much the leitmotif of the latter half of the 1970s as solidarity had been for the early period. Political parties' growing attention to women's issues drained moderate supporters away from the movement, leaving militants to continue the struggle alone. Moreover, the various factions concentrated on developing their positions rather than seeking permanent alliances. Almost all remained fiercely opposed to organizational hierarchy and authority and, for the most part, united only over specific issues such as abortion or rape. This antiestablishment position was Janus faced. On the positive side, it permitted feminist criticism—particularly radical feminist criticism—to flourish. Radical feminists, with their materialist arguments and frequent rapier wit, produced some of the most astute feminist analysis. On the negative side, trenchant criticism of all gender norms created a rarefied atmosphere that alienated would-be supporters.[67] The problem was both ideological and strategic. The antireformist wings of the movement, notably the radical feminists and Psych-et-Po, were operating at a theoretical pitch beyond the hearing range of the average French woman. Radical feminists' stridency and Psych-et-Po's late-night discussion-therapy groups and obfuscating language were also met with incomprehension and often hostility by women both within and outside the movement.

Radical feminism played a strange role in the feminist movement of the 1970s. Having no ambitions to political power, radical feminists articulated women's grievances and the problematic of sexism in the boldest and most uncompromising fashion, providing the movement with constant inspiration and theoretical strength. At the same time, however, radicals served as a scapegoat for the kind of "aggressive feminism" that Françoise Giroud claims French women always repudiated. When planning the "women's strike" that they called *grrr... rêve des femmes*, they suggested "bringing the kids to work so the boss can watch them" and "bringing your dirty laundry en masse to the may-

or's office until free and collective washing machines are installed." One of the militants' favorite strategies was parody, and for this strike they urged women to "play up the role that they want us to play," including actions like "putting on makeup ten times a day and laughing and gabbing with your friends."[68] In fact, the most radical women within the MLF did not believe that real equality was possible within a male-dominated world. This fervent conviction led some feminists to believe that fighting for "rights" was an exercise in futility because they understood that although the concept of equal rights asserts the principle of providing the same chances to all individuals, whatever their origins, such equality of opportunity was impossible in a patriarchal system that had as a primary aim the supremacy of one group over the other.[69]

Ordinary women were not necessarily inspired by the radicals' motive for the abortion legalization campaign: overthrowing male domination as it manifested itself in law, interpersonal relationships, the economy, language, and consciousness itself. For the radical feminists, half the point of legalizing contraception and abortion was to bring about the destruction of marriage and the family—for them the very foundation of women's oppression. While repudiation of republican principals and feminist agitprop threw the injustices of French society into relief, it was too much of a leap for most French women.[70]

Because of this, motherhood as experience and cultural identity divided some MLF militants from average women. Many women had the (generally) false impression that feminists were against maternity. But it's more accurate to say that feminists frequently criticized the centuries-old exhortation to reproduce. They wanted to glorify women's autonomy and freedom from involuntary reproduction and male authority—rather than taking a serious interest in desired childbearing and management of children.[71] Separatism was a consequence of militants' attempt to wed theory to political and personal practice. But for all but the most committed militants, these attitudes were a hard row to hoe. The gap between pure ideals and the complex reality of women's lives intimidated many women and frustrated others, and, in such a charged atmosphere, sisterhood seemed more theoretical than real.[72]

While some women in politics repudiated independent feminist activism, accusing it of being insufficiently political, many moderate feminists and apolitical French women saw feminism as too broadly political. The feminist argument that "the personal is political," which deeply politicized private as well as public acts, made it possible to criticize the complex nature of women's oppression and helped reconceive politics and social criticism. Yet within the movement, that revolutionary slogan was experiencing an inversion. Personal behavior was at times becoming conflated with political struggle and applied to analyze every sort of social oppression "from domestic tyranny to institutional dictatorship," as feminist academics Françoise Picq and Liliane Kandel have suggested. "Sisterhood" as collective identity at times became a club with a strict entry code that many could not meet. Identity politics, in which personal identity and experience moved beyond analysis to serve an exclusive political alliance, worked against many women's identification with feminism as a broad ideal and as a political mission. "Feminist" could be trivialized rather than broadened to attract more followers.[73]

Following the principle that the personal is political, certain strands within radical feminism began adopting separatism in their private lives. The Gouines rouges and later the Front des lesbiennes radicales (Radical Lesbian Front) are early examples of separatist groups. Combining their exploration of women's homosexuality with separatist politics, they argued that only lesbian identity and practice could sustain the radical feminist theory that "a political position is revolutionary only in the measure that it constitutes the negation of the social relations of capitalism or patriarchy or both." Both groups maintained that lesbianism refuted the patriarchal mythologies that oppressed women—that sexual pleasure is linked to reproduction, that gender roles are natural, and that the only possible loving relationships are heterosexual, monogamous, and oriented toward the traditional family. They believed that their lesbianism allowed them to develop what one member called "new roads for the social expression of the libido," which freed them to define themselves in relation to other women instead of to men. By refusing to marry, they explained, "We deny the rivalry and isolation of heterosexual women. Lesbianism refutes the notion that woman is the property of her husband and children, and the property of their parents."[74] But their rejection of heterosexuality as a legitimate sexual expression for feminists divided them from other MLF women who were unwilling to isolate themselves politically or socially from men or from heterosexual feminists. This division—which turned into a gulf by 1981—was one of the most painful conflicts within the movement.

Lesbian separatism came to a head at a meeting in June 1980, when the newly organized Groupe lesbiennes de Jussieu (The Lesbian Group of Jussieu) publicly condemned feminists for practicing "heterofeminism" and being complicit with the "heteropatriarchy." Using a combination of Marxist theory, which radical feminists had employed so deftly early in the movement, and language of the postwar period—speaking of the "occupation" of women's spirits and bodies by the patriarchy— lesbian separatists transformed lesbianism, once viewed as a sexual and emotional reality or preference, into a political weapon.[75] Lesbian feminists forced heterosexual feminists to acknowledge the role that institutionalized heterosexuality played in women's oppression. Yet this position was a double-edged sword because it sometimes painted heterosexual women as only half-committed to the feminist project.[76]

Thus, by the second half of the 1970s, participants in the MLF, like feminists elsewhere, often formed small factions based on shared visions of the world and of politics—visions that encompassed everything from fashion to manners of speech and that forged tight circles of like-minded women. This trend reinforced the image of the MLF as a movement that eroticized relations among women and downplayed or rejected heterosexuality. True or not, the creation of "antinorms" at the heart of the movement—viewing men as the enemy, dressing and acting in a rebellious fashion—alienated many heterosexual and, especially, married women. Feminists who were also mothers and spouses accused the MLF of being uninterested or unable to incorporate pregnancy and motherhood into the movement. Régine Dhoquois, sociologist and legal scholar, tells of one woman who said that while her feminist comrades offered her a chair during her pregnancy, the pregnancy itself and her experience of it was a taboo subject. "They treated me sometimes as if it didn't exist."[77]

As the midpoint of the decade approached, as less-dedicated supporters of the feminist movement returned to their everyday lives, and as MLF militants began to see the legitimacy of their movement funneled into government- or party-controlled organizations and campaigns, the movement entered a new and in many ways more circumspect phase. Militants retreated to groups whose participants and ideology they believed held the most promise, leaving feminists who remained uncommitted in a kind of political limbo. There were some exceptions. The Groupe de jeudi (Thursday's Group, sometimes called the Groupe politique extérieure, or External Policy Group), which existed from 1972 to 1974, tried to create a framework free from expectation and judgment, open to any woman who wanted to explore feminism but also critical of what it saw as feminists' Manichean vision. One of the few documents created by the group said, "We don't escape institutions; we struggle and debate with them." Thursday's Group was not able to stop the movement's fragmentation. When it joined together with a women's group from Marseilles to edit part of Le tôrchon brûle's seventh issue, they claim a representative of Psych-et-Po showed up while they were working, demanding that they reveal all the theses of the articles "that you are making on our backs." They were ridiculed as "the ones who are selling our struggle to the university," a small example of the petty power plays within parts of the movement weakening its already shaky reputation. Others tried to establish a "horizontal coordination of autonomous feminist groups" for women who "didn't recognize themselves in any of the tendencies to collaborate on feminist projects and make a public show of force." Other feminists turned to focus on a pragmatic agenda within state institutions to promote change.[78]

How are we to evaluate the scope and impact of feminist organizations by the end of the 1970s? In France, where the political victory of the Socialists allowed left-liberals to engage in leftist politics without having to "take on the system," groups who defied mainstream political language and avenues of power, such as the Féministes révolutionnaires and Psych-et-Po, seemed less and less politically relevant as the parties began adopting diluted feminist ideas. Groups such as the Ligue du droits des femmes, Choisir, and the PFU fought marginalization, finding that only some of their ideas were partially accepted. Concepts such as "women's insertion in society" became associated with a generalized reformist impulse that blunted their radical intent. The Ligue and the PFU had been born from the radical feminism that had created the women's liberation movement in the first place. Beauvoir's argument that women are made, not born—that "femininity" and even "woman" herself are social constructs—inspired the large majority of feminists in France. The paradox, however, is that radical feminism's attempt to overturn or abandon phallocratic society received no widespread support among women of any social class. For many participants in the MLF, the separatist theory that blurred the lines between patriarchy and patriarch, defining men and their world as the primary cause of women's oppression, turned into a refusal to consort with the enemy—a kind of personal rather than political separatism. This was a decidedly unpopular stance.

Sexual and personal freedom had served as a rallying point for the early movement, evident in the campaign to broaden contraception and legalize abortion and to force a greater acceptance of homosexuality in French culture. This focus led to concrete changes, such as the decline in the number of unwanted children, the reduction of gynecological complications and female mortality from botched abortions, equalizing working women's salaries, and a broader acceptance of educated women professionals. While some of these institutional changes had been made slowly and without fanfare before 1968, feminism—in little more than half a decade—had engaged in a kind of collective public consciousness-raising, making enormous strides. In only four short years, feminists had managed to win the passage of legislation that would radically alter the scope of all women's lives and their prospects for independence. The right to control one's own reproductive capacity seemed so fundamental to the vast majority of women active in the movement—and resonated so strongly among French women generally—that activists threw their weight behind the campaign despite all their philosophical or tactical differences. Feminists had myriad subjects to criticize, demands to make, and plans to hatch *because* French society needed to be changed in so many ways to render justice to women and equalize power between the sexes in the public and private worlds. French women needed feminism for precisely these reasons, yet because of all the competing ideas and solutions, feminism could not sustain itself as a strong, united movement. After the black years, feminism would not recover its broad popularity for decades. Instead, the black years left feminism—as theory, ideal, and individual practice—to be interpreted and adapted by a variety of forces for a variety of ends.

Fig. 1. Photo of the Arc de Triomphe protest: "More unknown than the unknown soldier—his wife." After a small newspaper announcement about a protest by the Women's Liberation Movement in New York City. *Left*: Emmanuelle de Lesseps; *Right*: Christine Delphy; *Behind*: Janine Serre; *Hidden behind policeman's arm*: Margaret Stephenson (American). Unknown Photographer.

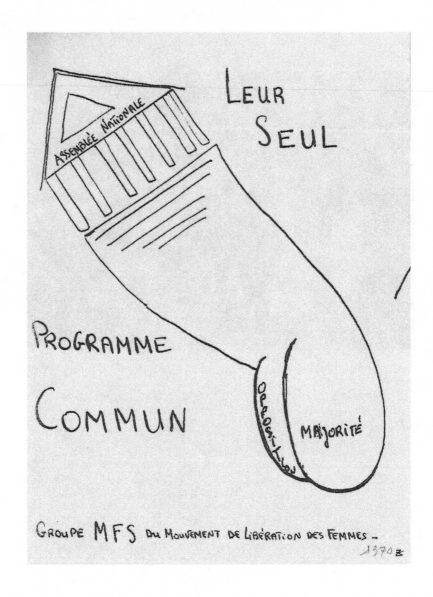

Fig. 2. Flyer: "Leur Seul Programme Commun" (Their Only Common Program), 1970. Unknown designer. Gift of Anne Zelensky.

Fig. 3. Women's strike at the Troyes Hosiery Factory, 1971. © Catherine
Deudon / Bibliothèque Marguerite Durand / Roger-Viollet.

Fig. 4. Protest against a radio show hosted by Ménie Grégoire
on homosexuality in March 1971. *Left to right*: Maffra, Christine
Delphy, behind her Christiane Dancourt, Monique Wittig, Elisabeth
Salvaresi, Antoinette Fouque, Anne de Bascher. © Catherine
Deudon / Bibliothèque Marguerite Durand / Roger-Viollet.

Fig. 5. Protest against Mother's Day, Paris, May 28, 1972. © Catherine
Deudon / Bibliothèque Marguerite Durand / Roger-Viollet.

Fig. 6. Poster protesting the registration and copyright of "MLF" and the women's sign and feminist symbol by Psych-et-Po, 1979. © Catherine Deudon / Bibliothèque Marguerite Durand / Roger-Viollet.

Fig. 7. (*top*) Fifty thousand women take to the streets of Paris for accessible and free contraception and abortion. © Catherine Deudon / Bibliothèque Marguerite Durand / Roger-Viollet.

Fig. 8. (*bottom*) Protest of March 8, 1980, on International Women's Day. "Here we fight against the patriarchy: the thousand and one coalitions of the (unregistered/uncopyrighted) Women's Liberation Movement." © Catherine Deudon / Bibliothèque Marguerite Durand / Roger-Viollet.

Fig. 9. Yvette Roudy, "Win in 2000." International Women's Day
Conference, March 8, 1985. Campaign for the Parity Law of June 6, 2000.
© Catherine Deudon / Bibliothèque Marguerite Durand / Roger-Viollet.

7 WHO OWNS WOMEN'S LIBERATION?

The Campaigns for French Women

Women's access to political power is only one essential aspect of the relationship between the sexes. It was always and everywhere difficult.

Michelle Perrot, "La démocratie sans les femmes" (Democracy without women) in Gisèle Halimi's *Femmes: moitié de la terre, moitié du pouvoir* (Women: Half the world, half the power) (1994)

By the end of the 1970s, as feminist discourse increasingly permeated French politics, the parties appealed to feminist ideals and some feminist factions began courting them. In fact, the influence of the movement had begun to shift to integration-oriented activists who believed that feminist theory and ideals were worth little if they could not be concretely and promptly integrated into existing French institutions. Thus, women like Yvette Roudy within the Socialist Party, Gisèle Halimi and her group Choisir, and the Ligue du droit des femmes, led by Anne Zelensky and Simone de Beauvoir, would increasingly grab the spotlight because their demands and policy ideas—including laws protecting women against sexual violence and policies ensuring equal education, training, and income—spoke to more French women. These activists believed, as did Suzanne Blaise of the PFU, that a movement for women's liberation would flourish only if it engaged politics at the same time as it made politics engage feminism.

Nevertheless, overall lack of agreement and communication among the many groups made it easier for one woman—Antoinette Fouque—to assert her authority in the movement and to gain more control over its products and its ideas. While denouncing feminism, from 1979 to 1980 Fouque or her partners registered the name *Mouvement de libération des femmes* as their own, declaring themselves the true prophets of women's liberation. They took a name that had embraced an entire political movement and gained legal control of its usage.[1] In reaction, feminists across the political spectrum exploded in rancor and disgust and, in turn, were caught up in legal cases unprecedented enough to make any future feminist action far more complicated and difficult than it had been for a decade. Torn apart by internal sabotage, shaken by an inability to find common ground, and diluted by the Socialist Party apparatus and business as usual, the independent women's liberation movement would cease to be a player in the national arena for the next three decades, even as diverse forms of feminism would continue to generate interest on the Far Left and be used by women in politics to gain recognition for all its causes.[2]

"A State of Siege"

By 1977 Antoinette Fouque seemed increasingly embattled and willing to act aggressively to maintain what she felt was her good name. That year Fouque and her publishing house, Éditions *des femmes*, sued four women for defamation. The suit grew out of Fouque's conflict with an employee, Mireille de Coninck, whom she had asked to open a bookstore in Lyon. According to news reports, in the winter of 1976, Fouque and Éditions *des femmes* hired de Coninck, a leading activist for prostitutes' rights (and a former prostitute herself) to lease a property in Lyon for a bookstore and to have the interior renovated. Over the spring and into the summer, relations between the two women soured. Fouque, it seems, almost immediately regretted handing the task over to de Coninck. According to journalist Martine Storti and others, the conflict between de Coninck and Fouque arose over their different visions for the bookstore: de Coninck saw it as a meeting place for all feminist groups in Lyon—including those with whom Fouque did not agree.[3] De Coninck, who had two children to support, complained that Fouque did not meet her legal or financial obligations. By de Coninck's account, she was frequently reproached when she would phone or visit the headquarters in Paris for being "too aggressive" or for not loving Fouque and the others enough. The last time she visited, she found herself "in front of a tribunal of five or six women" who proceeded to blame and insult her, not for her work but for her conduct and motivations. What eventually became known as the "Barbara affair" (Barbara was the name de Coninck had used as a prostitute) took on a darker dimension when de Coninck attempted suicide. Reporters snatched up the story. What had started as a labor conflict swiftly became a showdown between Psych-et-Po and other feminists. For them, the "Barbara affair" epitomized Éditions *des femmes*' commercial style— using politics as others used advertising to garner publicity and market share without regard to ethical standards or political integrity. Various women from within the movement were therefore only too eager to help de Coninck seek recompense.[4]

On October 12, 1976, de Coninck, along with a number of her friends and supporters, occupied the *des femmes*' bookstore in Paris, demanding payment of her salary and compensation for being unofficially fired. With the help of a lawyer she then sued Fouque and *des femmes*; a trial date was set for the following May.[5] From there the conflict escalated. Over the following months, de Coninck recorded her complaints on videotape, as did two other women, Erin Pizzey and Monique Piton, who both said they had similar difficulties with Fouque. Documentarian Carole Roussopoulos filmed the confessions (conducted by the actress Delphine Seyrig). Pizzey, an English domestic-abuse expert and activist who had written the book *Scream Quietly or the Neighbours Will Hear* (published in the UK in 1974) and who had a contract with *des femmes* to publish a French translation, declared that she too had not been paid. She also said that she had no idea how many copies of her book had been printed or sold, that her letters to *des femmes* had gone unanswered, and that she had never been able to reach the editors in charge of publication. Piton, a working-class militant who had participated in the prolonged strike at the Lip watch factory and written an account of her experiences, had similar complaints.[6]

The video of the interviews, entitled *Il ne fait pas chaud ou une édition contre des femmes . . .* (It's none too warm or a publisher against women . . .), was distributed by a "counterinformation militant distribution company" called Mon Oeil and shown in public on January 30, 1977. In addition, a transcript of the video (with the same title) was published as a large four-page pamphlet, adding the testimony of two other women, the writer and avant-garde musician Brigitte Fontaine and the writer Catherine Leguay. It contained a statement, signed by 343 women, that read, "We, women in struggle of all groups and of all factions and of no group nor any factions, have seen this videotape and have recognized in it part of our experience with Éditions and Librairie *des femmes*." Fontaine declared, presumably to *des femmes*, "I'm leaving you," saying that she had withdrawn a novel under negotiation from their editorship. "If after everything," she wrote in a postscript, "you decide to send me the money you owe me, good; do it! If you don't it's nothing anyway."[7] Within a month, Fouque sued de Coninck, Pizzey, Piton, and Roussopoulos, as well as Mon Oeil, for defamation. (Strangely, Seyrig was not named in the suit, perhaps because Fouque did not want to challenge a popular celebrity.) The case dragged on for two years, largely because the anti-Fouque feminists had drawn a line in the sand, committing themselves to making the conflict into a political showdown, but also because Fouque and *des femmes* refused to budge. During that time, many feminists condemned the way Fouque was trying to settle a matter of politics and ideology in the courts, using the "law of the father" that she had always vociferously condemned.[8]

Fouque and Psych-et-Po occupied an increasingly embattled position within the movement—what she called "a state of siege."[9] Fouque was harshly criticized in almost every feminist journal of the 1970s by the most influential feminists from different wings of the movement, and her bookstore on rue Jacob in the Sixth Arrondissement was vandalized five times in three years by feminists and antifeminists. Three men implicated in one attack, on December 22, 1977, signed their work with a swastika, demonstrating once again that antifeminism (and anti-Semitism) was alive and well in France—and that there were downsides to being the face of "feminism." The neo-Nazis clearly were uninterested in the finer points of the debate over women's liberation. In contrast, on May 12, 1978, the store was seriously defaced by women calling themselves Les Bombeuses à chapeau (a rough translation would be "The Classy Taggers"). They left a cryptic note: "If they share the dough, we will share the spray cans."[10] The feminist journal *Le temps des femmes* (Women's times) published their statement: "We do not recognize ourselves in an isolated feminism, a global questioning of social relationships that glorify the image of the emancipated woman, ... or other traps of fools. ... Watch out, these feminists and their sisters are false comrades." The store window was also sprayed with buckshot. Another time, on October 19, 1978, the stockroom was completely burned and the building filled with smoke. The vandals this time called themselves The Women's Movement against Abortion.[11]

In one strange reversal, after all the accusations against Fouque surrounding the defamation suit, Erin Pizzey wrote Fouque two deeply apologetic letters declaring that she herself had been misled and that her signature on certain contested documents had been forged by her husband. In May 1985 she wrote, "I have had an awful lot of trouble with cheating among my various agents ... and you have been excellent publishers." And then, a month later: "I have never been able to apologize for that awful deception."[12]

Throughout these events, Fouque's and Psych-et-Po's actions seem to have deepened conflicts between different factions in the women's movement by consistently making disputes broadly theoretical. For instance, in interpreting the "Barbara affair" we might view Fouque as an employer burdened with an irascible employee or de Coninck as an employee denied a proper labor contract. But it was more than that. The dispute embodied the movement's frequently casual mixture of politics, personal relationships, and business. "The contract that we had with Mireille," *des femmes* offered in its defense, "was first a contract of political confidence, that from the start ... she could not maintain and that she then actively broke." De Coninck also expressed her shock at what she believed was *des femmes*' unfair treatment of her in political terms: "I had confidence in them because they were women, women in struggle."[13]

That women's commerce should be a natural extension of politics and activism was one of Psych-et-Po's ideals, as it was for many feminists.

Even Georges Kiejman, Psych-et-Po's lawyer and a prominent spokesman for civil liberties, confused them. *Libération* quoted his argument in court that the "irregularities in pay and proper documentation are also due to the fact that the Librairie *des femmes* is an artisanal society in formation, . . . and if she [de Coninck] didn't understand [this situation] it was because she had tasted the sweet and bitter fruits and the sensual pleasure of stardom."[14] Despite their possible mutual miscommunication, news reports imply that Fouque's dealings with de Coninck showed little of the insight that feminists had gathered through the years—notably, that to hire a socially vulnerable woman without the proper documents was to reproduce the same kind of vulnerability and discrimination that men and patriarchal society had maintained. Such carelessness, de Coninck's supporters further implied, flew in the face of Fouque's purported commitment to women's liberation. As someone in the press commented, "One could never have imagined that a group of this same movement would one day, always by the intercession of a lawyer, demand in front of a legal tribunal the right to 'militant respect.'" None of this gave pause to the thirty or so women who supported *des femmes* by standing outside the court and holding up large placards that read, "2,000 Years of Feminism, That's Enough! Long Live Women's Liberation Movements."[15]

Criticism and bad feeling deepened when, as the scandal broke, the Psych-et-Po group remained incommunicado. The group called a press conference on March 25, 1977, promising to clear up any confusion. But when the press corps arrived, Psych-et-Po handed out a short, written statement that contained generally known information and refused to say anything further despite the journalists' vigorous requests. A reporter from *Libération* who asked Fouque to answer some questions was told that she "did not want to enter into a system of response, especially not in *Libération*."[16] Worse for its reputation within the movement, Psych-et-Po refused to try to reach an understanding in an out-of-court settlement with those they accused. When the judge left the courtroom, having annulled the first proceedings because *des femmes* refused to allow the possibility of reconciliation required in defamation suits, the women present suggested debating the issue right there. The group from *des femmes* refused, and as they left the courtroom were quoted as retorting, "You take the place of the judges"—a comment that struck at least one reporter as a curious irony since *des femmes* had initiated the defamation suit.[17]

Des femmes sued again, this time challenging the transcript of the videotape that had been distributed with signatures of supporters. They declined to accept the reconciliation offerings of the defendants. "We have refused the proposals that they made us respond to," *des femmes* explained in the introduction to its complete book catalogue in 1979. "Because it is necessary to limit the real prejudice against Éditions *des femmes*—suspicion, scandal-mongering, reduction, political censure, which is today still being referenced—we brought the complaint of defamation." The accused for their part vowed that they would not argue their case in court since their dispute was one of politics and ideology and not something that should be decided by a patriarchal judge. The four women were found guilty by default in May 1979. Yet it was Psych-et-Po that described itself as victimized at the hands of "ideological imperialism (totalitarian and monopolistic feminism)."[18]

Feminists were quick to find contradictions between Fouque's conduct during this affair and the theory she espoused. They pointed out that while Fouque had spent considerable energy over the previous decade denouncing feminism—which, she argued, collaborated with the bourgeoisie and with capitalism—she lost no time in mobilizing all the resources of bourgeois capitalism when it served her purposes. When she refused to open a dialogue with those she accused, feminists saw her as ignoring the welfare of the movement and working solely for her own interests. Fouque's newspaper the *Quotidien* had represented itself as the international voice of struggle against women's oppression. Yet during the defamation hearing Psych-et-Po appeared to trivialize other women's oppression and exaggerate the slights against its organizations by calling them "works of death, of destruction, and of Dachau in leaden wagons."[19] These contradictions and overblown claims confounded Fouque's adversaries and made it close to impossible—even if Fouque and her group had been amenable—to have a debate, let alone a constructive dialogue. The whole affair drained the movement of productive energy and dissipated its resources, contributing nothing to the ongoing discussion about feminism and the best kind of liberation for France's women.

The Heist of the MLF

Less than two years later, on October 6, 1979, members of Psych-et-Po joined with thousands of other women in Paris to march in defense of reproductive rights. The size of the crowd—forty thousand to fifty thousand—surpassed all expectations, and the march was considered a huge success: three months later on December 31, the Veil law would be renewed with revisions increasing access to abortion. But this would be the last time for a long while that Psych-et-Po and the rest of the movement would unite. The day before the march, Psych-et-Po had taken out an ad in *Le Monde* calling women to the "Mouvement de libération des femmes" and signing it "Politique et Psychanalyse et *des femmes en mouvements*." Many feminists were shocked or annoyed by the ad, which seemed to present the women's movement as having one leader.[20]

Psych-et-Po's motives became clearer after a reader of the feminist journal *Histoires d'elles* (Women's stories) came upon a strange announcement in the *Journal officiel* (Official law journal), the national bulletin in which new laws and decrees are published. On September 5, 1979, a month before the march, Marie-Claude Grumbach, Antoinette Fouque, and Sylvina Boissonnas from the group Psychanalyse et Politique had registered an association named "Mouvement de libération des femmes—Psychanalyse et Politique" at the Paris police prefecture. On October 16, they changed the registration to "Mouvement de libération des femmes—MLF," and on November 19 they entered the association "Mouvement de libération des femmes—MLF" at the Institut national de la propriété industrielle (National Institute of Industrial Property), creating the commercial brand name and limited partnership "Mouvement de libération des femmes—MLF (SARL)."[21]

Histoires d'elles immediately accused Fouque and Psych-et-Po of hijacking the women's liberation movement. Psych-et-Po responded saying, "We have not registered any title, we have created an association. . . . The MLF is not a trademark, but a space of struggle." "Space of struggle" or not, the trademark had very real legal and practical implications. At a women's forum in Creteil on November 11, where Psych-et-Po was asked publicly to explain its behavior, its members were quoted as saying, "Now that the MLF is inscribed in the *Journal officiel*, it can no longer disappear from history."[22] Participants in the movement were hardly satisfied with such explanations, not the least because Psych-et-Po had for years derided any engagement with the body politic. *Questions féministes* published a manifesto (printed by Éditions Tierce) against the registration. These feminists were convinced that Fouque's actions would create ideological and political misconceptions abroad. As one remarked, "In the United States, they have come to believe that Psych-et-Po's points of view are those of the entire French movement. There, it is called 'French feminism.'"[23] This was only partially correct, however. In the United States, French feminism was indeed believed to embody some of Fouque's guiding principles: the act of writing as central to women's liberation; the direct connection between sexuality, consciousness, and personality; and the importance of Lacanian psychoanalysis. Yet these ideas conjured up the names Irigaray and Cixous rather than Fouque, and American feminists were generally unaware of or indifferent to the politics behind the theoretical debates in France.

Long before Fouque registered the MLF as her trademark, she had been using the acronym MLF on many of Psych-et-Po's leaflets and documents because she had incorporated them into her trademarks for various publication series such as *Le quotidian des femmes, Du côté des petites filles,* and *Des femmes en mouvements*—and had been criticized for doing so. Standard practice among movement participants had been to identify themselves *as part* of the MLF—using names such as "women from the MLF" or "radical feminists of the MLF"—and not to claim to represent the whole movement. But Psych-et-Po had not followed this practice. At the International Tribunal of Crimes against Women in Brussels in March 1976, other women from the movement had distributed a tract that accused Psych-et-Po of monopolistic usage and explained to the uninitiated the degree to which French feminism was not organized or directed. They accused Fouque of playing on the fact that when the press wanted to contact a spokeswoman for the "feminists," they would turn to a group that used the title officially. "This is more dangerous," they said, "because they play into the hands of the enemies of our liberation." This might seem hyperbolic, but with Psych-et-Po's registration of MLF three years later, their worst fears were confirmed.[24]

It appears that Fouque intended to rewrite the history of the movement to place herself at the center. Book catalogues published by Éditions *des femmes* substantiate this claim. The epigraph for the 1978 catalogue stated, "The group Politique et Psychanalyse in the MLF is at the forefront of a specific and massive practice that has concrete accomplishments." In 1980 the statement was slightly modified, delineating the date of the beginning of the movement—a date that only Fouque and her supporters considered accurate: "In the Mouvement de libération des femmes, *born in October 1968*, the collective Politique et Psychanalyse is at the forefront of a struggle" (emphasis added). Two years later, in 1982, the catalogue no longer equivocated: "The Mouvement de libération des femmes, *created in October 1968 by Antoinette Fouque*, is at the forefront of a struggle" (emphasis added).[25]

The registration received some press coverage, most of it critical of Fouque and Psych-et-Po. But in July 1980, when the furor seemed to have died down, Fouque gave an interview to Catherine Clément in *Le matin*, in which she tried to explain further:

> By 1979 feminists had long abandoned the word "liberation." MLF became dishonorable. We had entered a period of large reversals with the International Year of the Woman (1975), then the creation of a secretariat of the feminine condition and the reburial of our victories. . . . We think that there is a necessity, an urgent need to give a minimal anchor to our movement.

Clément pressed her: "A minimal anchor, and yet you criticize institutions?" Fouque responded:

One cannot live in the perpetual negation of the institution. The association of the law of 1901 governs political parties as well as the associations of happy *boules* [bowling] players; it's the most flexible form that we could lend to our movement.

"But what is the need to exist legally?" Clément pursued. Fouque went on:

The MLF had been threatened with obliteration. We were in great danger. [Michel] Rocard [the Socialist Party leader who lost to Mitterrand in the first round of the presidential elections] spoke of incorporating women. Out of the question to let him. . . . And then, as a result of contradictions came divisions, the movement risked splitting up, self-destruction, sterility. It was the moment to realize . . . . It is to clarify by a gesture, that what I call the "revolution of the symbolic," has begun with this movement. . . . For it must be put behind us, this reality to which we women have been submitted, within feminist emancipation—as much a disguise as femininity.[26]

Fouque explained, but feminists outside her group objected to her actions and her symbolically freighted words. Her characterization of the MLF registration as an attempt to "simply affirm an existence," to give a "shot of reality" to a sinking, disappearing movement rang hollow. And her use of the word "we" in the interview—meaning her group, the movement as a whole, or both—inspired yet more outrage.[27] According to the law of 1901 governing associations, Fouque and the few other women who registered the name now had the right (which Fouque would publicly make use of) to publish their groups' ideas and activities under the MLF label; to use it as their trademark and signature, making them the sole representatives of all those using that name; to collect funds for the cause of the Mouvement de libération des femmes; to be able to sue in court over any unauthorized use of the name; to appropriate anything that was or had been previously created or published under the name; and, finally, if they chose, to put up candidates for election under the MLF banner.[28]

Half a year later at the Paris Police Prefecture, on July 23, 1980, Psychanalyse et Politique registered another variant, this one named "Confédération nationale—Mouvement de libération des femmes," which served as an extra precaution to prevent any unauthorized association from using the title *Mouvement de libération des femmes* or MLF. Article 7 of the bylaws required that "every association applying must be accredited by the bureau of the union; the refusal of accreditation will interdict the local association from using the title 'Mouvement de libération des femmes—MLF,'" meaning only *des femmes* and associates had the right to use the name or to grant permission to use it. Moreover, the design chosen for the MLF brand was a raised fist inside the female symbol—an emblem, originating in the United States, that had become an international symbol for feminists and women's liberation. As the editors of the *La revue d'en face* remarked, "It is to encroach on the market of 'women' of which this group intends to reserve the monopoly. That must be what we call to 'change politics': change it into commerce."[29]

During the July 1980 International Women's Conference in Copenhagen, eleven feminist publishers from various countries, including the small French feminist publishing house Éditions Tierce, wrote a statement condemning Psych-et-Po's registration of MLF. Three months later, in October 1980, the condemnation was circulated at the colloquium for feminist publishers at the Frankfurt Book Fair. Fouque lost no time in sending a message to Tierce and all the others who wanted to challenge her politics or her business. She sued Tierce (the only French publisher that had signed the petition), not for libel, but for *concurrence déloyale* (unfair competition). Fouque argued that Tierce's action went beyond political critique and constituted an unwarranted threat to her livelihood. *Nouvelles questions féministes* pointed out that Fouque deliberately avoided the Tribunal de grande instance (High Court of Justice), which usually dealt with thorny questions of defamation, and chose instead to sue through the Tribunal de commerce de Paris (Paris Commercial Court), which took a more cut and dried approach to commercial disputes. On June 25, 1981, Tierce was found guilty, fined 1 symbolic franc for damages and 8,000 francs to defray *des femmes'* legal costs, and was required to have the court's decision printed in three French newspapers.[30]

Feminists felt the verdict required an appropriate response. They hastily published a collection of documents, articles, and collections of quotations to build a political case against Psych-et-Po. The result, *Chroniques d'une imposture: Du mouvement de libération des femmes à une marque commercial* (Chronicles of an imposture: From the women's liberation movement to a commercial brand), could hardly be called a "book" with its lack of set type, pagination, or editor. Fouque and her supporters considered the work slanderous and cruel. Nevertheless, the collection damns the group with its own words, taken from various publications. It is left somewhat up to the reader to evaluate the—sometimes decontextualized—quotations. Its authors included the historian and philosopher Geneviève Fraisse, a member of the editorial collective of *La revue d'en face*; Marie-Jo Dhavernas, a researcher at CNRS; Nadja Ringart, a former member of Psych-et-Po; and Simone de Beauvoir, who wrote the preface:

> To face this threat, some authentic feminists, not directly implicated in the suit, have decided to bring this affair to the public's attention, so that no one may think that this is a petty quarrel only concerning a few. To reduce thousands of women to silence by claiming to speak in their place is to exercise a revolting tyranny.... This abuse is all the more intolerable given that Antoinette and her disciples claim to be enamored with social justice and to be rebelling against this world belonging to the rich and the powerful. In fact, it is their wealth that has allowed them to gain power, which has long been their only goal.[31]

The collective condemned them for using their money to "assure a monopoly over the movement," for using an identity that did not belong to them, for legally appropriating a name that was not theirs, and for infusing that name with their own peculiar doctrine.

Many women in the movement saw it as one thing for Fouque to have declared herself against the principles of the diverse feminist movement but quite another then to co-opt its name for her own use. The documentary group La Griffonne commented: "In effect, the group Psych-et-Po, owner of the corporation *des femmes*, not only itself used the gains of the movement for its own *private* commercial exploitation; but what's more, it is arming itself with legal means to attempt to prevent the same movement from appearing as it is: to use its own name."[32]

Feminists could not decide how to stop Fouque. Legal action seemed fruitless. The MLF was a political and social movement in the same way the May 1968 events had been, so there was no one group or person that could claim infringement or injury. Fouque and company had registered the association and trademark within the constraints of commercial law. But there was little talk of waging a legal fight even if there had been grounds for a legal case. That was because women in the movement remained staunchly opposed to settling their differences through the mediation of the patriarchal structures they believed maintained the status quo. They also wanted to avoid attracting ugly media attention or, as Beauvoir described it, "airing their dirty laundry in public, or giving their adversaries—male or female—the spectacle of their dissensions." But, Beauvoir also observed, this "politics of silence" did not pay off, since Psych-et-Po continued to pursue its agenda.[33]

Fouque found herself at the epicenter of a debate over "feminist excess" when she took up the defense of Jiang Qing, Mao Zedong's wife, with a full-page advertisement in *Le Monde*, headlined "Sauvez Jiang-Qing: Appel du MLF-International" ("Save Jiang-Qing: Appeal of MLF International") and signed "MLF-International," on January 15, 1981.[34] Jiang was being tried along with ten others for crimes against the Chinese state and its people. Psych-et-Po's advertisement claimed that Madame Mao was being tried by a patriarchal jury that was making her pay for her husband's crimes. Fouque's enthusiastic plunge into international politics was ridiculed by China experts and feminists in what they called Psych-et-Po's tardy and misplaced concern for Mao's wife and her collaborators. In *Le matin de Paris*, Claudie Brouyelle wondered why Fouque had not put out a call during the Cultural Revolution, when many of China's finest intellectual and cultural institutions were "cleansed" under Madame Mao's instructions: "Who protested to Jiang Qing demanding that she save Zhou Xinfang, famous actor of the Peking Opera, who slit his own throat rather than continue to submit to the tortures of his executioners?" It was Madame Mao, Brouyelle argued, who demanded that 450 million women submit to the absolute authority of one man—her husband—and that all Chinese children be considered the property of the nation and the state. Brouyelle railed against the small-mindedness of Fouque's appeal, reducing her strategy to three axioms: "1) One only allies with women; men, they're not our problem; 2) Among women, we are only interested in famous ones; 3) Among famous women, we only ally with the nice ones, the 'leftists,' the revolutionaries; in any case, those whom these ladies find nice, leftist, and revolutionary."[35] More than one writer spoke with outrage against the MLF International's praise of the Maoist motto "It is just to rebel," an expression that Mao had lifted from Stalin, who used it to justify sending political prisoners to the gulag. "If to be feminist is to encourage denunciation, deportations, and lynchings, well then I've been mistaken, I'm not feminist," the sinologist Marie-José Lalitte wrote in Le matin de Paris. "For me, feminism was a synonym for justice, today it is only a perverted word."[36]

Feminists' fear that Fouque would use the registration to defend causes with which not all women in the movement agreed was playing out in real time. From the beginning of the movement, feminists had been wary of being hijacked by the organized Left in the same way that the noncommunist Left had feared being swallowed up by the PCF decades before. In the early 1970s, feminists had discovered and expelled Trotskyist infiltrators who tried to gain influence over the movement's agenda. They also bristled at the thought that Fouque's claim on the women's movement—and the well-known MLF label— would enable her companies to sell more of their own books, journals, and other products. This prospect especially incensed them because Fouque had often attacked or ignored the name MLF and the feminist ideas the MLF had generated.[37]

Many feminists saw Fouque's words and behaviors as incompatible— for example, her speaking of inclusion and collective decision-making as she unilaterally registered the name MLF. Fouque's publications depicted a vision of harmony that downplayed the tensions and difficulties of women's liberation. Marie-Jo Dhavernas, an early participant in the movement and scholar at CNRS explained further: "The sleek, sometimes sickly sentimental, and always triumphant accounts of their practices, actions, and relations; the uniform character of the texts on top of which is the absence of a signature . . . an identical tone, texts in which the author never personally enters, dissolves itself entirely in the collective . . . no discord is apparent, no evolution, nor hesitations, nor debates, nor contradictory articles." In the end, Dhavernas concluded, Fouque found intolerable those who had another discourse of liberation: "Those who thought of liberating themselves away from the psychoanalyst's couch of Antoinette."[38]

It is difficult to evaluate certain parts of the saga leading up to 1979–1980. The history of the registration and the suit against Tierce could perhaps be viewed as an overreaction by individuals who believed themselves cornered or, as Psych-et-Po's suit alleged, attacked by a rival publisher that wanted to run them out of business. Whatever the case, the suit's result was to damage both the movement's ability to function and its image. After all, the success or failure of Fouque's publishing house would not affect the lives of most French women, and the public attention given to this conflict made feminism appear irrelevant and childish. The damage can be seen, for example, in the 1980 march, in Paris, for International Women's Day. Bad feelings over competitive preparations and reports that Psych-et-Po pushed and shoved its way to the front resulted in a split procession—much smaller than its predecessors: At its head was the Psych-et-Po contingent, composed of nearly a thousand women dressed in red and carrying banners that proclaimed, "The factory is for workers, the uterus is for women, the production of life belongs to us" (signed) "politique et psychanalyse MLF." Behind them, separated by a long gap, came, as *Les temps modernes* described it, "an incredible jumble of groups with banners, five to six thousand women, not aligned and not registered," that filled the Place Beaubourg, where the march ended.[39]

In the following years, French women who might potentially be sympathetic to the movement were instead further alienated by what appeared on the surface to be ineffective French politics. General participation in meetings and encounters fell off as the 1970s ended, and

Psych-et-Po's registration of MLF and then the electoral victory of the Socialists only accelerated the process. As all but the most institutionally affiliated women's groups became sucked into an internecine battle, feminist activists increasingly drove themselves away from the very women they claimed to defend.

"Feminism Is Political, and Politics Will Be Feminist or It Will Not Be Anything"

While a great deal of energy was consumed by militant feminists in combating the ideology and defensive swagger of Psych-et-Po, integration-oriented feminist activity of the 1970s continued along, mostly indifferent to it. France by the mid-1970s was presided over by the economically conservative but socially liberal Valéry Giscard-d'Estaing, and had witnessed an economic revival, a growth of women working outside the home, and liberal social reforms such as the liberalization of reproductive rights. Successful women professionals with political connections became more visible and assertive about their feminist politics and their desire for power as the 1970s continued.

Political women's efforts were even more significant when we consider that many of them were funneled into traditionally female domains, such as health and human services, also enduring ad hominem criticism in the press that passed for political commentary. In the 1980s, for example, Yvette Roudy would be called "a ball buster" for reintroducing the antisexism bill (commensurate with the already passed antiracism law), and Édith Cresson, who briefly served as prime minister under François Mitterrand, would be accused of having slept her way to the top. As late as 1995, under the government of Alain Juppé, the women appointed to his cabinet were referred to frequently as *les juppettes*, a play on the prime minister's name and the French word for short skirts. Women's ability to stay in the game while pushing forward a sometimes explicitly feminist agenda represented an extraordinary achievement for them and for feminists' ability to legitimize their cause in France.[40]

Gisèle Halimi and her group Choisir proved to be potent and long-lasting allies of the independent women's movement. She and her group's efforts are perhaps the best example of the positive intersection of materialist feminist theory and integration-oriented practice. While her strategy was pragmatic, she was unafraid of radical analysis and cutting criticism, and since she was not beholden to any organization larger than Choisir itself, she maintained a fiery independence. Choisir had started as a legal defense team, but it grew in the years after the Manifesto of the 343 into a combination of tough political lobbyist and legal watchdog, with Halimi fighting every test case on abortion and rape she could. By mid-decade, Choisir claimed to have ten thousand members, and it announced that its slogan for 1976 would be "From physical freedom to economic independence."[41] It had widened its objectives to encompass the full inclusion of women in social, political, and economic life; the elimination of rape and spousal abuse; and the adoption of other "cultural schemas" to replace destructive myths about women—in other words, the making good her claim that "feminism is political, and politics will be feminist or it will not be anything."[42] Far from retreating once the Veil law was passed, Choisir extended its demand for "the autonomy of women's bodies" to other realms of social action. It suggested that economic independence was "the essential condition for real social insertion" and broader independence and that women had to be incorporated into the productive realms of society. Choisir spoke out against pornography and inflexible gender roles in private and public life. Halimi successfully wove these battles together with her court cases as she defended abortionists or rape victims while demonstrating the essentially discriminatory nature of the current law.[43]

Choisir's strategy was to use institutions and the legal system to create real social change for women: to teach them how to grow their own rice, as Halimi often quoted from a Chinese proverb, rather than giving them a rice bowl. The group did not favor supporting one political party over another; in fact, Halimi had railed against all the parties for discriminating against women and not taking women's problems seriously. But Halimi had an appreciation for political power and saw women's liberation in concrete terms. A cartoon in the Choisir newspaper in July 1976 showed a woman being dragged by her hair by a man with a club. She says: "Freedom is a meaningless word when the means to assume it are lacking." He responds: "What are you complaining about? I love you."[44]

A few months before the March 1978 legislative elections, Choisir launched the Women's Common Program, a campaign to elect women who were dedicated to feminist concerns. "Politics is too serious a thing to be left to men alone," Halimi stated in the introduction to the published version of the Women's Common Program. One of the Women's Common Program candidates, Geneviève Pastre, suggested that the program was intended as much to "upset things" as to gain access to the lawmaking power structure. By February 1978, *Le Monde* reported that Choisir was in the process of amassing one hundred candidates on an independent list entitled Choisir la cause des femmes (Choose the Cause of Women). Consistent with the group's strategy, it refused to align itself with one particular party; rather, it presented its own program and urged the parties to follow it. "It's for the Left and the Right to say if the program that we present is a program of the Left or Right," Halimi remarked to *L'humanité* the day after Choisir's official presentation of its program.[45] The program included twelve proposals for legal reform, such as equality in marriage law, salaried parental leave, a more stringent pay-equity law to replace the ineffective 1972 and 1975 laws, and a law requiring an equal gender balance in criminal court juries.[46] Halimi's responses during the press conference introducing the program show her profound faith in the law as the final arbiter of change. "We are neither marginals, nor fanatics, nor crackpots. We are the living force of this country," she said. When asked her opinion about a ministry of women, she commented optimistically, "The women's ministry doesn't have to be a perpetual institution, it only has to last four or five years: the time it takes for women, who have always been in a disadvantaged position, to catch up to men."[47]

Throughout the election, Choisir fiercely maintained its independence, arguing that if it took up the banner of any one party "even while defending our program, we would be obligated in the case of conflicts between the interest of women and the interest of the larger politics to choose the political interest, in other words, to sacrifice the interests of women. But we want to act in complete liberty." Choisir also vowed to maintain the political separatism that had been a hallmark of the movement since the 1970s and refused to allow male candidates to run under its banner. "A man should not defend the program," Halimi asserted. "That he supports it, yes, but he should not speak for our real lives." Choisir sought to avoid becoming entangled in traditional party politics, she said, because in that arena personal power and the seduction of the electorate came as much into play as ideas and policies. If Choisir remained in an adversarial relationship to power, she concluded, the group would be able to speak out more freely.[48] But even Halimi's equivocal position regarding French politics had to be explained to many feminists. She admitted that it was risky to fight the system from within rather than from outside, but she explained that she could not wait for "the great eve of the Revolution" or "the rosy future." She understood the essential difficulty of utopian movements: that people live in the present and want to be able to experience change. As she wrote, "We know our power, and we women will use it and all its weight, to change centuries of women's condition. We also think that our final objectives are beyond and even elsewhere, but it appears impossible to us not to search to master lucidly today the infernal machinery in which we are trapped. In order to slow down the machine, to stop it, to put it on another track, we must not be completely outside it."[49]

In fact, it seemed that Halimi had little love for any of the political parties, Left or Right. *Le Monde* quoted her deriding them all in turn: The extreme Right, she said, believed "women are the noblest conquest of man." "The reformers" had created a secretariat of the feminine condition without giving it money to do anything, and the Left held that the future "is only created by the hand of men and women's patience." Yet despite her critiques, Halimi elicited praise from across the political spectrum. Georges Marchais published a letter to her in *L'humanité* declaring that the Communist electoral list would include 188 women, "more than all the other parties combined." This letter was intended for a wider audience, but it shows that Halimi and her feminist ideals were deemed worthy of acknowledgement and even support, if only superficially.[50]

Nevertheless, as the legislative campaigns heated up, Choisir faced an internal crisis that almost sent it the way of most other feminist groups. Several members of the organization and the executive committee tried to unseat Halimi, accusing her of creating a "Stalinist" rather than a "sisterly" structure and of having abandoned "the fundamental objectives of Choisir." They claimed that she no longer supported its larger goal of fighting for women's full participation in economic, political, social, and cultural life and that the group's journal had "fewer and fewer articles stimulating feminist reflection and action" (and that its price had tripled). They also charged that militants had not been encouraged to participate in decision making and that "the initiatives of regional coordinators had not been systematically encouraged." These women and their supporters had felt for years that they and other grassroots activists had done all the work of organizing protests and disseminating information only to see Halimi grab the spotlight and the reins. "We were never consulted to see if we agreed with the type of defense chosen," read one tract released during the decisive Bobigny court case seven years before.[51] The fact that Halimi was an experienced attorney and that she had won the case was, however, not lost on many of her supporters.

Halimi's troubles demonstrate a widespread distrust of authoritative women who had institutional power, as their behavior was viewed as a replication of the male authority that feminists rejected so strongly. Yet complaints voiced by Halimi's detractors also seemed directed against the force of her personality and her desire to shape the movement in line with her plans and expectations. "We refuse to substantiate the idea that feminism in France can be reduced to a monopoly of a few personalities," the opposition faction stated. In an open letter, they explained that they "would like to institute a democratic decision-making process not founded on relations of power and hierarchy like those practiced in the majority of institutions in today's society."[52] But Halimi, having weathered what seemed like much greater challenges in her own life and in the French courts, was not to be easily sidelined. She accused her would-be usurpers of trying to divide and conquer and of paralyzing the movement by sectarianism. The women resigned after much rumor and bad feeling, and Halimi managed to return to the political tasks at hand, commenting that had the faction really been concerned with democratic processes, they would have broached the problem in a general meeting of Choisir and worked to come to an agreement rather than act so divisively.[53]

Conflicts aside, Choisir's "Choose the Cause of Women" had little direct political success in electing the female candidates on the list. In the elections held between March 12 and 19, 1978, almost all its candidates lost in the first round. The forty-four candidates remaining received a little over 31,000 votes in total, which translated into just 1 percent of all votes nationwide. Nevertheless, Choisir continued to fight for its program. It proposed, for example, eliminating the distinction between rape and indecent assault; implementing the Swedish model of parental leave, in which both parents could share child-care responsibility for two years; and adding sanctions to the equal employment laws of 1972 and 1975 to force compliance. It also attacked government policies such as a proposal to reopen houses of prostitution. The Common Program's success also was mixed. The Communists delivered on their promise, producing the largest number of elected women among all the parties. In contrast, as *Le matin* magazine noted, "The Socialists, who didn't count among themselves one elected woman, refused to take such a 'risk,' offering the open seats to their young male pets such as Pierre Guidoni or Laurent Fabius, but never to women."[54]

The Women's Ministry

Feminists had reason to believe a fully engaged, integration-oriented strategy would be most effective. Leftist parties increasingly sought women's support through platforms invoking feminist issues. In 1978 the PS officially acknowledged that "feminism is neither a particular theme nor localized preoccupation, nor is it a series of categorical demands. It is nothing other than women's struggle against discrimination, oppression, and overexploitation to which they are subject because of their sex."[55] The same year, Georges Marchais declared his Communist Party's commitment to women's promotion: "It is the honor of our parliamentary group to be the only ones to have presented a bill entitled 'For the woman: equality, freedom, promotion at work, the family, and society.'" And he added, "If the Giscardian majority was not opposed to it because of their politics of austerity and democracy's limitations, many of these questions would have been resolved years ago." Marchais might boast, but in terms of feminist politics, the PCF had much to answer for in terms of a real commitment to feminist politics, and this was the contradiction that integration-oriented feminists sought to eradicate. A *Cahiers du féminisme* issue accused the CGT (the largest national trade union) of ridiculing feminists, quoting them calling feminists "hysterical, petit-bourgeois, dividing the working class" and, worse, accusing the CGT of allowing their security forces to violently expel feminists from their protest marches.[56] Such statements clearly showed that the Socialist and Communist parties would benefit from feminist reform.

"The women's struggle," Gisèle Halimi wrote, "is the most important event at the end of this century."[57] The fact that so many—from MLF militants to the French government—were trying to define feminism shows that by the second half of the 1970s, women's liberation had been accepted as a political and ideological force in contemporary society. Moreover, the years between 1977 and 1981, which coincided with municipal, legislative, and presidential elections, were considered critical by any feminist who understood the direct impact of the country's politics on French women. This period was all the more important as there was a growing hope among leftists that the PS would win in both local and national elections. Thus, early in 1977, when the Programme commun de la gauche (Common Program of the Left)—a coalition of the PS, PC, and the Mouvement des radicaux de gauche (Radical Leftist Movement)—won a majority of municipal elections, certain feminist groups began to consider an integration-oriented and mainstream strategy that would bring the Left to power and give feminists some influence once it was there. Choisir, for example, devised its own political program to embody its independent engagement with the political system and to demand changes for women's rights. "It is not the feminine commission of any political party," Halimi remarked to *Le quotidien de Paris* in October 1977. "If Choisir is independent, however, it is not apolitical." Adding to this rapprochement, the Left had begun to change its aggressive posture vis-à-vis women militants as it became evident that women might put the Left over the top. Both the PCF and the PS elaborated their own "feminist ideology." The Organisation communiste gauche ouvrière et populaire (Popular Communist Workers and Leftist Organization), for example, devoted a whole issue of *Cahier pour le communisme* to women's issues ranging from the double day to sexual harassment in the workplace, headlining the issue "Women, Exploited and Oppressed, Dare to Struggle."[58]

The older generation of leftist party women such as Audry (then on the executive committee of the PS) and Eyquem, as well as Roudy, Halimi, Édith Cresson, and Hugette Bouchardeau (who ran for president in 1981 on the Parti socialiste unifié's ticket), felt that having the Left in power would benefit women's liberation. "A party that wants to come to power by universal suffrage must ask itself how the Right retains women in their camp," Bouchardeau wrote in 1980.[59] Without women's votes for the Right, she argued, Mitterrand would have beaten de Gaulle in 1965 and Giscard in 1974, and the Left would have won the legislative elections of 1978.

The Socialist Party found it gained supporters by expanding the definition of "working class" beyond its original constituency of male industrial workers to include the growing ranks of female workers, who, despite their reputation for being indifferent to "bourgeois" feminism, generally supported the ideals of women's liberation. Employed women were more likely than unemployed women to become politically active as a result of trade union activities in their workplaces. In the 1970s the rapid expansion of the service sector and the proportional increase of low-wage industrial jobs filled largely by female labor dovetailed with new feminist analyses of women's subordination.[60] Working women often felt a double insecurity—anxiety caused by the French recession coupled with the knowledge that they were economically disadvantaged because of their sex. These very real material inequalities nourished support for feminism. In 1970, among the more than six million salaried women in France, industrial workers and employees earned 33 to 45 percent less than men in the same or comparable jobs. By 1976, when the recession had dug in, the CGT found that 75 percent of working women earned less than 2,500 francs per month, a relatively small salary. This disparity occurred despite the law of December 22, 1972, which guaranteed equal pay for equal work. Moreover, 40 percent of women lived alone and relied on their own relatively weak earning power to support themselves.[61] Between 1968 and 1975, the gap between women's and men's economic prospects grew larger. While the number of skilled male workers rose 17.3 percent during this time, the skilled female workforce dropped by 6.1 percent. In contrast, the number of unskilled male laborers diminished by 10.7 percent while the number of their female counterparts rose 27.7 percent. One study found that women accounted for 82 percent of unemployed persons under the age of twenty-five. Working women also became more convinced that the improvement of their economic and social position would not come from mere loyalty to the Communists or their unions. Women themselves would have to articulate the problem and formulate their own solutions and demands.[62]

Beginning in 1971, women went on strike at various factories to demand higher pay and better working conditions, but the resulting political message was disproportionately larger than their immediate gains. Striking women workers did not always claim allegiance to the MLF nor to feminism, but their demands and their statements erased any doubt that they were part of a broad women's movement. In *Les messagères* (The messengers), an account of working-class women and their independent struggles, Evelyne Le Garrec wrote that "women today want to define the battle themselves, from their own experience, refusing to copy their point of view and their demands from men's, and to feign a belief in the idea that only one legitimate point of view exists for all workers."[63]

Before 1968, workers who went on strike were mostly skilled, white, French adult males. After 1968, strikers were as likely to be women or immigrants, often young and unskilled. During the long strike at the Lip watch factory in Besançon in 1973, for example, women strikers gradually began to take organizing roles, publishing a brochure, *Lip au féminin* (Women's lip), and urging other working women to articulate their grievances about the double day and the lack of promotion to technical and scientific positions. While many working women may not have wanted to identify themselves as feminists, when they began to organize they articulated their claims in feminist terms. Women's sense of injustice was heightened when managers encouraged the view that striking women workers who occupied factories were licentious—as, for example, during a strike at a Peugeot factory, when managers reported that it was being "transformed into a brothel." When women workers adopted feminist positions, organized support structures were already in place: committees, bureaus, and journals within unions as well as within the Socialist and Communist parties. Women strikers ultimately were instrumental in creating feminist pressure groups within unions.[64] For example, union women lobbied hard to place women on the political map and managed to do so in the accord signed between the Confédération française démocratique du travail (French Democratic Confederation of Labor) and the CGT on December 19, 1974. Both union confederations officially agreed to try to eliminate wage discrimination by reworking professional classifications, to push for the enforcement of the equal pay for equal work law, and to offer more information on promotions and other employment possibilities to women. The accord also included demands for better, more affordable child care; education for girls and boys that was less sexist; and more opportunities for women's professional training.

By 1977 the CGT had begun to show greater interest in the status of working women, in part because of orders from the PCF, but also because of continuing pressure from women trade-unionists. At the sixth National Conference of Female Employees of the CGT, the "feminist question" was high on the agenda. The secretary of the CGT, Jean-Louis Moynot, denounced "the ideology of men's superiority."[65] The Socialists, with their rhetoric of *autogestion* and personal liberation, seemed to capture the spirit of change for many feminists, particularly young women. As the oil crisis, inflation, and deindustrialization swept over France in the 1970s, and as right-wing governments remained wedded to *dirigiste* (state-managed) economic policies that were less and less efficacious, the Left's program of *autogestion* led by the Socialists grew in popularity. The autogestionist ideal implicitly included an expanded conception of individualism and, hence, of women's rights and freedoms, which had the potential of attracting more women to the party.[66]

The mutual courtship that went on between self-proclaimed feminists and the Socialist and Communist parties during the last years of the decade was both delicate and stormy. One of the low points in the Left's relationship with the feminists occurred in 1978, when the Communists, refusing to play handmaiden to the Socialists (whose municipal candidates it had helped to elect a year before) and frustrated with the lack of progress on the nationalization of industries, backed out of the Common Program, and the Left lost the hotly contested and strategically important legislative elections. This failure confirmed for some that the strategy employed by integration-oriented feminists of kowtowing to institutional politics was no guarantee of a successful election. Roudy acknowledged that many feminists mistrusted the Socialist Party's embrace of feminism. "To say that we didn't communicate is an amiable way of saying that we detested each other cordially," Roudy remembers, referring to what she called the *pures et dures* (hard-line) women in the movement who saw Roudy and other feminists in the Socialist and Communist parties as traitors. Even though more women had faith in leftist parties and were willing to give them a vote of confidence, some feminists refused to lend their support because it seemed obvious that feminism was being used as a campaign tactic to be employed or abandoned according to its immediate usefulness.[67] The parties' leadership did include more women in their ranks and absorbed certain feminist demands, but this did not have much effect on the parties' structure, and there were feminists who had left the parties because of unequal treatment. Replicating the May 1968 hierarchies, party men encouraged women to be foot soldiers but were, for the most part, still unwilling to accept them in the executive bureaus, where real decisions were made. Those who were brought in, remembers Françoise Gaspard (who at the time was a member of the management committee of the PS executive bureau), were expected to stay silent.[68]

After the Left lost the legislative elections of 1978, many feminists regretted any lack of support. As an editorial in the Marxist feminist *Cahiers du féminisme* put it, "No one in the women's movement had thought that the [voting] urns would end our oppression; but many had considered that a leftist victory would signify new potential" and that "Feminism could impose itself as a fundamental given of the class struggle." *Politique hebdo*, the weekly newspaper of the LCR, pointed out that the results should be a lesson to the movement that "ambiguity doesn't pay. . . . When Gisèle Halimi says 'politics will be feminist or it won't,' we could retort, 'feminism will be political or it won't.'" Halimi agreed. Choisir's ultimate willingness to support the Socialists was pragmatic.[69] In legislative and municipal elections small parties had some chance, but in presidential elections they had none. In April 1981, before the presidential election, Halimi invited all the presidential candidates to a forum entitled "Which President for Women?" to discuss their commitment to women voters and to feminist issues. Françoise Parturier, writer and editorialist, led the discussion. Only Mitterrand chose to participate in the forum itself, and his speech and his answers to questions were published in a brochure under the same title. Mitterrand used the event as an opportunity to demonstrate his faith in the female electorate and to attack the male-dominated power politics that he knew feminists stood against. Here is one of his replies to the question of balancing women's reproductive and productive labor that received a rousing applause:

> A "housewife salary" is not a good way to approach the issue of women in the labor force. . . . Admittedly, I say . . . that a woman who . . . has a child, who must take care of his/her education . . . we can very well admit that it takes time for that, and therefore there should be remuneration for it. But the idea of a "housewife's salary" is a notion that seems to me dangerous, as it isolates women from the society in which they live, and basically, it is a means—for I cannot imagine that this remuneration would be considerable—it is a low-cost means of getting rid of women in the labor market.[70]

Through the voice of Mitterrand, the Socialists no longer seemed mired in class analysis, but as a party of new ideas and programs, the best hope of feminists.

In a stunning about-face, Psych-et-Po also decided to support Mitterrand in 1981. Its statement of support conscientiously appealed to women's pragmatism: "The heart says, no candidate for women. Reason says, Mitterrand's program in the primaries to be sure to win in the general election." The group's reasoning revealed a pragmatism similar to that of other groups.[71] Even the radical feminists of the renamed *Nouvelles questions féministes* (New feminist issues) journal were willing to allow the ends to justify the means by supporting the Socialists, but they were far more cynical about it. In an editorial soon after the election they explained: "We hoped for the victory of the Left without illusion about its feminism or socialism, but in order to reconquer spaces of struggle that were reduced under Giscard. . . . One of the aims of the movement is to obtain reforms in the short term."[72] By 1981 many more women had turned a corner and were willing to help bring the Left to power despite its shortcomings. As Colette Audry, who had committed herself to the cause, remarked, "The fact that socialism today is a dream should not prevent us from struggling for its implementation."[73]

Simone de Beauvoir credited Roudy with never renouncing feminism in the tough world of political gamesmanship. As a result, she brought many women to support the Socialists and was able to extract assurances from the party, for example that it would create a ministry of women with more clout, authority, and funds than its predecessors. "To change women's lives is to change everyone's, and this is at the center of socialism," Roudy concluded in *La femme en marge* (Women on the margins), her 1975 analysis of women's status and the ways to change it, for which François Mitterrand wrote the preface. Roudy argued that capitalism, the family as a societal institution, and men themselves were responsible for women's oppression, and new attitudes and behaviors would only come about through awkward struggle, slow reform, and women's full participation in the political process. The feminist strategy within the Socialist Party was to force the party to recognize women's problems and to act on them. But beyond this,

Roudy recalls, "We had to make feminism recognized as a coherent criticism of the world, as a cultural current, a fact of advancing civilization ... fulfilling the Socialist ideal ... to struggle against inequalities, to support progress, and to view feminism as humanism."[74] For other groups, including the Ligue du droit des femmes and MLAC, however, support came only after a good deal of soul searching. Hugette Bouchardeau, for example, felt the need to address the apparent contradiction between party politics and feminism in the first pages of her memoirs. "Is there a contradiction between my conviction of the necessity of an autonomous women's movement and my attachment to a political struggle begun a while ago?" she wrote. "No," she decided, "because no structure or movement is perfectly adapted to the problems that we [feminists and Socialists] pose." Roudy attributed this kind of turnaround to the force of good campaigning.[75]

Giscard, however, seemed fairly confident of winning another term in 1981, aided by his profeminist record. Feminists therefore believed they had to make a more convincing argument to the female electorate if they wanted to see the conservatives out of office. Toward election time, Giscard pushed harder for policies aimed at attracting women's votes—for example, proposing to reserve 20 percent of the places on municipal ballots for women (a proposition that the Left and the Right both objected to for opposite reasons)—and continued to appoint women to subministerial positions. His adversaries interpreted these actions as paternalist, not feminist, and were quick to take public note. "We have a strong tradition on the French Right," Halimi said in an interview with *The Guardian*. "You can see it in the Pétain regime and in modern Gaullism—of exaggerated deference to the family, which has always resulted in ruthless suppression of women."[76] Increasing numbers of women seemed to agree with her.

In the euphoria of Socialist victory, the Ministry of Women (Ministre déléguée aux droits de la femme), under Roudy's direction, did tap into the realism expressed by feminist electioneering. Right from the start, the new ministry was an improvement over the old secrétariat during Giscard's tenure. Provided with its own substantial budget, the ministry was expected to produce substantive results for women:

improved integration in the public sphere and better protection in the private. It was suggested that the ministry would actually be able to initiate changes in society at large and perhaps serve as a rallying point for feminists. Many feminists objected to its name, however. "*De la femme*" implied the abstract notion of "womankind" from which feminists had tried to escape. They were expecting the title to be constructed with "*des* femmes" ("women"), or all individual women in France. Pragmatists shrugged off the name, too elated by the ministry's potential. Radical feminists assumed that the anachronistic name was a presentiment of future relations between government and feminists. Would the Left really be "our land of birth and liberation," as Psych-et-Po had described it in its election posters?[77] Indeed, in the two years following Mitterrand's election in 1981, during which the government did *not* make the transformation of women's position in society a top priority, radical feminists came to believe their cynicism was well-founded. After all, a decade earlier, women participating in leftist parties and organizations had become radicalized because of the sexism of their male cohorts.

An antisexism bill, which sought to equalize punishment for sexism and racism, failed to pass despite acceptance from the Council of Ministers. Adapted from the 1972 antiracism law, it would have made discrimination against women subject to legal challenge. Cries of reverse sexism helped defeat the bill, much as Phyllis Schlafly's campaign helped defeat the Equal Rights Amendment in the United States around the same time. As Éliane Viennot argued in *Nouvelles questions féministes* in the autumn of 1981, men see "women" as a large abstract bloc, living in more or less equality to men, because they only see women's *capacity* for equality and not their actual equal authority. Then, she argued, men point to the few exceptions of women in power to defend the idea that women have already achieved equality. "Feminism," Viennot concluded, "is turned into a *discourse* on women, emptied of substance."[78] The ministry provided yet another reminder of how discourse could be a far cry from political or material reality. In 1986 the Right swept back to legislative victory without much of a nod to women's causes and with women representing a mere 6 percent of candidates in the two conservative parties, the Union pour la démocratie française (Union for French Democracy) and the Rassemblement pour la république (Rally for the Republic). Mitterrand began the arduous road of sharing power with the Right, and women's equality in society became the least of his worries.[79]

By the mid-1980s feminism was no longer the politics of the moment, and for feminists that was a painful reality. Halimi's struggles at Choisir and a lack of broad-based support for Choisir from women in the mainstream was just one symptom of this trend, demonstrating the entrenched interests that independent feminism was up against. Faced with competition from identity politics, separatism, internal conflicts, and the authority of the Socialist Party, Halimi's Choisir would lose its role as the leading force in the women's movement, a role that in the years leading up to the 1981 election it had seemed destined to play. The feminist movement had produced indisputable changes in French society, both concrete as well as ideological, from tighter laws on rape and assault to reduced tolerance for unequal pay scales. New women's publishing companies, women's centers, advocacy groups, and programs had sprung up. But the movement was in disarray. Its primary identity—namely the formerly unregistered Mouvement de libération des femmes, around which diverse feminist groups could rally—had been taken from it, and many feminists were exhausted by internal conflicts and uphill political battles. Only with the coming of age of a new generation at the end of the 1990s—one focused on widening the scope of women's rights to address issues of race and immigration as well as class, the renewed threat to reproductive rights, and the Left's increasing electoral losses—would the feminist movement begin to revive in France.

NOT A CONCLUSION

*The Socialist Party's Ascendancy and
French Feminism's Second Wave*

There exists a contradiction between the demand for universality in
a democratic society and the need for the legislator of today to create
a legal environment capable of eliminating specific discrimination of
which women are still the object. A growing feminine presence within
the politics of a country will resolve it.

Christine Fauré, *La démocratie sans les femmes* (Democracy without
women) (1985)

On May 10, 1981, François Mitterrand was elected president of the
French Republic. During the inauguration ceremonies on May 21, he
paraded down the Champs Elysées and then to the Panthéon, where
he paid homage to the memory of Socialist leader Jean Jaurès and
Resistance leader Jean Moulin. After twenty-five years of the Right in
power, French supporters of the Left burst into celebration. A month
later, the Left won again with the election of a new National Assembly in which the Socialists occupied the majority of seats—270 deputies out of 491, with the Communists claiming another 44. In the
next eight months the new government abolished the death penalty,
implemented a tax on large fortunes, began the process of nationaliz-
ing key industries and banks, and initiated a long-term plan of government decentralization.[1] Despite such notable signs of change, many
feminists eyed the new administration with suspicion, wary that the
Socialist Party's preelection interest in feminism would not translate

into a postelection commitment to feminism and its goals. In part they were right, and yet feminism had already transformed the laws, politics, and social morays of France.

In its first years Roudy's ministry attacked sexism and paternalism and enshrined more reforms in law. It established programs to improve women's education and professional training, initiated a new campaign to promote contraception and responsible sex education, and formally encouraged women to pursue degrees in male-dominated disciplines. It made abortion reimbursable, not through the public health system but through a special fund (a compromise with the conservatives); it established equality between the sexes in controlling their joint finances; and it funded women's advocacy organizations and a published guide to women's rights. Roudy and her team also began a long crusade for an antisexism bill and activated a discussion of France's deeply held prejudices against women's equality. Together with Halimi and Choisir, the ministry managed to force another revision of the Penal Code (in July 1982) that equalized civil rights between homosexuals and heterosexuals and spearheaded the first professional equality law in France, enacted in 1983. The "Roudy law" promoted negotiations between companies and trade unions to increase women's equal access to positions and promotions.[2]

Important as they were, many of these reforms were not fully elaborated. In the case of the Roudy Law, for example, hardly any company enacted regulations promoting equality and unions actually fought against them. In the French tradition of splitting the difference between universalism and particularism, the law did reaffirm the concept of "equal value" of work (plugging a loophole of the 1972 Equal Pay Act) and squashed the "legitimate grounds" provision for refusing women certain jobs or creating jobs to privilege one sex over the other. It did not, however, entirely remove "special provisions" regulations on night work, for example, which it maintained for the health of women, children, and the family. Referring to this law as part of the Socialist initiative of "symbolic reform," Amy Mazur suggests that the Socialist government was able to make very little change while claiming to make significant advances in women's rights, and, in fact, the Roudy law resulted in very few improvements to women's employment.[3] Nevertheless, Roudy was a dynamic politician and fought to make her ministry as visible and effective as possible. The ministry and its work was a far cry from the paternalism of the postwar period.

The feminism of the 1970s had been an aberration in France's feminist history, as anomalous as Beauvoir's *Second Sex* had been when it appeared in Paris in 1949. Both argued for an egalitarian world in which the independence and potential of both sexes would be accorded equal weight and in which men and women could construct a new era. Such ideas were based on a reappraisal of rights in French society, an appraisal at odds with the sensibility of a country that was concerned primarily with women's responsibilities rather than their freedoms. Most postwar advocates for the women's cause had been willing to accept an assessment of women's independence that was contingent on the expectations of French society. Feminists in the 1970s were not. So, when early in Mitterrand's administration he named Yvette Roudy as minister of women's rights, feminists were anxious to know to what extent Roudy would choose a path of accommodation trod by earlier generations of politicians who had taken up "the women's cause" within government.

Would integration into the power structure serve the feminist cause? Many feminist activists were faced with a decision their comrades had predicted: should they compromise on issues of fairness or justice or risk being shut out of influential positions altogether? This fundamental philosophical dilemma of the women's liberation movement was not resolved by the 1980s. I have argued that, ultimately, it was the integration-oriented feminists who managed this contradiction best, pushing the feminist agenda ahead by addressing the concrete needs of French women while insisting on an explicitly feminist vision.

Because of French society's entrenched sexism, as well as the robust political legacy of the French Left, the women's cause in France had a history of pragmatism that made French women much more receptive to the arguments of groups such as Choisir and the Ligue du droit des femmes, for example, than to the self-referential arguments of Psych-et-Po. The women's liberation movement, from its inception in the wake of the 1968 events to its ministerial debut in the Socialist government in 1981, had managed to nullify a century of pronatalist policies. It had created greater access to advanced education, to professional schools, and to traditionally male disciplines and professions; it had helped narrow the gap between male and female salaries; and it had succeeded in creating a legal system more favorable to women's independence, changing laws governing everything from reproduction to child care. To be sure, economic and social factors in France were moving in the direction of greater parity for women. More equal education and professional experience increasingly became the norm, and the family headed by a single male wage-earner became a social dinosaur. But a quick glance at the legislation passed between 1970 and 1985 shows feminist success in concrete measures that pushed for equal opportunity, from marital law reforms in the early 1970s to the 1980 law that updated the legal definition of rape and made it easier to prosecute accused attackers.[4]

Pragmatic and gradualist approaches within the political structure yielded the most concrete results, yet French radical feminism made an extraordinary contribution. It crystalized the terms of the debate and forced it into the public eye. Simone de Beauvoir, Andrée Michel, and Christine Delphy, for example, analyzed society with an unprecedented rigor, leveling uncompromising criticism and articulating women's oppression and the mechanisms that engaged it. Without these women, the feminist movement may not have emerged at all—or the women's cause would have remained a shallow, theoretically stunted collection of demands for equality. It is also true, however, that too much theorizing at the expense of inclusiveness and tolerance diminished feminism's successes. Marxist feminists and radical feminists rarely saw eye to eye on the source of women's oppression and, more significantly, many women from small-town France did not identify with feminism, in part because it was intellectual and urban. This profound antipathy—an antipathy mirrored in the United States and Britain by the same social class over similar cultural issues—limited the movement to large urban centers and mostly to middle-class women.

If many participants in the French women's movement seemed obsessed by theory and by "femininity," it is due in part to the complexity of French history. Some women engaged in "feminine writing" and embraced "femininity" or tried to reclaim it on their terms, while many feminists assailed it as the very root of oppression and of inequality. Women writers such as Luce Irigaray argued that repositioning the cultural values of "woman" was the only way to free women from the psychological value-system of the patriarchy; other feminists, such as Christine Delphy, argued in contrast that women's "femininity" historically had been used, in law and social convention, to constrain women to a biological destiny and a special sphere of influence. Such conflicting interpretations drove the two sides to greater antipathy and isolation. In short, questions of gender were particularly loaded for the French because of their country's history and culture, and they often presented an insurmountable barrier to women who found themselves on opposing sides.

It has been the intention of this study to restore the history of French feminism as an intellectual and political movement to its material roots as well as to clarify the label "French feminism." For what mattered most about feminism *in France* was not philosophy and theory but the ideas and actions of a fiercely political movement and the material and cultural changes that movement wrought. Just as the May 1968 events transformed French society, so did the feminist movement. During the 1970s feminism established new foundations for rebellion that permanently affected the way in which politicians framed their appeals to the electorate. It influenced the way the Right confronted women's inferior position in society and the way the Left analyzed women's oppression and sought to end it. Many feminists' experience in leftist parties and cells and in the anticolonization movement made them fluent in Marxist and anti-imperialist theory and able to manipulate and expand upon that theory to analyze the relationship between forms of labor, power, and authority more fully.

Despite considerable political and theoretical conflict, feminism of the 1970s marked a turning point in French culture. The expectations and demands of a generation of women permanently transformed the fabric of society—the ways men and women viewed themselves and engaged with each other. Feminist ideology permeated popular consciousness, winning broad acceptance of the notions that women's work should be respected and made equal to men's; that women need not tolerate being molested on a subway, or, in contrast, have to guard their virginity like a prize; and that women could expect to be treated as the intellectual and professional equals of men. Feminist criticism undermined previously unquestioned social behaviors and attitudes, forcing French society to reappraise and, often, to modify or discard them.

At the same time, what makes French feminism unusual is that many economic reforms passed in the wake of feminist activism in the postwar period followed in France's paternalist tradition—what the government called "measures to reinforce the social protection of women" or "measures to reconcile employment and other life priorities of women." The reforms were based not on 1970s feminist beliefs in the basic sameness between men and women or in women as separate individuals but rather on a pragmatic assessment of women's difference and their existence within families. During this period, increasing numbers of women worked outside the home while still bearing most of the responsibility for household maintenance and child care. Rather than pass legislation such as parental leave that assumed men partook equally in domestic labor (and encouraged their doing so), the French chose to officially recognize the social inequality and to compensate women for it with benefits such as maternity leave.[5] Thus feminists waged an uphill battle for equality and social change against laws that doled out incentives to women in traditional roles while at the same time giving lip service to women's "full insertion in society." Feminist criticism of this paternalism was not popular because these laws appealed to many women who either accepted or acquiesced to traditional gender roles.

Feminist criticism also called into question the ideological framework of the Left and permanently altered it. For over a century, radical French politics were founded on the critique of the social relations of production. The great social struggle was said to be between the traditional classes of labor and capital, with women belonging to one or the other, and if any critique of the relations between the sexes emerged, it was prudently shelved for the period after the revolution. Feminists expanded that debate to include the social relations of reproduction. The private sphere, which for the most part had been overlooked as a site of discrimination and oppression, became the focus of a critique that tore at the very essence of the way human beings organized their world. Andrée Michel once remarked that "thanks to women's analysis of their specific oppression, they demystified an economic science that only took into consideration market production and mystified all others."[6] Feminists did not revolutionize party programs or doctrine (much to Marxist feminists' disappointment), yet, conversely, they did force political parties to acknowledge women's claims to justice. In the French Left, this was no small task.

Feminism also helped break down the traditional structure of French society, which had long separated the private from the public sphere. "Perhaps more than in any other major country in the world," the historian Karen Offen wrote, "French women have regularly been accorded recognition by men as being vastly powerful and influential, even as they were being stripped of institutional power. This immediately puts French women in a different position with reference to politics and power than they occupy in cultures that render women invisible or that immobilize them far more successfully."[7] As a result, French women's expectations vis-à-vis their own society have been especially complex. They have willingly embraced, and indeed have been indoctrinated with, the belief in universalist principles to which they have been encouraged to aspire. At the same time, they have been thrown back on the fact of their sex by being denied the fruits of those same ideals. The French historian Mona Ozouf exposed this contradiction when she quoted George Sand as saying, "There is only one sex," implying that women invested meaning in a standard they believed transcended male or female. But Sand's statement obscures half the story. That other half finds, for example, the president of Simone de Beauvoir's *agrégation* jury recounting that, although it gave Jean-Paul Sartre first place and Beauvoir second, "everybody agreed that, of the two, she was the real philosopher." Yet they reasoned that "he was the *normalien* [male student] and, besides, he was taking [the exam] for the second time." Unstated, but clearly understood, was that women were expected to settle for second place. Men and women might both have agreed that French culture and politics were universal, but they did so by deliberately accepting their particular positions.[8] In this intentionally constructed world where women's seductive qualities and intrinsic beauty were valorized while men ran the show, feminism demanded an account. The movement not only encouraged women's release from subordination in the private sphere and attendant service to men, it also gained acceptance for the notion that men should share power and time in both the public and private spheres. Perhaps most important, feminists defeated men in their attempt to keep the private sphere off limits from political criticism.[9]

Last, feminists helped create a new terrain of political engagement. The slogan of the 1970s movement, "the personal is political," opened the realm of the private to political analysis and established a parallel field of battle. Casting off traditional party scenarios of a utopian future and inherited prescriptions for revolution, feminists argued that women themselves could better speak of their oppression and likewise should be the sole interlocutors of their liberation. In a few short years, the Right became hard-pressed to invoke women's maternal instinct without recognizing women as individuals, and the Left abandoned its paternalist tone in appealing to women's good nature and asking them to sacrifice their needs for the good of the revolution. The fiction that socialism would bring an end to women's oppression by men had thinned to the point of transparency. Although "the personal is political" proved to be the most useful theoretical tool for unmasking women's second-class status in society, it could also encourage an almost boundless solipsism. When personal behavior became synonymous with politics, this field of battle could rapidly shrink to individual experience. "Far from being a guarantee of authenticity," the political scientist and MLF participant Françoise Picq noted, "the subjective approach opened a field of partiality, dishonesty, and falsification."[10] Radical politics in the traditional sense of social revolution were increasingly channeled into the politics of identity, which caused the movement to become politically isolated and cut off from the concerns of many progressive French women.

Despite its importance to fundamental changes in France, the popularity of the 1970s feminist movement didn't continue the way it did in the United States—infused into progressive institutions such as universities, foundations, and liberal discourse (however superficial), and fashionable among leftists. In the decades after its birth, no real counterpart in France emerged to rival the National Organization for Women; Planned Parenthood; respected, well-staffed, and well-funded women's studies departments and institutes at top universities; or affirmative action policies or programs for women such as Title IX. It is particularly interesting to note the gap that existed in twentieth-century France between the serious gains for women achieved through feminist influence and feminism's relatively limited appeal. The reasons for this failure must be sought in French society as well as in the movement itself. A constellation of forces curtailed feminism's appeal but intensified its impact: the power of the state and the breadth of its influence, the politicization of any kind of public or voluntary association, the end of the Left's status as an opposition party, and the weight of French culture and social standards. The movement's internal problems also blunted its popularity and fed the mistrust and dismissal that suffused feminism's reception in France. This was evident in many feminists' refusal to compromise on long-term strategy, the tension among feminist groups, and feminists' apparent intolerance of reticent, centrist women. With the Socialists' victory, however, these difficulties were thrown into relief, and many analysts have said that, at least initially, the Socialist success was the cause of the movement's submersion in the 1980s.

Many women across France who identified with feminism were excited by the leftist victory and thrilled about the official public recognition the Socialists gave feminism and the potential such glamour added to the cause. But many others at the core of the movement— enough to make a considerable impact—cried takeover. Feminists in the Socialist Party (such as those who launched Courant III) increasingly came to view the Ministère des droits de la femme as the party's effort to ghettoize feminism rather than to incorporate its critique into the party's overall political theory. Despite party rhetoric, feminists continued to experience antifeminism and were at a loss as to how to combat it. They argued that the Socialists' promotion of the "women's cause" relieved the party from having to examine the ideological as well as the material aspects of male-dominated French society. Granted, feminism was not the only internal critique to be repressed as the Socialists streamlined their policies to become a party in power rather than in opposition. At the PS Congress in 1981, the three principal party wings decided to bury their differences and collaborate on a single policy program. Ideological differences after that were considered unconstructive dissent and treated as such. The party's wholehearted supporters were rewarded with government posts, while feminists, who had had a contentious relationship with the party, were shunned.[11]

Some feminists argued that the institutionalization of feminism restricted rather than disseminated the feminist message—first, because one of feminism's goals was to recast institutions in a different form, and, second, because feminism was an evolving praxis and, as such, had emerged out of constant debate. They believed that the breadth of dissent had produced feminism's sophisticated political analysis—that its gadfly position had created much of its richness. Moreover, feminists doubted that the ministry would really be in a position to level criticism.[12] Other feminists argued that it was not so much that feminism had been "institutionalized" by the Socialist victory but that the movement was unable "to define itself clearly in relation to political institutions." Historian Françoise Ducrocq speculated as early as 1983 that the change in government had come at a time when the women's movement was particularly divided and thus incapable of relaunching itself. French feminism could learn from the more "communitarian" example of feminists in Great Britain, Ducrocq suggested: "Only the resolution of structural conflicts, and a clear approach to feminists' relationship as individuals and groups, will permit this necessary transfusion."[13] French feminists achieved much through their uncompromising radicalism, but when the Socialists came to power, this hard-line position crippled the movement by preventing its further evolution.

Rather than developing a new kind of feminist coalition to work with the Socialists, most feminists remained fearful of formal structures and saw those who were not as elitists or collaborators. When a collective of women from the 1979 abortion rights march formed a federation of feminist groups called Féminisme et politique (Feminism and Politics), organizers barely got through their first meeting before being attacked as "intellectuals." Some of those in the group were lawyers, journalists, and professors who declared themselves willing to work together with the government.[14] At the same time, Antoinette Fouque's consortium of publishing houses and publications and her professionally printed banners solidified the public's association of "feminism" with Éditions des femmes. The lack of cooperation and intolerance among feminists played into the hands of Fouque and her supporters, making them more visible and seemingly better organized than anyone else, even as they disavowed feminism.

Historians and political scientists have tried to explain the seeming contradiction between the movement's foundering and its electoral "success." Françoise Picq argued that the women's movement was not prepared for the possibility that the Left would win. In her view, feminists needed "to replace their defunct revolutionary project" and "to reinvent a moderate and progressive feminism."[15] But they were not particularly successful in this. The PS had spent at least a decade fashioning a transition from being the party of revolutionaries to becoming the governing party. In contrast, 1970s French feminism had for the most part never been interested in being in a dominant position, and it was not prepared to suddenly do so with the election of Mitterrand and a Socialist National Assembly. The unfailingly revolutionary character of French feminism was confronted with a new Left that had gradually been abandoning the radicalism of its original ideals. American historians Laura Frader and George Ross point out that by 1980 the "second Left" of the triumphant Socialist Party no longer believed in radical change; it simply opposed the "statist politics" of the "first Left" of George Marchais and the Communist poet Louis Aragon. As Frader and Ross saw it, the problem was not a lack of feminist accommodation but—as had been the case with the Third Republic a century before—the move toward the center by the Left now in power, which alienated itself from any radical dogma.[16]

As it had in the postwar period, the women's movement in the 1980s (and even in the 1970s) also foundered because feminism suffered from a general lack of popular interest. Feminism continued to be associated with man-hating, with the extreme Left, and with extraordinary social behavior. The power of French feminism was in its uncompromising radicalism, but this also proved to be its albatross. The reality is that feminism as trenchant social critique is not an easy politics to swallow, and its spokespeople—even the polished professional Halimi of Choisir and Zelensky from the Ligue du droits des femmes—were unwavering in their criticism of male-dominated institutions and of women's inferior status in society. The average French woman also remained entirely disinterested in Psych-et-Po. Antoinette Fouque presented a joyous, if abstract, image of women's liberation and had the finances to promote it, but it seems most women were unable to see themselves in her ideal, and, notwithstanding the success of certain books she published, she never gained broad-based support. Dorothy McBride and Amy Mazur have demonstrated that the way feminism was "framed" (publicly defined) influenced the impact of the French feminist movement. It was most successful when framed through the idiom of "equality"—identifying women "as potential target groups in a given policy." But feminism in France was often framed in other ways, either as intensely critical of gender relations or through overly academic language celebrating "womanness" that appeared obtuse and thus unattractive.[17]

Françoise Picq suggested in 1982 that the fear of elitism in the early movement created unnecessary divisions among feminists. "The old suspicion of institutions and of individual promotion is still there: to write a thesis in 1974, to aspire to a teaching post in women's studies today, these appear equally suspect; and those who refuse this suspicion don't always manage to avoid feeling guilty."[18] A decade later, Marie-Victoire Louis gently reproached feminists for retreating into themselves and allowing a few women to speak in their name. She saw this as a general refusal to create a constructive dialogue about feminist goals and strategy: "This visibility of a few rare women socially legit-imized as empowered to speak 'on women,'" Louis wrote, "contrib-utes to the accentuation of a perception of feminism as elitist, which squares badly with antiestablishment demands."[19]

There were larger, structural reasons for feminism's limited popu-larity in France. Some of the most concrete lie in the French people's relationship to government, specifically in the cohabitation in France of corporatism and universalism. Paradoxically, a country that had proclaimed a radical definition of universalism at the end of the eigh-teenth century had not cast off the mantle of particularism in the twen-tieth, or not where women were concerned. What the universalist state gave with one hand—equality of rights in the constitution and the law, for example—it took away with the other, by inscribing women's role as child-bearers and nurturers in various pieces of protective legisla-tion. Both popular and elite culture allowed these contradictory visions of individuals to coexist, and each was employed to defeat claims of the other. Women's complex relationship to French universalism also worked to discourage interest in feminism in a number of ways. "Nous sommes tous des citoyens" ("we are all citizens"), antifeminists fre-quently said to convey the assurance that France believed in human equality above all other human divisions—man and woman, European and non-European. This did not mean these divisions did not exist. As we have seen, for much of the twentieth century the French state maintained a particularist notion of women and their special role. But above such state-sponsored particularism floated the concept of a basic humanity in which everyone was believed equal. Therefore, to recognize women's ontological interests as separate from men's was, in a sense, to deprive every individual in the collectivity a claim to the rights of citizenship. This contradiction between universalist ideal and particularist practice was never resolved either philosophically or in law. One small example of this unresolved tension was illustrated in the government's response to the decision by Psych-et-Po's "MLF" to found a "women's union" in 1982. Fouque's Confédération syndicate des femmes (Confederate Syndicate of Women) was intended to pro-mote women's interests in paid as well as unpaid employment, in the public sphere and at home. But soon after Psych-et-Po declared its intentions, the Labor Ministry outlawed the Confédération syndicate des femmes, arguing that defending the interests of "women's condition" was the role of associations, not unions.[20]

An abiding belief in universalism kept women from seeing their social status as a political issue and from joining with other women to improve it. "The personal is political," the rallying cry of second-wave feminists from New York to Rome, which enabled women to connect how they were treated in the boardroom with how they were treated in the bedroom, never gained common currency in France despite its power as an analytical tool. In fact, the French remained vigorously attached to drawing a wall of separation between the two—which was why the angry reaction by many French women to the 2011 Dominique Strauss-Kahn scandal seemed so out of character. French universalism remained tempered by a national commitment to collective solutions and communal ways of living, balancing personal freedom with social responsibility, and, as unscientific as this might seem, a bit of that old romantic French "je ne sais quoi" mentioned in the introduction to this book. Although some scholars have argued that corporatism was effectively stamped out by the 1970s and 1980s and replaced by universalism, this book has argued that relations between men and women were slow to change, and that men hid behind constructions of universalism to justify their dominance while only symbolically acknowledging women's rights.[21] Feminist rebellion was viewed by many (women as well as men) as going too far—as an ugly exhibition of self-aggrandizement and . . . bitchiness.

Historian and critic of the French Left Tony Judt took the analysis of French universalism a step further, observing that "the French have not in recent generations concerned themselves overmuch with the topic of rights: what they are, who has them, whence they derive and how they should be protected." This might explain why there was not much ideological and political room for French feminists' claim to a constellation of rights, from the right to walk safely on the streets at night to the right to be paid wages commensurate with men's. Such demands were never weighed independently from a concomitant discussion about women's obligations and relationship to the state. If rights were largely articulated, as Judt argued, by "the claims of citizens upon the state," then the welfare state, more than any other institution in France, sidelined feminism. French Social Security benefits and public child care provided what has been one locus of feminist demands in the United States and United Kingdom. French feminists ridiculed the state for doling out bonuses to large families and criticized French society for ignoring the many hours that women labored in the domestic sphere, but in fact the French state recognized women's labor and rewarded it. French mothers have long had social benefits for which feminists elsewhere continue to fight. The French state provides many with affordable, high-quality day care, plus financial compensation for bearing children in the form of tax breaks and monthly allowances. French paternalism made it worthwhile for women to maintain the state's protection rather than to fight to be respected as free and non-gendered individuals without it.[22]

Young women of the 1980s could perceive an enormous gulf between their lives and those of young women a half-century earlier in terms of rights, freedoms, and state-sanctioned protections, which made earlier struggles appear out of date. Yet while bourgeois mothers were no longer clipping together the pages containing questionable material in the novels their daughters were reading—as Beauvoir in her memoirs described her mother doing—the French seemed to maintain a fairly strict and widely accepted notion of proper behavior, against which it was considered bad taste to rebel. Such things should not be taken lightly. In the same decade, Elaine Marks and Isabelle de Courtivron, in their introduction to a collection of French women's writing, hypothesized that "the notion of working without, or doing without men is more scandalous in France than in the United States where there is the precedent of the black separatists and a less excessive need for male approval."[23] The pressure on women to be sexy, to accept public demonstrations of men's desire, and to be, above all, the companions of men affected a broad range of women's expectations.

It is important to consider that although most French women ceased to be interested in feminism as a political movement during the 1980s and through much of the 1990s, they continued to be deeply affected by it. And it was easier for French women to ignore the difference feminism made in their lives precisely *because* of the changes it wrought. "There are already 18-year-old women who do not understand the founding principles of a movement that is barely ten years old," Delphy wrote in *Questions féministes* in 1980. "When they say that their lives are not— not exactly anyway—what ours were at their age, they are right. The tragedy is that the changes—whatever they are and whether they are thought of as big or small—are being used as arguments against the struggle." Thus, as Delphy explained, achieving small successes and basking in them erased the understanding that more change would come only through continued exertion.[24]

The cultural feminism (and the search for a separate female identity as a means of liberation) that developed during the 1970s within the Psych-et-Po group could also be charged with draining support from feminism. But this strand was also easy to consider separate from the movement, since half of its adherents repudiated feminism, and their ideas were an odd blend of a conservative vision of the ideal woman who possessed a kind of intrinsic female power but engaged in post-modern semantics and left politics up to the men.[25] Radical feminist separatists' criticism of heterosexual women as traitors only added to feminism's marginalization. The "personal is political" had served as one of the radical wing's most potent weapons, but as cultural feminism took hold, the political came to be inscribed onto the personal: it was less necessary to act in solidarity with others and to launch mass campaigns if personal behavior and beliefs were the most potent forms of political expression. Cultural feminism in fact paralleled the rise of identity politics on the Far Left in France. The change was not as striking as in America; nevertheless, the gay rights movement and, to a lesser extent, French-African and immigrant feminist groups all began organizing on their own with the express understanding that their needs were not being met within standard political organizations or umbrella groups, and so they required their own political agenda. At its best, then as now, feminism championed the inquiry and the defense of marginalized groups at the intersection of other groups, not always regarded as sufficiently important. Some of these efforts, such as the antiracist coalition that sprung up and died in the 1980s, addressed the problems of populations that had been ignored both by French universalism and by the Left in general. American sociologist Todd Gitlin describes "the separatist impulse" according to a feminist model in which "subordination on the basis of sex and sexuality became the basis for a liberationist sequence: first, the discovery of common experience and interests; next, an uprising against a society that had imposed inferior status; finally, the inversion of that status, so that distinct qualities once pointed to as proof of inferiority were transvalued into the basis for positive distinction."[26]

Some separatism was helpful in developing specialized advocacy groups, which were effective in bringing still-taboo subjects such as female genital mutilation out of the shadows and forcing some public discussion. Organizations such as the watchdog group SOS-Sexisme; the Mouvement d'information et d'expression des lesbiennes (Movement of Lesbian Information and Expression), a clearinghouse for information on lesbian-feminist solidarity; the Groupe pour l'abolition des mutilations sexuelles (Group for the Abolition of Sexual Mutilation), which worked to educate certain ethnicities in France about the dangers of female genital mutilation; and the Mouvement pour la défense des droits de la femme noire (Movement for the Defense of Black Women's Rights) targeted their activities at particular populations or issues. At the end of the 1970s, Maghreban and African women began organizing in Paris to discuss problems specific to women who had recently immigrated. They often collaborated with non-African French feminists and allowed men in their group. Members felt they had to link the struggle against women's oppression to the struggle against imperialism and colonialism—an argument that Beauvoir had made in the 1950s, long before "intersectionality" had become a common analytical approach. Yet because of France's deep ambivalence about its colonial past and its postcolonial population, this broader focus limited popular interest. And because many of these women saw themselves as temporary residents whose primary locus of concern was their home country, this also limited their impact. For instance,

Choisir incorporated some concerns of French-African feminists in its platform, but most of the French population was (and continues to be) indifferent or hostile to African immigrants or French-African nationals in France and thus had little interest in what Choisir had to say about them.[27]

The fault lines of intersectionality were not over race but, in fact, between feminists. At the beginning of the 1980s, some radical feminists created a separate political movement called Le front radical lesbien (The Radical Lesbian Front). Françoise Picq recalls that in June 1980 the walls of Jussieu University in Paris were covered with slogans such as "A Woman Who Loves Her Oppressor, That's Oppression; A 'Feminist' Who Loves Her Oppressor, That's Collaboration"; and "Hetero-Feminists = Kapos of the Patriarchy." Radical lesbian feminists such as Monique Wittig argued that lesbians had laid aside their own demands for recognition while fighting for heterosexual causes such as unrestricted access to abortion and contraception. As women on the Left had said ten years earlier about their male comrades, they no longer wished to fight the battles of others. Moreover, if women truly were a separate class, as radical feminists had been arguing, then women—certainly feminists—should not consort with the enemy at home or in politics.[28]

The conflict between the original radical feminist position and that of radical lesbian separatism played out most dramatically among participants in the *Questions féministes* editorial collective, with one side arguing that the group had to divorce itself completely from men and the women who associated with them and the other asserting feminism's commitment to all women. The debate burst into public view in 1980 with Wittig's publication in *QF* of an article called "The Straight Mind," in which she argued that feminism (and even some lesbian feminism) had remained enraptured by patriarchal thinking, and then, a few months later, another article, "One Is Not Born a Woman," in which she went so far as to argue that lesbians were not women since "woman" was defined by the patriarchy. Some of the movement's original militants, such as Wittig and Christine Delphy, who had embraced each other at the first meetings at Vincennes University in 1970, now faced each other across a wide divide. Moreover, their differences could not be construed as a problem of "heterosexism," since women on both sides of this ideological dispute were lesbians. *Questions féministes* folded with the breakup of the collective during the summer of 1980 and restarted as *Nouvelles questions féministes* (NQF) less than a year later, prompting a lawsuit by the dissenting lesbian separatists of the original collective, who said they had been promised that the journal's new name would not resemble the old. It was one more feminist dispute to drag through the courts, and it further suggested that the movement was caught up in irrelevancies.[29]

The remaining *Questions féministes* collective—radical feminists who had argued against the lesbian separatist position—were not willing to give up a name that had exemplified one of the only radical feminist reviews in France. "As necessary as the critique of heterosexuality is," the re-formed collective wrote in its first editorial,

> no theoretical necessity can justify the exclusion of any woman from the oppressed, from the group to defend, in short, from the class of women. We refuse the obligatory link between the critique of heterosexuality and the condemnation of heterosexual women; on one hand because this conclusion is straightaway unacceptable; on the other hand, because "radical lesbians" have not reached it except by a series of shifts and sophisms which imply the negation of principles of radical feminism, including the centrality of the concept of oppression and the theory of sex classes.[30]

The re-formed QF collective refused to abandon its principles, the judge ruled in their favor, and *Nouvelle questions féministes* continued to publish. But its voice became somewhat lost between the mercurial voice of cultural feminism on the one hand and self-restrained state feminism on the other.

Feminism did not fare well when promoted by radical lesbians because the French found their separatist ideals so unpalatable and because the radicals' lesbianism had a political edge (unlike Psych-et-Po's euphemistic homosexual practice, which seemed more inwardly focused and romantic). Many women rejected the idea of consciously making their personal lives conform to a political vision, especially when that vision denied them some of the most fundamental human relationships. Even radical feminists agreed. In its first editorial, the NQF collective wrote, "[These] principles [of radical lesbianism] lead us to commit violence against individual experience, not by the fact of *speaking* of them or *analyzing* them but in establishing the obligation to conform to 'the line.'" Radical feminists registered the fact that one of the founding principles of post-1968 feminism, "the personal is political," was undergoing "an insidious and extremely dangerous reversal."[31] Based on the radical lesbian position, the slogan had come to mean "the political must be personal." Many people on the Left, including feminists, saw cultural feminism as a trap, and they defied being caught in it.

Alice Echols has described how a similar situation developed within American feminism, and her analysis contains many parallels to the French case. "By equating feminism with the so-called reassertion of a female identity and culture," Echols writes, "cultural feminism seems to promise an immediate solution to women's powerlessness in the culture at large. Its growth is attributable to the frustrating fragmentation of the women's movement and the erosion of feminist gains in the recent past. Cultural feminism represents a retreat from the difficulties of political struggle into the self-validation that community-building offers. It further substitutes the fantasy of a united sisterhood for political theory."[32] Cultural feminism—that term used to denote the "female essence" to the ideas or social activities around and among women—served to create vibrant communities (the Psych-et-Po group, for example) but alienated a broad swath of women.

Cultural feminism could be the purview of lesbian separatists as well as social conservatives. The first chapter of this book, which focused on French society and feminist activity in the postwar period through the 1950s, showed that most of the French, including some feminists, could not entirely conceive of a world in which, on the most important levels, men and women were equals. The modern feminist equivalent believed that feminism must be approached in a less demanding and more consensual manner. Gabrielle Rolland, for example, the author of *Seront-elles au rendez-vous? La nouvelle cause des femmes* (Will they be up to the task? The new women's cause), published in 1995, wrote in a section entitled "A Serene Femininity" that in the 1970s "feminists for the most part stuck to their egalitarian demands while neglecting their bodies and refusing the traditional flashy togs of seduction." In contrast, she said that women today "play on the register of difference, for they have come around to love their body, their beauty, and their radiance." This, for Rolland, was the force women would use in the future: women could demand "parity" (not equality) while "at the same time enjoying their difference, keeping their identity, and sharing responsibilities and decisions that engaged the future."[33]

Like the activists of earlier generations, second-wave feminists of many stripes displayed a particularly French preoccupation with the issue of exclusion and the belief that men and women have more in common than they have differences. In the early 1990s Christine Planté, in the critical journal *Futur antérieur*, noted this French distaste for excluding men from a mass feminist movement. She argued that since the French rejected separatism and militancy as solutions to the problems identified by feminism, it led them to highlight the "difference" between men and women rather than their simple "equality." Yet she viewed this as a positive sign: it is not that the French wanted "difference" to be socially valorized, she argued, but rather that they "preferred to approach problems from a more *scientific* rather than political point of view" (emphasis added). "To reflect in terms of difference(s)," Planté reasoned, "is to be interested in two, in a relationship, an interaction, and thus to refuse problematics of the feminine." She conceded, however, that "difference" was in vogue among a certain set of academics, from literary critics to anthropologists. Around the same time, Marie-Victoire Louis, sociologist and longtime feminist, also recognized the difficulties of gaining mass support with a politics of separatism. She said women could articulate their demands alongside men: "We must consider that feminist groups' fear of invasion by men is silly, and the fear of not being able to face them a mark of insufficient self-confidence, and finally, we must acknowledge as a political problem continual 'antimale' reactions in associations. The exclusion of men does not have to be the last foundation necessary for associations insecure about their purpose to affirm their identity."[34]

In part because of the voices like Rolland's, by the 1990s many women in some way sympathetic to women's liberation saw French feminism as a movement that had run its course. "The French feminist movement is at an impasse," conservative feminist Élisabeth Badinter said in an interview in 1994 with *Le nouvel observateur*, commenting that it had stalled for "the best possible reason." The problem, Badinter offered, was that from a legal standpoint, women had nothing more to fight for. An "arsenal of very powerful laws" against sexual harassment, for equality in marriage, and for equal salaries existed in France. "All is now a question of personal negotiation between men and women," she cautioned. "The most difficult [achievement] remains precisely that of salaries, because this equality will signify definitively that our society has internalized that men and women in the family and at work are worth the same. Two generations are needed, I believe, for it to enter into fact. In France, feminism is only a question of vigilance—but quotidian!"[35]

The historian Dominique Frischer saw, on the contrary, powerful interests at work in minimizing the effect of social transformation through feminism, highlighted by the women's magazines' announce-ment of the return of "real women" in the 1990s: "Stripped of their warlike armor, accepting without psychological complex their phys-ical, emotional, and social difference, pacified in their relations with men, reconciled with family values, it only remains for real women to harmonize their inner selves with their outward appearance so that society can finally find its bearings."[36] Of course, much—for good or ill—could happen over Badinter's "two generations," and as Frischer pointed out, it appeared possible that women could be lulled back into a state of irenic acceptance of their singular but unequal fate. Chris-tine Delphy, equally critical in her ten-year assessment of feminism in France, hardly believed that feminist work was over: first, because the "arsenal of laws" was not sufficiently powerful to assure women jus-tice, and, second, because feminism offers a critique of the relations between men and women that is crucial if society expects to change those relations. Thus, Delphy suggested, feminists needed to ask the question, "Where can we go from here?" As she wrote, "[This] implies that we ask how, in what conditions, our achievements can be used as a basis for new struggles. And for them to be used as such we must first and foremost assert and reassert the very idea of the struggle, the need for it, and its effectiveness. . . . And we must write into history all the different moments of the struggle and especially the most important of them—the process of collective reflection through which we arrived at the positions that we later defended."[37]

Delphy's urging to continue the struggle resonated among feminists in the last decade of the twentieth century, at a time when the daughters of those who marched on the streets for abortion's legalization in the early 1970s came of age. Their mothers reared them to take pride in being girls and to expect equal treatment as women. They found themselves faced with a wider range of professional prospects and personal choices than their mothers did a generation before. They believed—and continue to believe—that they may and should expect more of their lives and, accordingly, had less tolerance for injustice. But they also were faced with an increasingly competitive job market, a rising unemployment rate, and a resurgence of social conservatism articulated by the Far Right. By the end of the century, critics of abortion rights had become more vocal in France. Women continued to earn proportionally less than men, and poverty in France remained disproportionately female. In this atmosphere, growing numbers of women began voicing their support for feminist ideals, even calling themselves feminist. During the public-sector strikes and protests that paralyzed France during November and December 1995, a march for widening reproductive choice, organized by a coalition of feminist groups, drew approximately forty thousand men and women, many of them in their twenties. It was the largest feminist march in over a decade.[38]

Many feminists disagreed with Badinter's suggestion that no further institutional changes were necessary or that the central problem was wage inequality. But it is true that many people in France—even some feminists—now spoke of the women's movement as a historical relic. A collective of university-age women formed in 1991 to publish a feminist magazine called *Marie pas Claire* (a spoof on the name of the women's fashion magazine *Marie Claire*). The collective saw itself as the heir to the legacy of its 1970s feminist mothers, crediting them with "being everything, having invented and discovered everything." But the collective also referred to the 1970s feminists as "the old ones." "We've never had an easy relationship with them," Sabine, a member of the collective, recounted in an interview. "We have trouble doing things together. . . . Having known a great moment and then its ebb, [1970s feminists] have difficulty believing that we represent something." "And," she added, "three-quarters of the young women who want to be in [our] group don't know what the MLF is. It's 'Liberation year zero' all over again." The old feminists ruefully agreed. In an interview, Liliane Kandel remarked, "It's true that certain young feminists today shock me with their ignorance of what came before."[39]

This cynicism during the 1990s cut a wide swath: feminists spoke with regret not just about the apathy or ignorance among a new generation of women but about the overall lack of tolerance on the Left, which dismantled coalitions among feminists and other groups. SOS-Racisme and the Union des étudiants juifs de France (Jewish Student Union of France) were two organizations that managed to hold together a coalition of French Muslims and Jews united in combating prejudice and misunderstanding. But the campaign "The Right to Be Different" launched by the Union des étudiants juifs de France in 1981 fell apart by the end of the decade amid the rise of the National Front, leftist antipathy toward Israel, and the popular fear of a Muslim invasion. The ousting of three Muslim girls from school for wearing headscarves and the greater support for France's integrationist model of citizenship demonstrated how easy it was for intersectional campaigns to fail.[40]

Moreover, the indifferent public, aided by a press that had reduced feminist arguments to stereotypical generalities, tended to view feminism as either a vague force for promoting women's economic equality or a doctrine of uncompromising man-haters. In 1994, at the time of the fiftieth anniversary of women's suffrage in France, many voices were raised about the meager number of women representatives in Parliament; some, like Simone Veil, suggested that political parties be required to place women on their candidate lists. A parity bill stipulating the equal distribution of men and women on electoral lists within municipal areas was defeated in 1995 when it was first proposed by the Chirac administration.[41] The eventual adoption, in 2000, of the Loi sur la parité (parity law) as well as of other laws relating to women's legal and employment status point to the continuing influence of feminism in law.[42] But as the DSK incident showed, a gap remained between statute and status quo in terms of relations and expectations between men and women.

The debate over parity reveals the rifts over feminist theory crossing both political and business practices. But it also represents the continuity of feminist public policymaking since the Liberation—from changing laws to creating institutionalized channels of feminist advocacy for gender equality.[43] In the most general sense, consensus about how to increase female representation in the body politic as well as in positions of corporate authority broke down at the end of the century between the "universalists" (or "indifferents"—as in indifferent to gender distinctions) and the "*paritaires*" (parity advocates) who believed that it was possible at the same time to avoid particularist or naturalist categorizing of women, institutionalize women's fuller participation, and end men's domination of politics. Constitutional support for parity lay in the preamble of the 1946 Constitution itself, which reads, "The law guarantees women in all domains, rights equal to those of men." Parity, Gisèle Halimi and others argued, only fulfills the letter of the law, and thus the constitution did not have to be amended to put in place such prescriptive measures. Halimi proffered some of the most interesting arguments for parity, perhaps because as a lawyer she experienced both the discrimination and the potential for equality under French law. In her view, the universalist argument had this fundamental flaw: "The abstract and total assimilation of one sex with another, . . . the refusal to take into account the existence of injustice, although it is real, concrete, and proven. . . . Disoriented, diminished in their difference, and pilloried by the impalpable universalist theory, women are swept away beyond their control. The *real* confinement of women is exacerbated by the fact of being confined within the *abstract* principles used to oppose that confinement."[44]

Françoise Collin put it another way when she argued that the "indifference between the sexes risks hiding, confirming, and even strengthening the privileged status of one section of the community. There is a gulf between metaphysical truth and political truth." And that is because, in the words of philosopher Sylviane Agacinski, sex is a different kind of difference inscribed on half of humanity.[45]

Feminist theory aside, the figures on the lack of gender equality in politics and business spoke for themselves. In 1946 female deputies represented 5.6 percent of the National Assembly. This book began with the moment of exultation for women as they cast their first ballots and imagined their lives filled with possibilities in a reborn France; at the end of this book, statistics show that there was still much more work to be done. After the parliamentary elections of 1993, female deputies totaled 6.1 percent. Almost fifty years had gone by since women had achieved political majority, but the number of women elected to office remained about the same. Why French politics and business remained so male dominated up through the end of the twentieth century has a lot to do with what Raylene Ramsay describes as the French paradox—pioneer of democracy in Europe but late on women's suffrage—combined with the Latin character of French culture, the ongoing Catholic influence, and a staunch belief in the concept of individualism.[46]

Feminist support for parity began growing after the publication in 1992 of a political call to arms, *Au pouvoir citoyennes! Liberté, égalité, parité* (To power women citizens! Liberty, equality, parity), by feminist journalists Françoise Gaspard, Claude Servan-Schreiber, and Anne Le Gall. They demanded that parity be concretely implemented in the law for elected local and national assemblies as the only way to affect profound change to social norms of patriarchy (literally, men's rule). Throughout the 1990s, major papers published various manifestos on parity, and feminists kept insisting that parity become a national conversation.[47] By July 1999, *paritaires* had managed to successfully push through an amendment to Articles 3 and 4 of the 1958 Constitution stating that "the law favors equal access of women and men to electoral mandates and elected office" and that the parties must "contribute to the development work" of this principle. The net result was the parity

law of June 6, 2000, which, in typical French fashion, created a pragmatic compromise between the absolute institutionalization of equal
numbers of elected officials—something the French majority found to
be against the fundamental principles of democracy—and nothing at
all. The law required political party candidate lists for local and national
elections to have equal numbers of men and women starting with the
municipal elections of 2001, and it added teeth to the law by fining parties for noncompliance by depriving them of government stipends.[48]

The initial success of the parity law was modest, not least because
as long as women were on electoral lists, parties could say they were
following the letter of the law (while not promoting them in the spirit
of it). Women were not appointed to cabinet posts with any greater
frequency, because they didn't match the image of an *homme politique*
("male" politician). But over its first ten years, the parity law did in fact
bring women into the political arena, especially in local elections. Joan
Scott has pointed out that in the little cantonal elections (where the
law didn't even apply), women seemed to be taking the initiative and
using the law as impetus to become more politically active. In less than
a decade, the percentage of female local elected officials had grown
by more than half and the percentage of women on boards of publicly
listed companies had more than tripled. Nationally, men remained
in more positions of power, but that number had also diminished,
from upward of 95 percent in 1999 down to 75 percent in 2015. These
advancements have encouraged women's belief in the success of the
"quotidian vigilance" to which both Badinter and Delphy referred.[49]

Since approximately 2010, there has been a growing consensus that
both essentialism and accommodation marginalized feminism and
prevented it from addressing the heart of politics, society, and culture.
The intellectuals and politicians of the 1970s who argued for a "wom-
en's voice" and women's special contribution to the broader struggle
seemed increasingly outmoded simply because of the advancement of
legal and economic rights for women, which reduced "separate spheres"
and mitigated the attractiveness of cultural feminism. One powerful
twenty-first century example of this repudiation of "difference" was
provided by the group Ni putes ni soumises (NPNS; Neither Whores

nor Submissives), an organization founded in 2003 by a mixed-gender group of second-generation North Africans. NPNS activists applied Beauvoir's feminist theory to challenge the violence and sexism of the suburban ghettos that ringed Paris. In its first years, NPNS convened special assemblies and demanded government action on schooling, jobs, and housing in poor neighborhoods, drawing upon the support of thousands of women within and outside of the slums to march in solidarity. NPNS emphasized their French identity, supported the ban on religious symbols and headscarves in public schools, and opposed affirmative action (*discrimination positive*) as well as any law or policy that made special accommodations for ethnic, cultural, or religious groups. NPNS saw itself as carrying on the legacy of feminism combined with antiracism. "We have fed off their experiences, . . . and yet, at the same time, we see the relationship as a sort of apprenticeship, because with a few exceptions, many of their gains were not concretely solidified."[50] These activists challenged not just the sexist behavior of the men in the slums but also the destructive social climate of all its inhabitants in a multilayered critique of their own culture as well as the analyses of contemporary social science. If the feminist movement took society to task for maintaining women in a kind of "liminal" status (as it did its immigrants), North African women immigrants represented yet another challenge to both feminist and French presumptions of the status quo.

As the twenty-first century continued, the only kind of feminism that appeared to have any mass appeal combined Beauvoir's assertion of women's independence and her egalitarian hopes for the future with a consensual social and political model. In this supposed middle ground, however, there is lots of slippage. Conservative feminist Mona Ozouf, who devoted her 1995 book *Les mots des femmes: Essai sur la singularité française* (Women's words: Essay on French singularity) to the subject of women's identity in the twentieth century, argued that this feminism is universalist and not particularist. Ozouf reminded her readers that the feminism of the future is "for all," finding universalist goals "in the hope of exchange, in the certitude of a shared language, and of a common conscience." This makes sense if interpreted critically through

Joan Scott's observation that "feminism is not a reaction to republican-ism, but one of its effects, produced by contradictory assertions about the universal human rights of individuals . . . and exclusions attributed to 'sexual difference.'" Nevertheless, as far back as the 1940s, Beau-voir had argued a position, reiterated in this book, that may offer the greatest promise for a feminism that addresses both egalitarianism and the social contract. It can be found in the words of Lori Jo Marso and Patricia Moynagh, scholars of Beauvoir and French feminism: that we should "resist philosophical analysis that fails to attend to the circum-stances in individuals' lives." There is still resistance to this principle both by French thinkers and by American scholars of French feminism, but the body of work that takes into account French women's mate-rial circumstances is growing and garnering increasing interest. Par-ity might be the feminist campaign that attends to both the universal and particular because, in Gaspard's words, it "does not only question politics, but the public sphere. It forces us to reconsider the boundaries between public and private as they have been defined in the 'Enlight-enment.' It leads to a destruction of both the legal abstraction that has been the individual . . . and the social abstraction of a 'postmodern' individualism that wants to surpass the categories of sex even before it critically examines them."[51]

In the first decade of the twenty-first century, French feminist intel-lectuals began a process of forging an ontological conciliation between individualist (universalist) and particularist (differentialist) under-standings of women and gender. For some, gender is hypothesized in more open terms to accommodate the problematic of sexual or at least social difference, as in the feminist philosophy of Sylviane Agacinski, but, to use Françoise Collin's words, this project is always "haunted by the specter of naturalism." Here again, Scott reminds us that fem-inism has been most useful in the spaces opened by "republican's insufficient universalism." Nevertheless, Collin, Agacinski, and those Colin calls the "new" French feminists also recognize the disjuncture between the philosophical and the political, and between republican universalism and particularism—another area of friction in French feminism that has dogged the movement yet has been overlooked by scholars of French feminism. Defenders of parity, a practical means for redress and the construction of new norms, have developed perhaps the most sophisticated articulation of "French feminism": "Parity imposes itself," political scientist Janine Mossuz-Lavau reminds us in a discussion of men and women and gender equality, "because, in their *gender*, men and women are . . . the same."[52]

Feminism in France has had a passionate history since Simone de Beauvoir took up the old *querelle* after the Liberation and then, years later, the women's movement declared it would put many of her book's claims into political action. From the end of World War II, women have been as divided over the ways to remake society as has the rest of France. In sorting through their various arguments, I have agreed with some and criticized others, not only because of the ideas themselves but because of the way these ideas have been articulated and used politically. Intellectual fashion often obscures real consequences. Ultimately, I concur with Christine Delphy when she argued that "the great danger lying in wait for the women's struggle today is that the 'before' of the feminist question [what Delphy refers to as naturalist assumptions of women's subjugated position] can be presented as its 'after'—sparing us, or seeming to spare us, the trouble of fighting." This book is hardly a call to arms. But it eventually points toward the same conclusion. Women in France, in the second half of the twentieth century, were confronted with a devil's bargain: take a back seat to political power, accede to a low glass ceiling in the working world, and accept a greater burden of child care and, in return, gain considerable recognition, protection, and state support for that maternal and feminine sacrifice. In this world, the ideology of "womanhood" or "womanness"—as attractive as these concepts appeared to many— ultimately weakened women's ability to attain true equality *and* the redefinition of male and female roles. Feminists' ability to engage with French law, economic policy, and society, and to implement concrete changes in them, served in many ways as the measure of their and French feminism's success.[53]

APPENDIX

The Feminist Press in France, 1968–1981

In her article "L'explosion de la presse féministe," Liliane Kandel remarked that the profusion of feminist writings mirrored the psychological release that street protests had for so many women. It was a transformative moment in their understanding of themselves and their evaluation of French society and its expectations. Women found their voices on the pages of these publications, reveling in seeing their ideas and feelings in print, and they built solidarity and a political movement by reading the ideas and experiences of women that had so many parallels to their own. The collection of writings is rich and varied, from tight political criticism to raw emotional outpourings. The list below is not comprehensive but should serve as a starting point for anyone interested in understanding how women became feminists in France.

Journals of Feminism and the Women's Movement
(dates marked are the years concerned with this study)

Antoinette, 1966–1980
Les cahiers du féminisme, 1977–1981
Les cahiers du grif, 1973–1981
Choisir : La cause des femmes, 1976–1981
Elles voient rouges, 1979–1981
des femmes en mouvements, 1978–1982
Les femmes s'entêtent, 1975
Femmes françaises, 1945–1948
F Magazine, 1978–1982
Histoires d'Elles
L'information des femmes, 1975–1977

Jamais contentes!, 1979–1981

Mignonnes, allons voir sous la rose . . . , 1980–1982

Les nouvelles . . . *féministes*, 1974–1977

Nouvelles questions féministes, 1981–1982

Les pétroleuses, 1974–1976

Questions féministes, 1977–1980

Le quotidien des femmes, 1974–1976

La revue d'en face, 1977–1983

Les temps des femmes (replaced by *L'information des femmes*), 1978–1983

Le torchon brûle, 1971–1973

La voix des femmes, 1975

Journals with Special Issues Focused on Women and Feminism (1981 and before)

Action socialiste. (September 19, 1971).

Alternatives. "Face à femmes." 1 (June 1970).

Antoinette. Magazine féminin édité par la CGT. (July 1967–August 1969).

Après-demain. "La condition de la française." 140 (January 1972).

L'arc. "Simone de Beauvoir et la lutte des femmes." 61 (1975).

Avenirs. "Les carrières féminines." 93–95 (April–June 1958).

Les cahiers de l'IHTP. "Questions à l'histoire orale: Table ronde du 20 juin 1986." 4 (June 1987).

Le débat: Histoire, politique, société. "Notre histoire: Matériaux pour servir à l'histoire intellectuelle de la France, 1953–1987." 50 (special issue) (May–August 1988).

Dialogue des femmes. "L'engagement politique des femmes à partir de 1968: L'explosion féministe." (April 29, 1984).

———. "Libération des femmes: Année zéro." 54–55 (July–October 1970).

L'idiot international. (November 1970).

La nef. "La condition féminine." 26, no. 38 (October–December 1969).

Partisans. "Sexualité et répression." 32–33 (October–November 1966).

La pensée. "Un débat sur la presse féminine." 124 (December 1965).

Revue française des affaires sociales. "Le travail des femmes." 4 (October–December 1981).

———. "La famille en 1975." 177 (October 1976).

NOTES

Introduction

1. Coignard and Guichard, "Vive les françaises," 44–53; Scott, *Fantasy of Feminist History*, 117–18. Among French women, antifeminism continues to be alive and well. See Lucile Quillet, "Ces jeunes filles," *Madame figaro*, November 1, 2014, http://madame.lefigaro.fr/societe/ces-jeunes-filles -qui-detestent-feminisme-180714-898871.

2. See the collection of feminist statements responding to the DSK affair: Delphy, *Troussage de domestique*; Long, *Women Intellectuals*, 93–94.

3. Callu, *Le mai 68*, 178–81; Le Dœuff and Deutscher, "Feminism Is Back."

4. Ben McPartland, "France Bids Adieu," France 24, February 23, 2012, http://www.france24.com/en/20120222-france-strikes-out -mademoiselle-coup-feminism.

5. Aubin and Gisserot, *Les femmes en France*, 65–66; "L'inégale répartition," April 29, 2016, http://www.inegalites.fr/spip.php?article245; "Inégal- ité homme-femme," March 8, 2011, http://www.inegalites.fr/spip.php ?article1381&id_mot=27.

6. Pizan, *City of Ladies*, 63.

7. Klejman and Rochefort, *L'égalité en marche*, 17–18. Also see Offen, "His- tory of Feminisms," 326.

8. Klejman and Rochefort, *L'égalité en marche*, 342; Kimble, "No Right to Judge"; Mansker, *Sex, Honor, and Citizenship*, 43–45, 63–64, 178–81; Bard, El Amrani, and Pavard, *Historie des femmes*, 10–11; Offen, *Woman Question*.

9. Bard, *Les femmes*, 12–28, 48–52; Schwartz, "Redefining Resistance," 141– 53; Offen, "Des modèles nationaux," 70–71; Opello, *Gender Quotas*, 16–17; Gerhard, "Concepts et controverses," 70–72.

10. See especially Moses, *French Feminism*; Hause and Kenney, "Suffragist Behavior," 781–806; Offen, "Women, Citizenship, and Suffrage," 162–63.

11. Among other social guarantees: the paid maternity and adoption leave, the longer (up to two years) postnatal leave, the parental child-rearing

leave, and the 1972 law of equal pay for equal work with a clause establishing the idea of comparable worth. Throughout much of the twentieth century, jobs banned for women included underground work in mines and craters, dangerous work with chemicals and compressed air, and night work between 10 p.m. and 5 a.m. except for exempted professions such as nursing. See Pollard, *Reign of Virtue*, 203.

12. Stuart, *Health and Beauty*, 37; Bock, *Women in European History*, 164; also see Offen, "Theory and Practice of Feminism," 343, 350–51.

13. Voldman, "Mai 68," 44; also see Picq, "Le féminisme bourgeoise," 391–406. The Union féminine civique et sociale, and its journal, *La femme dans la vie sociale*, promoted women's interests to the extent that they fell within Catholic doctrine of women's role. The Union des femmes françaises, despite its support for improving conditions in the home, at work, with child care, etc., did not form coalitions with other groups. Duchen, *Women's Rights*, 168–70.

14. Duchen, *Women's Rights*, 171.

15. Essentialist feminism has also been called "cultural feminism." See Alcoff, "Cultural Feminism;" Mazur, *Theorizing Feminist Policy*, 7; Scott, *Only Paradoxes to Offer*, 165; Scott, *Politics of History*, 49.

16. Bard, *Les filles de Marianne*, 383–436; Sowerwine, *Sisters or Citizens?*, 12–13, chaps. 3 and 4; Moses, *French Feminism*, 229–37; Bidelman, *Pariahs Stand Up!*; Hilden, *Working Women*; Hause, *Women's Suffrage*; Michel, "Ideologies, Pressure Groups," 3.

17. Jardine and Menke, *Shifting Scenes*, 59.

18. See, for example, Burke, "Report from Paris," 843–55; Marks and Courtivron, *New French Feminisms*; Moi, *Sexual/Textual Politics*; Eisenstein and Jardine, *Future of Difference*. For a contemporary analysis of the interpretation of feminism in France see Möser, *Féminismes en traduction*, 31–35.

19. Jardine and Menke, "Interview with Christiane Rochefort," 184. For the theories within historical narrative (without the political context) see Long, *Women Intellectuals*.

20. French feminism, together with philosophy and literature, was promoted largely within American linguistic and philosophy departments rather than in departments of political science or history. See Schrift, "French Philosophy," 8. For the counterargument see Offen, "The History of Feminism."

21. Françoise Collin outlines this misunderstanding in "Question philosophique," 293–304; see also, Moi, *Sexual/Textual Politics*; Butler, *Gender Trouble*; Turkle, *Psychoanalytic Politics*; Gallop, *Thinking through the Body*; and Gallop, *Daughter's Seduction*.

22. See Duchen's *Women's Rights* for the continuity of generations.

23. Delphy, *Un universalisme*, 8.

24. Chaperon, "Reprendre l'histoire du féminism," 206–8.

25. See Marks and Courtivron, *New French Feminisms*. This has led many 1970s feminists to don the title "feminist" as a badge of honor.

26. Voldman and Vandecasteele-Schweitzer, "Oral Sources." Also see Thompson, Voice of the Past, 137.

27. Chaperon, "Reprendre l'histoire du féminism," 206–8; for a discussion of universalism and feminism see Zancarini-Fournel, "Les feminismes," 237 as well as Scott, *Politics of History*, 39

1. Rethinking Gender Roles

1. See Pollard, *Reign of Virtue*, 197; Roberts, *Civilization without Sexes*; and Chaperon, "Feminism is Dead," 151–53.

2. Drake, *Intellectuals and Politics*, 23–24.

3. Paul Archambault, *La famille*; Fougeyrollas, "Prédominance du mari." See Bard, *Les filles de Marianne*, 385 and Fishman, Sexual Revolution, 114–32.

4. Machard, *Les françaises*; Philippon, *L'esclavage* and *La jeunesse coupable*, for which she won the Prix Jean Finot and the Prix de l'académie d'éducation et d'entraide sociales.

5. Pollard, *Reign of Virtue*, 200; Roberts, *What Soldiers Do*; Lowe, *Savage Continent*, 6–13, 22–27, 280–83, 362.

6. Judt, *Past Imperfect*, 49–50; Jobs, *Riding the New Wave*, 193–94; Foley, *Women in France*, 241; Lowe, *Savage Continent*, 39, 164–69; Diamond, *Second World War*, 131–54. Those who had been true to their spouses were not always happy to find them home again. Pollard and Fishman point out that despite the euphoric pictures, the Liberation was not a happy time, especially for women. See Pollard, *Reign of Virtue*, xiii, 197–200; Fishman, *We Will Wait*, 165.

7. Herzog, *Sexuality in Europe*, 99; Pollard, *Reign of Virtue*, 197. Nevertheless, popular sentiment supported the idea that the Catholic religion and rebuilding the French nation trumped Jewish restitution—even of rescued Jewish children to their living relatives after the war. See Doron, Jewish Youth and Identity, 108–10.

8. Crouzet, *Bachelières ou jeunes filles*, 106.

9. Robcis, *Law of Kinship*, 54, 143–44; Jobs, *Riding the New Wave*, 190; Pollard, *Reign of Virtue*, 200.

10. Gennari, *Le dossier*, 297; Dyer, *Population and Society*, 123–26; Larkin, *Popular Front*, 117–18; Pauline Archambault, *Deux mondes*, 4; Robcis, *Law of Kinship*, 29–30.

11. Larkin, *Popular Front*, 3-4. See also Steck, "Les prestations familiales." With their strident calls for world peace, women seemed to suggest that men would have been better off avoiding war in the first place rather than forcing women to repopulate after it.

12. Pedersen, *Origins of Welfare State*, 387; Graziella, *Demography*, 482; Diamond, *Second World War*, 64-66, 162-64; Robcis, *Law of Kinship*, 54-60.

13. Lacroix, *Force et faiblesses*, 13.

14. Weitz, "Heroic Man," 316, 339-41; Bard, *Les filles de Marianne*, 428-33, 444-48; Reynolds, *France between the Wars*, 210-12; Chaperon, "Feminism is Dead," 148-49; Jacquemart, *Les hommes*, 63-64.

15. Bard, *Les filles de Marianne*, 448-49; Scott, *Only Paradoxes to Offer*, 162; Foley, *Women in France*, 248.

16. Women were granted suffrage by an ordinance of April 21, 1944. See Collette-Kahn, "Femme, tu vas voter"; Lacore, *L'émancipation de la femme*; Masson, "Je suis socialiste"; and Saumoneau, "Le devoir civique."

17. Roberts, *What Soldiers Do*, 5-6, 96-97, 162; Adereth, *French Communist Party*, 144-46; Djelic, *American Model*, 250-57.

18. Lacroix, *Force et faiblesses*, 14, 28-30.

19. Sauvy, "Préface," 9-18; Bresard, "La famille," 330-42; Stoetzel, "Les fonctions familiales," 343-69.

20. Crouzet, *Bachelières ou jeunes filles*, 97-98; Jobs, *Riding the New Wave*, 71.

21. Rauze-Comignan, *Pour la paix universelle*, 5.

22. Herzog, *Sexuality in Europe*, 3; Lacroix, *Force et faiblesses*, 153.

23. Guéraiche, "Les femmes de la vie," 92; Rauch, *Politics and Belief*, 41, 112-17; also see Moyn, "Origins of Human Rights." Mounier and Archambault were competitive proponents of an anti-individualist philosophy they called "personalisme," which Archambault developed in the 1920s and 1930s and Mounier elaborated upon in the 1940s and 1950s.

24. Crouzet, *Bachelières ou jeunes filles*, 101.

25. Crouzet, *Bachelières ou jeunes filles*, 99, 172-74, 195.

26. Crouzet, *Bachelières ou jeunes filles*, 172, 195, 295-98. Ironically, Crouzet also admired women's schools in England and the United States, such as Middlesex, Barnard, and Wellesley, but did not seem to notice differences in their philosophies or missions.

27. Crouzet, *Bachelières ou jeunes filles*, 33-36, 110-112, 170, 324-25. Crouzet considered men equally responsible for women's abandonment of their maternal posts and their forays into the male world when men enjoyed their wives' salaries rather than allowing them to fulfill their feminine

mission. The first iteration of the Fourth Republic Constitution had a "right to work clause." Chaperon, "Feminism Is Dead," 156–57.

28. See Lévy-Bruhl, "Les carrières féminines," 16–17; Beevor and Cooper, *Paris after the Liberation*, 366.

29. Chaperon, *Les années Beauvoir*, 97.

30. Dyer, *Population and Society*, 133–57. Reynolds, *France between the Wars*, 89–90. The *allocation familiale* (family allowance), paid on a flat-rate, tax-free basis for each child, formed the basis of the natalist policy. See Steck, "Les prestations familiales," 3–38; Larkin, *Popular Front*, 117; Clark, *Rise of Professional Women*, 300–301; Le Bras, *Marianne et les lapins*; Laubier, *Condition of Women*; Pulju, *Mass Consumer Society*, 98–99. Women advocated for maternity subsidies. See Offen, "Body Politics,"152.

31. Bessières, *Le vote des femmes*, 10. Bessières was a Jesuit, but he did not outwardly argue for women's vote as a bulwark against republicanism. For a discussion of antisuffrage popular sentiment, see Barral, *Partis et élections*, 185.

32. Machard, *Les françaises*, 100–101.

33. Machard, *Les françaises*, 99–100.

34. Henri Calet, "Les Parisiens votent," *Combat*, April 30, 1945, 1–5.

35. Collette-Kahn, "Femme, tu vas voter," 4; Diamond, *Second World War*, 196–97.

36. Lacore, *L'émancipation de la femme*, 2.

37. Quoted in Bouchardeau, *Un coin*, 120; Saumoneau, "Civique des femmes," 4; Boxer, "Socialist Construction," 131–58.

38. Suffrage decree, August 25, 1944. See Bruhl-Lehmann, "Responsabilité civique," 7–10; Barral, *Partis et élections*, 191. Also see Dogan and Narbonne, *Les françaises face*, preface; Plantey, *Prospective de l'etat*, 18–21.

39. Dogan and Narbonne, *Les françaises face*, 41–43, 191.

40. Bessières, *Le vote des femmes*, 34–37. Also see Louise Weiss, "Lettre sur la participation des femmes aux élections," *Les nouvelles epitres*, July 15, 1945.

41. Bessières, *Le vote des femmes*, 27–29, 33.

42. Foley, *Women in France*, 247–48; Diamond, *Second World War*, 198–99.

43. The first article of the 1946 Constitution states: "The law guarantees to women, in all domains, equal rights to those of men." This intense contradiction between constitutional rights and codified law persisted through the 1970s. Morriandpre, "Reform of Civil Code," 1–21.

44. Rauze-Comignan, *Pour la paix universelle*, 17–18, 26. Françoise d'Eaubonne's *Le complexe de Diane* stands as a powerful exception.

45. Dogan and Narbonne *Les françaises face*, 40–41; Rauze-Comignan, *Pour la paix universelle*, 27–28.

46. Pauline Archambault, *Deux mondes*, 117; Claudine Chomat, "Unies, nous pouvons tout sauver: Le bonheur, la paix," *Femmes françaises*, June 11, 1949. Also see Vaillant-Couturier, "Amies de la paix" and Bernard, *Paris rouge*, 114–15 for a description of women's contradictory role in the postwar French Communist Party.

47. Nouvion, "Fémininité et autonomie," 65; Choisy, "Féminité et psychologie," 39.

48. Nouvion, "Fémininité et autonomie," 53–54.

49. Jacqueline Martin, "L'epouse," 277.

50. Nouvion, "Fémininité et autonomie," 63–64.

51. Quoted in Le Cormier [Pauline Archambault], "Au delà du féminisme," 15–16; Pauline Archambault, *Deux mondes*, 39–41, 44–45; Klejman and Rochefort, *L'égalité en marche*, 344.

52. See Doron, Jewish Youth, 22–26, 76; for an examination of the Catholic Left in postwar France, see Tranvouez, "Left Catholicism," 91–94.

53. Atkin, "Rallié and Résistants," 110–12; Tippett-Spirtou, *French Catholicism*, 98–99, 109.

54. Bard, *Les femmes*, 53; Hellman, "Jacques Chevalier," 139–53; Kelly, "Catholicism and the Left," 149–50; Judt, *Past Imperfect*, 29–30, 86; Wilkinson, *Intellectual Resistance*, 17–21; Offen, "Ernest Legouvé," 452–84. Christianity, however influential, remained a quiet affair during the Fourth Republic due to its association with Vichy. See Byrnes, *Catholic and French Forever*, 215. For Christian women's articulation of gender in the 1950s see Dubesset, "Les figures du féminin."

55. Bruhl-Lehmann, "Responsabilité civique," 4.

56. Le Cormier, "Au delà du féminisme," 16–17; Picard, "L'indépendance économique," 156; Rudolph, *Postwar France*, 152.

57. Rauze-Comignan, *Pour la paix universelle*, 3.

58. Drake, *Intellectuals and Politics*, 145–46; Francis and Gontier, *Les ecrits de Beauvoir*, 156–60; Chaperon, "Une génération d'intellectuelles," 99–116; Sanos, *Simone de Beauvoir*, 102–3.

59. Beauvoir, *La force des choses*, 197–98; see Gennari's assessment of the book in the 1960s: *Le dossier de la femme*, 298. Butler, "Performative Acts," 519–20; Albistur and Armogathe, *Histoire du féminisme français*, 611. Beauvoir had significant influence among her students and followers from the intellectual circles of St. Germain des Prés. See Webster and Powell, *Saint-Germain-des-Prés*, 94; Moi, *Simone de Beauvoir*, 190; Marso, "Thinking Politically"; Sanos, *Simone de Beauvoir*.

60. The novelist and essayist Françoise d'Eaubonne early on articulated an explicit feminist critique. See, for example, d'Eaubonne, *Le complex de Diane* and *Y a-t-il encore des hommes?* Marks, *Critical Essays*; Moi, *Feminist Theory*; Reineke, *Beauvoir and Her Sisters*, 22–25; Tidd, *Simone de Beauvoir*, 54.

61. Moynagh, "Beauvoir on Lived Reality"; Simons, *Beauvoir and the Second Sex*, xv–xvii, 8, 25. See also Stavro, "Use and Abuse," 263–80.

62. Gennari and Pauline Archambault were the only conservative writers of the 1950s who mention her ideas. See Pauline Archambault, *Deux mondes*, 65; Moi, *Simone de Beauvoir*, 179–85; Bauer, Simone de Beauvoir, 22–23. See Offen, "Before Beauvoir," 11–36, on the historical uses of sex and gender.

63. Sanos, *Simone de Beauvoir*, 101–5. For a description of the intellectual and material context in which Beauvoir was writing, see Moi, *Simone de Beauvoir*, 185–90; Beauvoir, *Le deuxième sexe*, 655. Also see Simons, *Beauvoir and the Second Sex*, 7. Beauvoir clung to Communism despite mounting evidence that its practice did not live up to her ideals.

64. On particularism, see Célestin and DalMoulin, *France from 1851*, 17.

65. Jacqueline Martin references Hubertine Auclert, nineteenth-century feminist, suffragist, and founder of the group Le droit des femmes, and Olympe de Gouges (although Martin spells her name "Ganges"), Girondin and author of the *Déclaration des droits de la femme*, who was guillotined during the French Revolution. Martin, "L'epouse," 277. Choisy agreed: "Women must deepen their understanding of themselves to the point where . . . they authentically express their 'being,' and not only their talents." Choisy, "Feminité et psychologie," 65.

66. Jacqueline Martin, "L'epouse," 272–73, 277.

67. Le Cormier, "Conclusion,"430.

68. Le Cormier, "Conclusion," 430.

69. Le Cormier, "Conclusion," 431.

70. Le Cormier, "Conclusion," 436–37; Paul Archambault, *La famille*; Fougeyrollas, "Prédominance du mari," 83–102.

71. See, for example, Michel, "Ideologies, Pressure Groups," 7; Fagnani, "L'intégration progressive."

72. Beauvoir, *Second Sex*, 663.

73. See especially Bruhl-Lehmann, "Responsabilité civique," 179–98.

2. Reform and Consensus

1. In the past two decades, Sylvie Chaperon, Judith Coffin, Sarah Fishman, and Miranda Pollard have examined women's experience from the Liberation to the 1970s; Foley, *Women in France*, 255.

2. Duchen, *Women's Rights*, 168–70.

3. Dubesset, "De la citoyenneté," 272. Allwood and Wadia, *Women and Politics*, 29–32.

4. Knibiehler, *Qui gardera les enfants?*, 122. Continuities with the Third Republic and Vichy in terms of family policy were easily apparent. Robcis, *Law of Kinship*, 48.

5. For the traditional view, see Vincent, "Pour la reduction," 21–30; Grégoire, "Résponses à l'enquête," 771–83. Otherwise, see Michel, "Prospective du travail féminin."

6. Lagrave, "Une émancipation sous tutelle," 431–33, 436–37.

7. Maurice Duverger, *Participation des femmes*.

8. Rocard, "Sur le travail," 501–2.

9. Fishman, *We Will Wait*; Bettelheim, "Economic and Social Policy," 3–4, 154; École de haut enseignement, *La condition*, 25. Also Ministère du travail, *L'évolution*, 3.

10. A 1947 study performed by the Institut français d'opinion publique. See Girard, "Le travail féminin," 31–32; Guilbert, "L'emploi féminin," 26, 32. Also see Marzellier, "Une enquête," 1397.

11. A study from the early 1970s showed that at technical high schools, 83 percent of women trained for the tertiary sector, half as secretaries. At the next level of professional training (the CAP V), 66 percent trained for the tertiary sector. Even in university institutes of technology, where only 21 percent of students were women, two-thirds followed tertiary sector courses. Comité du travail féminin, "Formation professionnelle," 41. Law for equal pay for equal work, December 22, 1972. Also see INSEE, *Annuaire rétrospectif*, 99–100; Regnaut, "Les femmes enseignantes," 21–29 and Fishman, *Sexual Revolution*, 54–59, 133–137.

12. Lévy-Bruhl, "L'activité professionnelle," 19–20; Girard, "Le travail féminin," 31, 108; Guilbert, *Les fonctions des femmes*, 232; Ministère du travail, "Formation professionnelle," 53; Longone, *53 millions de français*, 74; Jenson, Hagen, and Reddy, *Feminization of the Labor Force*, 155–58; See Comité du travail féminin, *L'evolution*, 13–15; Girard, "Le travail féminin," 175–77; Lazar, "Cold War Culture," 220–22; Gienow-Hecht, "Cold War," 410–12.

13. Guilbert, "L'emploi féminin," 26–27. Also, Laubier, *Condition of Women*, 114; Gregory and Tidd, *Women in Contemporary France*, 5; Sohn, *Age tendre*, 195.

14. Guilbert, "L'emploi féminin," 26; Sohn, *Age tendre*, 361–62; Pulju, *Mass Consumer Society*, 65–72.

15. Bettelheim, "Economic and Social Policy," 6, 723, 728–29; Steck, "Les prestations familiales," 7. Also see Yves Martin, "Niveau de vie," 407–28.

Martin concludes that using allowances in a natalist policy is justified as it augments the quality of life of families.

16. In the 1920s in France many still viewed the idea of government subsidies as a Communist plot, but such attitudes were changed by pronatalists. The family allowances law of March 11, 1932, combined with pressure on business to enroll in Social Security funds, served as the cornerstone of social welfare between the wars, elaborated upon in the Family Code of 1939. See Pedersen, *Family, Dependence*, 373–87.

17. Pedersen, *Family, Dependence*, 420; Caisse nationale des allocations familiales, "Historique," 29–38; Steck, "Les prestations familiales," 15–17; Dupâquier et al., *Histoire*, 4. Also see Stoetzel, "L'étude du budget-temps," 47–62.

18. Based on review of student admissions and alumni records from 1945 to 1981. Ministère de l'éducation nationale, "Résultats à l'examen," 89, and "Recrutement des professeurs," 398; Sénat, *Rapport*, "Reforme de l'enseignement." Also see Girard, "Le travail féminin," 280–81.

19. École nationale d'administration, *Concours étudiants* (admissions exam), 1956: Male: candidates registered (for exam): 528, admitted (to ENA): 30; Female: candidates registered: 41, admitted, 2; *Concours fonctionnaires* (civil service exam), 1956: Male: candidates registered (for exam): 254, admitted (as state functionary): 24; Female: candidates registered: 18, admitted, 4. Disinterest in educated women was demonstrated in a variety of ways; see "Les intellectuelles,"1–10; Clark, *Rise of Professional Women*, 75, 281; Girard, "Le travail féminin," 40–42; Guilbert, "L'emploi féminin," 28; Duchen, *Women's Rights*, 150–54; Girard, "Le travail féminin," 280–81.

20. Michel and Texier, *La condition*, 185.

21. Dogan and Narbonne, *Les françaises face*, 88, 90–91, 187–88; Michel and Texier, *La condition*, 175–210; Brimo, *Les femmes françaises*, 56–84; Allwood and Wadia, *Women and the State*, 27.

22. Robcis, *Law of Kinship*, 19–20; Soubbotitch, "Recent Important Reforms," 248–49; Offen, *Woman Question*, 51–52. Since a woman could not open a bank account without her husband's consent, and any assets from their earnings were considered part of the community and subject to a husband's discretion, the revisions had little effect.

23. Machard, *Les françaises*, 154.

24. Catholic and feminist, Poinso-Chapuis was the first woman to hold a cabinet post. The Marthe Richard law, April 1947, made houses of prostitution (*maisons closes*) illegal. See Dubesset, "De la citoyenneté," 271–72; Grégoire, "Mariage et régimes matrimoniaux," 693–700.

25. "Réforme des régimes matrimoniaux," *Journal officiel*, Sénat, Rapport no. 144 (April 24, 1965): 6; Michel and Texier, *La condition*, 41–54; L. Neville Brown, "Matrimonial Property Law," 309–10; Hamiaut, *Régimes matrimoniaux*, 20–22. Also see Grégoire, "Mariage et régimes matrimoniaux," 693. Ironically, a revised version of the first draft of the bill, proposed in 1965, departed even further from the old standard, although it still retained the primacy of the community over women's freedoms. See Sénat, *Projet de loi*, "Réforme des régimes matrimoniaux," *Journal officiel*, no. 131 (March 17, 1965): 3.

26. Sénat, *Projet de loi*, "Réforme des régimes matrimoniaux," *Journal officiel*, no. 131 (March 17, 1965): 3; Sénat, *Rapport*, 2; Law no. 65–570, July 13, 1965.

27. Jeannette Prin, "Rappel au règlement," Assemblée nationale, Débats parlementaires, *Journal officiel*, no. 26 (June 1965): 2584. The RDR was composed of Communists who rejected the Stalinism of the PCF as well as other leftists.

28. Jean Foyer, "Discussion d'un projet de loi adopté par le Sénat," Assemblée nationale, Débats parlementaires, *Journal officiel*, June 26, 1965, 2584.

29. Jean de Broglie, "Discussion d'un projet de loi," Débats parlementaires, Sénat, *Journal officiel* (May 6, 1965): 175.

30. Jean Foyer, "Discussion d'un projet de loi adopté par le Sénat," Assemblée nationale, Débats parlementaires, *Journal officiel*, June 26, 1965, 2584–85.

31. Duchen, *Women's Rights*, 177; Offen, *Woman Question*, 617–18.

32. Collette, "Discussion d'un projet de loi adopté par le Sénat," Débats parlementaires, *Journal officiel* (June 26, 1965): 2588. Collette belonged to the UNR, the party founded by de Gaulle in 1958; Foyer, "Suite de la discussion d'un projet de loi adopté par le Sénat," Débats parlementaires, *Journal officiel* (June 26, 1965): 2606.

33. See Glendon, "Matrimonial Property," 25–28.

34. Prin and Collette, Débats parlementaires, Assemblée nationale, *Journal officiel* (June 26, 1965): 2608.

35. Marcel Molle, "Reforme des régimes matrimoniaux," Débats parlementaires, Sénat, *Journal officiel* (May 6, 1965): 184.

36. Jean de Broglie, "Discussion d'un projet de loi," Débats parlementaires, Sénat, *Journal officiel* (May 6, 1965): 176.

37. Dekeuwer-Defossez, *Dictionnaire juridique*, 355, 361.

38. Prin, Launay, and Thome-Patenôtre, "Rappel au règlement," Assemblée nationale, Débat parlementaires, *Journal officiel* (June 26, 1965): 258–65.

39. The *dénatalité* debate continued even when abortion was legalized, but the subject shifted to the state's role in enticing families to have more children. See, for example, "La stagnation des prestations familiales n'est

pas la principale cause de la chute de la natalité en France," *Le Monde*, December 5, 1970, 33; Michel Debré, "Pour une politique de la famille," *Le figaro*, February 26, 1974; Debré, *Ami ou ennemi*; Yvette Roudy, "Deux ou trois choses que l'on oublie," *Le Monde*, December 29, 1978, 2. For a discussion of feminist pronatalism see Pedersen, *Family, Dependence*, 368.

40. Jobs, *Riding the New Wave*, 187–89.

41. Modern concerns with *dénatalité* began in the nineteenth century with France's defeat in the Franco-Prussian War. Fortescue, *Third Republic*, 94–95; Jobs, *Riding the New Wave*, 189; Bard, *Les filles de Marianne*, 209–17; Jenson, "New Rights for French Women," 281; Dourlen-Roullier, *La vérité sur l'avortement*, 26; Odile Dhavernas, *Droits des femmes*, 144–45; Marie-France Callu, *Le nouveau droit*, 170; Guéraiche, *Les femmes et la République*, 91–92

42. Odile Dhavernas, *Droits des femmes*, 146–47; Marie-France Callu, *Le nouveau droit*, 171.

43. The decrees of October 5, 1953, and May 11, 1955, codified legislative texts concerning public health. Dourlen-Roullier, *La vérité sur l'avortement*, 24–26; Odile Dhavernas, *Droits des femmes*, 141–42, 148. Mossuz-Lavau, *Les lois de l'amour*, 18; and McLaren, "Abortion in France," 461–85. See Shepard, *Invention of Decolonization* and "'Something Notably Erotic.'" Also see Marsh and Frith, *France's Lost Empires*.

44. Valabrègue, *Contrôle des naissances*, 153.

45. Herzog, "Abortion, Christianity, Disability," 249–63; Herzog, *Sexuality in Europe*, 100.

46. Herzog, *Sexuality in Europe*, 212; Leclercq, *Le contrôle des naissances*; Valabrègue, *Contrôle des naissances*, 212.

47. Littré, a group of Freemason doctors in France, Switzerland, and Belgium, worked on spreading birth control information and devices, inspiring some interest among the French Left but no serious political action. Mossuz-Lavau, *Les lois de l'amour*, 21; Valabrègue, *Contrôle des naissances*, 10.

48. Valabrègue, *Contrôle des naissances*, 115.

49. Lagroua Weill-Hallé, "Du conflit"; Valabrègue, *Contrôle des naissances*, 114; Michel and Texier, *La condition*, 55. Some doctors were already arguing that the legalization of birth control would help lower the unconscionably high abortion rate, but they were not in the majority. See Péquignot, "Simple remarques," 175–81.

50. Derogy, *Des enfants*, 20–45. He claimed the Ministry of Public Health counted sixty thousand abortions in 1947. I have been unable to confirm the statistics. They are nevertheless consistent with nineteenth-century medical statistics on abortion rates in France. In contrast, half this num-

ber was estimated in 1950. See McLaren, "Abortion in France," 479; Mignon, "Lutte contre l'avortement," 489-90.

51. Derogy cited a sample of one hundred hospitals in which the majority of women suffering from abortion complications comprised workers, employees, and domestics from poor to moderate income. Derogy, *Des enfants*, 63-65, 72-73. See Texier, "Quelques indications" and Geisendorf, L'OURS, 1-APO-75.

52. Jobs, *Riding the New Wave*, 185-89; Colin Roberts, "Secularization and (Re)Formulation," 264-68; Derogy, *Des enfants*, 241, 247. Also see Daric, "Niveau de vie," 425-27.

53. Bard and Mossuz-Lavau, *Le planning familial*, 21-23; Chaperon, "Le MFPF face," 21; also see Muller, "Etre féministe en France; Michel, "Evaluation du rapport."

54. Beauvoir, "Préface," *Le planning familial*, 4-5; MFPF, "Instructions à l'usage," L'OURS, 1-APO-71; also see Offen, "Depopulation, Nationalism," 675.

55. Odile Dhavernas, *Droits des femmes*, 145-46; Mossuz-Lavau, *Les lois de l'amour*, 39.

56. André Berge, paper read during "Journées d'etudes du groupe Lyonnais d'études médicales," April 1957, in Valabrègue, *Controle des naissances*, 135.

57. Michel, "A propos du contrôle," 1201-18; Valabrègue, *Controle des naissances*, 154-56.

58. Union nationale des caisses d'allocations familiales sponsored the survey. Lagroua Weill-Hallé, *Le planning familial*, 85; Valabrègue, *Controle des naissances*, 157.

59. See Fabre's arguments on contraception and abortion in Pascal and Fabre, "Contraception et problèmes démographiques," 49-53; Mutuelle générale de l'education nationale, L' OURS, 1-APO-76; Michel, "Evaluation du rapport," 2; Rochefort, "Le rôle laïcisateur," 60-61.

60. Auclair, *Le livre noir*; Dourlen-Rollier, "La vérité sur l'avortement"; Zancarini-Fournel, Rochefort, and Pavard, *Les lois Veil*.

61. Valabrègue, *Contrôle des naissances*, 205-6, 213, 224; Thébaud, "Réflexions," *Le planning familial*, 98.

62. Valabrègue, *Contrôle des naissances*, 191-95.

63. See Dumont, "Le combat national," 1081-92. The law of May 25, 1956, was proposed by prominent Communists: National Assembly Deputy Waldek Rochet and Secretary General Jeannette Vermeersch. They called for the expansion of the definition of "therapeutic abortion" but argued against the legalization of contraception. They were willing to allow abortion for a woman with three children, in poor health, unmarried, or with

economic difficulties—similar in principle to the arguments made for contraception. Mossuz-Lavau, *Les lois du l'amour*, 28; Mazelin, "Pour une maternité," 873; Vincent, "La restauration," 20–38.

64. Vincent, "La restauration," 29; also see *Journal officiel*, Assemblée nationale, Documents, 2203 (April 4, 1967), 1027; Dubois, "La france a besoin," 85–95; Legay, "La question des naissances," 74–75.

65. *L'humanité*, January 26, 1965; Mossuz-Lavau, *Les lois du l'amour*, 34; Chaperon, "La radicalisation," 63.

66. Odile Dhavernas, *Droits des femmes*, 150; Mossuz-Lavau, *Les lois du l'amour*, 27–29, 37. Assemblée nationale, *Proposition de loi* 1285 (December 17, 1964); 1678 (November 3, 1965); 1680 (November 16, 1965); 1710 (November 27, 1965) and Sénat, *Proposition de loi* 82 (December 6, 1965); 104 (April 26, 1966); Valabrègue, *Contrôle des naissances*, 191. In November 1965 Jacqueline Thome-Patenôtre, Radical-Socialist deputy, proposed law no. 1680 modifying the law of 1920 in the name of the newly formed Rassemblement démocratique. Also see Vauthier, "Famille et socialisme," 548. Between 1957 and 1967 a total of eleven laws attempting to liberalize contraception or abortion were proposed by the Left and summarily killed by the government.

67. Rabaut, *Histoire des féminismes*, 319–31, 343–47; Mossuz-Lavau, *Les lois du l'amour*, 41–44. *Journal officiel*, Assemblée nationale, Documents, 2203 (April 4, 1967), 1013.

68. Numbers are approximate. In the 1950s the birthrate declined slightly, but the mortality rate dropped in half. Only after 1975 did the birthrate fall significantly. See Dupâquier et al., *Histoire*, 214; *Journal officiel*, Assemblée nationale, Documents, 2203 (April 4, 1967): 1022–27; Valabrègue, *Contrôle des naissances*, 164; Lagroua Weill-Hallé, "Du conflit," 431.

69. Guislain also happened to be a member of many remembrance organizations such as l'Union nationale des victimes de guerre and l'Union nationale des déportés, internés et anciens résistants du nord, leaving us to speculate that *dénatalité* and defeat must have been closely linked in his mind. Guislain argued that factors others than contraception, television, and the loosening of public morality posed a greater threat to the French birthrate; *Journal officiel*, Sénat, "Régulation des naissances et usage des contraceptifs," 585 (December 5, 1967), 2033–35.

70. *L'express*, June 19–25, 1967, 34; "Rapport fait au nom de la commission spéciale chargée d'examiner la proposition de loi de M. Neuwirth," *Journal officiel*, Assemblée nationale, Documents, 2203 (April 4, 1967), 1013.

71. Coquille, "Naissance du mouvement," 11.

72. Mossuz-Lavau, *Les lois du l'amour*, 56; Odile Dhavernas, *Droits des femmes*, 153–54.

73. It is necessary to distinguish somewhat between the "old Left" of established political parties and the "new Left" of 1968, which spoke in grander, more abstract terms about women's liberation but offered little if any change. French women's issues paralleled larger French state-building efforts such as Gaullism and the "Third Way." See Gallois, "Against Capitalism?," 49–72.

74. Guilbert, *Les fonctions des femmes*. See also Chombart de Lauwe et al., *La femme* and Marie-José and Paul-Henri Chombart de Lauwe, *La vie quotidienne*; Michel and Texier, *La condition*; and Michel, *Famille, industrialisation, logement*.

75. Guilbert, *Les fonctions des femmes*, 1–2. She analyzes studies performed by INSEE in the 1950s as well as the historical evolution of the sector from 1866.

76. See, among others, Marie-José and Paul-Henri Chombart de Lauwe, *Images de la femme*, 384; Sartin, *La promotion des femmes* and *La femme libérée?*; Pulju, *Mass Consumer Society*, 66.

77. Marie-José and Paul-Henri Chombart de Lauwe, *Images de la femme*, 369. Surveys showed that women's expectations were rising; Giroud, *La nouvelle vague*, 1.

78. For a fascinating analysis of the recreation of "feminine sexuality," see Weiner, *Enfants Terribles*; Salomon-Bayet, "La neutralité est impossible," 13, 18; Michel and Texier, *La condition*, 6, 52; Beauvoir, "La condition féminine," 120–27; Vincendeau, "Brigitte Bardot," 363–76; Niel, *Le drame*.

79. Audry also published Lagroua Weill-Hallé's *La grand peur d'aimer* and Maria Montessori's *L'enfant*.

80. Michel and Texier, *La condition*, 232–33.

81. Michel, "La française," 20–30.

82. Salomon-Bayet, "La neutralité est impossible," 18; Grégoire, *Le métier*, 7–8.

83. Grégoire, *Le métier*, 7–8; Salomon-Bayet, "La neutralité est impossible," 13. See also Texier, "Virilité et fémininité," 81–93.

84. See especially Moses, *French Feminism*; Giroud, La nouvelle vague, 1.

85. Aumont, "Jeune fille, lève-toi!" 18. Netter, *La femme face*. The latter is a clear, easy-to-read outline of women's rights (regarding divorce and marriage, for example), as well as an explanation of the functions of French institutions such as banking and Social Security. For more examples, see, among others, Sartin, *La promotion des femmes* and *La femme libérée*; Lagroua Weill-Hallé, *Le guide*; Villeneuve, "La femme et le Code civil,"

Dossier Suzanne Blaise, BMD. Also see Michel, "La française," 20–36 and Maria Craipeau, "Une femme," 101–8.

86. Marzellier, "Une enquête," 1400–1401. According to Marzellier, traditional political groups aimed at women did little to promote their concerns, and L'Union des femmes françaises, formed after the Liberation to educate women to accept their new status, did good work but ignored women as individuals.

87. d'Eaubonne, *Le complex de Diane*, 301.

88. See Moi, *Simone de Beauvoir*; Bair, *Simone de Beauvoir*; Tristan and Pisan, *Histoires du MLF*.

89. See, among many others, Derrick, "The Dissenters," 65; Andrée Michel, *Les travailleurs algérians*.

90. Audry, "Dix ans après," 120. Also see Michel, "Famille, société industrielle." She argued that greater sexual or individual freedom or professional success did not necessarily translate into liberation.

91. Chaperon, "La radicalisation," 62; LeCoultre, "La condition féminine."

3. Birth of Second-Wave Feminism

1. See Bourg, *From Revolution to Ethics*, to understand the impact and some of the limits of thought and action during this era; Reineke, *Beauvoir and Her Sisters*, 24–25; Wadia, "Events of May," 148–66. Wadia argued that women's participation in and ideas on the 1968 events have been so overlooked that it is difficult to draw a clear or comprehensive picture of their role. This is still largely true. Wadia is a notable exception. Other exceptions are Picq, *Libération des femmes*; Duchen, *Women's Rights*; Artières and Zancarini-Fournel, *68: Une histoire collective*.

2. Jobs, *Riding the New Wave*, 24, 36, 39, 48; Sohn, *Age tendre*, 361; Kristin Ross, *Fast Cars*, 1–13, 149; Servan-Schreiber, *Spirit of May*, 22–25; Gombin, *Modern Leftism*.

3. Scioldo-Zürcher, "Cost of Decolonization," 111. Also see Kristin Ross, *Fast Cars*, 4, 78, 152–53.

4. Reader, *Intellectuals and the Left*, 13; Ross and Frader, "May Generation," 108–9; Jackson, Milne, and Williams, *May '68*, 52–53; Maruani, *Les syndicats*, 29; Remy, *De l'utopie*, 49.

5. Reader, *Intellectuals and the Left*, 13; Ross and Frader, "May Generation," 108–9.

6. Jackson, Milne, and Williams, *May '68*, 53; Touraine, *May Movement*, 239.

7. Kurlansky, *1968*, 211–19; Célestin and DalMolin, *France from 1851*, 270; Scioldo-Zürcher, "Cost of Decolonization," 99–111; Hamon and Rotman, "Rise and Fall," 12–13.

8. Quoted in Bourges, *Student Revolt*, 33–39. Julian Bourg stresses that the events revived a discussion of ethics and its parameters in France that was crucial to its development of late-twentieth-century philosophy. Bourg, *From Revolution to Ethics*, 3–18.

9. Author interview with Christine Delphy, Paris, May 19, 1992.

10. Jenson, Hagen, and Reddy, *Feminization of the Labour Force*, 155–63; Maruani, *Les syndicats*, 26–27; Confédération générale du travail, "Les femmes salariées"; author interview with Chantal Rogerat, Paris, March 26, 1992.

11. Delphy, "Le MLF en France," manuscript, Delphy private collection.

12. An exception was around the issue of genital mutilation. See, among others, "Elements de bibliographie" and "Lettre de 24 Octobre 1979," *Collection mutilation sexuelles* 391.7 MUT; MFPF, "Centre de documentation," 4; Mandel, *Muslims and Jews*, 127; Nicollet, *Femmes d'Afrique*, 63–64; Gordon, "From Militancy to History," 115–23.

13. Mouvement démocratique féminin, "Les buts et l'organisation du MDF," 1963, Q pièce 8209, BDIC.

14. MDF, "Article destiné au premier numéro du bulletin," BDIC, 4°962; Feldman. "De FMA au MLF"; Duchen, *Women's Rights*, 171–73. Marguerite Thibert, one of the directors of the NGO International Labor Bureau, was also a member.

15. See, for example, Eyquem, "Le travail à temps partiel: Un expédient," *Le Monde*, January 2, 1970, 10; Albistur and Armogathe, *Histoire du féminisme français*, 654–60; Le Mouvement démocratique féminin, "Les régimes matrimoniaux," 1965. 4*D 1145, BDIC.

16. Marie-Thérèse Eyquem and MDF, "Chère amie," February 3, 1971, Delphy private collection. Also see Picq, *Libération des femmes*, 265.

17. FMA, "Pensez-vous que tout a été dit sur l'homme et la femme?," Delphy private collection; Roger Rebes founded the group Mouvement de liberation des hommes. See Jacquemart, *Les hommes*, 82.

18. FMA, "Pensez-vous." Colette Audry, Gallimard's editor of the series Collection femme, recruited Yvette Roudy to translate it; it appeared as *La femme mystifiée* in 1964.

19. FMA, "Pensez-vous"; FMA, "FMA se propose de lutter contre l'inégalité," Delphy private collection; Muller, "Etre féministe en France."

20. FMA, "Notre point de départ est féministe," Zelensky and Delphy private collections. "Letter addressed to Messieurs," dated by Zelensky as February 18, 1970, Zelensky private collection.

21. Delphy, "L'ennemi principal," 157–72. Also see Wittig et al., "Combat pour la libération," 16; Perrot, "Écrire l'histoire," 52–53.

22. Alice Schwarzer's interview with Beauvoir for *Ms.* and reprinted in Marks and Courtivron, *New French Feminisms*, 143, explains Beauvoir's support for feminism and her seeming disinterest in it before 1971.

23. Sexual liberation meant that women were not at the beck and call of men. See Gildea, Mark, and Warring, *Europe's 1968*, 247-52; Bard, "Le lesbiennisme," 114.

24. FMA, "Notre point de départ est féministe," 2, Zelensky and Delphy private collections.

25. Delphy, "Les origines," 139; FMA, "Notre point de depart est féministe," 3, Zelensky private collection.Ample precedent was set for this position, principally by Friedrich Engels, who in his treatise *The Origins of Private Property* argued that throughout history and up to the present women's relationship to men was similar to the relationship of the proletariat and the bourgeoisie. See Wittig, Rothenburg, and Stephenson,"Combat pour la libération," 13-16; Elles voient rouge, *Féminisme et marxisme/journées*.

26. FMA, "Sexualité. Couple. Famille," Delphy private collection; Chaperon, "La radicalisation," 66; Zancarini-Fournel, "Notre corps," 210.

27. FMA, "Notre point de départ est féministe," 1, Zelensky and Delphy private collections.

28. Alice Schwartzer, "La femme révoltée: Interview with Simone de Beauvoir," *Le nouvel observateur*, February 14, 1972, 48; Beauvoir quoted in Roudy, *A cause d'elles*, 113-14.

29. Beauvoir quoted in Roudy, *A cause d'elles*, 113-14; Reineke, *Beauvoir and Her Sisters*, 72; Chaperon, "La radicalisation," 68; Bair, *Simone de Beauvoir*, 543-47; Marso, "Beauvoir on Mothers"; Picq, "Simone de Beauvoir," 175-85.

30. See Evans, *Personal Politics*.

31. The French, German, and Italian feminist movements all were born of the social conflict of the late 1960s but developed differently. For a brief overview see Smith, *Changing Lives*, 524-39.

32. "Une révolte des femmes américaines: Contre le 'chauvinisme male,' des dizaines de milliers de 'guérillères' américaines ont commence revolution,'" *Le nouvel observateur*, February 16, 1969, 51-56; Letter from FMA to "Messieurs," February 1, 1970, Zelensky private collection; Marianne Lohse, "Les manifestantes féministes de Paris: 'Il y a plus inconnu que le Soldat inconnu: c'est la femme'," *France-Soir*, August 28, 1; "Dépôt d'une gerbe à la femme du soldat inconnu," ORTF (Collection: JT 20H), August 26, 1970, http://fresques.ina.fr/elles-centrepompidou/fiche-media /ArtFem00101/depot-d-une-gerbe-a-la-femme-du-soldat-inconnu.html.

33. Letter from FMA to "Messieurs, February 1, 1970, Zelensky private collection.

34. Groupe MLF du lycée Claude Monet, "A quand nôtre libération?," Zelensky private collection.

35. In 1962 and again in 1968 the number of employed women increased, and from 1968 onward, specifically numbers of women twenty-five to thirty-five years old were employed whether or not they had children. They continued to be paid far less than men, however. See Laubier, *Condition of Women*; Maruani, *Les syndicats*, 26–27; Mendras, *La sagesse*, 163–72. Also see Andrée Michel, "Naissance du conscience féministe," 31–38 and Jacquemart, *Les hommes*, 153–85 on who were the militant feminists.

36. Mouvement de libération des femmes, "On n'appelle pas ça du travail," 1970, BDIC.

37. Jackson, Milne, and Williams, *May '68*, 52–53; Maruani, *Les syndicats*, 29; Remy, *De l'utopie*, 49.

38. Mossuz-Lavau and Sineau, *Enquête sur les femmes*, 221–22; Eyquem broached the subject once more in "Un expédient," 1–7. Also see the September 1969 issue of *Antoinette*. From 1969 to 1982, Rogerat was the editor in chief of *Antoinette*, which became more ambitious and explicitly feminist under her direction.

39. Chaplin, *Turning On the Mind*, 131; Jenson, "One Robin," 62–64. It was the Socialists, in contrast, who adopted the radical philosophy and rhetoric of women's liberation.

40. Flyer from the University of Vincennes meeting around the summer of 1970, Zelensky private collection.

41. Voldman, "Mai '68," 46; Gibbon, "Trade Unions," 139–51; Le Garrec, *Les messagères*, 138–39.

42. Originally founded by the Italian Communist Amadeo Bordiga. Author interview with Danièle Voldman, Paris, May 19, 1992.

43. Author interview with Christine Delphy, Paris, May 19, 1992.

44. Tristan and Pisan, *Histoires du MLF*, 37–39; author interview with Christine Delphy; also see Zelensky, "Féministe de naissance," Zelensky private collection, ca. 1975.

45. *Le livre de l'oppression*, 10; "Premières journées de dénonciation des crimes contre les femmes," "Femmes, célibataires ou mariées, avons-nous vraiment le choix?," and "Des crimes! Quels crimes?," Zelensky private collection.

46. "Que voulez-vous exactement Daniel Cohn-Bendit?," *Le nouvel observateur*, May 8–14, 1968, 18–19; Daniel Cohn-Bendit, "Notre com-

mune du 10 mai," *Le nouvel observateur*, May 15–21, 1968; "Une crèche à Nanterre," pamphlet, BDIC; Duchen, *Feminism in France*, 6; Voldman, "Mai '68," 45. Also see Reader, "Symbolic Violence"; Centre d'études et de recherches marxistes, *La condition féminine*, 4.

47. Chambers and Carver, *Judith Butler*, 31–33, 57–59; see also Jagger, *Judith Butler*.

48. FMA, "Perspectives," Delphy private collection.

49. FMA, "Pourquoi FMA," May or June 1968, Delphy private collection. Jacquemart, *Les hommes*, 82–95.

50. Dhoquois, *Appartenance et exclusion*, 123–26; Duchen, *Feminism in France*, 8; Picq, *Libération des femmes*, 15; Guadilla, *Libération des femmes*, 30–31. As Keith Reader suggests, the slogan is a play on Mao's "Power grows out of the barrel of a gun."

51. See "Organiser une crèche 24hrs sur 24hrs," Delphy private collection; Roudy and Maignial, "Des crèches à l'université et sur les lieux de travail," Zelensky private collection.

52. Picq, "Le mouvement," 29; "Nécessité de la non-mixité," Zelensky private collection; Rochefort, "La non-mixité," handwritten manuscript, ca. 1970, Zelensky and Delphy private collections.

53. "Nécessité de la non-mixité," Zelensky private collection; letter from J. Feldman-Hogason to Delphy, August 7, 1970, Delphy private collection; *Le livre de l'oppression*, 51.

54. FMA, "Notre point de départ," 3; Cohn-Bendit, *Obsolete Communism*, 29.

55. "F.M.A. Paris, B.P." Delphy private collection; Chaplin, "Orgasm," 385–90; Robcis, "Republicanism," 225.

56. Wadia, "Events of May," 153–54; Jobs, *Riding the New Wave*, 189. See Comité d'action de corbeille pour la libération de la sexualité, "Apprenons à faire l'amour, car c'est le chemin du bonheur, c'est la plus merveilleuse façon de se parler et de se connaître," Zelensky private collection.

57. FMA, "Perspectives," 1, Delphy private collection.

58. FMA, "Notre point de départ est féministe," 3, Zelensky and Delphy private collections; Daniel and Gabriel Cohn-Bendit, *Obsolete Communism*, 29.

59. Dekeuwer-Defossez, *Dictionnaire juridique*, 24–26.

60. "La sexualité est à la mode," 7, Delphy private collection; Bouchoux, "Gabrielle Russier," 56–64.

61. See, for example, "Devenir capable de toucher nos corps," Zelensky private collection.

62. Sexuality Commission members: Emmanuelle de Lesseps, Danièle Levy, Paul Casassus, Serge Rasko, Julien Romere, Roger Ribes, Yvonne Simon, and Dominique Gensac. See documents, "La sexualité est à la mode,"

manuscript; "Sexualité, couple, famille"; "Révolution sexuelle ou erotisme bourgeois"; Révolution sexuelle: Acte ou parole"; Titres provisoires,
"Sexualité, qu'est-ce que le désir pour une fille? (enquête), 1969; Notes:
"Réunion du 2 septembre 1970, group sexualité"; "Réactions au questionnaire sur la sexualité"; Collectif famille-sexualité, "Groupe (polymorphe
pervers) sur une politique sexuelle," Zelensky private collection. Letter
from Feldman-Hogason to Zelensky, Oslo, November 10, 1969, Zelensky
private collection.
63. FMA, "Notre point de départ est féministe," 4, Delphy and Zelensky private collections.
64. The four regular members remaining were Delphy, Zelensky,
Lesseps, and Feldman-Hogasen. Response to letters: Bernard Lauzanne,
Le Monde, April 22, 1969 and September 12, 1969; Francine Lazurick, *L'au-
rore*, September 12, 1969. See "Vous invite à participer au débat organ-
isé sur: Echec au couple avec Albert Memmi, auteur de *L'homme dominé*,"
February 10, 1969; "L'éducation différentiante ou le soldat et la poupée,"
Delphy and Zelensky private collection.
65. Wittig et al., "Combat pour la libération," 13–16; Thibaut, "Entretien," 66–70.
66. Wittig et al., "Combat pour la libération," 13.
67. Tristan and Pisan, *Histoires du* MLF, 59; Picq, *Le mouvement*, 31.
68. The expression also implied conflict such as "the sparks fly."
69. "Letter from Oslo," August 7, 1970; FMA, "Culture," Delphy private
collection.
70. "Préparation du 3e *Torchon brûle*," "Comment s'est fabriqué le journal," Zelensky private collection.
71. "Deux analyses," 5.
72. Author interview with Michèle Le Dœuff, Paris, May 14, 1992.
73. Bourg, *From Revolution to Ethics*, introduction.

4. Feminist Theory and Practice

1. Christine Delphy, Christiane Rochefort, Anne Zelensky, Monique Wittig, Julie Dassin, Monique Bouroux, Cathy Bernheim, Emmanuelle de
Lesseps, and Jeanine Serre.
2. "La journée de la libération des femmes," *Le Monde*, August 28, 1970, 4;
"Arrest Follows Tribute to Wife of Unknown Soldier," *International Herald
Tribune*, August 27, 1970; Pierre Paraf, "La révolte des femmes," *Combat*,
August 29–30, 1971, 1–2.
3. "Metro-Pince-Fesses, y en a marre!," Delphy private collection.
4. Zancarini-Fournel, "Notre corps," 217.

5. France had held other États généraux de la femme during 1929 and 1931. See Bard, *Les filles de Marianne*. See Marie-José Chombart de Lauwe, "Les femmes," 30.

6. Roudy, a journalist and Socialist Party member, was later appointed Ministre déléguée, Chargée des droits de la femme from 1981 to1986; Vaillant-Couturier was a long-time deputy and vice president of l'Union des femmes françaises; Weiss had been a prominent journalist, pacifist, and feminist since the 1920s. *Elle*, Etats généraux de la femme, Versailles, November 1970. "Conférence de presse" and "Organisation et programme" from this conference are in the Delphy private collection. Simone de Beauvoir was conspicuously absent from the meeting.

7. "Les etats généraux de la femme: Arriver à l'égalité sans passer par la lute des sexes," *France soir*, November 24, 1970.

8. "Une grande enquête du service études et sondages vous interroge sur la condition féminine et prépare avec vous *Les états généraux de la femme*, Delphy private collection. For the results of the survey see Elle, *La grande venture*.

9. "Nous dénonçons la campagne des états généraux," notes for the speech, "Questionnaire," Zelensky private collection.

10. "Nous dénonçons," Delphy private collection.

11. Célestin and and DalMolin, *France from 1851*, 327–28.

12. By 1965 the children of the baby boom began arriving at university. See Mendras, *La sagesse*, 18; "Notes," Delphy private collection.

13. Mauduit and Raimond, *Elle*, 233–38. For a record of the proceedings see Mauduit, *La révolte*. Feminists put on their own États généraux du féminisme in 1929, 1930, and 1931. See Offen, *Woman Question*, 614–15.

14. Le Dœuff, "Hiparchia's Choice," 48.

15. Groupe MLF du lycée Claude Monet, "A quand notre libération" and "Nous sommes 27 millions," Zelensky private collection.

16. Picq, *Libération des femmes*, 190. Feminists rebelled from the start against hierarchy and traditional organizations as essentially patriarchal and controlling. "Ras le bol des histoires de tendances," Zelensky private collection.

17. Picq, *Le mouvement*, 55–60; Remy, *De l'utopie*, 46–47; "Deux analyses," 5.

18. Cercle Elisabeth Dimitriev, "Sortir de l'ombre"; "Texte du Cercle Élisabeth Dimitriev: Qu'est ce que le Cercle Elisabeth Dimitriev" was republished under the title *Brève histoire du MLF*; "Elizaveta Dmitrieva," Russian exile, member of the First International, and friend of Louise Michel, was called Madame X by communards who fought with her at the barricades.

19. Des ex-militantes du MLF, "Ras le bol de la révolution femino-sexuelle *ou* comment faire la révolution en se masturbant le clitoris!," Delphy private

collection; Un groupe de femmes, "Proposition de discussion à propos de l'A.G.," Zelensky private collection.

20. "Qu'est ce que le Cercle Élisabeth Dimitriev," Zelensky private collection.

21. See Simone, "La prise de parole comme prise de pouvoir (à propos de la réunion sur la Mutu)" and "Ras l'bol des organisatrices qui, d'un côté récupèrent les idées en les enrobant dans tout un discours vachement structuré," Zelensky private collection.

22. Dhoquois, *Appartenance et exclusion*, 122.

23. It is not always easy to pinpoint exactly who were founders of every group owing to the rapid changes and crossovers between them. I've done my best. Stevi Jackson, *Christine Delphy*, 5. "Féministes révolutionnaires," *Torchon brûle* 5, 7–9. Also see "Réflexions sur le féminisme. Féministes radicales. Recueil de textes diffusé à la Conférence nationale du mouvement anglais, Londres 1972," and Féministes révolutionnaires, "Pourquoi un groupe sur l'exploitation domestique?," Delphy private collection.

24. Author interview with Christine Delphy, May 19, 1993.

25. "We Are 27 Million," Zelensky private collection. Also, *Bulletin of the Women's Liberation Movement* 2 (December 10, 1970); Christiane, "Pour les féministes révolutionnaires, schéma du travail," November 1970, Delphy private collection.

26. Delphy, *Un universalism*, 12–14; Bard, "Le lesbiennisme," 145.

27. Mother's Day, May 28, 1972: "Comme c'est gentil, la fête des mères!" and "Ma fille, mon fis," Zelensky private collection.

28. "Journées de dénonciation des crimes contre la femme," BDIC, papiers Françoise Picq, Mfc 0198, tracts; "Pourquoi ce texte?," 3–5. Members of the group had also participated in the actions against "Maisons maternels" for young unwed mothers. See *Action socialiste* 19 (September 1971), L'OURS.

29. Féministes révolutionnaires, "Processus pour soumettre," 9; "Pour un mouvement féministe révolutionnaire," October 1970, Delphy private collection.

30. Letter from Feldman-Hogason to Delphy, Oslo, August 7, 1970, Dephy private collection.

31. For a discussion on some of radical feminism's contributions, see Flamant, *À tire d'elles*, 27, 56–57.

32. Möser, *Féminismes en traduction*, 49–60, 198–202, 215–19.

33. See Fouque, "Le mouvement," 226; Des femmes du MLF, "Politique et Psychanalyse," BMD, Dossier Antoinette Fouque; "D'une tendance," 18; "Féminisme ou lute de femmes: Débat avec Benoîte Groult," *Quotidien des femmes*, March 6, 1976, 7. "Féminisme ou lute de femmes," 7. Coquille,

Naissance du mouvement. Every account I have read of this group estab-
lishes Fouque as its leader, although she asserted that it had no leader.

34. See Fouque, "Femmes en mouvements," 128; Roudinesco, *Jacques Lacan*,
444-45; Remy, *De l'utopie*, 38.

35. Fouque, "Une expérience," 9-10, 25.

36. Remy, *De l'utopie*, 39-40; Roudinesco, *Jacques Lacan*, 472; Duchen, *Feminism in France*, 32-34. Fouque, "Le mouvement," 227.

37. Chaperon, "Antoinette Fouque," 207-9; "La situation et notre politique . . .
ni victims, ni complices," *Quotidien des femmes*, March 3, 1975, 3-5.

38. Fouque used the lowercase *des femmes* in the names of her journals
and her publishing house (Éditions *des femmes*) to imply inclusion of all
women without hierarchy. Coquille, "Naissance du mouvement," 98;
Remy, *De l'utopie*, 61; see Kaufmann-McCall, "Politics of Différence,"
287-92; Fouque, "Le mouvement," 180.

39. The director of research is listed as Francine Demichel (from the Political
Science Department), but Fouque claimed Cixous as the chair of the committee, although she is not listed as such in the dissertation. Fouque, 2 *Sexes*.

40. "La difference internée," 13; Remy, *De l'utopie*, 41. Fouque reserved
her most strident criticism for the Féministes révolutionnaires, who she
believed corrupted women's liberation with their critique of the feminine.

41. Association la griffonne, *Douze ans de femmes*, 64; also see Psyche-et-Po/
des femmes, "Le revolution est en travail," *Libération*, June 10, 1974,
and "Antoinette Fouque, entretien avec Kate Millett," *des femmes en
mouvements-hebdo*, May 16, 1980, respectively; Fouque, "Une experience," 21; Coquille, "Naissance du mouvement," 95-96.

42. des femmes du MLF, "Politique et Psychanalyse," BMD, Dossier Antoinette Fouque. The tract closes with "long live women's struggle, long live
the class struggle." Including disparate, unexplained, or contradictory
elements in her writings (or writings by the group) gave her theory and
her politics a flexibility she would not have had otherwise. See Coquille,
"Naissance du mouvement," 97-100.

43. Offen, "Defining Feminism," 149. Gauchet and Nora, "Femmes en mouvements," 7-46. This article was originally published in *Le débat* 59
(March-April 1990): 22-23.

44. Offen, "Defining Feminism," 135-36, 147, 152.

45. See Moses, "Made in America," 241-74; Fouque described her difficulties
in the interview with *Le débat*.

46. Fouque, "Femmes en mouvements," 128-29.

47. See Fouque, *2 sexes*. Fouque was elected in June 1994 on the Energie radicale list with Bernard Tapie, and to the vice presidency of the Commission des droits de la femme au Parlement européen. Mazur, *Gender Bias*, 193.

48. Picq, *Le mouvement*, 40; Annette Lévy-Willard, "Quand on réécrit l'histoire du féminisme avec Antoinette Fouque," February 22, 2014, http://www.liberation.fr/societe/2014/02/22/quand-on-reecrit-l-histoire-du-feminisme-avec-antoinette-fouque_982274.

49. "Quand j'entends," August 30, 1980. BMD, 396 PSY.

50. Roudinesco, *Jacques Lacan*, 506. For a more positive account of these early meetings, see Sweatman, *Risky Business*, 32–35.

51. Coquille, "Naissance du mouvement," 100–101; Coquille reports that, in 1973, Fouque was accused by some members of the group of "appropriating power over militants through psychoanalysis." She decided to end analysis with members of the group and then to take a hiatus from it altogether.

52. Martine Storti, "Politique et Psychanalyse: Coupable ou non coupable?," *Libération*, January 8, 1975, 3.

53. Translation of "Mais toi, d'où tu parles?" Nadja Ringart, "La naissance d'une secte," *Libération*, June 1, 1977. Also see the recollections of Jackie in "Des oubliettes," 28–29.

54. Boissonnas, Book Event; Fouque and Boisonnas's relationship has found its way into many sources. See, for example, Mouvement de libération des femmes, *Génération* MLF, 68–71; Salvaresi, *Mai en heritage*, 134–36; Natalie Brochard, "Antoinette Fouque, décès et controverse," *Site De L'emiliE*, February 25, 2014, http://www.lemilie.org/index.php/ailleurs/556-antoinette-fouque-deces-et-controverse. This contrasts with Jennifer L. Sweatman's argument that feminists simply resented Fouque's well-funded organizations; see *Risky Business*, 53.

55. Guadilla, Libération des femmes, 72. Fouque herself denied that she held such influence over the group. See also Association mouvement pour les luttes féministes, *Chroniques d'une imposture*.

56. For an evaluation of Beauvoir and her analysis of lesbian sexuality, see Tidd, *Simone de Beauvoir*, 53–56; Bard, "Le lesbiennisme," 113.

57. Cruikshank, *Gay and Lesbian*, 1–12; "Un appel de 343 femmes," *Le nouvel observateur*, April 5–11, 1971, 5; Xavier Héraud, "Mort de Ménie Grégoire, à l'origine malgré elle du FHAR," Yagg, August 16, 2014, http://yagg.com/2014/08/16/mort-de-menie-gregoire-a-lorigine-malgre-elle-du-fhar/; Bécar and Legrand, "Menie Grégoire," 7–13; Herzog, *Sexuality in Europe*, 168–69; Robcis, *Law of Kinship*, 203–7.

58. Bard, "Le lesbiennisme," 118.

59. Gunther, *Elastic Closet*, 48-49; Bonnet, "Les gouines rouges (1971-1973)," https://mariejobon.net/2009/08/les-gouine-rouges-1971-1973/; Bard, "Le lesbiennisme," 111-26; Chaperon, "L'histoire," 27, 47-59.

60. Londeix, *Le manifeste lesbien*, 21-26; Bernheim, *L'amour*; Martel, *Pink and Black*, 43-46.

61. Martel, *Pink and Black*, 46-47. See Bourg, *From Revolution to Ethics*, 186-87; Sibalis, "Spirit of May '68." Twenty-first-century gay rights movements, in contrast, moved back to a more culturally conservative position, advocating, for example, right to marry—closer to what Sibalis calls the "homophile" movements of the 1950s.

62. "Présentation du groupe 'femmes mariées,'" Zelensky private collection.

63. "Freedom of abortion is the first stage of our liberation because the interdiction of abortion is but one material oppression which constrains women and forces them to live exclusively as spouses and mothers" in "Mis au point du mouvement de libération des femmes sur ses positions sur l'avortement," Zelensky private collection.

64. Concerning the development of the modern welfare state, see Pedersen, *Family, Dependence*, 413-26.

65. Hamon and Rotman, *Génération 2*, 197-98.

66. Efforts toward solidarity, at least among nonparty feminists, were made from the beginning. See, for example, a pamphlet from 1969, "Appel à une rencontre nationale des féministes indépendantes," which calls feminists who are "truly autonomous" (free from ties with other political groups and men) to meet together to share ideas and combat their self-imposed isolation, Delphy private collection; MLF. Partout, "Le mouvement de libération des femmes, c'est toi, c'est moi," Zelensky private collection.

5. Fight for Reproductive Freedom

1. Françoise Collin, response to author's questionnaire on feminism, 1992; Gubin, "Pour le droit," 164; Picq, "Two or Three Things," 5.

2. The Ligue was an organization to fight sexism and discrimination and to disseminate information on women's rights. Long, *Women Intellectuals*, 27-29.

3. It is important to examine the political fault lines rather than see "feminism" as a monolith. See Kristin Ross, *May '68*, 125-26 for the parallel of 1968 intellectuals.

4. Halimi and Choisir, *Choisir de donner*, 18.

5. Picq, "Two or Three Things," 4; Herzog, *Sexuality in Europe*, 112; Bernheim et al., *Mouvement de libération*, 171.

6. "Mise au point du mouvement de libération des femmes sur ses positions sur l'avortement," Zelensky private collection.

7. See, for example, "Coordination Parisienne," 17–18" and "Pour une coordination," 19; Cercle Élisabeth Dimitriev, "Finie . . . la préhistoire"; MLF, "Contraception pour toutes et pour tous"; MLF, Bulletin d'informations (May 1–15, 1971); "Quelques réflexions sur la signification politique du mot d'ordre: 'Avortement et contraception libres et gratuits,'" Zelensky and Delphy private collections.

8. Herzog, *Sexuality in Europe*, 249–63; Evans and Godin, *France since 1815*, 138.

9. Marie-France Callu, *Le nouveau droit*, 170–71. Also see Fuchs, *Poor and Pregnant*, 11–17. In 1923 abortion cases were transferred from the Cour d'assises (where juries often acquitted the accused out of sympathy and because of the severe penalties attached) to the Tribunaux correctionnels, which produced more guilty verdicts.

10. MLF, "Contraception pour toutes et pour tous" and "Femmes," Zelensky private collection; Mossuz-Lavau, *Les lois de l'amour*, 61. The MLF eventually estimated that 1.5 million women underwent clandestine abortions, with five thousand fatalities per year (a statistic they arrived at by multiplying the official figure by two or three). See Club de l'observateur, *Le livre blanc*, 33.

11. Members of the "groupe avortement" included Zelensky, Delphy, Anna de Bascher, Christiane Rochefort, Simone de Beauvoir, Delphine Seyrig, and Maryse Arditi; "Un appel de 343 femmes," *Le nouvel observateur*, April 5–11, 1971, 5. Statistics exaggerated for effect. See Reineke, *Beauvoir and Her Sisters*, 6; Picq, *Libération des femmes*, 56.

12. Picq, *Libération des femmes*, 56–63.

13. Isambert-Jamati, "Adaptation au travail," 104–5, 109, 201; Institut français d'opinion publique survey: only 38 percent opposed. Club de l'observateur, *Le livre blanc*, 199 (originally published in *Le nouvel observateur*, April 26, 1971, 42–43). Lagroua Weill-Hallé, founder of the MFPF, joined the debate. See Lagroua Weill-Hallé, *L'avortement de papa*.

14. "252 médicins: L'avortement doit être libre!," *Le nouvel observateur*, May 3, 1971, 48–49; Sénat, *Proposition de loi tendant à permettre l'IVG*, 2768 (June 1971). Although the government didn't prosecute the 343, they pursued others. See MLAC, "La repression contre l'avortement!"; Zelensky private collection; "Reprise de la polémique sur l'avortement libre," *Le figaro*, February 5, 1973; "Des médecins s'accusent," *Le nouvel observateur*, February 5, 1973, 21–22; "La charte de l'association pour l'étude de l'avortement," *Le Monde*, February 8, 1973, 10; Rameau, "Pratiques illegals," 133–46.

15. The film's title was a play on the title of the erotic novel (and, later, film) *Histoire d'O (Story of O)*; "Les protestations contre l'interdiction du film 'liberté au féminin,'" *Le Monde*, November 13, 1973; *L'express*, December 24–30, 1973, 35. Directed by Charles Belmont and Marielle Issartel and eventually banned from being shown and distributed, *Histoires d'A* was nonetheless supported by all the reproductive rights groups, which said they would continue distributing it.

16. Halimi reports Choisir's founding membership to be herself, Beauvoir, Christiane Rochefort, and Jean Rostand (of the Academie française). Halimi, *La cause*, 296–302.

17. Kunkle, "'We Must Shout,'" 5–24; Khanna, *Algeria Cuts*, 78–83; Khanna, *Dark Continents*, 227–28.

18. Caputi, "Case of Djamilia Boupacha"; Murphy, "Algerian War," 263–64.

19. See Informations centre des femmes Berlin, "Crimes contre des femmes," 25; MLF and MLA, "November 20, 1971," Zelensky private collection.

20. Groupe communiste libertaire, "Avortement de classe, 6; Remy, *De l'utopie*, 55–58; MLF, "Je suis enceinte, je ne veux pas d'enfant," "Nous en avons assez de nous taire!," "Un million de femmes par an avortent seules," and Choisir, "Pourquoi une loi?, 1973," Zelensky private collection.

21. Some accounts state that Marie-Claire's abortion and subsequent complications landed her in the hospital, provoking an inquest; others claim the rapist tipped off the authorities. The judge was permitted to order moral inquiries to help place the case in the context of the defendants' lives. "Le combat de Bobigny," *Le nouvel observateur*, November 12, 1973, 74; Angeloff and Maruani, "Gisèle Halimi," 5–25; Herzog, *Sexuality in Europe*, 156–57.

22. Association Choisir, *Avortement*, 110–11; *des femmes*, "Marie-Claire, 17 ans, va être jugée pour avoir avorté," Zelensky private collection.

23. Association Choisir, *Avortement*, 102–5.

24. "Front libertaire de luttes des classes, July 10, 1973," Zelensky private collection; Halimi, *La cause*, 169–82. Another advocacy group formed "to continue the struggle" was called Comité pour la libération de l'avortement et de la contraception.

25. "La reforme de la loi de 1920 sera soumise en juin au Parlement," *Le Monde*, May 17, 1973. See "Avortement: Les députés s'en lavent les mains dans le sang," *Libération*, December 16, 1973; "Laissez-les mourir . . . voici comment les adversaires de l'avortement ont torpillé les projets de libéralisation, *Le nouvel observateur*, December 17, 1973. The Neuwirth abortion law authorized abortion if the physical, moral, or psychological health

of the mother was in danger or if the fetus was found to have serious abnormalities.

26. Halimi, *La cause*, 296–302; "Combien d'avortements en France," *Le Monde*, October 23, 1973; Angeloff and Maruani, "Gisèle Halimi," 5–25; Picq, "Two or Three Things."

27. "La législation sur l'avortement doit être libéralisée déclare M. Giscard d'Estaing," *Le Monde*, February 18–19, 1973.

28. André Aubry, Sénat, Débats, "Interruption volontaire de la grossesse,"-*Journal officiel 76* (December 14, 1974): 2869.

29. The Left rallied together despite serious ideological conflicts among members. Hirsh, *French Left*, 178–207. See, for example, the article "Citoyennes a part entière," *L'humanité*, February 2, 1973, 6.

30. Mossuz-Lavau, *Les lois du l'amour*, 80–86; Assemblée nationale, *Proposition de loi*, 1710 (November 27, 1965); Sénat, *Proposition de loi 82* (December 6, 1965); Choisir-La Cause des femmes, *Le programme commun*, 13.

31. Gisèle Moreau, Assemblée nationale, Débats, "Interruption volontaire de la grossesse,"*Journal officiel*, 92 (November 27, 1974): 7026–27; McBride and Mazur, *Politics of State Feminism*, 200.

32. "L'association pour l'étude de l'avortement demande aux partis politiques de se prononcer 'nettement' avant les élections," *Le Monde*, February 16, 1973. The main political parties were willing to respond to a questionnaire sent by the National Association for the Study of Abortion outlining their willingness (or unwillingness) to reform the law, and under what criteria. See "L'Association pour l'étude de l'avortement demande aux partis politiques de se prononcer 'nettement' avant les élections," *Le Monde*, February 16, 1973, 25; "Les partis politiques répondent au questionnaire de l'association pour l'étude de l'avortement," *Le Monde*, March 4–5, 1973. Marie-Victoire Louis explains this point in detail; see "Recherches féministes," 4.

33. Picq, *Libération des femmes*, 62; Beauvoir, "Préface," *Avortement*, 12–14.

34. Simone Iff, Besse, and Werner Iff, *Demain la société sexualisée*, 21, 120, 219. The statistics are taken from the period October 1972 to November 1973.

35. Picq, *Libération des femmes*; also see "Le libéralisation de l'avortement," *Le Monde*, February 22, 1974; McBride and Mazur, *Politics of State Feminism*, 96–215.

36. For some of the historiography of this theory, see Canning, *Gender History*, 24–28; Agacinski, "Turning Point," 18. Also, Butler and Scott, *Feminists Theorize the Political*.

37. Michel Debré, Assemblée nationale, Débats, "Interruption volontaire de la grossesse," 1974, *Journal officiel 93* (November 28, 1974): 7107. Even

those opposed to abortion after the war knew how widespread it was. See Mignon, "Lutte contre l'avortement," 489–90 and Pequignot, "Simple remarques," 175–81.

38. Mouvement français pour le planning familial, *D'une révolte*, 133; for an analysis of the law's strictures, see especially Dickens, "Right to Conscience," 221; Mossuz-Lavau, "La loi et les mœurs," 150.

39. Hélène Constans, Assemblée nationale, Débats, *Journal officiel*, 93 (November 28, 1974): 7139.

40. Veil suffered anti-Semitic attacks during the debates (among them swastikas drawn on her car and building and receiving death threats on her children). Hottell, "Sharing Stories."

41. Jacques Henriet, Sénat, Débats, "Interruption volontaire de la grossesse," *Journal officiel* 76 (December 14, 1974): 2864. Veil, *A Life*, 251; Herzog, *Sexuality in Europe*, 159.

42. Lagroua Weill-Hallé, *L'avortement de papa*, 16; *Projet de loi*, "Relatif a l'interruption volontaire de la grossesse," présenté par Mme. Simone Veil au nom de M. Jacques Chirac, Première Ministre, *Journal officiel* 1297 (November 15, 1974): 2.

43. Sénat, Rapport, "Fait au nom de la commission des affaires sociales sur le projet de loi adopté par l'Assemblée nationale relative a l'interruption volontaire de la grossesse par Jean Mézard, Sénateur," *Journal Officiel* 120 (December 19, 1974), 70.

44. Halimi, *La cause*, 235–36; Zancarini-Fournel, Rochefort, and Pavard, *Les lois Veil*.

45. Veil, *A Life*, 269. For a clear discussion of French abortion law, see Glendon, *Abortion and Divorce*; Roujou de Boubée, "L'interruption volontaire," 210–20.

46. Article no. 1, see Glendon's translation in *Abortion and Divorce*, 16; Roujou de Boubée, "L'interruption volontaire," 212. For criticism of the law see Michel, "Ideologies, Pressure Groups," 6.

47. There were an estimated 68,778 doctors in France at the time. Mossuz-Lavau, *Les lois du l'amour*, 100; "Dès sa conception, l'individu est une entité déclare le professeur Lejeune devant l'académie des sciences morales et politiques," *Parisien libéré*, October 1973; Conseil constitutionnel, "Décision du 15 janvier 1975," *Journal officiel* (January 1975): 671. Also see commentary in Conseil constitutionnel, "Jurisprudence"; Veil, *A Life*, 262.

48. Isambert-Jamati, "Adaptation au travail," 85.

49. "The Black Years"; Secrétariat d'etat à la condition féminine. Annie de Pisan is the pseudonym for Annie Sugier. Beauvoir, "Pré-

face," *Histoires du* MLF, 10–11. See also Remy, *De l'utopie*, 73; "Feministes: Mégalodossier,"16–59.

50. Picq, *Libération des femmes*, 169; Delphy, *Un universalisme*, 10.

51. Giscard's government created a Secrétariat d'etat à la condition féminine (secretary of state for the "feminine condition" or "female condition") on July 16, 1974, but the position continued to be renamed and dumped onto various ministries. In August 1976 Giroud was replaced by Nicole Pasquier, who was named Déléguée nationale à la condition féminine and stuck out in Lyon, far from the corridors of power. In September 1978 Pasquier was named Secrétaire d'etat à l'emploi féminin under the Ministère du travail but was replaced by Jacqueline Nonon, who only stayed at her post for six months. Monique Pelletier followed her to become Ministre déléguée à la condition féminine in September 1978, and in February 1980, Ministre déléguée chargée de la famille et de la condition féminine. Secrétariat d'etat chargé des droits des femmes, "Condition féminine (1975-1990)," Service de documentation, 1992. See Allwood and Wadia, *Women and Politics in France*, 29–32; Rabaut, *Histoire des féminismes*, 358.

52. Popkin, *Modern France*, 318; Picq, *Libération des femmes*, 175. See law of July 11, 1975; "Le secrétariat d'etat à la condition féminine"; Giroud, *Cent mesures*; Pelletier, "Bilan de l'application." Duchen claims that Giroud's proposals ("Projet pour les femmes") were accepted and approved by Parliament in principle, but no action was ever taken to realize any of her suggestions. Duchen, *Feminism in France*, 127.

53. Author interview with Françoise Giroud, Paris, November 22, 1996; Michele Cotta, "Un programme pour la moïté des français," *L'express*, May 31, 1976, 72–74; "Gadfly of French Cabinet Françoise Giroud," *New York Times*, October 21, 1974, https://www.nytimes.com/1974/10/21/archives /gadfly-of-french-cabinet-has-a-tiny-staff.html.

54. Giroud, "Discours de clôture des journées internationales," March 3, 1975, excerpted in Albistur and Armogathe, *Le grief*, 268–72; "La delegation générale à l'information," Secrétariat d'etat chargé des droits des femmes, archives.

55. Author interview with Françoise Giroud, November 22, 1996; "M. Giscard d'Estaing souhaite que de nombreuses femmes se présentent aux prochaines élections municipales," *Le Monde*, February 22, 1975; Picq, *Libération des femmes*, 284.

56. Sung to the tune of "Il était une bergère qui allait au marché."

57. Picq, *Libération des femmes*, 172–73; Remy, *De l'utopie*, 75; "Ce numéro special contre l'année international de la femme' a été écrit par des femmes,"

Le quotidien des femmes, March 3, 1975, 3–13; Association la griffonne, *Douze ans de femmes*, 14.

58. "Manifestation MLF à l'occasion de la fête des mères," Le point du 7ème jour, Émission, June 11, 1972, http://www.ina.fr/audio/p14356816.

59. Tristan and Pisan, *Histoires du MLF*, 153–54. La ligue du droit des femmes was launched on March 8, 1974, and the "grrr . . . rève des femmes" on June 8–9. They held a "take back the night march" to highlight the problem of women and violence.

60. Mouvement français pour le planning familial, *D'une révolte*, 169, 185–87.

61. Mouvement français pour le planning familial, *D'une révolte*, 172–77.

62. "Le MFPF face au problème de l'avortement" and other papers, MFPF archive, L'OURS, 1.APO-71; Mossuz-Lavau, *Les lois du l'amour*, 91. The MLAC coalition included groups from the MLF, the Groupe-Information-Santé, CFDT, Parti socialiste unifié, and LCR.

63. "Charter du MLAC." See also "Compte rendu de la commission sur le contrôle des femmes réunie au MLAC le 22 septembre 1979," L'OURS, 1.APO-71; Mouvement français pour le planning familial, *D'une révolte*, 187–202. Also see Picq, *Libération des femmes*, 155. Monique Antoine, lawyer, and Simone Iff, both the vice president of MFPF and the secrétaire confédérale of the CFDT, founded MLAC.

64. Mouvement français pour le planning familial, *D'une révolte*, 187, 195, 202; Picq, *Libération des femmes*, 159.

65. Herzog, *Sexuality in Europe*, 166–68.

66. This style of meeting began with the Journées de dénonciation des crimes contre les femmes on March 13–14, 1972, at the Mutualité. "Manifest contre le viol," Delphy private collection. Mossuz-Lavau, "La loi et les mœurs," 145–56.

67. Solveig Gerfaut, "La définition du viol, une longue construction juridique," Libération.fr, February 20, 2014, http://www.liberation.fr/societe/2014/02/20/la-definition-du-viol-une-longue-construction-juridique_981774; Bourg, "'Your Sexual Revolution,'" 85–114; Bourg, *From Revolution to Ethics*, 193–203.

68. Picq, "Two or Three Things."

69. "Le travail des femmes," 161; van der Poel, *Une revolution*, 24–30.

70. Beauvoir, "Préface," *Histoires du MLF*, 11.

6. Takeover?

1. See Dogan and Narbonne, *Les françaises face*, préface; Sineau, *Des femmes*, préface; Brimo, *Les femmes françaises*, 67–75.

2. Johnson, *Long March*, 195; Judt, *Marxism*, 279–80; Picq, *Libération des femmes*, 178.

3. "Résumé de la proposition" and Comité pour la creation, "Du nouveau à Lariboisiere?," L'OURS, Pachkoff archives, APO-2, Autumn 1979; Marie-Odile Fargier, Claude Weil, and Bernard Veillet-Lavallee, "Le début de la grande enquête du matin: Les femmes face à la politique," *Le matin*, December 5, 1977, 13–18.

4. Allwood and Wadia, *Gender and Policy*, 70; Evans and Godin, *France since 1815*, 136–38.

5. *Pour la femme: Une vie heureuse, libre et responsable dans l'égalité.* The conference was held at the Centre d'études et de recherches marxistes, November 9-10, 1976. Marchais, "Discours: Femmes pour changer votre vie," Paris, December 3, 1977. An earlier speech was published as Marchais, "Le parti de la liberté pour les femmes"; Vincent and Marchais, "Pour la femme." A later pamphlet, also edited by Vincent, was entitled "Pour les femmes: Promotion . . . egalité . . . liberté. . . ." See Herzog, *Sexuality in Europe*, 100.

6. "Femmes: Le grand chambardement," 15.

7. Letter to Suzanne Blaise-Rigail, Front féministe, from François Mitterrand, May 11, 1974; Blaise-Rigail and Front féministe, "Questions posées par les femmes," Dossier Suzanne Blaise, BMD. See Parti socialiste, *Femmes en lutte*. See also Evans and Godin, *France since 1815*, 179.

8. Delphy, *Close to Home*, 106. Delphy had reason to question the depths of Mitterrand's commitment, because although he claimed to be interested he also said he had "reservations." Delphy mentions, among other authors, Claude Alzon, a sociologist, who became quite well known for his books and articles on the "woman question": *La femme potiche* and *Femme mythifiée*. For a good illustration of Delphy's criticism, see Alain de Benoist, "Le féminisme au bain-marie: Deux hommes de gauche, Claude Alzon et Julien Cheverny, mettent le MLF au pied du mur; Entre la 'différence' et la 'similitude' existe-t-il une troisième voie pour le féminisme contemporain?," *Le figaro*, November 25, 1978, 85–87.

9. Foley, *Women in France*, 268; La gaffiche, *Les femmes s'affichent*, 60.

10. Lorwin, "Trade Unions," 9.

11. See Remy, *De l'utopie*, 96; Michèle Guenoun et al., "Le parti communiste mis à nu par ses femmes," *Le Monde*, June 12, 1978. For the standard ideology for women in the party see Centre d'études et de recherches marxistes, *La condition féminine*, 373: "Contrary to the feminists . . . we don't think that the ideology of inequality is caused by a collective conspiracy of

men. . . . [If this is the case] it closes all real possibilities to change the way things are." Also see Macciocchi, "Quelque thèmes autour," 387–432.

12. Martine Storti, "Féministe et communiste: Une toute petite mauvaise graine," *Libération*, May 9, 1979; Ligue communiste révolutionnaire, *Conférence femmes*, 1. It is an extraordinarily detailed document describing their theory, the history of the feminist movement, its strategy, and its political future.

13. Françoise Gaspard, Cécile Goldet, and Edith Lhullier of Courant III du Parti socialiste, "Lettre ouverte," June or July 1987; Journées nationales du Courant III, October 7–8. They presented the formal proposal at the national congress at Metz, April 1979; "Le 'Courant' III aujourd'hui?," L'OURS, Pachkoff archives, APO-2; Guéraiche, *Les femmes et la République*, 238–250. Duchen, *Feminism in France*, 110–11, 129.

14. "Schéma d'une motion de politique générale proposé par des femmes du PS," manuscript for *Mignonnes, allons voir sous la rose . . .* , January 1979, written in December 1978, L'OURS, Pachkoff archives, APO-2.

15. "Untitled," Delphy private collection, ca. 1977. Some of those who left with the group began publishing their own newspaper, *Mignonnes, allons voir sous la rose . . .* (Cute Girls, Let's Look Under the Rose . . .); those who stayed in the party, such as Yvette Roudy and Françoise Gaspard, continued to climb the party ladder.

16. Tristan and Pisan, *Histoires du MLF*, 118–21; Ligue du droit des femmes, "Nous vous proposons le projet suivant," May 30, 1974; "La ligue du droit des femmes," pamphlet, 1974, Zelensky private collection.

17. "Lettre ouverte à mesdames, messieurs les députés et sénateurs," Paris, June 10, 1977. Secrétariat d'etat chargé des droits des femmes, archives; Picq, *Libération des femmes*, 206–7.

18. Albistur and Armogathe, *Histoire du féminisme français*, 673–74. The first number of *L'information des femmes du GLIFE* appeared in November 1975; "Le GLIFE a fermé ses portes," *Le Monde*, August 12, 1976, 8; author interview with Anne Zelensky, Paris, May 29, 1992.

19. Remy, De l'utopie, 75; Herzog, *Sexuality in Europe*, 166–67; SOS-Femmes-Alternative, "Le feminisme face aux realités," 1975, Zelensky private collection; Association la griffonne, *Douze ans de femmes*, 16.

20. Women staged a protest on the same day the article "SOS femmes battues" appeared in *Paris Match*, April 21, 1978, 104–6. The article begins, "Mrs. Gisèle Halimi gets on my nerves with her circus and all her stories of phallocracy, of millennial oppression, and sexist terrorism." The article argued that very few women were beaten and that such violence was a

problem in the relationship between the specific man and woman. It was followed by another article, "Le proces des avocates," *Paris Match*, June 30, 1978, 61–62, suggesting that women did not have the psychological constitutions to be attorneys. The following November, twenty-one lawyers took him to court: "In an injurious and sexist way it calls into question women who are exercising their profession, implying that women are incompetent and frivolous and use their charms and the vulnerability of their sex," "Pétition de solidarité," November 1978, BMD, Dossier Gisèle Halimi. The women won. See Remy, *De l'utopie*, 99.

21. Front féministe, "Aux femmes travailleuses, aux ouvriers en lutte!" (tract distributed during the Besançon Street March, May 30, 1973); Blaise, "Histoire du Parti féministe unifié," 3; Bihin-Jourdan, "Les origines," 43–47. It is difficult to find statistics on the number of women involved, but it had outsize influence due to the relative prominence of its members.

22. "France: Parti féministe unifié," c.1976; "Parti féministe unifié (France). Plate-forme politique," Paris, December 1975, 2; "Communique. Constitution d'une internationale féministe," Paris, May 21, 1977; "Parti féministe unifié," May 1, 1978; Blaise, "Histoire du Parti féministe unifié," 21; "Bilan de six mois d'existence," January–June, 1976; Parti féministe unifié, "Définition d'un parti féministe unifié." BMD, Dossier Suzanne Blaise.

23. These groups joined together at times to take action on specific issues such as their protest against a specific maternity-leave bill that they found insufficient and discriminatory. See letter dated June 15, 1977, to the President du groupe parlementaire and signed by representatives of the PFU and the Ligue as well as feminists from other political parties and syndicates. BMD, Dossier Suzanne Blaise. See also "Un projet de loi: Le congé de mère: Pourquoi les féministes sont contre"; Blaise, "Histoire du parti féministe unifié," 20; "Statuts déposés à la Préfecture de Bobigny," BMD, Dossier Suzanne Blaise.

24. "Les féministes radicales face aux élections," signed by the PFU, Ligue du droit des femmes, SOS-Femmes-Alternatives, Féministes radicales, Groupe liaison du 13e, Groupe liaison du 5e, BMD, Dossier Suzanne Blaise.

25. "Féministe internationale: May 28–30, 1977." Remy, *De l'utopie*, 102-3; Blaise, "Histoire du Parti féministe unifié," 22, 23, 70; Blaise, "Au collectif de coordination aux membres du PFU française," letter, Paris, June 22, 1977, BMD, Dossier Suzanne Blaise.

26. Kandel speculates that such magazines had not kept up with the issues that increasingly occupied women, such as divorce, sexuality, and public

life. Kandel, "L'explosion," 105–6; Bonvoisin and Maignien, *La presse fémi-nine*, 25–31; Drake, *Intellectuals and Politics*, 208.

27. Kandel, "L'explosion," 105–6.

28. Many of these journal titles were plays on words, some quite *recherché*, such as the reference to Pierre de Ronsard's sixteenth-century poem "Mignones . . . ," which was adopted by the Socialist Party and then readopted in name with a layer of irony by the socialist-feminists.

29. Kristeva, "Un nouveau," 2; see also Cixous, "Poésie e(s)t politique," 29–30; Cixous, *Le troisième corps*, 12–16; Braidotti, "Interview," 39.

30. "Editorial," 4. The initial editorial collective consisted of Colette Capitan Peter, Christine Delphy, Emmanuelle de Leseps, Nicole-Claude Mathieu, and Monique Plaza. Peter eventually left and Monique Wittig, Colette Guillaumin, and Claude Hennequin joined.

31. "Editorial,"3–8.

32. Guillaumin plays on the word "slavery" (*esclavage*) in "Les corps appropriés," 9.

33. Plaza, "Pouvoir 'phalomorphique,'" 117; Hanmer, "Violence et con-trôle," 69–88.

34. "Editorial," 5, 9. Also see Delphy, "Proto-féminisme," 1471. See also Echols, "New Feminism," 65.

35. "Editorial," 12.

36. Guillaumin, "Question de différence," 2–21.

37. "Editorial," *La revue d'en face*, 4; Navarro, "Questions," 36.

38. Lapierre, "A partir," 20.

39. *Les cahiers du* GRIF; see especially 1 (November 1973), 4 (October 1974), and 5 (December 1974); Remy, *De l'utopie*, 81.

40. "'Les femmes' sont l'avenir," 3. Margaret Gibbon notes that femi-nists had good reason to doubt the motives of trade unions, although she notes rightly that the CFDT pursued a more radical line on feminism than the CGT. "Trade Unions," 145–49.

41. *Les pétroleuses* referred to the female communards who, at the fall of the commune, purportedly set fire to much of Paris. The journal ran until December 1976 and was then replaced by *Cahiers du féminisme* in Novem-ber 1977. See especially, "Editorial," 3; "'Les femmes' sont l'avenir,'" 2; "L'équipe," 119.

42. "De l'art d'accompagner," 15–17 and "Chronique de Mittard," 3. Other leftist women's journals such as *Femmes travailleuses en lutte* hewed more closely to the Socialist line and thus developed less of an independent cri-tique of socialism and men. They concentrated their criticism on the state and on capitalism.

43. Reader, *Intellectuals and the Left*, 70. Also see Gallop, *Daughter's Seduction*, 20, on Lacan's belief in the phallus as privileged signifier—what Gallop calls "Lacanian conceit." For an elaboration on both the romance and the disconnect between French psychoanalytic philosophy and American feminism, see Feher-Gurewich, "Lacan," 239–60.

44. Selous, *Other Woman*.

45. Wittig, *Les guérillères*, 19; originally published by Éditions de Minuit, 1969.

46. Wittig, *Les guérillères*, 108.

47. Chetcuti and Amaral, "Monique Wittig," 93–98; Marks and Courtivron, "Introduction III," *New French Feminisms*, 37; Gauthier, "Creations," 163; Jardine and Menke, *Shifting Scenes*, 195. Also see Slama, "De la 'littérature féminine'," 51–71.

48. Fisher, *La cosmogonie*, 46–47; Cixous, Gagnon, and Leclerc, La venue, 44–47; Cixous, "Extreme Fidelity," 15–19; Cixous, "Entretien avec Françoise"; Moi, *Sexual/Textual Politics*, 102, 108.

49. Cixous, "Le rire," 39; Cixous, "Je n'ai lâché," 37. Also see Ozouf, *Les mots*, 384–85.

50. Irigaray, *Ce sexe*, 29, 159–60.

51. Jardine and Menke, *Shifting Scenes*, 103.

52. She was also rebuffed by many participants. See Berg, "Luce Irigaray's 'contradictions,'" 50–70; Le Dœuff, "Hiparchia's Choice," 51–54; Mazur, *Theorizing Feminist Policy*, 7.

53. Kristeva, *Séméiôtiké*; Moi, *Kristeva Reader*, 150–73; Zakin, "Beauvoir's Unsettling."

54. Kristeva was criticized by sociologists and anthropologists for the same lack of social or historical perspective when she wrote *Des chinoises*; Kristeva, "Un nouveau type," 6–7; Kristeva, "Le temps des femmes," 5–19; Also see Moi, *Kristeva Reader*, 187–88.

55. American theorists have tended to overlook the essentialist qualities of writers such as Irigaray, noting that because she offers "a multiplicity of essentialisms" her propositions for women are "de-essentialized." See Schor, "Cet essentialisme," 85–109.

56. Servan-Schreiber, "Editorial," 3; Bonvoisin and Maignien, *La presse féminine*, 34, 47.

57. *La revue d'en face* attempted to print a variety of articles, some of which included "women's writers," but this was less a dialogue than a forum and the slant of the *Revue* was largely materialist and antiessentialist. See, for example, Ravelli, "De l'intérêt," 18–23.

58. Introduction, *des femmes, Catalogue*. Also see Pavard, *Les éditions*.

59. Arnaud Spire, "Antoinette Fouque: Mon ambition 'historique' de femme" (interview), *L'humanité*, September 4, 1995, 10–11.

60. Pavard, *Les éditions*, 166–67. Forrest was arrested, imprisoned, and tortured for her alleged terrorist activities with Euskadi ta Askatasuna, a Basque nationalist group. *Libération*, June 2, 1977, 1.

61. "Mon ambition 'historique' de femme: Je suis moi-même la matière de mes luttes." Arnaud Spire, "Antoinette Fouque: Mon ambition 'historique' de femme," interview, *L'humanité*, September 4, 1995, 10–11; Sweatman, *Risky Business*, 29, 79.

62. Xavière, "Fabrication écriture," *Le quotidien des femmes*, May 3, 1975, 12.

63. "Une femme . . . une analyst," *Le quotidien des femmes*, September 22, 1975, 20. Reproduced in Fouque, "Une expérience," 65–74; also see Duchen, *Feminism in France*, 35–36.

64. "Menacées de chômage," *Le quotidien des femmes*, September 22, 1975, 2–5; "Le quotidien des prostituées," *Le quotidien des femmes*, November 18, 1975, 2–5, 9; see, for example, "Conçus par l'opération," 2; Pratique Politique et Psychanalyse, "C'est l'économie," 83.

65. Victoria Thérame's *Hosto-Blues* sold all twenty thousand copies of its first printing; Kristeva's *Des chinoises* had a first printing of twenty-five thousand. Claude Mauriac, "Un autre regard," *Le figaro*, December 2, 1974. For an in-depth study of *des femmes* publishing success, refer to Sweatman, *Risky Business*.

66. *des femmes en mouvements*, 1978–1982.

67. Fougeyrollas-Schwebel, "Controverses et anathèmes, 13–26. See, for example, "Contribution à l'élaboration d'un projet de manifeste contre le viol," signed by Groupes femmes de quartier, entreprise, lycée, faculté, June 26, 1976; the manifesto of "Mouvement féministe libertaire." Zelensky, private collection. Picq, *Libération des femmes*, 185.

68. Association la griffonne, *Douze ans de femmes*, 41. "Grrr . . ." is a play on the word *strike* and the onomatopoeia of frustration. Rêve is dream.

69. Dhoquois, "From formal equality," 3; Odile Dhavernas, "Pour une recherche," 358; La ligue du droit des femmes, "Quelque réflexions," 86–90.

70. Delphy, *Close to Home*, 93–105.

71. "Un groupe femmes, 349; Picq, *Libération des femmes*, 190.

72. Dhoquois, *Appartenance et exclusion*, 132–47. In Zelensky's words, "It is difficult to describe the paroxysms of hate reached in certain meetings where the so-called pure revolutionary feminists, and the vile reformists, to which Anne, Colombe, and myself belonged, had a go at one another." See Tristan and Pisan, *Histoires du MLF*, 119.

73. Picq, *Libération des femmes*, 187; Kandel, "Du politique," 26; also see Ellen Willis, "Foreword," in Echols, *Daring to be Bad*, 16–18; Reineke, *Beauvoir and Her Sisters*, xxiii, 69–70.

74. See Vicky, "Harmonie ou si l'homosexualité," 398; Margaret, "Quelques réflexions," Delphy private collection; Picq, *Libération des femmes*, 188; Bernheim, *L'amour* and Bard, "Le lesbiennisme," 117.

75. Bourg, *From Revolution to Ethics*, 186–87; see especially chap. 15, "Gender and '68: Tensions from the Start"; Sibalis, "'Our' Problem?"; Bourg, "'Your Sexual Revolution,'" 85–113.

76. The lesbian separatist Front des lesbiennes radicales (Radical Lesbian Front) formed in the spring of 1981 and then disbanded a year later, together with much of the rest of the MLF, over various internal disagreements on policy and practice. Political lesbianism in France did not exist in isolation; it echoed ideological and practical struggles of women in other countries. Echols, *Daring to Be Bad*, 211–20, 239–40. See also Butler, *Gender Trouble*. For contemporary French analyses of gender and language, see Chetcuti, Amaral, and Greco, *La face cachée*.

77. Dhoquois, *Appartenance et exclusion*, 148, 153, 158.

78. Dhoquois, *Appartenance et exclusion*, 194–96; Picq, "Du mouvement."

7. Who Owns Women's Liberation?

1. At the time that I was first researching this book, Fouque's actions were virtually unknown to Anglophone scholars. By now, a number of social scientists are aware of their broad outlines. See, for example, Allwood, *French Feminisms*. For more sources see Zancarini-Fournel, *Le moment*, 131–33.

2. Josseline Abonneau, "Mais qu'est devenu le MLF," *Le figaro*, October 16, 1984.

3. Martine Storti, "Des femmes, des librairies, un monopole," *Libération*, October 19, 1976; Sweatman, Risky Business, 106, 115.

4. "La réinsertion des ex-prostituées ne vas," *Libération*, July 31, 1976, 4; Marie-Odile Fargier, "La complainte de Barbara," *Le matin de Paris*, March 18, 1977, 12. I have used the spelling of her name from her book *La partagée*, written by Barbara (pseudonym for Mireille de Coninck) and Christine de Coninck, about her experiences as a prostitute and in the movement to defend prostitutes. Other newspapers and books spell it differently.

5. Monestier, "Qui a peur?" 33–34. De Coninck claimed to have never received a pay slip or other necessary employment documents between the time that she was hired in February 1976 and when she was fired in October. See also Picq, *Libération des femmes*, 250; Roger-Po Droit, "Des

femmes occupent la librairie . . . des femmes," *Le Monde*, October 14, 1976; "Retrouvez plus d'informations sur Antoinette Fouque," http://www.antoinettefouque-desfemmes.com/chronologie/.

6. Marie-Odile Delacour and Martine Storti, "des femmes contre quatre femmes," *Libération*, June 2, 1977; Le collectif de solidarité avec Mireille, Monique, Erin, Carole, et Mon Oeil, "Mireille contre ses anciennes employeuses," *Rouge*, May 18, 1977; Martine Storti, "Des femmes, des librairies, un monopole," *Libération*, October 19, 1976. Pizzey's book was translated by Benoîte Groult as *Crie moins fort, les voisins vont t'entendre* (Paris: Éditions *des femmes*, 1975). Pizzey had founded Chiswick Women's Aid in 1971. Piton, *C'est possible*.

7. "Il ne fait pas"; "International Women's Liberation Movement Inc.," English version, Zelensky private collection; Monestier, "Qui a peur?" 33–34; Picq, 252. The French idiom "Mon Oeil" translates as "my ass" or "yeah, sure."

8. Also see Rose Prudence and Catherine Crachat, "Une libraire pas comme les autres: Trois points du vue," *Libération*, May 18, 1977, 4–5 (pullout section); Jeanne Favret, "Allonge-toi tu seras emballée," *Libération*, October 27, 1976, 3; "Les conflits des femmes."

9. Pratique Politique et Psychanalyse, "Enoncer, de plein chant," 6.

10. "Du rififi," 5; "La librairie des femmes saccagée par un commando de huit femmes," *Libération*, May 13–15, 1978; Fouque, "Une experience," 33–35.

11. L'union des femmes contre l'avortement. *Des femmes*' bookstore was not the only place to be harassed. The offices of GRIF were also broken into and vandalized. See *des femmes en mouvements* 2 (February 1978).

12. Erin Pizzey, "Letter to dear sisters, *des femmes*," May 3, 1985; "Letter to Florence Prudhomme and *des femmes*," June 11, 1985. Gift of Antoinette Fouque.

13. "*La réinsertion des ex-prostituées ne vas pas de soi même parmi des feministes*," *Libération*, July 31, 1976. For an elaboration of *des femmes*' position, see Sweatman, Risky Business, 105–16.

14. "Le 1er procès du féminisme," *Libération*, May 20, 1977, 8. Kiejman was also an attorney for the Mitterrand family.

15. The defense also had prominent attorneys: Colette Auger, Paule Alcabas, Stephanie Bordier, and Roland Dumas. Françoise Picq and Nadja Ringart, "Les femmes et le tribunal," *Libération*, June 4–5, 1977, 7; "Une société a responsabilité limitée," *Libération*, July 31, 1976, 4; "Le 1er procès du féminisme," *Libération*, May 20, 1977, 8; Auger, "De la diffamation," 1213–18.

16. Rose Prudence and Catherine Crachat, "*La réinsertion des ex-prostituées ne vas pas de soi même parmi des féministes*," *Libération*, July 31, 1976, 4.

17. "Les femmes et le tribunal," *Libération*, June 4–5, 1977, 7; "Le procès de 4 femmes par des femmes n'a pas eu lieu," *Libération*, June 3, 1977, 9. Women who were part of the movement hated that such political debate would be played out in the courts and urged *des femmes* to freely debate their adversaries or to use women's mediation groups to find a settlement. See "Courrier," *Libération*, June 6, 1977, 2; Marion G., "Un proces avorté, un débat," *Rouges*, June 3, 1977.

18. "All therapeutic and diplomatic tactics at reconciliation will not have any other effect but to reinforce or displace the symptom or both and to immobilize the movement." See *des femmes*, "Histoire en mouvement," 24–25; The defendants had offered to distribute the videotape accompanied by a response from *des femmes* and to suppress the passages that touched on private life. The judge had found these proposals constructive, but *des femmes* rejected them. Picq, *Libération des femmes*, 258.

19. Françoise Picq and Nadja Ringart, "Les femmes et le tribunal," *Libération*, June 4–5, 1977, 7; Monique Piton, "Monique Piton s'adresse aux femmes de province," *Libération*, June 6, 1977, 4.

20. Another march for abortion rights was held on November 24. For a discussion of the changes in the abortion law, see Mossuz-Lavau, *Les lois de l'amour*, 112–15. On Fouque's registration, see Katia D. Kaupp, "Bataille pour un drapeau," *Le nouvel observateur*, December 31, 1979; Picq, *Libération des femmes*, 295. According to several feminists, the Psych-et-Po group had joined the march's organizing collective at the last minute.

21. The acronym SARL stands for Société à résponsabilité limité (limited partnership). *Bulletin officiel de la propriété industrielle*, June 18, 1982, 5 (bulletin where property is registered); Association la griffonne, Douze ans de femmes, 63–64; "Sexisme ordinaire," 1145–59; L'Association mouvement pour les luttes féministes, *Chroniques d'une imposture*; "Le pouvoir," 8.

22. Marie-Jo Dhavernas, "Des divans profonds," 34; L.K., "Post-scriptum," 37–44; Ringart, "La naissance d'une secte." Also published under the same title in *Libération*, June 1, 1977.

23. "Front Matter." See also Kandel, "Une presse 'anti-féministe,'" 37–46.

24. "Annex no. 3." This story has been chronicled by political scientist Françoise Picq, who also lived through it.

25. Éditions *des femmes* catalogues for the years 1978, 1980, and 1982, respectively.

26. Catherine Clément, "'Notre ennemi n'est pas l'homme, mais l'impérialisme du phallus,' nous dit Antoinette Fouque," *Le matin*, July 16, 1980,

13. Historian Michele Perrot has analyzed Fouque's decision in Perrot, "Antoinette Fouque," 19–20.

27. Clément, "'Notre ennemi n'est pas l'homme,'" 13.

28. "MLF: Propriété privée, défense d'afficher sans autorisation?," *Libération*, January 8, 1980.

29. "Année du patrimoine," 62.

30. "Le procès de 'des femmes,'" 120–24; Picq, *Libération de femmes*, 310. Sweatman sees this first and foremost as a problem of the MLF's inability to "adequately address the movement's problematic relationship to capitalism and consumerism"; see Risky Business, 55–56.

31. Beauvoir, "Préface," *Chroniques*.

32. Association la griffonne, *Douze ans de femmes*, 63–64.

33. Beauvoir, "Préface," *Chroniques*.

34. Groupe notre mouvement nous appartient, "Le commerce des femmes"; "Simone de Beauvoir contre la SARL des femmes," *Le Monde*, May 8, 1981, http://www.lemonde.fr/archives/article/1981/05/08/simone-de-beauvoir-contre-la-s-a-r-l-des-femmes_2721509_1819218.html.

35. Claudie Broyelle, "La cabale des dévotés," *Le matin de Paris*, January 26, 1981, 13.

36. Cheng Ying-Hsiang, "Le MLF s'est déshonoré," *Le Monde*, January 28, 1981, 2; Marie-José Lalitte, "Jiang Qing féministe?," *Le matin de Paris*, January 19, 1981, 15. Several celebrities, including Élisabeth Badinter, Yvette Roudy, Sonia Rykiel, and Jo Richardson (Labour Party MP), signed the petition for clemency.

37. Association la griffonne, *Douze ans de femmes*, 64; "'MLF': Propriété privée, defense d'afficher sans autorisation?," *Libération*, January 8, 1980.

38. Marie-Jo Dhavernas, "Des divans profonds," 36–37.

39. The celebration of International Women's Day had historically been organized by a coalition of groups from the movement. "Chroniques du sexisme ordinaire," 1905–20; Vinteuil, "De psychanalyse et politique," 5–9. See also Groupe notre mouvement nous appartient, "Le commerce des femmes."

40. Scott, *Parité!*, 140; Allwood and Waida, *Women and Politics*, 45–48.

41. "Après la libéralisation de l'avortement: Le mouvement Choisir veut obtenir 'l'indépendance économique des femmes," *Le Monde*, December 23, 1975, 9.

42. Halimi, "Mouvement de femmes?," 277.

43. "Après la libéralisation de l'avortement: Le mouvement Choisir veut obtenir 'l'indépendance économique des femmes," *Le Monde*, December 23, 1975, 9.

44. "La liberté au féminin," 1.

45. Walter Schwartz, "Opinion Polls Lump Them with the Extreme Left and Right and Other Marginals," *The Guardian*, March 10, 1978; Choisir–La Cause des femmes, "Une interview," 9–11. See, for example, Choisir, "Pourquoi une loi?," BMD; Halimi, *La cause*, 296–302; Claudine Ducol, "Le refus de Choisir: Gisèle Halimi a présenté, hier, un programme et des candidates," *L'humanité*, February 7, 1978.
46. Choisir–La Cause des femmes, *Le programme commun*, 27; "75 candidates pour la cause des femmes," *Le matin*, February 6, 1978. The antidiscrimination laws she called ineffective were the December 22, 1972, law on *l'égalité des rémunérations* (equal pay law) and the December 11, 1975, law on *la discrimination fondée sur le sexe* (sex discrimination law). Her other law proposals included abrogating the death penalty, permitting female and feminist associations to sue in civil court, an antisexism law, liberalizing abortion, and requiring that a child carry the patronymic of both parents.
47. Luc Bernard, "100 candidates Choisir aux élections législatives," *Le Monde*, February 7, 1978; Jane Friedman, "French Women Have Vote— Now Want Votes," *International Herald Tribune*, February 7, 1978; Claudine Ducol, "Le refus de Choisir," *L'humanité*, February 7, 1978; Anne Chaussebourg, "Les femmes 'au charbon' électoral," *Le Monde*, February 7, 1978.
48. Choisir–La Cause des femmes, "Une interview," 10–11.
49. Loosely translated as "A brighter future," the expression was taken from the Communist poet Louis Aragon's ballad about the Communist deputy Gabriel Peri, who was martyred by Vichy in 1941. His last letter before his execution spoke of waiting for "des lendemains qui chantent," representing revolutionary hopes for the day of liberation; Halimi, "Le programme commun des femmes," 275–80.
50. Luc Bernard, "Gisèle Halimi et le mouvement Choisir proposent," *Le quotidien de Paris*, October 26, 1977, 5; Georges Marchais, "Le choix des femmes: Le groupe parlementaire communiste sera le plus féminisé répond Georges Marchais à Gisèle Halimi," *L'humanité*, February 18, 1978. Marchais might boast, but even the women representatives of the PCF seemed out of touch with feminism. "Nous refusons," 9; "Femmes à la CGT," 10–14, reported that Gisèle Moreau, Communist deputy, ignorantly cited November 18, 1978, as the "first time in years that women in the Paris region had protested."
51. Choisir, "Procès-verbal de réunion du conseil d'administration de Choisir," March 7, 1977; Thalmann et al., "Pourquoi nous quittons

Choisir"; and "Des explications," Zelensky private collection; Bruno Frappat, "Les difficultés des mouvements féministes: Choisir déchiré," *Le Monde*, May 28, 1977, 31.

52. Bruno Frappat, "'Chosir' déchiré," *Le Monde*, April 28, 1977; "Des explications" and Thalmann et al., "Pourquoi nous quittons Choisir," Zelensky private collection.

53. Frappat, "Les difficultés des mouvements"; "Des explications" and Thalmann et al., "Pourquoi nous quittons Choisir," Zelensky private collection; Choisir, "Procès-verbal de réunion"; Bobigny trial flyer: "Who makes decisions in Choisir? Why has the defense been organized without consulting the members of the association? Halimi made decisions alone to defend the accused. We were never consulted." Zelensky private collection.

54. "Les femmes grandes vaincues des élections," *Le matin*, March 20, 1978; Zarrouk, "Femmes: Un échec." For a list and description of most of the candidates, see *Choisir–La Cause des femmes* 31 (March 1978). See G.C., "75 candidates pour la cause des femmes," *Le matin*, February 6, 1978, 6; Anne Chaussebourg, "Le programme de 'Choisir': Les femmes 'au charbon' electoral," *Le Monde*, February 7, 1978, 5.

55. Roudy, *A cause d'elles*, 119. On paper, the PS appeared extraordinarily progressive. See François Mitterrand and PS, *Changer la vie*.

56. Georges Marchais, "Le choix des femmes: Le groupe parlementaire communiste sera le plus féminisé répond Georges Marchais à Gisèle Halimi," *L'humanité*, February 18, 1978. "Syndiquées à la CGT," 10.

57. Halimi, *La cause*, 200.

58. Organisation communiste gauche ouvrière et populaire, "Femmes exploitées," 5; Remy, De l'utopie, 101–2; See, for example, Barbara, "Le Féminisme ne répond plus?," 6–7; "Une interview de Gisèle Halimi," 9.

59. Bouchardeau, *Un coin*.

60. See, for example, Zylberberg-Hocquard, *Femmes et féminisme*; Maruani, "Grèves de femmes, 25–35; Moses, *French Feminism*; Kergoat, "Une expérience," 274–92; Derbyshire, *Politics in France*, 23; Gibbon, "Trade Unions," 140.

61. Charraud and Saada, "Les écarts," 4; Luce Irigaray, "A quand notre majorité?," *Le matin*, December 10, 1977; Moreau-Bourles and Sineau, "Les femmes," 694–719; Gibbon, "Trade Unions," 142–43; Le Garrec, *Les messagères*, 63; "Le travail des femmes," 163.

62. Colette Audry, "Dans le combat socialiste," *Le Monde*, January 27, 1978; Kergoat, "Industrie de pointe," Ministère du travail, de l'emploi et

de la formation professionnelle; Laot, *Stratégie*; Kergoat, "Ouvriers = ouvrières?," 65–97.

63. This did not, however, mean declaring themselves alone responsible for "women's issues such as child care. They aimed to integrate the principles of feminism in across-the-board reforms." Le Garrec, *Les messagères*, 138.

64. "Le travail des femmes, repères historiques," 162; Julian Jackson, Milne, and Williams, *May '68*, 52; Remy, De l'utopie, 95; Jean-Loup Craipeau, *Lip au féminin*. For example, women in the CGT created Le club Flora Tristan, led by Chantal Rogerat (former editor in chief of *Antoinette*, the CGT's women's magazine) to address specific women's concerns but on a clearly feminist basis. See Rogerat, "Club Flora Tristan," manuscript, IRESCO; Mariella Righini, "Les ouvrières aussi," *Le nouvel observateur*, May 22–28, 1968.

65. Laot, *Stratégie*, 239–40. Maria Antonietta Macciocchi claims that Lip workers had long doubted the goodwill of the PCF. *De la France*, 156–63. Rogerat, "Club Flora Tristan," manuscript; Remy, De l'utopie, 96; "Le viol: Les femmes s'entendent," *L'information des femmes*, October 19, 1977, 7.

66. See Jenson, "French Left," 97–98, 103; "Le travail des femmes," 162; McMillan, *Dreyfus to De Gaulle*, 178.

67. Roudy, *A cause d'elles*, 119–20.

68. Sineau, Des femmes en politique, 43–44; Gaspard, Madame Le . . . , 230; Picq, 313.

69. "Editorial," *Cahiers du féminisme*, 1.

70. Institute François Mitterrand, "François Mitterrand au débat 'Choisir la cause des femmes,'" April 29, 1981, http://fresques.ina.fr /mitterrand/fiche-media/Mitter00143/francois-mitterrand-au-debat -choisir-la-cause-des-femmes.html; Choisir–La Cause des femmes, *Quel président?*, 122–23, 146. Also see Halimi, *Une embellie perdue*, 31–47.

71. Annik, "Qu'est-ce qui?,"14–15; Picq, *Libération des femmes*, 313. Psychet-Po invited the PS to a "historic encounter" at which Catherine Lalumière, Véronique Neïertz (Socialist and Radical Party deputies, respectively), and Edith Cresson were in attendance.

72. "Editorial: Féminisme," 5. Also see Viennot, "Féminisme et partis politiques," 35–46.

73. Colette Audry, "Dans le combat socialiste," *Le Monde*, January 27, 1978. Also see Bridgford, *French Trade Unionism*, 51–54; Sineau, Des femmes, 43–44; Gaspard, Madame Le . . . , 230; Picq, Libération des femmes, 313.

74. Roudy, *A cause d'elles*, 7–11, 118–19, 150; Roudy, *La femme en marge*, 76, 113.

75. Bouchardeau, *Un coin*, 11; See "Une loi pour l'égalité des femmes," *L'hu-manité*, May 11, 1980. Also refer to the discussion of Courant G and the feminist critique of the Communist Party earlier in this book. Picq, *Libéra-tion des femmes*, 286; Aubry, "Des 'bleues,'" 29; R. Ustarroz, "H Bouchard-eau entre le féminisme et un congrès," *Libération*, February 4, 1981, 10; Roudy, *A cause d'elles*, 119-20.

76. He installed Alice Saunier-Seïté as Ministre des universités, Monique Pel-letier as Secrétaire d'etat auprès du ministre de la justice, and Nicole Pas-quier as Secrétaire d'etat chargée de l'emploi féminin. See also Georges Vedel, "Le 'quota' aux élections municipales," *Le Monde*, February 3, 1979: 9; Annie Kriegel, "Femmes: L'égalité soldée à 20 percent," *Le figaro*, Feb-ruary 9, 1979; Storti, "Giscard," 58-59; Walter Schwartz, "Opinion Polls Lump Them with the Extreme Left and Right and Other Marginals," *The Guardian*, March 10, 1978.

77. Duchen, *Feminism in France*, 126-27; Allwood and Wadia, *Women and Poli-tics*, 187-90.

78. Viennot, "Féminisme et partis politiques," 44.

79. Jenson and Sineau, *Mitterrand*, 202-7; Marie-Jo Dhavernas, Kandel, and Slama, "Sexisme et loi anti-sexiste," 1-61; "La discorde chez les fémin-istes," *Le figaro*, March 8, 1982; Emma Henderson, "France Is Destined to Swing to the Right at the March Elections—And Women Will Be the Los-ers," *The Guardian*, January 7, 1986.

Not a Conclusion

1. Guillaume, *La France contemporaine*, 331-50.

2. Ministère des droits de la femme, *Les femmes en France*; Projets économiques et sociaux, "L'égalité professionnelle entre les femmes et les hommes," Projet de loi adopté par le Conseil des ministres on November 3, 1982, 134, no. 82 (November 24, 1982); Ministre des droits de la femme, *Une annoncée pour les femmes, 1981-1985*; Simone de Beauvoir, "Le pro-jet de loi antisexiste: La femme, la pub, et la haine," *Le Monde*, May 4, 1983; Christiane Chombeau, "Les remous provoqués par le projet de loi antisexiste," *Le Monde*, May 24, 1983; "Yvette Roudy: Les puritains ridi-cules," *Le figaro*, April 18, 1983; "Dix articles de loi qui veulent combattre le sexisme," *Libération*, April 10, 1983, 2-6; "La loi cache-sexe," *Libération*, March 10, 1983, 2-6; Marie-Jo Dhavernas, Liliane Kandel, and Béatrice Slama, "Sexisme et loi anti-sexiste," 1-61; Christiane Chombeau, "Une loi pour favoriser l'égalité professionnelle entre l'homme et la femme," *Le Monde*, December 7, 1982, 11-13; Foley, *Women in France*, 268-71.

3. Allwood and Wadia, *Gender and Policy*, 41–45; Bard, "Le lesbiennisme," 119–20; Mazur, *Gender Bias*, 227–28, 256–57.

4. The law of June 4, 1970, on parental authority (from paternal power); the law of January 9, 1973, on maternal transmission of nationality (from systematic paternal transmission); and the law of July 11, 1975, on choice of conjugal domicile (from husband as arbiter, to couple) and legalizing uncontested divorce. The law of December 23 defined rape as "all acts of sexual penetration, whatever the nature, committed on another person, by violence, constraint or surprise." Billeta, "Evolution des droits des femmes," Secrétariat d'etat chargé des droits des femmes archives, 1BVG.

5. Ministère des droits de la femme, Service de documentation, "Une politique pour les femmes," 202–12.

6. Andrée Michel, "Mouvements féministes," 1277.

7. Offen, "Comment," 90.

8. Bair, *Simone de Beauvoir*, 145–46; Sand, *Correspondance*, 297; Ozouf, *Les mots*, 383. Also see Cairns, "Sexual Fault Lines," 85–87.

9. Louis, "Recherches féministes," 1–2.

10. Picq, "Le mouvement," 12–16.

11. *Mignonnes, allons voir sous la rose* . . . 6 ("special congrès") 7 (December 1981). See, for example, Marie-Jo Dhavernas, "Une seule solution," 29–36; "Editorial," *Cahiers du féminisme*, 1–2; Duchen, *Feminism in France*, 129–30.

12. Odette, "Lettre ouverte," 14; Duchen, *Feminism in France*, 130–34.

13. Ducrocq, "Mouvement de libération," 103, 112.

14. Picq, *Libération des femmes*, 317.

15. Picq, *Libération des femmes*, 315–16 and "1970–1980," 11–24; Marie-Jo Dhavernas, "Une seule solution," 29–36.

16. Ross and Frader, "May Generation," 114.

17. See Ducrocq, "Mouvement de libération," 103–14; McBride and Mazur, *Politics of State Feminism*, 202–15.

18. Picq, "Quelques réflexions," 917.

19. Louis, "Eléments," 10.

20. Picq, *Libération des femmes*, 324–25.

21. Robcis, "Republicanism," 226–27; Cairns, "Sexual Fault Lines," 85; Mendras and Cole, *Social Change*, 226–46.

22. Judt, "Rights in France," 67, 101. The statement "La loi garantit à la femme, dans tous les domaines, des droits égaux à ceux de l'homme" (the law guarantees women, in all areas, rights equal to those of men) is found in the preamble of the Fourth Republic's constitution (October 27, 1946).

The Fifth Republic's preamble (October 4, 1958) proclaims its attachment to the principles defined by the Declaration of 1789, confirmed by the preamble of 1946.

23. Marks and Courtivron, *New French Feminisms*, 33. Mendras and Cole, *Social Change*, 229–30 also point out the French "curious mélange of opposing principles" between libertarian values and pleasure and comfort on one hand and French puritanism and "respect for rigorous moral codes" on the other.

24. Delphy, "Nouvelles du MLF," 3–13. Quotes from translation in Duchen, *French Connections*, 33, 35–36.

25. For further discussion of the pernicious effects of postmodern ideas on politics and history see Hoff, "Gender," 149–68 and Hoff, "A reply," 25–30.

26. Mandel, *Muslims and Jews*, 125–27; Gitlin, *Twilight of Common Dreams*, 285.

27. See, for example, Commission femmes immigrées, "Pourquoi la commission"; Monique Dental, "Notes of meeting, October 28, 1978," and Association Choisir-La Cause des femmes, "Toutes et tous solidaires . . . venez dire non à l'excision," Monique Dental private collection; M. O. Delacour, "Des groupes femmes Algériennes s'organisent à Paris," *Libération*, July 17, 1978; "Des millions de jeunes supplicées," *Le Monde*, November 2, 1978; "Journée des femmes mutilées," *Rouges*, October 26, 1978; "Meeting samedi du Mouvement de femmes noires," *Rouges*, October 30, 1978; Groupe femmes pour l'abolition des mutilations sexuelles, "Mutilations sexuelles," 17; Béatrice Vallaeys, "Le tribunal de Paris tarifie l'excision: Un an avec sursis," *Libération* January 30, 1984; Christiane Chombeau, "Le tribunal corretionnel de Créteil s'estime incompétent dans une affaire d'excision ayant entraîné la mort," *Le Monde*, March 3, 1984; Claude Varène, "Excision: Les parents risquent les assises," *Le matin*, March 2, 1984; Châabane, "Diversité des mouvements."

28. Picq, *Libération des femmes*, 305–9; Delphy, "Nouvelles du MLF," 8; "Editorial," *Nouvelles questions feministes*, 3–15; "Féminisme: Quelles politiques,"3–8.

29. Wittig, "La pensée straight" and "On ne naît." Feminists were painfully aware of their failures. See, for example, Annette Levy-Willard, "Le Women's Council: L'arbitrage entre femmes," *Libération*, June 2, 1977, 4, and Bard, "Le lesbiennisme," 118; Delphy, "Trente ans," 4–22.

30. "Editorial," *Nouvelle questions féministes*, 7.

31. "Editorial," *Nouvelle questions féministes*, 10.

32. Echols, "New Feminism," 77.

33. Rolland, *Seront-elles?*, 141–43.

34. Planté, "Questions de différences," 112–13; Louis, "Recherches féministes," 17.

35. Elisabeth Schemla, "Ici, en droit, nous avons tout obtenu," *Le nouvel observateur*, April 19–25, 1994, 102–5.

36. Frischer, *La revanche*, 226.

37. Delphy, *Un universalisme*, 39.

38. Roudy, "Rapport d'information"; de Vendeuil, "La longue marches," 2–3; Philippe Flamand, "Les inégalités entre hommes et femmes à la loupe," *La tribune des fossés*, October 20, 1995, 43; "Avortement, emploi, égalité . . . Les revendications des femmes mobilisent," *Libération*, November 27, 1995, 4–5.

39. Les *Marie-pas-Claire* and Anne Dhoquois, "Nouvelle génération," 154–55; "Les féministes ripostent aux anti-IVG," *Libération*, November 26, 1995, 21; Stanislas Noyer, "Les *Marie-pas-Claire*: Féministes, et alors?," *Le jour*, April 7, 1993, 2; Kandel, "Génération MLF," 5–24; Valérie Cadet, Débats and Décryptages, "Simone de Beauvoir: L'aventure d'être soi," *Le Monde*, March 5, 2011, 19.

40. Mandel, *Muslims and Jews*, 126–27; Derderian, *North Africans*, 3–12; Dedieu, *La parole immigrée*, 24–29.

41. Christiane Chombeau, "Mme. Veil se prononce pour un quota de représentation politique des femmes," *Le Monde*, April 23, 1994; "Mme. Halimi plaide pour la 'parité hommes et femmes dans les assemblées élues," *Le Monde*, October 19, 1994; Gisèle Halimi, "Un référendum pour les femmes," *Le monde diplomatique*, October 1994: 3; Michelle Coquillat, "Parité, quotas: La démocratie des femmes," *Libération*, May 22, 1995; "La politique et les 'machos,'" *Le figaro*, November 9, 1995; "Bachelot, 'L'égalité hommes-femmes existe dans la loi, pas dans les faits,'" *InfoMatin*, September 28, 1995.

42. June 6, 2000: political parity law; May 9, 2001: the Génisson law concerning professional equality between men and women (following the legislation proposed by Roudy in 1983); March 1, 2004: national interprofessional accord relating to professional equality between men and women; March 23, 2006: law concerning the equal salary between women and men; April 4, 2006: law reinforcing the prevention and repression of domestic violence between couples and committed against minors; August 6, 2012: law relating to sexual harassment.

43. Reineke, *Beauvoir and Her Sisters*, 74–75.

44. Sineau, "*Parité*," 113–26. See note 22 above.

45. Oliver and Walsh, *Contemporary French Feminism*, 21–22; Ramsay, *French Women*, 80. Agacinski has been critiqued by radical feminists like Christine Delphy (who is for parity) as essentialist, but this might be a less nuanced reading than what Agacinski is trying to convey. See Delphy, "Parité, procreation, prostitution," 179–81.

46. Ramsay, *French Women*, 29, 73; Mossuz-Lavau, "La parité en politique," 41–57; Sénac, *L'égalité*, 147–48.

47. See among others, Gaspard, *Au pouvoir*; Gaspard, "De la parité"; Praud, "Gendering."

48. Mossuz-Lavau, "La parité en politique," 41–57; Scott, *Parité!*, 127–40; Praud, "Gendering," 38–39.

49. Scott, *Parité!*, 130–39; Caroline Ressot, "Rapport sur la parité: Le HCEfh appelle les partis politiques à s'engager pour le partage du pouvoir entre les femmes et les hommes," press release on website of Haut conseil à l'égalité entre les femmes et les hommes, February 26, 2015, http://www.haut-conseil-egalite.gouv.fr/parite/actualites/article/rapport-sur-la-parite-le-hcefh; Picq, "Parité"; Long, *Women Intellectuals*, 103.

50. Murray and Perpich, *Taking French Feminism*, 1–3, 10–11, 14, 90; Scott, *Politics of the Veil*, 68–69.

51. Ozouf, *Les mots*, 397; Scott, *Only Paradoxes to Offer*, 117–18, 168–69; Marso and Moynagh, "Introduction," 1–10; Cairns, "Sexual Fault Lines," 85; Mossuz-Lavau, "La parité," 169–87; Gaspard, "De la parité," 42–43. See Mossuz-Lavau's argument that women increasingly accept feminism because they like their rights: Mossuz-Lavau and Sineau, "Le vote," 688.

52. Collin, "Difference/Indifference," 13–30; Agacinski, "Versions of Difference," 40–55; Agacinski, *Femmes entre sexe*; Mossuz-Lavau, "Preface," 16; Scott, *Parité!*, 151.

53. Christine Delphy put it this way: "The ideology which oppresses women— or rather the entire system of which ideology is but a part—may be presented as an *invention* . . . and as a *means* to women's liberation; for *proto*-feminism promoted as *post*-feminism and becoming militant is *anti*-feminism." Delphy, "Proto-féminisme," 1499–1500. For English translation, see Delphy, "Protofeminism and Antifeminism," translated by Diana Leonard, in Moi, *French Feminist Thought*, 80–109.

BIBLIOGRAPHY

Manuscripts, Archives, and Government Documents

Anne Zelensky, private collection

Bibliothèque de documentation internationale contemporaine (BDIC)

    Archives des collectivités, mémoires de 68, archives d'associations, Mouvement de libération des femmes, papiers Françoise Picq (1970–1976), Mfc 0198, tracts.

    Citoyennes. *Propagande du mouvement républicain populaire.* 1945. BDIC Q.Piece 4305.

    Les cocottes éclatent! Brochure du MLF. Nanterre. 1973. BDIC. D62533.

    Dossier femmes.

    Dossier Union des femmes françaises.

    Ministère du travail de l'emploi et de la population; Comité du travail féminin, "Formation professionnelle: Rapport de la commission, March 1972. Folio 104/9 BDIC.

Bibliothèque Marguerite Durand (BMD)

    Assemblée consultative provisoire. "Commission de législation et de réforme de l'état. December 22, 1943.

    Cercle Elisabeth Dimitriev. "Sortir de l'ombre," May 1972.

    Choisir. "Pourquoi une loi?," 1973. Pamphlet.

    Collection mutilation sexuelles 391.7 MUT.

    Comité d'entente des associations féminines." "Françaises."

    Commission de législation et de réforme de l'état. "Procès-verbal de la séance du March 2, 1944."

    Dossier 396 vot.

    Dossier documentaire: Recueil. Antoinette Fouque.

    Agence femmes info. "MLF contre le Mouvement de libération des femmes." ca. 1979.

    Des femmes du MLF. "Politique et Psychanalyse: Mouvement de libération des femmes." Tract.

Dossier documentaire: Recueil. Gisèle Halimi.

Dossier Éditions *des femmes*.

"Pétition de solidarité," November 1978.

Dossier Suzanne Blaise.

"Au collectif de coordination aux membres du PFU française." Letter, Paris, June 22, 1977.

Blaise, Suzanne, "Histoire du Parti féministe unifie (PFU) 1975-1979: Du comportement des partis traditionnels à l'égard des partis féministes, en démocratie." Manuscript.

Blaise-Rigail, Suzanne, and Front féministe. "Questions posées par les femmes à François Mitterrand S.G. du Parti socialiste français." Paris, April 29, 1974.

"Les féministes radicales face aux élections."

Parti féministe unifié. Tracts. 1970s.

Parti socialiste.Tracts. 1974.

"Statuts déposés à la Préfecture de Bobigny."

"Un projet de loi: Le congé de mère; Pourquoi les féministes sont contre."

Villeneuve, Suzanne. "La femme et le Code civil," *Union feminine, civique, et sociale*, February 17, 1964, 1-12.

Gouvernement provisoire de la République française. "Ordonnance du August 9, 1944." 1944.

Lagroua Weill-Hallé, Marie-Andrée. "Du conflit entre la loi et la conscience professionnelle du médecin." ca. 1955. Dossier MFPF.

Le torchon brûle (1970-1971).

Luttes de femmes. "Plate-forme pour un centre d'initiatives et de coordination." n.d.

Muller, Martine. *Etre féministe en France: Contribution à l'étude des mouvements de femmes, 1944-1967*. Paris: Institut d'histoire du temps présent, 1987.

Regnaut, Françoise. "Les femmes enseignantes." *L'US: Dossier de documentation* 3 (October 1968): 21-29.

"Une crèche à Nanterre." Pamphlet.

Union des femmes françaises. "Programme de l'Union des femmes françaises." Adopté par le 7ème congrès national. Asnières, November 18-20, 1960.

———. *Traits de propagande de l'Union des femmes françaises, 1944-1945*.

Union féminine, civique, et sociale. "College civique feminine: La femme droits et valeurs." February 17, 1964.

———. "La femme et le Code civil." *Fiches documentaires d'action sociale et civique* 3 (May–June 1960).

———. "La participation des femmes à la vie de la cité." *Fiches documentaires d'action sociale et civique* 10 (April–June 1962).

———. "Moralité publique: Lois et moyens d'action." *Fiches documentaires d'action sociale et civique* 7 (July–September 1961).

Centre national de la recherche scientifique (CNRS) archives

Enquête 3: Le "fonds Slama." http://legs.cnrs.fr/spip.php?article133.

Loos, Jocelyne, and Marie-Victoire Louis. "Recherches sur les femmes, recherches féministes." Manuscript. La découverte. Laboratoire d'études de la sexualite. Axe 1.

Christine Delphy, private collection

Ecole normale supérieure de jeunes filles, boulevard Jourdain

"Anciennes élèves de l'école au CNRS directeurs de recherche en 1981."

"Anciennes élèves de l'école dans l'enseignement supérieur en 1981."

Bellina, Mme. "La dernière promotion des sevriènes." 1987.

"Débouchés des élèves scientifiques entrées à l'ENSJF en 1973. 1977."

Ecole normale supérieure des jeunes filles, pour le 75ᵉ anniversaire. *D'un anniversaire à l'autre (1931–1936).* 1959.

"Note d'information pour les enseignants scientifiques: Rentrée 1980."

"Places offertes aux concours d'entrée des ecoles normales supérieures (sections littéraires)."

"Résultats des dernières agrégations: 1973–1981."

Serre, Josianne. "Discours prononcé par Mme. Serre." December 3, 1981, à l'occasion du centenaire de l'école.

Institut de rechèrches sur les sociétés contemporaines (IRESCO)

Rogerat, Chantal. "Club Flora Tristan." Manuscript. October 1985.

———. "De la construction de manières de voir et de dire: Le cas du syndicalisme et des femmes." Les sociologues dans le débat social en Europe, *Institut de recherche sur les sociétés contemporaines,* Paris, September 30–October 3, 1991. IRESCO.

———. "Le mouvement des femmes en France et la recherche: Un repérage de circonstance." Manuscript for *Arguments,* 1987.

Institut national de la statistique et des études économiques (INSEE)

Annuaire rétrospectif de la France. Séries longues, 1948–1988. INSEE, 1990.

Bulletin mensuel de statistique. 1961–1970.

Caisse nationale des allocations familiales. "Historique: L'evolution des prestations." *Extraits du guide des prestations familiales* 1: 29–38.

Huet, Maryse. Archives et documents: La concentration des emplois féminins; Ampleur, analyse, évolution. Manuscript. Paris: INSEE, 1983.

"La carrière des femmes." *Population et sociétés* 146 (April 1981).

Les femmes. Collection "Contours et caractères." INSEE, 1991.

Recensement général de la population. For years 1946, 1953, 1954, 1962, 1968, 1972, 1975.

L'Office universitaire de recherche socialiste (L'OURS)

Action socialiste 19 (September 1971) (four-page pamphlet)

Cahier et revue nos. 170–77, 1986–1987.

Cahiers mensuels d'éducation socialiste féminine publiés par Suzanne Lacore. 1951.

Commission national des femme socialistes. La condition des femmes.

Comité pour la creation d'un centre de contraception et d'interruption volontaire de grossesse (IVG) à l'hopital Lariboisière, "Du nouveau à Lariboisiere?" L'OURS, Pachkoff archives, APO-2, Autumn 1979

Documents planning familial. 1-APO-71–75.

Mutuelle générale de l'education nationale. L'OURS, 1-APO-76.

Parti socialiste SFIO; Bureau national des femmes. Conférence nationale des femmes du PS.

"Résumé de la proposition de loi Socialiste sur la contraception et l' IVG: thèmes principaux et argumentaires," Pachkoff archives, APO-2, Autumn 1979.

Ministère de la santé et du travail

Centre d'études et de recherches marxistes. "L'importance décisive de la crèche: Sa valeur actuelle." *Les cahiers du CERM*, no. 87. 1970.

Confédération générale du travail. *Les femmes salariées.* Travaux de la ve conférence nationale, Paris (May 17–18, 1973). Paris: Éditions sociales, 1973.

Ministère de l'education nationale

Bureau universitaire de statistique et de documentation professionnelles. Concours d'entrée et effectifs. 1954–1955. Diplômes délivrés en 1954, 1960–1961. Diplômes 1960, 1964–1965. Diplômes délivrés en 1964.

———. Ecoles publiques d'enseignement supérieur et d'enseignement technique supérieur en France. Statistique des cours d'entrée, des effectifs, et des diplômés, 1948–1951.

———. Recueil de statistiques scolaires et professionnelles, 1949–1951.

Relevé général des étudiants des universités français depuis 1990.

"Les étudiants: Effectifs des élèves de l'enseignement public dans les classes préparatoires aux grandes ecoles; Année scolaire, 1945–1975." *Statistiques des enseignements* 10 (1977).

"Origine sociale des effectifs par discipline: Enseignement supérieur public." *Informations statistiques* 76 (December 1965).

"Recrutement des professeurs certifiés en 1964"; "Étudiants français en valeurs absolues." *Informations statistiques* 69 (April 1965).

"Recrutement des professeurs certifies en 1964"; "Agrégations, session de 1964." *Informations statistiques* 72 (July 1965).

"Résultats à l'examen du baccalauréat: June 1965." *Informations statistiques* 78 (February 1966).

"Résultats à l'examen du baccalauréat: Année 1966." *Informations statistiques* 88 (January 1967).

"Résultats de l'examen du baccalauréat: Année 1967." *Informations statistiques* 100 (February 1968).

Service central des statistiques et de la conjoncture. Tableaux de l'education national. 1966.

Service central des statistiques et sondages. Tableau des enseignement et de la formation, 1970, 1972, 1976, 1980, 1982.

Service des études informatiques et statistiques. "Effectifs des élèves dans les grandes écoles publiques et privée." Année scolaire 1977–1978.

Tableau 34. Enseignement supérieur public, 1899–1964.

Tableaux statistiques. "Écoles normales supérieures: Analyse du concours d'entrée diplômes." Délivres en 1969, February 1971, 1971–1972. April 1973.

Ministère du travail, de l'emploi et de la formation professionnelle

Kergoat, Danièle. "Industrie de pointe, revendications gestionnaires et classe(s) ouvrière(s): Le cas de la raffinerie antar à Danges." Paris: Centre national de la recherche scientifique–Groupe de sociologie des organisations, 1978.

Ministère des affaires sociales. "Le travail des femmes."

Ministère d'état chargé des afaires sociales. "Le Comité du travail féminin." Notes 9 (March 5–11, 1973). 104/2.

———. Rapport sur les équipements d'accueil de la petite enfance. January 1973.

Ministère du travail, de l'emploi et de la population. Comité du travail féminin. L'évolution de la situation des femmes dans la société française. January 1975.

———. Enquête nationale sur les femmes demandeurs d'emploi, November 1973–March 1974. Rapport. November 1975. 104/3.

———. La situation de l'emploi féminin en March 1974, June 1974. 104/5.

———. Le rôle des femmes dans l'économie: Synthèse du rapport de la France à l'OCDE. June 1973.

———. Programme de travail pour l'année 1973–1974. 104/1.

Ministère du travail. Derniers chiffres sur l'emploi des femmes en France. January 1976.

Ministère du travail. Études. 1970–1980.

Sullerot, Évelyne, and the Conseil économique et social. *Avis et rapport: Les problèmes posés par le travail et l'emploi des femmes.* October 1975.

Monique Dental, private collection

Commission femmes immigrées. "Pourquoi la commission femmes immigrées au sein des assises." Assises nationales sur les femmes et le travail, November 14–15, 1981.

Parlement français

Avice, Edwige, et al. "Proposition de loi tendant à favoriser l'insertion professionnelle des femmes et à leur assurer une garantie contre toutes les discriminations sexistes." Assemblée nationale. 1223 (June 28, 1979).

Journal officiel. Assemblée nationale. *Débats parlementaires.* Compte rendu intégral des séances. "Réforme des régimes matrimoniaux." Rapport no. 1475. June 1965.

Journal officiel. Assemblée nationale. *Débats parlementaires.* "Réforme des régimes matrimoniaux. Discussion." 1e séance. June 26, 1965.

———. "Garantie de l'emploi en cas de maternité." June 7, 1966.

———. Molle, Marcel. Sénat. "Reforme des régimes matrimoniaux." *Débats parlementaires.* May 6, 1965.

———. "Prophylaxie anticonceptionnelle." 2e et 3e séances. July 1, 1967.

———. "Réforme des régimes matrimoniaux." 2e séance. June 26, 1965.

———. "Réforme des régimes matrimoniaux." 3e séance. June 26, 1965.

———. "Réforme des régimes matrimoniaux." 2e séance. June 29, 1965.

———. "Régulation des naissances." 2e séance. December 14, 1967.

———. "Régulation des naissances." 1re séance. December 19, 1967.

———. "Scrutin no. 224." 3e séance. June 26, 1965.

Journal officiel. Assemblée nationale. *Documents de l'assemblée nationale.* "Divorce par consentement mutuel." Annexe no. 6141. December 12, 1957.

———. Collette, "Discussion d'un projet de loi adopté par le Sénat," *Débats parlementaires. Journal officiel.* June 26, 1965.

———. "Construction et fonctionnement de crèches." Annexe no. 65. October 21, 1969.

———. "Femmes salariées: Deux jours de repos hebdomadaire." Annexe no. 65. October 21, 1969; annexe no. 1408. September 21, 1966.

———. "Femmes salariées: Deux jours de repos hebdomadaire." Annexe no. 1974. 27 September 1966.

———. "Femmes salariées . . . droit à la pension de retraite." Annexe no. 412. June 26, 1969.

———. Foyer. "Suite de la discussion d'un projet de loi adopté par le Sénat." *Débats parlementaires.* June 26, 1965.

———. "Garantie de l'emploi en cas de maternité." Annexe no. 1964. April 9, 1966.

———. "L'article 757 du Code Civil." Annexe no. 1409. September 21, 1966.

———. "L'assurance-maternité aux femmes salariées." Annexe no. 600. July 3, 1969.

———. "Livret de famille aux mères de famille non mariées." Annexe no. 7244. June 3, 1958.

———. "Loi du 31 juillet 1920." Annexe no. 1870. September 20, 1966.

———. "Mères de famille exerçant un emploi salarié." Annexe no. 315. May 28, 1969.

———. "Prestations familiales." Annexe no. 442. June 26, 1969.

———. "Principe de non-discrimination du travail féminin." Annexe no. 2010. September 29, 1966.

———. "Prophylaxie anticonceptionnelle." Annexe no. 2203. April 4, 1967.

———. Proposition de loi. "L'autorité parentale." Annexe no. 642. October 21, 1969.

———. "Régimes matrimoniaux." Annexe no. 6259. December 26, 1957.

———. "Tableau 2: Montant des prestations légales versées par le régime général de sécurité sociale au titre des assurances sociales." July 10, 1965.

Journal officiel. Sénat. Documents. Discussion d'une proposition de loi. "Lutte contre la discrimination sexiste." (June 29, 1980): 3372–78.

———. "Annexe au procès verbal." May 11, 1965.

———. Broglie, Jean de. Discussion d'un projet de loi. "Réforme des régimes matrimoniaux." May 6, 1965.

———. Projet de loi. "Garantie de l'emploi en cas de maternité," no. 253. June 24, 1966.

———. Projet de loi. "Réforme des régimes matrimoniaux," no.131.

———. Rapport. "Réforme de l'enseignement (textes de bases)," no. 297. August 9, 1966.

———. Rapport. "Réforme des régimes matrimoniaux," no. 144. April 29, 1965.

———. "Réforme des régimes matrimoniaux." May 11, 1965.

———. "Régulation des naissances et usage des contraceptifs." 1ᵉ séance. December 5, 1967.

Moreau, Gisèle, et al. Assemblée nationale. *Journal officiel.* "Proposition de loi sur le respect de l'application du principe de l'égalité des sexes." 1538 (October 4, 1958).

Projets économiques et sociaux. "L'égalité professionnelle entre les femmes et les hommes." Projet de loi adopté par le Conseil des ministers, November 3, 1982. 134, no. 82 (November 24, 1982).

Serusclat, Frank, et al. "Proposition de loi tendant à lutter contre la discrimination sexiste." Sénat. *Journal officiel.* 346 (May 23, 1979).

———. "Rapport fait au nom de la Commission des lois constitutionnelles, de législation du suffrage universel, du règlement et d'administration générale." Sénat. *Journal officiel.* 316 (June 17, 1980).

Vincent, Madeleine. "Pour les femmes: Promotion . . . egalité . . . liberté . . . Extraits de la proposition de loi générale du PCF déposée au Parlement le 14 juin 1979."

Robert W. Woodruff Library, Emory University, Special Collections

Dorothy Kraus French Political Collection. "May 1968."

Secrétariat d'etat chargé des droits des femmes. Archives. (Collections from all past women's ministries and secretariats.)

Billeta, Isabella. "Evolution des droits des femmes." September 2,1988.

Comité du travail féminin. "Mesures protectrices et égalité professionnelle entre hommes et femmes." March 3, 1981.

Giroud, Françoise. "Bilan de l'application des "cent mesures." July 1979.

La delegation générale à l'information, Secrétariat d'état à la condition feminine, July 1974–July 1975, *Les actions nouvelles,* n.d.

Legislation/femmes (see files).

"Lettre ouverte à mesdames, messieurs les députés et sénateurs." Paris, June 10, 1977. Secrétariat d'etat chargé des droits des femmes.

Ministère des droits de la femme. Service du documentation.

"L'évolution de la place des femmes sur le marché du travail en France."

"Une annonce pour les femmes." 1981–1985.

"Une politique pour les femmes." Actualités documents. 1974–1981.

Ministre délégué à la condition féminine. Documentation.

"L'opinion des femmes (1974–1978). Famille, travail, politique. Paris, December 8, 1978.

"Une politique pour les femmes. Bilan (1974–1978) et perspectives."

Ministre délégué auprès du Premier ministre, chargé des droits de la femme.

"Bilan des actions menées en faveur des femmes et des familles depuis 1974." March 12, 1985.

"Onze fiches pratiques sur la loi d'égalité professionnelle." Conférence de presse. October 11, 1983.

Newspaper clips file.

Parti socialiste. "L'action du Parti socialiste depuis 1971 et du gouvernement depuis 1981 en faveur des droits des femmes." November 1985.

Parti socialiste. Ministère des droits de la femme.

———. Service de documentation. "Bilan de la politique de promotion de la condition féminine depuis 1974." March 7, 1985.

———. "Une politique pour les femmes." Actualités documents; Secrétariat d'etat chargé des droits des femmes, "L'evolution de la protection légale de la grossesse dans le travail (1909-1981), annexe 2: 202-12. 1981.

Pelletier, Monique. Ministre déléguée à la condition féminine. "Bilan de l'application des 'cent mesures.'"

Roudy, Yvette. "Rapport d'information sur l'égalité professionnelle entre les femmes et les hommes: Déposé à l'Assemblée nationale par la Commission des affaires culturelles, familiales, et sociales." Manuscript. Secrétariat d'état chargé des droits des femmes. Service de documentation, 1989.

———. "Un ministère pas comme les autres: Un projet, une stratégie pour les femmes." Colloque FEN, March 1988.

Roudy, Yvette, and Jane Maignial. "Des crèches à l'université et sur les lieux de travail: Rencontre avec Françoise Lenoble Pradine." *La femme du 20ě siècle* 15 (December 1969).

Roujou de Boubée, G. "L'interruption volontaire de la grossesse: Commentaire de la loi no. 75-17 of January 17, 1975." *Recueil dalloz sirey: Chronique* 36 (1975).

Secrétariat d'état auprès du Premier ministre. Condition féminine. "Le programme français pour l'année internationale de l'effort de la femme." January 1975.

Socialist Party archives (also archives for Section française de l'internationale ouvrière—SFIO)

"Conférence nationale des femmes du Parti socialiste SFIO." Le Pré St. Gervais, May 2-3, 1964.

"Congrès national du Parti socialiste." 1944-1960.

Parti socialiste, ed. *Femmes en lutte: Pour le droit à l'information sexuelle à la contraception et à l'interruption de grossesse.* Paris: Parti socialiste, 1979.

Published Works

Adereth, Maxwell. *The French Communist Party: A Critical History (1920–1984), from Comintern to the "Colors of France."* Manchester UK: Manchester University Press, 1984.

Agacinski, Sylviane. *Femmes entre sexe et genre.* Paris: Éditions du Seuil, 2012.

———. "The Turning Point of Feminism: Against the Effacement of Women." In Roger and DalMolin, *France from 1851 to the Present,* 17–22.

———. "Versions of Difference." In Oliver and Walsh, *Contemporary French Feminism,* 40–55.

Albistur, Maïté, and Daniel Armogathe. *Histoire du féminisme français: De l'empire napoléonien à nos jours.* Vol. 2. Paris: Éditions des femmes, 1977.

———. *Le grief des femmes: Anthologie des textes féministes de l'empire napoléonien à nos jours.* Vol. 2. Paris: Éditions hier et demain, 1978.

Alcoff, Linda. "Cultural Feminism versus Post-Structuralism: The Identity Crisis in Feminist Theory." *Signs* 13, no. 3 (1988): 405–36. http://www.jstor.org/stable/3174166.

Allwood, Gill. *French Feminisms: Gender and Violence in Contemporary Theory.* London: UCL Press, 1998.

Allwood, Gill, and Khursheed Wadia. *Gender and Policy in France.* Basingstoke UK: Palgrave Macmillan, 2009.

———. *Women and Politics in France 1958–2000.* New York: Routledge, 2000.

Alzon, Claude. *Femme mythifiée, femme mystifiée.* Paris: Presses Universitaires de France, 1978.

———. *La femme potiche et la femme bonniche: Pouvoir bourgeois et pouvoir mâle.* Paris: Éditions François Maspero, 1973.

Amiel, Simonne, and Ligue des droits de l'homme. *Ce qu'une française doit savoir.* Paris: Éditions L.D.H., 1945.

Andrews, William G., and Stanley Hoffmann. *The Impact of the Fifth Republic on France.* Albany: State University of New York Press, 1981.

Andrieu, Claire. "Les résistantes, perspectives de recherche." *Le mouvement social* (July–September 1977): 69–96.

Angeloff, Tania, and Margaret Maruani. "Gisèle Halimi: La cause du féminisme." *Travail, genre et sociétés* 14, no. 2 (2005): 5–25.

"Année du patrimoine: Une éclatante apothéose." *La revue d'en face* 9–10 (1st trimester 1981), 61–63.

"Annex no. 3." In Association mouvement pour les luttes féministes, *Chroniques d'une imposture,* unpaginated.

Annik. "Qu'est-ce qui nous réunit ce soir?" *Le temps des femmes* 12 (1980): 14–15.

Archambault, Paul. *La famille: Œuvre d'amour*. Paris: Éditions familiales de France, 1950.

Archambault, Pauline. *La femme entre deux mondes*. Paris: Éditions Jeheber, 1955.

Armogathe, Daniel. *Le deuxième sexe: Simone de Beauvoir; Analyse critique*. Paris: Éditions Hatier, 1977.

Artières, Philippe, and Michelle Zancarini-Fournel, eds. *68: Une histoire collective, 1962–1981*. Paris: Éditions La Découverte, 2008.

Association Choisir. *Avortement: Une loi en procès; L'affaire de Bobigny*. Preface by Simone de Beauvoir. Paris: Éditions Gallimard, 1973.

Association des anciens Science Po. *Annuaire de anciens science po*. Paris: Association des anciens élèves de Sciences Po, 1991.

Association la griffonne. *Douze ans de femmes au quotidien: Douze ans de luttes féministes en France*. Paris: Éditions la griffonne, 1981.

Association mouvement pour les luttes féministes. *Chroniques d'une imposture: Du mouvement de libération des femmes à une marque commerciale*. Paris: Association mouvement pour les luttes féministes, 1981.

Association mouvement pour les luttes féministes. "Il ne fait pas chaud contre des femmes," in, *Chroniques*, n.p.

Associations familiales protestantes. *Mesdames vous allez voter . . . Pourquoi? Comment?* Paris: Éditions J. E. P., 1945.

Atkin, Nicholas. "Rallié and Résistants: Catholics and Vichy France: 1941–1944." In Chadwick, *Catholicism, Politics and Society*, 97–118.

Aubin, Claire, and Hélène Gisserot. *Les femmes en France: 1985–1995; Rapport établi par la France en vue de la quatrième conférence mondiale sur les femmes*. Paris: La Documentation française, 1994.

Aubry, Marielle. "Des 'bleues' à l'Assemblée: 18 candidates qui ont une chance." *F Magazine* 3 (March 1978): 29.

Auclair, Marcelle. "La presse féminine." *La nef* 17, no. 4 (October–December 1960): 89–95.

Auclair, Marcelle, with Jeanne Dodeman. *Le livre noir de l'avortement*. Paris: Librairie Arthème Fayard, 1962.

Audry, Colette. "Dix ans après *Le deuxième sexe*." *La nef* 17, no. 4 (October–December 1960): 120–28.

———. *Les militants et leur morales*. Paris: Éditions Flammarion, 1976.

———. "Les pièces du dossier." *Après-Demain* 140 (January 1972): 1–41.

Auger, Colette. "De la diffamation." *Les temps modernes* 34, no. 391 (February 1979): 1213–18.

Aumont, Michèle. *Femmes en usine*. Paris: SPES, 1953.

———. *Jeune fille, lève-toi!* Paris: Librairie Arthème Fayard, 1962.

Avril, Pierre, et al. *Personnel politique français, 1870-1988*. Paris: Presses Universitaires de France, 1989.

Baczko, Bronislaw. "Femmes: Une singularité francaise?" *Le débat: Histoire, politique, société* 87 (November–December 1995): 117–46.

Bair, Deidre. *Simone de Beauvoir: A Biography*. New York: Summit Books, 1990.

Barbara, "Le féminisme ne répond plus?" *Histoires d'elles* 3 (February–March 1978): 6–7.

"Barbara," and Christine de Coninck. *La partagée*. Paris: Éditions de Minuit, 1977.

Bard, Christine. *Le féminisme au-delà des idées reçues*. Paris: Éditions Broché, 2012.

———. "Le lesbiennisme come construction politique." In Gubin et al., *Le siècle des féminismes*, 111–26.

———, ed. *Les féministes de la deuxième vague*. Rennes: PUR, 2012.

———. *Les femmes dans la société française au vingtième siècle*. Paris: Librairie Armand Colin, 2001.

———. *Les filles de Marianne: Histoire des féminismes, 1914-1940*. Paris: Éditions Fayard, 1995.

———, ed. *Un siècle d'antiféminisme*. Paris: Éditions Fayard, 1999.

Bard, Christine, Fréderique El Amrani, and Bibia Pavard. *Historie des femmes: Dans la France des XIXE et XXE siècles*. Paris: Éditions ellipses, 2013.

Bard, Christine, and Janine Mossuz-Lavau. *Le planning familial: Histoire et mémoire, 1956-2006*. Paris: Presses Universitaires de Rennes, 2006.

Barral, Pierre. "Pour qui votent les femmes? . . . à Vienne (Isère)." In *Nouvelles études de sociologie*, edited by François Goguel, 185–193. Paris: Librarie Armand Colin, 1954.

Barsy, Martine de [interviewer]. "Connaître et comprendre: Simone de Beauvoir." *Pénéla* 16 (September 1968): 8–17.

Barthas, Françoise. *Paroles de "bonne-femme."* Villejuif: IMPO, 1979.

Bauer, Nancy. *Simone de Beauvoir, Philosophy, and Feminism*. New York: Columbia University Press, 2001.

Beauvoir, Simone de. "La condition féminine." *La nef* 18, no. 5 (January–March 1961): 120–27.

———. *La force des choses*. Vol. 1. Paris: Éditions Gallimard, 1963.

———. *Le deuxième sexe*. Paris: Éditions Gallimard, 1949.

———. "Brigitte Bardot et le syndrome de Lolita." In *Les écrits de Simone de Beauvoir*, edited by Claude Francis and Fernande Gontier, 363–76. Paris: Éditions Gallimard, 1979.

———. ed. *Les femmes s'entêtent*. Paris: Éditions Gallimard, 1975.

———. "Préface." In Association Choisir, *Avortement*, 12–14.

———. "Préface." In Association du mouvement pour les luttes féministes, *Chroniques.*

———. "Préface." In Bard and Mossuz-Lavau, *Le planning familial,* 4–5.

———. "Préface." In Tristan and de Pisan, *Histoires du* MLF, 10–11.

Bécar, Florence, and Bernadette Legrand. "Menie Grégoire, une première: Son émission à la radio sur la sexualité." *Dialogue* 3, no. 193 (2011): 7–13. https://www.cairn.info/revue-dialogue-2011-3-page-7.htm.

Beevor, Antony, and Artemis Cooper. *Paris after the Liberation: 1944–1949.* London: Penguin, 1994.

Bell, D. S., and Byron Criddle. *The French Socialist Party: The Emergence of a Government.* Oxford: Clarendon Press, 1988.

Bell, Susan G., and Karen M. Offen. *Women, the Family, and Freedom, 1750–1880.* Stanford CA: Stanford University Press, 1983.

Berg, Maggie. "Luce Irigaray's 'Contradictions:' Postculturalism and Feminism." *Signs: Journal of Women in Culture and Society* 17, no. 1 (Autumn 1991): 50–70.

Bergevin, Annette de. "Pour une éthique de la femme." *Esprit* 23, no. 226 (May 1950): 740–758.

Berlioz, Johanny. "Les femmes dans la nation." *Cahiers du communisme* 22, no. 11 (September 1945): 43–51.

Bernard, Jean-Pierre Arthur. *Paris rouge: 1944–1964; Les communists français dans la capitale.* Paris: Éditions Champ Vallion, 1991.

Bernheim, Cathy. *L'amour presque parfait.* Paris: Éditions du Félin, 1991.

———. *Perturbation ma soeur: Naissance d'un mouvement de femmes.* Paris: Éditions du Seuil, 1983.

Bernheim, Cathy, Liliane Kandel, Françoise Picq, and Nadja Ringart, eds. *Mouvement de libération des femmes: Textes premièrs.* Paris: Éditions Stock, 2009.

Bertin, Celia. *Le temps des femmes.* Paris: Hachette, 1958.

Bertrand, Mireille. "Femmes: Égalité et personnalité." *Cahiers du communisme* 51, nos. 7–8 (July–August 1975): 38–44.

———. "La lutte des communistes français pour l'émancipation de la femme." *Cahiers du communisme* 12 (December 1970): 118–27.

Bertrand, Simone. "La promotion de la femme dans le monde." *Cahiers du communisme* 34, no. 4 (April 1958): 593–613.

Bessières, Albert, SJ. *Le vote des femmes.* Paris: Éditions spes, 1945.

Bettelheim, Charles. "Economic and Social Policy in France." *International Labour Review* 51, no. 6 (June 1945): 722–740.

————. "Economic and Social Policy in France." *International Labour Review* 54, nos. 3–4 (September–October 1946): 139–59.

Bidelman, Patrick Kay. *Pariahs Stand Up!: The Founding of the Liberal Feminist Movement in France, 1858–1889*. Westport CT: Greenwood Press, 1982

Bihin-Jourdan, Claire. "Les origines du parti féministe unifié." *Les cahiers du GRIF* 6 (1975): 43–47.

Bisseret, Noëlle. Les inégaux ou la sélection universitaire. Paris: Presses Universitaire de France, 1974.

Bize, P. R. "Sélection et orientation professionnelles: Quelques aspects particuliers de la sélection professionnelle." In *Les cours du conservatoire national des arts et métiers*. Centre de documentation universitaire, 1960.

Blaise, Suzanne. *Des femmes de nulle part*. Paris: Éditions Tierce, 1981.

Bloch-Lainé, François, and Jean Bouvier. *La france restaurée, 1944–1954: Dialogue sur les choix d'une modernisation*. Paris: Éditions Fayard, 1986.

Blum, Léon. "La femme dans la société socialiste." *Revue socialiste* 11(May 1947): 513–22.

Bock, Gisela. "Poverty and Mother's Rights in the Emerging Welfare States." In *A History of Women in the West*, edited by Georges Duby and Michelle Perrot, 402–32. Vol. 5. Cambridge MA: Harvard University Press, 1994.

————. *Women in European History*. Translated by Allison Brown. Oxford: Blackwell, 2001.

Boissonnas, Sylvina. Book Event: Remarks about *There Are Two Sexes: On the Thought and Commitments of Antoinette Fouque*. La Maison Française, New York University, New York, March 10, 2015.

Bontemps, Charles-August. *La femme et la sexualité*. Paris: Les Cahiers francs, 1956.

Bonvoisin, Samra-Martine, and Michèle Maignien. *La presse féminine: Que sais-je*. Paris: Presses Universitaires de France, 1986.

Boons, Marie-Claire. "Des femmes dans l'extrême-gauche française." Actes du colloque national. *Femmes, féminisme et recherches*, 111–17. Toulouse, December 1982. Toulouse: AFFER, 1984.

Borzeix, Anni, and Margaret Maruani. *Le temps des chemises: La grève qu'elles gardent au coeur*. Paris: Éditions Syros, 1982.

Bouchardeau, Huguette. "Le rôle économique de la femme." *Perspectives socialistes* 55 (December 1955): 7–13.

————. *Pas d'histoire, les femmes . . . 50 ans d'histoire des femmes, 1918–1968*. Paris: Éditions Syros, 1977.

————. *Un coin dans leur monde*. Paris: Éditions Syros, 1980.

Bouchardeau, Huguette, Suzanne Goueffic, and Geneviève Thouvenot. *Pour une politique des femmes, par les femmes, pour les femmes: Les propositions du PSU*. Paris: Éditions Syros, 1981.

Bouchoux, Corinne. "L'affaire Gabrielle Russier." *Vingtième siècle, revue d'histoire* 33 (January–March) 1992: 56–64.

Bouma, Saïd. *Les discriminations racists: Une arme de division massive*. Preface by Christine Delphy. Paris: Éditions L'Harmattan, 2010.

Bourg, Julian ed. *After the Deluge: New Perspectives on the Intellectual and Cultural History of Postwar France*. New York: Lexington Books, 2004.

———. *From Revolution to Ethics: May 1968 and Contemporary French Thought*. Montreal: McGill-Queen's University Press, 2007.

———. "'Your Sexual Revolution Is Not Ours': French Feminist 'Moralism' and the Limits of Desire." In Frazier et al., *Gender and Sexuality in 1968*, 85–113.

Bourges, Hervé, ed. *The Student Revolt: The Activists Speak*. Translated by B. R. Brewster. London: Panther Books, 1968.

Braidotti, Rosi, with Judith Butler. "Interview: Feminism by Any Other Name." *Signs: Journal of Women in Culture and Society* 6, nos. 2–3 (Summer–Fall 1994): 27–61.

Braitberg, Alice. "Jalons dans l'histoire du travail des femmes." *Revue française des affaires sociales* 4 (October–December 1981): 153–64.

Braye, Pierre. "Le rôle économique et social des allocations familiales." *Droit social* 8, no. 3 (March 1945): 116–20.

Bridgford, Jeff. *The Politics of French Trade Unionism*. London: Leicester University Press, 1991.

Brimo, Albert. "La femme dans le droit public français." *Annales de la faculté de droit de Toulouse* 14, no. 2 (1966): 184–221.

———. *Les femmes françaises face au pouvoir politique*. Paris: Éditions Montchrestien, 1975.

Brisac, Geneviève, Marie-Jo Dhavernas, and Irène Théry. "Sur quelques problèmes du féminisme: Entretien avec Simone de Beauvoir." *La revue d'en face* 9–10 (1st trimester 1981): 3–14.

Boxer, Marilyn J. "Rethinking the Socialist Construction and International Career of the Concept 'Bourgeois Feminism.'" *American Historical Review* 112, no. 1 (2007): 131–58.

Bresard, Marcel. "La famille, cellule sociale." In Prigent, *Renouveau des idées*, 330–42.

Brown, Bernard E., ed. *Eurocommunism and Eurosocialism: The Left Confronts Modernity*. New York: Cyrco Press, 1979.

Brown, L. Neville. "The Reform of French Matrimonial Property Law." *American Journal of Comparative Law* 14 (1965–1966): 308–22.

Bruhl-Lehmann, Suzanne. "Responsabilité civique et politique de la femme." In *Conscience de la féminité*, edited by Maryse Choisy, Janick Arbois, and Suzanne Bruhl-Lehmann. Paris: Éditions familiales de France, 1954.

Brun, Odette, Marie-Elisabeth Duffeteau, and Monique Dental. *Ruptures . . . et féminisme en devenir*. Paris: Éditions Voix off, 1984.

Brunschvicg, Betty. "A propos de la réforme des régimes matrimoniaux." *La revue socialiste* 132 (April 1960): 405–8.

Bureau international du travail. "La législation relative aux allocations familiales en 1947." *Revue internationale du travail*. Part 1: 57, no. 4 (April 1948): 354–75; Part 2: 57, no. 5 (May 1948): 505–29.

———. "La participation des femmes mariées et des mères de famille à l'activité économique." *Revue internationale du travail* 63, no. 6 (June 1951): 735–57.

———. "L'emploi des femmes en France." *Revue internationale du travail* 55, no. 6 (June 1947): 606–12.

———. "Le relèvement des salaires et traitements à la libération de la France." *Revue internationale du travail* 51, no. 5 (May 1951): 662–78.

———. "Les allocations familiales en France." *Revue international du travail* 52, nos. 2–3 (August–September 1945): 218–34.

Burke, Carolyn Greenstein. "Report from Paris: Women's Writing and the Women's Movement." *Signs: Journal of Women in Culture and Society* 3, no. 4 (1978): 843–55.

Butler, Judith. *Bodies that Matter: On the Discursive Limits of "Sex."* New York: Routledge, 1994.

———. *Gender Trouble: Feminism and the Subversion of Identity*. New York: Routledge, 1990.

———. "Performative Acts and Gender Constitution: An Essay in Phenomenology and Feminist Theory." *Theatre Journal* 40, no. 4 (1988): 519–31. doi: 10.2307/3207893.

Butler, Judith, and Joan Wallach Scott. *Feminists Theorize the Political*. New York: Routledge, 1992.

Byrnes, Joseph F. *Catholic and French Forever: Religious and National Identity in Modern France*. Philadelphia: University of Pennsylvania Press, 2011.

Cairns, Lucille. "Sexual Fault Lines: Sex and Gender in the Cultural Context." In Kidd and Reynolds, *Contemporary French Cultural Studies*, 81–90.

Calas, Raoul. "La journée internationale des femmes et la lutte pour la paix." *Cahiers du communisme* 26, no. 3 (March 1949): 298–305.

Callu, Agnès. *Le mai 68 des historiens: Entre identités narratives et histoire orale.* Villeneuve: Presses Universitaire Septentrion, 2010.

Callu, Marie-France. *Le nouveau droit de la femme.* Lyon: Éditions l'Hermès, 1978.

Canning, Kathleen. *Gender History in Practice: Historical Perspectives on Bodies, Class, and Citizenship.* Ithaca NY: Cornell University Press, 2006.

Caputi, Mary. "Beauvoir and the Case of Djamila Boupacha." In Marso, *Simone de Beauvoir's Political Thinking,* 109–26.

Carbognani, Marie-Thérèse. "Les communistes et l'emancipation des femmes de 1945 à 1959." Master's thesis, Université de Paris VIII. 1975.

Célestin, Roger, and Eliane DalMolin. *France from 1851 to the Present: Universalism in Crisis.* New York: Palgrave Macmillan, 2007.

Célestin, Roger, Eliane DalMolin, and Isabelle de Courtivron, eds. *Beyond French Feminisms: Debates on Women, Politics, and Culture in France, 1981–2001.* New York: Palgrave Macmillan, 2003.

Centre d'études et de recherches marxistes. *La condition féminine.* Paris: Éditions sociales, 1978.

Cercle Elisabeth Dimitriev. *Brève histoire du MLF: Pour un féminisme autogestionnaire.* Rome: Éditions Savelli, 1976.

Châabane, Nadia. "Diversité des mouvements de 'femmes dans l'immigration.'" *Les cahiers du CEDREF* 16 (2008): 231–50. http://journals .openedition.org/cedref/601#tocto3n5.

Chabal, Emile, ed. *France since the 1970s: History, Politics, and Memory in an Age of Uncertainty.* London: Bloomsbury Academic, 2015.

Chadwick, Kay, ed. *Catholicism, Politics and Society in Twentieth-Century France.* Liverpool: Liverpool University Press, 2000.

Chambers, Samuel A., and Terrell Carver. *Judith Butler and Political Theory: Troubling Politics.* New York: Routledge, 2008.

Chaperon, Sylvie. "1945–1970, reprendre l'histoire du féminism." In *L'histoire sans les femmes: Est-elle possible?,* edited by Anne-Marie Sohn and Françoise Thélamon, 205–16. Paris: Éditions Perrin, 1998.

——. "Antoinette Fouque (1936–2014): Une féminologue." *Hermès: La revue* 3, no. 70 (March 2014): 207–9. https://www.cairn.info/revue-hermes-la -revue-2014-3-page-207.htm.

——. "'Feminism Is Dead. Long Live Feminism!': The Women's Movement in France at the Liberation, 1944–1946." In *When The War Was Over: Women, War and Peace in Europe, 1940–1956,* edited by Claire Duchen and Irene Bandhauer-Schöffmann, 146–160. London: Leicester University Press, 2000.

——. "La radicalisation des mouvements féminins français de 1960 à 1970." *Vingtième siècle: Revue d'histoire* 48, no. 1 (1995): 61–74.

──. "Le MFPF face au féminisme (195-1970)." In *Le planning familial: histoire et mémoire, 1956-2006*, edited by Christine Bard and Janine Mossuz-Lavau, 21-26. Rennes: Presses Universitaires de Rennes, 2006.

──. *Les années Beauvoir: 1945-1970*. Paris: Éditions Fayard, 2000.

──. "L'histoire contemporaine des sexualités en France." *Vingtième siècle: Revue d'histoire 75*, no. 3 (July-September 2002): 47-59. https://www.cairn.info/revue-vingtieme-siecle-revue-d-histoire-2002-3-page-47.htm.

──. "*Momone* and the *bonnes femmes;* or Beauvoir and the MLF." In *The Women's Liberation Movement: Impacts and Outcomes*, edited by Kristina Schulz, 73-90. Oxford: Berghahn Books, 2017.

──. "Une génération d'intellectuelles dans le sillage de Simone de Beauvoir." CLIO: *Femmes, genre, histoire* 13 (2001): 99-116.

Chaplin, Tamara. "Lesbians on Line: Queer Identity and Community Formation on the French Minitel." *Journal of the History of Sexuality* 23, no. 3 (September 2014): 451-72.

────. "Orgasm without Limits: May '68 and the History of Sex Education in Modern France." In Jackson et al., *May '68*, 376-97.

──. *Turning On the Mind: French Philosophers on Television*. Chicago: University of Chicago Press, 2007.

Chapsal, Madeleine. *Les écrivains en personne*. Paris: Éditions René Julliard, 1960.

Charraud, Alain. "Travail féminin et revendications féministes." *Sociologie du travail* 3 (1974): 291-318.

Charraud, Alain, and Kathy Saada. "Les écarts de salaires entre hommes et femmes." INSEE: *Economie et statistique* 59 (September 1974): 3-17.

Chazalette, Andrée. "La femme dans la vie sociale et politique." *Perspectives socialistes* 55 (December 1955): 13-20.

Chenal, Odile, and Danièle Kergoat. "Production et reproduction: Les jeunes travailleuses, le salariat et la famille." *Critiques de l'économie politique* 17 (September-December 1981): 118-39.

Chérel, Albert. "Essais d'humanités féminines." *Revue des travaux de l'académie des sciences morales et politiques et comptes rendus de ses séances* 102, no. 4 (1979): 30-40.

Chetcuti, Natacha, and Maria-Teresa Amaral. "Monique Wittig, la tragédie et l'amour." *Corps* 1, no. 4 (2008): 93-98.

Chetcuti, Natacha, Maria-Teresa Amaral, and Luca Greco, eds. *La face cachée du genre: Langage et pouvoir des norms*. Paris: Presses de la Sorbonne Nouvelle, 2012.

Choisir-La Cause des femmes. *Quel président pour les femmes? Résponse de François Mitterrand*. Preface by Gisèle Halimi. Paris: Éditions Gallimard, 1981.

———. "Une interview de Gisèle Halimi: 'Pourquoi le programme commun des femmes; Pourquoi Choisir sera présent aux élections législatives?'" *Choisir: La Cause des femmes* 29 (December 1977): 9–11.

Choisy, Maryse. "Feminité et psychologie." In Choisy et al., *Conscience de la féminité*, 37–50.

Choisy, Maryse, Jean Viollet, Pauline Le Cormier, and Institut des hautes études familiales, eds. *Conscience de la féminité*. Paris: Éditions familiales de France, 1954.

Chombart de Lauwe, Marie-José. "Les femmes en 1971: Images d'une oppression, images d'une libération." *La nouvelle critique* 53, no. 234 (May 1972): 30–42.

———. "Les femmes: Oppression et liberation." *La nouvelle critique* 53, no. 234 (May 1972): 30–43.

———. "Les nouvelles images de la femme." *La nef* 26, no. 38 (October–December 1969): 154–58.

Chombart de Lauwe, Marie-José, and Paul-Henri Chombart de Lauwe. *Images de la femme dans la société: Enquête internationale*. Paris: UNESCO, 1962.

———. *La vie quotidienne des familles ouvrières*. Paris: Centre national de la recherche scientifique, 1956.

Chombart de Lauwe, Marie-José, Philippe Robert, Colette Guillaumin, Nicole Mathieu, and Centre national de la recherche scientifique (França). *La femme dans la société: Son image dans différents milieux sociaux*. Paris: CNRS, 1963.

"Chronique de Mittard et Roquerand, militants de base du PS." *Mignonnes, allons voir sous la rose . . .* 4:3.

"Chroniques du sexisme ordinaire." *Les temps modernes* 35, no. 405 (April 1980): 1905–20.

Cixous, Hélène. "Entretien avec Françoise van Rossum-Guyon." *Revue des sciences humaines* 44, no. 168 (October–December 1977): 479–92.

———. "Extreme Fidelity." In *Writing Differences: Readings from the Seminar of Hélène Cixous*, edited by Susan Sellers, 9–36. Oxford: Open University Press, 1988.

———. "Je n'ai lâché l'un que pour l'autre." In Cixous et al., *La venue à l'écriture*.

———. *Le prénom de dieu*. Paris: Éditions Bernard Grasset, 1967.

———. "Le rire de la méduse." *L'arc* 61 (1975): 39–54. Translated by Keith and Paula Cohen. *Signs: Journal of Women in Culture and Society* 1, no. 4 (1976).

———. *Les commencements*. Paris: Éditions Bernard Grasset, 1970.

———. *Le troisième corps*. Paris: Éditions Bernard Grasset, 1970.

———. "Poésie e(s)t politique." *des femmes en mouvements hebdo*, November 30, 1979, 29–31.

Cixous, Hélène, and Catherine Clément. *La jeune née*. Paris: Union générale d'éditions, 1975.

Cixous, Hélène, Madeleine Gagnon, and Annie Leclerc. *Dedans*. Paris: Union générale d'éditions, 1977.

———. *La venue à l'écriture*. Paris: Union générale d'éditions, collection "10/18," 1977.

Clark, Linda L. *The Rise of Professional Women in France: Gender and Public Administration since 1830*. Cambridge: Cambridge University Press, 2000.

Club de l'observateur. *Le livre blanc de l'avortement*. Paris: Le N.O., 1971.

Cohn-Bendit, Daniel, and Gabriel Cohn-Bendit. *Obsolete Communism: The Left-Wing Alternative*. Translated by Arnold Pomerans. New York: McGraw-Hill, 1968.

Coignard, Sophie, and Marie-Thérèse Guichard. "Vive les françaises: Enquête sur le rôle des femmes dans la société et leurs relations avec les hommes." *Le point* 1119 (February 26, 1994): 45–51.

Colin, Madeleine. "La femme dans la société contemporaine et les voies de son affranchissement." *Cahiers du communisme* 10 (October 1962): 97–110.

———. "La travailleuse peut-elle être mère?" *Perspectives socialistes* 55 (December 1955): 21–26.

Collectif féministe du mouvement de libération des femmes. *Ruptures . . . et féminisme en devenir*. Paris: Éditions Voix off, 1984.

Collette-Kahn, Suzanne. *Femme, tu vas voter: Comment?* Problèmes d'aujourd'hui, no. 5. Paris: Éditions de la liberté, 1945.

Collin, Françoise. "Difference/Indifference between the Sexes." In Oliver and Walsh, *Contemporary French Feminism*, 13–30.

———. "Féminitude et féminisme." *Les cahiers du* GRIF 1 (November 1973): 5–22.

———. "L'oubli d'une vieille question philosophique." In *De l'égalité des sexes*, edited by Michel de Manassein, 293–304. Paris: Centre national de documentation pédagogique, 1995.

———. "Pluralité différence identité." *Tiré à part de la contribution de Françoise Collin à Présences 1991*. In *Deux sexes, c'est un monde*, edited by Jil Silberstein and Silvia Ricci. Lempen Genève: Alliance culturelle romande, 1991.

———. "Praxis de la différence: Notes sur le tragique du sujet." *Les cahiers du* GRIF 46 (Spring 1992): 125–41.

Colombel, Jeannette. "Sartre et Simone de Beauvoir vus par Francis Jeanson." *La pensée* 129 (October 1966): 91–100.

Comité central du Parti communiste français. "Résolution." *Cahiers du communisme* 23, no 11 (November 1946): 1010–13.

Comité d'action féminine. *Appel du comité d'action féminine*. Toulouse: Comité d'action féminine, 1944.

"Conçus par l'opération du Saint-sème." *des femmes en mouvements* 2 (February 1978): 12.

Conley, Verena Andermatt. *Hélène Cixous: Writing the Feminine*. Lincoln: University of Nebraska Press, 1991.

Conseil constitutionnel. "Jurisprudence." *Recueil dalloz sirey* 31 (1975): 529–32.

Constans, Ellen. "Propositions et moyens d'action pour l'égalité." *Cahiers du communisme* 56, no. 5 (May 1980): 56–62.

"Coordination Parisienne des groups femmes." *L'information des femmes* 19 (October 1977): 17–18.

Coquille, Sylvie. "Naissance du mouvement de libération des femmes en France 1970–1973." Master's thesis, Université de Paris X. 1982.

Cowans, Jon. "French Public Opinion and the Founding of the Fourth Republic." *French Historical Studies* 17, no. 1 (Spring 1991): 62–95.

Craipeau, Jean-Loup, ed. *Lip au féminin*. Paris: Éditions Syros, 1977.

Craipeau, Maria. "Une femme à 'part entière.'" *La nef* 17, no. 4 (October–December 1960): 101–9.

Crevot, A., and M. Colson, eds. *Une aide semblable à lui: La femme dans la société*. Paris: Éditions ouvrières, 1960.

Crouzet, Paul. *Bachelières ou jeunes filles*. Toulouse: Éditions Privat-Didier, 1949.

Crozier, Michel. "The Cultural Revolution: Notes on Changes in the Intellectual Climate of France." *Daedalus* 93, no. 1 (1964): 514–42.

Cruikshank, Margaret. *The Gay and Lesbian Liberation Movement*. New York: Routledge, 1992.

"Culture des femmes: Une gestation; Entretien avec Antoinette Fouque." *des femmes en mouvements hebdo*, August 7–21, 14–16.

Cyfer-Diderich, G., Monique Basch, and Commission sociale de la fédération belge des femmes diplômées d'université. "Les jeunes femmes diplômées d'université: Leur ménage, leur vie professionnelle, leurs problèmes." *Revue de l'institut de sociologie* 33, no. 1 (1960): 103–56.

Danguy, M.-L. *Les femmes et l'action syndicale*. Paris: Éditions CFTC, 1945.

Daric, Jean. *L'activite professionnelle des femmes en France: Etude statistique; Evolution-comparisons internationales*. Paris: Presses Universitaires de France, 1947.

———. "Le travail des femmes: Professions, métiers, situations sociales et salaires." *Population* 10, no. 4 (October–December 1955): 675–90.

———. "Niveau de vie des familles suivant le nombre d'enfants." *Population* 11, no. 3 (July–September 1956): 425–27.

———. "Quelques vues sur le travail féminin non agricole en divers pays." *Population* 13, no. 1 (January–March 1958): 69–78.

Dauphin, Cécile, Arlette Farge, Geneviève Fraise, Christiane Klapisch-Zuber, Rose-Marie Lagrave, Michelle Perrot, Pierrette Pézsert, Yannick Ripa, Pauline Schmitt-Pantel, and Danièle Voldman. "Women's Culture and Women's Power: Issues in French Women's History." In *Writing Women's History: International Perspectives*, edited by Karen Offen, Ruth Roach Pierson, and Jane Rendall, 107–133. London: Macmillan, 1991.

d'Eaubonne, Françoise. *Le complexe de Diane: Erotisme ou féminisme*. Paris: Éditions René Julliard, 1951.

———. *Y a-t-il encore des hommes?* Paris, Éditions Flammarion, 1964.

Deboisvieux, Gilberte. "Un divorce si banal." *Actes: Les cahiers d'action juridique* 16 (Autumn 1977): 19–23.

Debré, Michel. *Ami ou ennemi du peuple?* Paris: Éditions Plon, 1975.

Dedieu, Jean-Philippe. *La parole immigrée: Les migrants africains dans l'espace public en France, 1960–1995*. Paris: Klincksieck, 2012.

"De l'art d'accompagner les femmes dans la rue sans y descender vraiment ou PPS (Parti papa socialiste) et la marche des femmes du 6 octobre." *Mignonnes, allons voir sous la rose . . .*, no. 2:15–17.

Delphy, Christine. *Close to Home: A Materialist Analysis of Women's Oppression*. Translated and edited by Diana Leonard. Amherst: University of Massachusetts Press, 1984.

———. "L'ennemi principal." *Partisans* 54–55 (July–October 1970): 157–72.

———. "Les femmes et l'état." Actes du colloque national. *Femmes, féminisme, et recherches*, 347–56. Toulouse, December 1982. Toulouse: affer, 1984.

———. "Les origines du mouvement de libération des femmes en France." *Nouvelles questions féministes* 16–18 (1991): 137–48.

———. "Libération des femmes ou droits corporatistes des mères." *Nouvelles questions féministes* 16–18 (1991): 93–118.

———. "Nos amis et nous: Les fondements cachés de quelques discours pseudo-féministes." *Questions féministes* 1 (1977): 21–49.

———. "Nouvelles du mlf libération des femmes an dix." *Questions féministes* 7 (February 1980): 3–13.

———. "Proto-féminisme et anti-féminisme." *Les temps modernes* 30, no. 346 (May 1975): 1469–1500.

———. "Trente ans de Nouvelles questions féministes." *Nouvelles questions féministes* 30, no. 2 (2011): 4–22.

———. "Un féminisme matérialiste est possible." *Nouvelles questions féministes* 4 (Autumn 1982): 51–86.

———, ed. *Un troussage de domestique*. Paris: Éditions Syllepse, 2011.

———. *Un universalisme si particulier: Féminisme et exception française, 1980–2010*. Paris: Éditions Syllepse, 2010.

Dekeuwer-Defossez, Françoise. *Dictionnaire juridique: Droits des femmes*. Paris: Éditions Jouve, 1985.

Deniel, Raymond. "Femmes dans la ville." *Revue de l'action populaire* 176 (March 1964): 273–93.

Derbyshire, Ian. *Politics in France from Giscard to Mitterrand*. Edinburgh: W. R. Chambers, 1990.

Derderian, Richard L. *North Africans in Contemporary France: Becoming Visible*. New York: Palgrave Macmillian, 2004.

Derogy, Jacques. *Des enfants malgré nous*. Paris: Éditions de Minuit, 1956.

Derrick, Jonathan. "The Dissenters: Anti-Colonialism in France." In *Promoting the Colonial Idea: Propaganda and Visions of Empire in France*, edited by Tony Chafer and Amanda Sackur, 53–70. New York: Palgrave, 2002.

des femmes. Catalogue, 1974–1979. Paris: Éditions *des femmes*, 1979.

———. "Histoire en mouvement." In *des femmes, Catalogue, 1974–1979*, 24–25.

Deudon, Catherine. *Un movement à soi: Images du movement des femmes, 1970–2001*. Paris: Éditions Syllepse, 2003.

"Deux analyses sur l'oppression feminine faites par des groups de quartier." *Le torchon brûle* 2:5.

Dhavernas, Marie-Jo. "Des divans profonds comme des tombeaux: Ideologie des femmes en mouvements hebdo." *La revue d'en face* 8 (1st trimester 1980): 36–44.

———. "Une seule solution: Autre chose." *La revue d'en face* 11 (1st trimester 1981): 29–36.

Dhavernas, Marie-Jo, and Liliane Kandel. "Quelques réflexions autour de la notion de 'sexisme.'" Actes du colloque national. *Femmes, féminisme et recherches*, 749–54. Toulouse: December 1982. Toulouse: AFFER, 1984.

Dhavernas, Marie-Jo, Liliane Kandel, and Béatrice Slama. "Sexisme et loi anti-sexiste: Contributions au débat." *Les temps modernes* 40, no. 444 (July 1983): 1–61.

Dhavernas, Odile. *Droits des femmes, pouvoir des hommes*. Paris: Éditions du Seuil, 1978.

———. "Pour une recherche féministe dans le domaine du droit." Actes du colloque national. *Femmes, féminisme et recherches*, 357–66. Toulouse, December 1982. Toulouse: affer, 1984.

Dhoquois, Régine. *Appartenance et exclusion*. Paris: Éditions L'Harmattan, 1989.

____. "From Formal Equality to Real Equality." Paper presented at Colloque: "Le féminisme en France, en Inde et en Russie," Paris, May 20, 1992.

Dhoquois, Régine, and Marie-Ange Leprince, eds. "Evolution du droit de la famille." *Actes: Les cahiers d'action juridique* 35-36 (February 1982): 12-64.

Diamond, Hanna. *Women and the Second World War in France, 1939-1948: Choices and Constraints.* Edinburgh: Longman, 1999.

Dickens, Bernard. "The Right to Conscience." In *Abortion Law in Transnational Perspective: Cases and Controversies,* edited by Rebecca J. Cook, Joanna N. Erdman, and Bernard M. Dickens, 210-38. Philadelphia: University of Pennsylvania Press, 2014.

Djelic, Marie-Laure. *Exporting the American Model: The Post-War Transformation of European Business.* Oxford: Oxford University Press, 2001.

Dogan, Mattei, and Jacques Narbonne. *Les françaises face à la politique: Comportement politique et condition sociale.* Paris: Librairie Armand Colin, 1955.

Dogan, Mattei. "Causes of the French Student Revolt in May 1968." In *The Tasks of Universities in a Changing World,* edited by Stephen D. Kertesz, 306-22. Notre Dame IN: University of Notre Dame Press, 1971.

Doron, Daniella. *Jewish Youth and Identity in Postwar France: Rebuilding Family and Nation.* Bloomington: Indiana University Press, 2015.

Dourlen-Roullier, Anne-Marie. *La vérité sur l'avortement: Deux enquêtes inédites.* Paris: Librairie Maloine, 1963.

Drake, David. *Intellectuals and Politics in Post-War France.* London: Palgrave, 2002.

Dr. J. V. "Réflexions sur la contraception." *Partisans* 32-33 (October–November 1966-1967): 65-68.

Dubesset, Mathilde. "De la citoyenneté à la parité." In Gubin et al., *Le siécle des féminismes,* 269-82.

———. "Les figures du féminin à travers deux revues féminines, l'une catholique, l'autre protestante, la femme dans la vie sociale et jeunes femmes, dans les années 1950-1960." *Le mouvement social* 198 (2002): 9-34. doi:10.2307/3780250.

Dubois, Juliette. "La France a besoin d'une politique au service de l'enfance." *Cahiers du communisme* 42, no. 4 (April 1966): 85-95.

———. "Le congrès mondial des mères: Étape importante de la lutte des femmes pour la défense de la paix." *Cahiers du communisme* 31, no. 9 (September 1955): 1064-74.

Duchen, Claire. *Féminism in France: From May '68 to Mitterrand.* London: Routledge & Kegan Paul, 1986.

———. *French Connections: Voices from the Women's Movement in France.* Amherst: University of Massachusetts Press, 1987.

———. "Une femme nouvelle pour une France nouvelle?" CLIO: *Histoire, femmes, et sociétés* 1 (1995): 151–64.

———. *Women's Rights and Women's Lives in France, 1944–1968*. New York: Routledge, 1994.

Duchen, Claire, Ben Mandelson, and les Chimères. *Maternité esclave: Les chimères*. Paris: Union générale d'éditions, 1975. First published as "Avortement, contraception, sexualité, réformisme" by Collective féministes révolutionnaires in *Le torchon brûle*, no. 5, 1972.

Ducrocq, Françoise. "Mouvement de libération des femmes en France socialiste." *La revue d'en face* 14 (Autumn 1983): 103–12.

Duhamel, Oliver. *La gauche et la Ve République*. Paris: Presses Universitaires de France, 1980.

Dumas, André. *Le contrôle des naissances, opinions protestantes*. Paris: Les Bergers et les mages, 1965.

Dumas, Francine. "L'avortement, il faut en parler!" January 23, 1964. http://www.protestants.org/index.php?id=932.

Dumont, Yvonne. "La femme devant son avenir." *Cahiers du communisme* 49, no. 3 (March 1973): 31–40.

———. *Les communistes et la condition de la femme: Étude de la Commission centrale de travail du Parti communiste français parmi les femmes*. Paris: Éditions sociales, 1970.

———. "Les femmes dans le combat national." *Cahiers du communisme* 33, nos. 7–8 (July–August 1957): 1081–92.

———. "Les femmes, leurs problèmes, et leurs luttes." *Cahiers de communisme* 43, no. 1 (January 1967): 75–84.

"D'une tendance." *Le torchon brûle* 3:18.

Dupâquier, Jacques, Alain Drouard, Maurice Garden, and Hervé Le Bras. *Histoire de la population française*, vol. 4: *De 1914 à nos jours*. Paris: Presses Universitaires de France, 1988.

"Du rififi rue des Saints-Pères." *Le temps des femmes* 3 (June 1978): 5.

Duverger, Maurice. *La participation des femmes à la vie politique*. Paris: UNESCO, 1955.

Duverger, Sylvia. "Simone Iff: Du protestantisme au féminisme (1924–2014)." *Nouvelles questions féministes*, 34, no. 1 (2015): 158–66.

Dyer, Colin. *Population and Society in Twentieth Century France*. London: Hodder and Stoughton, 1978.

Echols, Alice. "Cultural Feminism: Feminist Capitalism and the Anti-Pornography Movement." *Social Text* 7 (Spring–Summer 1983): 34–53. doi: 10.2307/466453.

———. *Daring to Be Bad: Radical Feminism in America 1967–1975*. Minneapolis: University of Minnesota Press, 1989.

———. "The New Feminism of Yin and Yang." In *Desire: The Politics of Sexuality*, edited by Ann Snitow, Christine Stansell, and Sharon Thompson, 62–81. London: Virago, 1983.

École de haut enseignement commercial pour les jeunes filles. *La condition de la française aujourd'hui et demain*. Paris: Imprint coopérative arpajonaise, 1964.

"Édito." *Cahiers du féminisme* 3 (March 1978): 1–2.

"Editorial." *Cahiers du féminisme* 2 (January 1978), 3.

"Editorial: Féminisme: Quelles politiques?" *Nouvelles questions féministes* 2 (October 1981): 3–8.

"Editorial." *La revue d'en face* 1 (May 1977): 3–6.

"Editorial." *Nouvelles questions féministes* 1 (March 1981): 3–15.

Ehrmann, Henry W. *Politics in France*. Boston: Little, Brown, 1983.

Eisenstein, Hester, and Alice Jardine, eds. *The Future of Difference*. New Brunswick NJ: Rutgers University Press, 1985.

Elle (under the direction of Jean Mauduit). *La grande aventure du travail féminin*. Paris: Éditions Fayard, 1974.

Elles voient rouge. *Féminisme et marxisme/journées "Elles voient rouge," 29 et 30 novembre 1980 [Paris]*. Paris: Éditions Tierce, 1981.

"Employment of Women in France." *International Labour Review* 55, no. 6 (June 1947): 549–55.

"Employment of Women in Free French Territory." *International Labour Review* 49, nos. 4–5 (April–May 1944): 516–17.

"Entrevue avec Antoinette Fouque." *Gravida* 1 (Autumn 1983): 22–42.

"Entrevue avec Antoinette Fouque: Suite et fin." *Gravida* 2 (Winter 1984): 55–74.

Evans, Martin, and Emmanuel Godin. *France since 1815*. 2nd ed. New York: Routledge, 2014.

Evans, Sara M. *Personal Politics: The Roots of Women's Liberation in the Civil Rights Movement and the New Left*. New York: Knopf, 1979.

Eyquem, Marie-Thérèse. "Un expédient: Le travail à temps partiel." *La femme du 20ᵉ siècle* 16 (March 1970).

Fagnani, Jeanne. "L'intégration progressive du modèle de 'la mère qui travaille': Trente ans de politique familiale en France." *Spirale* 2, no. 18 (February 2001): 139–55. doi: 10.3917/spi.018.0139.

"Family Allowance Schemes in 1947." *International Labour Review*, pt. 1, 57, no. 4 (April 1948): 315–33; pt. 2, 57, no. 5 (May 1948): 456–77.

"Family Allowances in France." *International Labour Review* 52, nos. 2–3 (August–September 1945): 196–210.

Fauré, Christine. *La démocratie sans les femmes: Essai sur le libéralisme en France.* Paris: Presses Universitaires de France, 1985.

Feher-Gurewich, Judith. "Lacan and American Feminism: Who Is the Analyst?" In Célestin et al., *Beyond French Feminisms*, 239–60.

Feldman, Jacqueline. "De FMA au MLF: Un témoignage sur les débuts du mouvement de libération des femmes." *CLIO: Femmes, genre, histoire* 29 (2009): 193–203. http://journals.openedition.org/clio/9326.

Féminisme et marxisme. "Journées 'Elles voient rouges,'" November 29 and 30, 1980. Paris: Éditions Tierce, 1981.

"Feministes: Mégalodossier." *Les temps des femmes* 12 (1980): 16–59.

"Féministes révolutionnaires." *Le torchon brûle*, nos. 5, 7, and 9.

Féministes révolutionnaires, "Processus pour soumettre les groups." *Le torchon brûle* no. 5, 9.

"Femmes à la CGT." *Cahiers du féminisme* 7 (December 1978–January 1979): 10–14.

"Femmes en mouvements: Hier, aujourd'hui, demain; Entretien avec Antoinette Fouque." *Le débat: Histoire, politique, société* 59 (March–April 1990): 126–43.

"Femmes: Le grand chambardement." *Politique hebdo*, February 7–13, 1977, 15.

"Femmes, une autre écriture?" *Magazine littéraire* 180 (January 1982): 17–31.

Ferry, Luc, and Alain Renaut. *La pensée 68: Essai sur l'anti-humanisme contemporain.* Paris: Éditions Gallimard, 1985.

Firestone, Shulamith. *The Dialectic of Sex.* New York: William Morrow, 1970.

Fisher, Claudine Guégan. *La cosmogonie d'Hélène Cixous.* Amsterdam: Rodopi, 1988.

Fishman, Sarah. *The Battle for Children: World War II, Youth Crime, and Juvenile Justice in Twentieth-Century France.* Cambridge MA: Harvard University Press, 2002.

———. *From Vichy to the Sexual Revolution: Gender and Family Life in Postwar France.* Oxford: Oxford University Press, 2017.

———. *We Will Wait: Wives of French Prisoners of War, 1940–1945.* New Haven CT: Yale University Press, 1991.

Flamant, Françoise. *À tire d'elles: Itinéraires de féministes radicales des années 1970.* Rennes: Presses Universitaires de Rennes, 2009.

Foley, Susan K. *Women in France since 1789: The Meanings of Difference.* New York: Palgrave Macmillan, 2004.

Folliet, Joseph, ed. *Morale sexuelle et difficultés contemporaines.* Paris: Éditions familiales de France, 1953.

Fortescue, William. *The Third Republic in France, 1870–1940: Conflicts and Continuities.* New York: Routledge, 2002.

Fougeyrollas, Pierre. "Prédominance du mari ou de la femme dans le ménage." *Population* 6, no. 1 (January–March 1951): 83–102.

Fougeyrollas-Schwebel, Dominique. "Controverses et anathèmes au sein du féminisme français des années 1970." *Cahiers du genre* 2, no. 39 (2005) :13–26. https://www.cairn.info/revue-cahiers-du-genre-2005-2-page-13.htm.

Fougeyrollas-Schwebel, Dominique, and Maryse Jaspard. "Critique féministe des statistiques: Jalons pour une confrontation européenne." *Cahiers du GRIF* 45 (Autumn 1990): 137–48.

Fouque, Antoinette. "Enoncer, de plein chant, nos revivances, toutes." In *des femmes, Catalogue des femmes*, 421. https://www.desfemmes.fr/wp-content/uploads/2014/11/6-nos-journaux.pdf.

———. "Féminisme et/ou mouvement de libération des femmes." In *Images de femmes mythe et histoire*, edited by Martine de Gaudemar, 177–87. Aix-en-Provence: Centre d'études féminines de l'Université de Provence, 1982.

———. "Femmes en mouvements: Hier, aujourd'hui, demain—An interview with Antoinette Fouque." In *Women in Movements: Yesterday, Today, Tomorrow, and Other Writings*, edited by Antoinette Fouque. Translated by Anne Berger, Arthur Denner, and Nina McPherson. Paris: *des femmes* USA, 1992.

———. *Il y a 2 Sexes*. Paris: Éditions Gallimard, 1995.

———. "Le mouvement des femmes: Féminisme et/ou MLF." In *Mouvements sociaux d'aujourd'hui: Acteurs et analystes*, edited by Alain Touraine, 225–49. Paris: Éditions ouvrières, 1982.

———. "Une expérience du mouvement des femmes en France 1968–1991 de la libération à la démocratisation." PhD diss., Université de Paris VIII, 1992.

Fraisse, Geneviève. "La solitude volontaire (à propos d'une politique des femmes). *Les révoltes logiques* (special issue) (February 1978): 49–58.

Francis, Claude, and Fernande Gontier. *Les écrits de Simone de Beauvoir*. Paris: Éditions Gallimard, 1979.

Frazier, Leslie Jo, and Deborah Cohen, eds. *Gender and Sexuality in 1968: Transformative Politics in the Cultural Imagination*. New York: Palgrave Macmillan, 2009.

Freundlich, Emmy. "Social Security for Housewives." *International Labour Review* 50, no. 2 (August 1944): 160–68.

Frischer, Dominique. *La revanche des misogynes: Où en sont les femmes après trente ans de féminisme?* Paris: Éditions Albin Michel, 1997.

Frischmann, Georges. "Le parti communiste et les femmes." *Cahiers du communisme* 1 (January 1960): 48–61.

"Front Matter: Le mouvement de libération des femmes devient la propriété privé d'un groupe." *Questions féministes* 7 (February 1980).

Fuchs, Rachel. *Poor and Pregnant in Paris: Strategies for Survival in the Nine-teenth Century*. New Brunswick NJ: Rutgers University Press, 1992.

Gabin, Laurent. *Simone de Beauvoir ou le refus de l'indifférence*. Paris: Éditions Fischbacher, 1968.

Gallois, William. "Against Capitalism? French Theory and the Economy after 1945." In Bourg, ed., *After the Deluge*, 49–72.

Gallop, Jane. *The Daughter's Seduction: Feminism and Psychoanalysis*. Ithaca NY: Cornell University Press, 1982.

———. *Thinking through the Body*. New York: Columbia University Press, 1988.

Garaudy, Roger. *Le communisme et la renaissance de la culture française*. Paris: Éditions sociales, 1945.

Gaspard, Françoise, ed. "De la parité: Genèse d'un concept, naissance d'un movement." *Nouvelles questions féministes* 15, no. 4 (November 1994): 29–44.

———. *Les femmes dans la prise de décison en France et en Europe: Demain la parité*. Paris: Éditions L'Harmattan, 1997.

———. *Madame Le . . .* Paris: Éditions Grasset, 1979.

Gaspard Françoise, Claude Servan-Schreiber, and Anne Le Gall. *Au pouvoir citoyennes! Liberté, égalité, parité*. Paris: Éditions Seuil, 1992.

Gauchet, Marcel, and Pierre Nora. "Femmes en mouvements: Hier, aujo-urd'hui, demain: An interview with Antoinette Fouque." In *Women in Movements: Yesterday, Today, Tomorrow, and Other Writings*, edited by Antoinette Fouque and translated by Anne Berger and Arthur Denner, 7–46. Paris: des femmes USA, 1992.

Gauthier, Xavière. "Creations." In *New French Feminisms: An Anthology*, edited by Elaine Marks and Isabelle de Courtivron, 161–64. Brighton UK: Harvester, 1986.

Gennari, Geneviève. *Le dossier de la femme*. Paris: Librairie Académique Per-rin, 1965.

———. *Simone de Beauvoir: Classiques du vingtième siecle*. Paris: Éditions Univer-sitaires, 1958.

Gerhard, Ute. "Concepts et controverses." In Gubin et al., *Le siècle des féminis-mes*, 47–63.

Gibbon, Margaret. "The Trade Unions and Women Workers after 1968." In *May '68 Coming of Age*, edited by D. L. Hanley and A. P. Kerr, 139–51. Lon-don: Macmillan, 1989.

Gienow-Hecht, Jessica C. E. "Culture and the Cold War in Europe." In *The Cam-bridge History of the Cold War*, edited by Melvyn P. Leffler and Odd Arne Westad. Vol. 1, Origins, 406–11. Oxford: Oxford University Press, 2010.

Gildea, Robert, James Mark, and Anette Warring, eds. *Europe's 1968: Voices of Revolt*. Oxford: Oxford University Press, 2013.

Girard, Alain. "Le travail féminin et l'opinion publique." *Avenirs* 93-95 (April–June 1958): 31-83.

Giroud, Françoise. *Cent mesures pour les femmes*. Paris: La Documentation française, 1976.

———. *La nouvelle vague: Portraits de la jeunesse*. Paris: Éditions Gallimard, 1958.

Gitlin, Todd. *The Twilight of Common Dreams: Why America is Wracked by Culture Wars*. New York: Metropolitan Books, 1995.

Glendon, Mary Ann. *Abortion and Divorce in Western Law*. Cambridge MA: Harvard University Press, 1987.

———. "Matrimonial Property: A Comparative Study of Law and Social Change." *Tulane Law Review* 49, no. 1 (November 1974): 21-83.

———. *The Transformation of Family Law: State, Law, and Family in the United States and Western Europe*. Chicago: University of Chicago Press, 1989.

Gobeil, Madeleine. "Entrevue avec Simone de Beauvoir." *Cité libre* 16, no. 69 (August–September 1964): 30-31.

Goguel, François. "Pour qui votent les femmes? . . . à Belfort." In *Nouvelles études de sociologie électorale*, edited by François Goguel, 197-98. Paris: Librarie Armand Colin, 1954.

Gombin, Richard. *The Origins of Modern Leftism*. Translated by Michael K. Perl. New York: Penguin, 1975.

Gordon, Daniel. "From Militancy to History: Sans Frontière and Immigrant Memory at the Dawn of the 1980s." In Chabal, *France since the 1970s*, 115-28.

Gouffe, Marthe. *La promotion féminine en France depuis la Libération*. Paris, 1952.

Graziella, Caselli, Jacques Vallin, Guillaume Wunsch, and Daniel Courgeau. *Demography—Analysis and Synthesis: A Treatise in Population*. Boston: Elsevier, 2006.

Greenwald, Lisa. "Not 'Undifferentiated Magma': Refashioning Women in France, 1945-1955."*Historical Reflections/Réflexions historiques* 22, no. 2 (Spring 1996): 407-30.

Grégoire, Ménie. "Enseignement et condition féminine." *Esprit* 11 (November 1958): 708-14.

———. *Le métier de femme*. Paris: Éditions Plon, 1965.

———. "Mariage et régimes matrimoniaux." *Esprit* 29, no. 295 (May 1961): 693-706.

———. "Réponses à l'enquête." *Esprit* 29, no. 295 (May 1961): 771-83.

Gregory, Abigail, and Ursula Tidd. *Women in Contemporary France*. New York: Berg, 2000.

Groult, Benoîte. *Ainsi soit-elle*. Paris: Éditions Grasset & Fasquelle, 1975.

———. "Préface." *Nouvelles femmes*. Paris: F Magazine, 1979.

Groupe communiste libertaire. "Avortement de classe: La Suisse pour les riches, les procès pour les autres." *Front libértaire des lutes de classe* 29 (July 10, 1973), 6.

Groupe femmes pour l'abolition des mutilations sexuelles. "Mutilations sexuelles, mutilations sexists." *Mignonnes, allons voir sous la rose*... 10–11 (December 1982): 17.

Groupe notre mouvement nous appartient. "Le commerce des femmes." In Association du mouvement pour les luttes féministes. *Chroniques*, unpaginated.

Guadilla, Naty Garcia. *Libération des femmes: Le MLF*. Paris: Presses Universitaires de France, 1981.

Gubin, Elaine. "Pour le droit au travail: Entre protection et égalité." In Gubin et al., *Le siècle des féminismes*, 179–93.

Gubin, Elaine, Catherine Jacques, Florence Rochefort, Brigitte Studer, Françoise Thébaud, and Michelle Zancarini-Fournel, eds. *Le siécle des féminismes*. Paris: Éditions de l'Atelier, 2004.

Guélaud-Leridon, Françoise. *Recherches sur la condition féminine dans la société d'aujourd'hui*. Travaux et documents. Cahier no. 48. Paris: Presses Universitaires de France, 1967.

Guéraiche, William. "Les femmes de la vie politique française, de la Libération aux années 1970-1992: Essai sur la répartition du pourvoir politique." PhD diss., Université de Toulouse le Mirail, Toulouse, 1992.

———. *Les femmes et la République: essai sur la répartition du pouvoir de 1943 à 1979*. Paris: Éditions de l'Atelier, 1999.

———. "Les femmes politiques de 1994 à 1947: Quelle libération?" *CLIO: Histoire, femmes et sociétés* 1 (1995): 165–86.

Guerin, Rose. "Pour le relèvement des allocations familiales." *Cahiers du communisme* 5 (May 1958): 841–47.

Guilbert, Madeleine. "Aspects de l'emploi féminin." *Avenirs* 93–95 (April–June 1958): 25–30.

———. *Les fonctions des femmes dans l'industrie*. Paris: Éditions Mouton, 1966.

Guillaume, Sylvie. *La France contemporaine: La Ve République*. Paris: Éditions Perrin, 1991.

Guillaumin, Colette. "Femmes et théories de la société: Remarques sur les effets théoriques de la colère des opprimées." *Sociologie et sociétés* 13, no. 2 (October 1981): 19–31.

———. "Les corps appropriés." *Questions féministes* 2 (February 1978): 5–30.

———. "Question de différence." *Questions féministes* 6 (September 1979): 2–21.

Gunther, Scott. *The Elastic Closet: A History of Homosexuality in France, 1942–Present*. New York: Palgrave Macmillian, 2009.

Habib, Claude. "Souvenirs du féminisme." *Esprit* 6 (June 1988): 7–17.

Halimi, Gisèle. *Djamila Boupacha*. Preface by Simone de Beauvoir. Paris: Éditions Gallimard, 1962.

———. *Droits des hommes et droits des femmes: Une autre démocratie*. Montréal: Éditions Fides, 1993.

———. *Fini le féminisme?* Compte rendu intégral du colloque international "Féminisme et socialism," October 13–15, 1983. Paris: Éditions Gallimard, 1984.

———. "Ici finit le roman de chevalerie." *La nef* 17, no. 4 (October–December 1960): 37–43.

———. *La cause des femmes: Propos recueillis par Marie Cardinal*. Paris: Éditions Bernard Grasset, 1973.

———. *La nouvelle cause des femmes*. Paris: Éditions du Seuil, 1997.

———. *Le lait de l'oranger*. Paris: Éditions Gallimard, 1983.

———. "Le programme commun des femmes." In Albistur and Armogathe, *Le grief des femmes*, 275–80.

———. *Le programme commun des femmes*. Paris: Éditions Bernard Grasset, 1978.

———. "Les femmes parlent (d'abort) aux femmes." In Albistur and Armogathe, *Le grief des femmes*, 275–79.

———. *Une embellie perdue*. Paris: Éditions Gallimard, 1995.

Halimi, Gisèle, and Choisir–La Cause des femmes, eds. *Choisir de donner la vie*. Colloque international de "Choisir," October 5–7, 1979, à l'UNESCO. Paris: Éditions Gallimard, 1979.

———. *Viol: Le procès d'Aix*. Paris: Éditions Gallimard, 1978.

Hamiaut, Marcel. *Le réform des régimes matrimoniaux*. Paris: Jurisprudence générale dalloz, 1965.

Hamon, Hervé, and Patrick Rotman. "'68: The Rise and Fall of a Generation." In *May '68 Coming of Age*, edited by D. L. Hanley and A. P. Kerr, 10–22. London: Macmillan, 1989.

———. *Génération: 1. Les années de rêve*. Paris: Éditions du Seuil, 1987.

———. *Génération: 2. Les années de poudre*. Paris: Éditions du Seuil, 1988.

Hanmer, Jalna. "Violence et contrôle social des femmes." *Questions féministes* 1 (November 1977): 69–88.

Hause, Steven C. *Women's Suffrage and Social Politics in the French Third Republic*. Princeton NJ: Princeton University Press, 1984.

Hause, Steven C., and Anne R. Kenney. "The Limits of Suffragist Behavior: Legalism and Militancy in France, 1876–1922." *American Historical Review* 86, no. 4 (October 1981): 781–806.

Hazareesingh, Sudhir. *Intellectuals and the French Communist Party: Disillusion and Decline*. Oxford: Clarendon, 1991.

H.B. "Bibliographie critique." *Population* 6, no. 1 (January–March 1951): 148–49.

Hellman, John. "Jacques Chevalier, Bergsonism, and Modern French Catholic Intellectuals." *Biography* 4, no. 2 (Spring 1981): 138–53.

Henry, Louis, and Jacques Voranger. "La situation démographique." *Population* 4, no. 2 (April–June 1949): 333–48.

Herzog, Dagmar. "Abortion, Christianity, Disability: Western Europe, 1960s–1970s." In *Sexual Revolutions*, edited by Gert Hekma and Alain Giamin, 249–63. New York: Palgrave Macmillian, 2014.

———. *Sexuality in Europe: A Twentieth-Century History*. New York: Cambridge University Press, 2011.

Higonnet, Margaret Randolph, Jane Jenson, Sonya Michel, and Margaret Collins Weitz. *Behind the Lines: Gender and the Two World Wars*. New Haven CT: Yale University Press, 1987.

Hilden, Patricia. *Working Women and Socialist Politics in France, 1880–1914*. Oxford: Clarendon, 1986.

Hirsh, Arthur. *The French Left*. Montréal: Black Rose Books, 1982.

Hoff, Joan. "A Reply to My Critics." *Women's History Review* 5, no. 1 (1996): 25–30.

———. "Gender as a Postmodern Category of Paralysis." *Women's History Review* 3, no 2 (1994): 149–68.

Hoffman, Stanley, and William G. Andrews, eds. *The Impact of the Fifth Republic on France*. Albany: State University of New York Press, 1981.

Hoffner, Claire. "Le développement de la législation sur les allocations familiales au cours des années récentes." *Revue internationale du travail* 41, no. 4 (April 1940): 361–85.

Hollifield, James F., and George Ross. *Searching for the New France*. New York: Routledge, 1991.

Horer, Suzanne, and Jeanne Socquet. *La création étouffée: Femmes en mouvement*. Paris: Éditions Pierre Horay, 1973.

Hottell, Ruth. "Sharing Stories Inspiring Change." *Simone Veil: Jewish Women's Archive*, https://jwa.org/encyclopedia/article/veil-simone.

Howorth, Jolyon, and George Ross, eds. *Contemporary France: An Interdisciplinary Review*. London: Frances Pinter, 1989.

Hunebelle, Danielle. "La femme indépendante." *La nef* 17, no. 4 (October–December 1960): 109–14.

Huss, Marie-Monique. "Pronatalism in the Interwar Period in France." *Journal of Contemporary History* 25 (1990): 39–68.

Iff, Simone, Marcel Besse, and Werner Iff. *Demain la société sexualisé: Le combat du mouvement français pour le planning familial*. Paris: Éditions Calmann-Levy, 1975.

"Immigration féminine et statut des femmes étrangères en France." *Revue français des affaires sociales* (special issue) (December 1992): 29–53.

"Industrial Home Work." *International Labour Review* 58, no. 6 (December 1948): 735–51.

Institut national d'études démographiques. *Les travaux du Haute comité consultatif de la population et de la famille en 1945*. *Cahier* no. 1. Paris: Presses Universitaires de France, 1946.

International Labour Office and Mr. Préville, eds. "Family Allowances in France." *International Labour Review* 52, nos. 2–3 (August–September 1945): 196–210.

——. "The Employment Situation in France." *International Labour Review* 52, no. 1 (July 1945): 29–39.

——. "Social Security in France." *International Labour Review* 52, no. 5 (November 1945): 541–44.

"Interview with Simone de Beauvoir." *Pénéla: Connaître et comprendre* (September 1968): 8–17.

Irigaray, Luce. *Ce sexe qui n'en est pas un*. Paris: Éditions de Minuit, 1977.

——. "L'identité féminine: Biologie ou conditionment social?" In *Femmes moitié de la terre, moitié du pouvoir*, edited by Choisir and Gisèle Halimi, 101–8. Paris: Éditions Gallimard, 1994.

——. *Speculum de l'autre femme*. Paris: Éditions de Minuit, 1974.

Isambert, François, and Paul Ladriere. *Contraception et avortement: Dix ans de débat dans la presse (1965-1974)*. Paris: Centre national de la recherche scientifique, 1979.

Isambert-Jamati, Vivianne. "Adaptation au travail et niveau de qualification des femmes salariées." *Revue française de sociologie* 1, no. 1 (January–March 1960): 45–59.

Jackie. "Des oubliettes au fond de ma cour." *Les temps des femmes* 12 (1981): 28–29.

Jackson, Julian, Anna-Louise Milne, and James S. Williams, eds. *May '68: Rethinking France's Last Revolution*. London: Palgrave Macmillian, 2011.

Jackson, Stevi. *Christine Delphy*. London: Sage, 1996.

Jacquemart, Alban. *Les hommes dans les mouvements féminists: Socio-histoire d'un engagement improbable*. Rennes: Presses Universitaires de Rennes, 2015.

Jacquemyns, G. *Le travail de la femme hors du foyer: Un sondage d'opinion pub-lique au sujet de son opportunité, de sa rémunération, et de son organisation.* Bruxelles: Éditions Parc Léopold, 1950.

Jagger, Gill. *Judith Butler: Sexual Politics, Social Change and the Power of the Per-formative.* New York: Routledge, 2008.

Jardine, Alice A., and Anne M. Menke. "Interview with Christine Rochefort." Translated by Carrie Noland. In Jardine and Menke, *Shifting Scenes*, 174–91.

Jardine, Alice A., and Anne M. Menke, eds. *Shifting Scenes: Interviews on Women, Writing, and Politics in Post-68 France.* New York: Columbia University Press, 1991.

Jenson, Jane. "Feminism in France since May '68." In *Contemporary France: An Interdisciplinary Review*, edited by Jolyon Howorth and George Ross, 55–67. London: F. Pinter, 1989.

———. "The French Left: A Tale of Three Beginnings." In Hollifield and Ross, *Searching for the New France*, 85–112.

———. "The Liberation and New Rights for French Women." In Higonnet et al., *Behind the Lines*, 272–84.

———. "One Robin Doesn't Make Spring: French Communist Alliance Strat-egies and the Women's Movement." *Radical History Review* 23 (Spring 1980): 57–75.

Jenson, Jane, Elisabeth Hagen, and Ceallaigh Reddy, eds. *Feminization of the Labour Force: Paradoxes and Promises.* Oxford: Oxford University Press, 1988.

Jenson, Jane, and Mariette Sineau. *Mitterrand et les françaises: Un rendezvous manqué.* Paris: Presses de Sciences Po, 1995.

J.H. "Avortement." *Population* 11, no. 4 (October–December 1956): 769–70.

Joannes, Gisèle. "Ce que veulent les femmes travailleuses." *Cahiers du com-munisme* 7 and 8 (July–August 1967): 99–102.

Jobs, Richard Ivan. *Riding the New Wave: Youth and the Rejuvenation of France after the Second World War.* Stanford CA: Stanford University Press, 2007.

Johnson, Richard W. *The French Communist Party Versus the Students.* New Haven CT: Yale University Press, 1972.

———. *The Long March of the French Left.* London: Macmillan, 1981.

Judt, Tony. *Marxism and the French Left: Studies in Labour and Politics in France, 1830-1981.* Oxford: Clarendon, 1986.

———. *Past Imperfect: French Intellectuals, 1944-1956.* Berkeley: University of California Press, 1992.

———. "Rights in France: Reflections on the Etiolation of a Political Language. *La revue Tocqueville/The Tocqueville Review* 14, no. 1 (1993): 67–108.

Kahler, Miles. *Decolonization in Britain and France: The Domestic Consequences of International Relations.* Princeton NJ: Princeton University Press, 1984.

Kammerman, Sheila B., and Alfred J. Kahn. *Child Care, Family Benefits, and Working Parents.* New York: Columbia University Press, 1981.

Kandel, Lilian. "Du politique au personnel: Le prix d'une illusion." In *Crises de la société féminisme et changement,* edited by Groupe d'etudes féministes de l'Université Paris VII (GEF), 21–34. Paris: Éditions Tierce, 1991.

———. "Génération mlf." *Travail, genre et sociétés* 24, no. 2 (2010): 5–24.

———. "L'explosion de la presse féministe." *Le débat: Histoire, politique, société* 1 (May 1980): 104–19.

———. "Une presse 'anti-féministe' aujourd'hui: Des femmes en mouvements." *Questions féministes* 7 (February 1980): 37–45.

Kaufmann-McCall, Dorothy. "Politics of Différence: The Women's Movement in France from Mai 1968 to Mitterrand." *Signs: Journal of Women in Culture and Society* 9, no. 2 (1983): 282–93.

Kelly, Michael. "Catholicism and the Left in Twentieth-Century France." In *Catholicism, Politics, and Society,* edited by Kay Chadwick. Liverpool: Liverpool University Press. DOI:10.5949/liverpool/9780853239741.003.0008.

Kergoat, Danièle. "Femmes ouvrières 1981: Interview de Danièle Kergoat." *Que faire aujourd'hui* 15 (1981): 15–19.

———. *Les ouvrières.* Paris: Éditions Le Sycomore, 1982.

———. "Ouvriers = ouvrières? Propositions pour une articulation théorique de deux variables: Sexe et classe sociale." *Critique de l'économie politique* 15 (October 1978): 65–97.

———. "Une expérience d'autogestion en mai 1968 (émergence d'un système d'action collective)." *Sociologie du travail* 3 (September 1970): 274–92.

Kesler, Jean-François. *l'ENA, la société, l'état.* Paris: Éditions Bergev-Levrault, 1985.

Khanna, Ranjana. *Algeria Cuts: Women and Representation, 1830 to the Present.* Stanford CA: Stanford University Press, 2008.

———. *Dark Continents: Psychoanalysis and Colonialism.* Durham NC: Duke University Press, 2004.

Kidd, William, and Siân Reynolds. *Contemporary French Cultural Studies.* London: Arnold Press, 2000.

Kimble, Sarah. "'No Right to Judge': Feminism and the Judiciary in Third Republic France." *French Historical Studies* 31, no. 4 (January 2008). https://www.researchgate.net/publication/31096824_No_Right_to_Judge _Feminism_and_the_Judiciary_in_Third_Republic_France.

Klejman, Laurence. "Orientation bibliographique pour l'histoire du féminisme en France, de 1945–1985." *Bulletin de l'institut d'histoire du temps présent* 23 (March 1986): 31–70.

Klejman, Laurence, and Florence Rochefort. *L'égalité en marche: Le féminisme sous la troisème République.* Paris: Presses de la Fondation nationale des sciences politiques–des femmes /Antoinette Fouque, 1989.

Knibiehler, Yvonne. *Qui gardera les enfants? Mémoires d'une féministe iconoclaste.* Paris: Éditions Calman-Lévy: 2007.

Koven Seth, and Sonya Michel. "Womanly Duties: Maternalist Politics and the Origins of Welfare States in France, Germany, Great Britain, and the United States, 1880–1920." *American Historical Review* 95 (October 1990): 1076–1108.

Kristeva, Julia. *Des chinoises.* Paris: Éditions des femmes, 1974.

———. "Le temps des femmes." *Cahiers de recherche de sciences des textes et documents* 33–34, no. 5 (Winter 1979): 5–19.

———. *Polylogue.* Paris: Éditions du Seuil, 1977.

———. *Séméiôtiké: Recherches pour une sémanalyse.* Paris: Éditions du Seuil, 1969.

———. "Un nouveau type d'intellectuel: Le dissident." *Tel quel* 74 (Winter 1977): 3–8.

Kunkle, Ryan. "'We Must Shout the Truth to the Rooftops:' Gisèle Halimi, Djamila Boupacha, and Sexual Politics in the Algerian War of Independence." *Iowa Historical Review* 4, no. 1 (2013): 5–24.

Kurlansky, Mark. *1968: The Year That Rocked the World.* New York: Random House, 2005.

La condition de la française aujourd'hui et demain. Paris: Imprint coopérative arpajonaise, 1964.

"La condition féminine." *La nef* 38 (October–December 1969).

Lacore, Suzanne. *L'émancipation de la femme.* Paris: Éditions de la Perfac, 1945.

Lacroix, Jean. *Force et faiblesses de la famille.* Paris: Éditions du Seuil, 1948.

"La difference internee." *des femmes en mouvements* 2 (February 1978): 13.

La Documentation française illustrée. La femme dans la vie française. Paris: La Documentation française, 1952.

———. *Le travail des femmes en France.* Paris: La Documentation française, 1973.

"La française et l'amour: L'enquête." *Sondages* 23, no. 1 (1961): 37–50.

La Gaffiche. *Les femmes s'affichent.* Paris: Association la gaffiche–Éditions Syros, 1984.

Lagrave, Rose-Marie. "Une émancipation sous tutelle." In *Histoire des femmes,* edited by George Duby and Michèle Perrot, 431–63. Paris: Éditions Plon, 1991.

Lagroua Weill-Hallé, Marie-Andrée. *Gynécologie pratique.* Paris: Vigot frères, 1955.

———. *La contraception et les français: Evaluation de leur possibilité d'adaption d'après une expérimentation de 10 ans: Etude de 7,600 couples (1956–66).* Paris: Librairie Maloine S.A., 1967.

———. *La grande peur d'aimer: Journal d'une femme médecin.* Paris: Éditions Gonthier, 1964.

———. *Le guide de la femme seule.* Paris: Éditions Neyret, 1968.

———. *Le planning familial.* Strasbourg: Imprimerie des Dernières Nouvelles de Strasbourg, 1959.

Lagroua Weill-Hallé, Marie-Andrée, with Jacques Derogy and illustrations by Maurice Siné. *l'Avortement de papa.* Paris: Éditions Fayard, 1971.

"La liberté au féminin." *Choisir* 19 (July 1976), 1.

La ligue du droit des femmes (MLF). "Quelque réflexions sur l'action du secrétariat d'état à la condition feminine." *Droit social* 1 (January 1976): 86–90.

Lancelot, Alain, and Marie Thérèse Lancelot. *Annuaire de la France politique: Mai 1981–Mai 1983.* Paris: Presses de la Fondation nationale des sciences politiques, 1984.

Lanquetin, Marie-Thérèse. "De l'égalité professionnelle entre les femmes et les hommes: A propos d'un projet de loi." *Droit social* 4 (April 1983): 238–44.

Laot, Jeannette, with Dominique Pélegrin. *Stratégie pour les femmes.* Paris: Éditions Stock, 1977.

Lapierre, Catherine. "A partir du 'droit au travail.'" *La revue d'en face* 1 (May 1977): 17–21.

"La résolution du Comité central sur le travail du parti parmi les femmes: Aubervilliers, October 19, 1956." *Cahiers du communisme* 32, no. 11 (November 1956): 1241–47.

"La résolution du Comité central du Parti communiste français: Puteaux, November 27, 1946." *Cahiers du communisme* 23, no. 11 (November 1946): 1010–13.

Larkin, Maurice. *France since the Popular Front: Government and People, 1936–1986.* Oxford: Clarendon, 1988.

Laroque, Pierre. "From Social Insurance to Social Security: Evolution in France." *International Labour Review* 57, no. 6 (June 1948): 565–90.

L'Alternative. *Libérer nos corps ou libérer l'avortement.* Paris: Éditions des femmes, 1973.

Laubier, Claire, ed. *The Condition of Women in France 1945 to the Present: A Documentary Anthology.* London: Routledge, 1990.

Lazar, Marc. "The Cold War Culture of the French and Italian Communist Parties." In *The Cultural Cold War in Western Europe, 1945–1960,* edited by Giles Scott-Smith and Hans Krabbendam, 176–85. Portland OR: Frank Cass, 2003.

Lazard, Françoise. "Le travail de la femme est-il un progrès? Est-il nuisible à l'enfant?" *Les cahiers du Centre d'études et de recherches marxiste* 64 (April 1968): 1–40.

Le Bras, Hervé. *Marianne et les lapins: L'obsession démographique.* Paris: Olivier Orban, 1991.

Leclercq, Jenny. *Le contrôle des naissances et le malaise conjugal.* Paris: Éditions Select, 1946.

Le Cormier, Pauline [Pauline Archambault]. "Au delà du féminisme." In Choisy et al., *Conscience de la féminité*, 11–18.

———. "Conclusion." In Choisy et al., *Conscience de la féminité*, 419–44

LeCoultre, Denise. "La condition féminine." *La nef* 38 (October–December 1969): 5–11.

Le Dœuff, Michele. "Hiparchia's Choice." In *French Feminism Reader*, edited by Kelly Oliver. Lanham MD: Rowman & Littlefield, 2000: 35–58.

———. *L'étude et le rouet: Des femmes, de la philosophie, etc.* Paris: Éditions du Seuil, 1989.

Le Dœuff, Michele, and Penelope Deutscher. "De l'existentialisme au deuxième sexe." *Magazine littéraire* 145 (February 1979): 18–27.

———. "Feminism Is Back: Or Is It?" *Hypatia* 15, no. 4 (Autumn 2000): 243–55.

"Le droit des ascendants aux allocations familiales et à l'allocation de la mère au foyer." *Droit social* 7, no. 8 (September–December 1944): 261–67.

"Le féminisme à la saucialiste: Quand les femmes découvriront-elles le potlitique aux roses?" *des femmes en mouvements*, 2 (February 1978): 16.

Le féminisme et ses enjeux: Vingt-sept femmes parlent. Paris: Éditions centre fédéral FEN, Edilig, 1988.

"Le féminisme, pour quoi faire?" *Les cahiers du GRIF* 1 (November 1973).

Le Garrec, Evelyne. *Les messagères.* Paris: Éditions des femmes, 1976.

Legay, Jean-Marie. "La question des naissances." In *La femme à la recherche d'elle-même: Semaine de la pensée marxiste de Lyon*, edited by Marie-Claire Herman, Maurice Moissonnier, Roger Arnaldez, and Renée Rochefort. Paris: La Palatine, 1966.

Leger, Danìele. *Le féminisme en France.* Paris: Éditions Le Sycomore, 1982.

Lehmann, Andrée. *Le rôle de la femme française au milieu du vingtième siècle.* Paris: Éditions de la Ligue française pour le droit des femmes, 1950.

Le livre de l'oppression des femmes. Paris: Éditions Pierre Belfond, 1972.

Lemerre, Sébastien. "A propos du travail des femmes: Une enquête dans une classe de l'enseignement technique supérieur." *La pensée* 120 (April 1965): 132–35.

Leleu, Claude. "Pour qui votent les femmes? . . . à Grenoble." In *Nouvelles études de sociologie électorale*, edited by François Goguel, 194–96. Paris: Librarie Armand Colin, 1954.

"Le travail des femmes: Repères historiques." *Revue française des affaires sociales* 4 (October–December 1981): 163.

"L'emploi des femmes en France." *Revue internationale du travail* 55, no. 6 (June 1947): 606–12.

"Le pouvoir au bout du 'MLF'?: Les tendances contre le movement." *Les femmes s'entêtent* 1:8–9.

"Le procès de 'des femmes' contre les Éditions Tierce." *Nouvelles questions féministes* 2 (October 1981): 120–24.

"L'équipe des Cahiers du féminisme, revue de la lcr." Actes du colloque national. *Femmes, féminisme et recherches*, 118–29. Toulouse, December 1982. Toulouse: affer, 1984.

"Les conflits des femmes passent maintenant par voie de justice: Un procès en diffamation contre un procès en prudhomme." *L'information des femmes* 17 (May–June 1977).

"Les carrières féminines: L'activité professionnelle." *Aveniers* 93–95 (April–June 1958).

Les femmes en France dans une société d'inégalités: Rapport au ministère des droits de la femme. Paris: La Documentation française, 1982.

"'Les femmes' sont l'avenir de . . . la femme." *Elles voient rouges* 0 (May 1979): 2–5.

"Les intellectuelles." *La nouvelle critique* 161–62 (December–January 1964–1965): 1–10.

Les Marie-Pas-Claire and Anne Dhoquois. "Nouvelle génération, nouvelles féministes?" *Cahiers du CEDREF* 4–5 (1995): 149–70.

"Les salaires féminins." *Droit social* 10, no. 11 (January 1947): 26–30.

"Le secrétariat d'etat à la condition féminine: Un an d'action." Supplement to *Cahiers français* 171 (May–August 1975): Vivre au feminine, notice 1, unpaginated.

"Le travail des femmes: Repères historiques." *Revue française des affaires sociales* 4 (October–December 1981): 163.

Lévy-Bruhl, Raymond. "L'activité professionnelle des femmes en France." *Avenirs* 93–95 (April–June 1958): 16–24.

———. "Les carrières féminines." *Avenirs* 16–17: 119–21.

Ligue communiste révolutionnaire. "Mouvement des femmes et lutte de classe." *Conférence femmes de la LCR: Résolution et débats.* Éditions de la Taupe Rouge, 1978.

Lilar, Suzanne. *Le malentendu du deuxième sexe.* Paris: Presses Universitaires de France, 1970.

L.K. "Post-scriptum: Une presse 'anti-féministe' aujourd'hui; 'Des femmes en mouvements.'" *Questions féministes* 7 (1980): 37–44.

Londeix, Pauline. *Le manifeste lesbien.* Édition Mathieu Garrigues, 2008.

Long, Imogen. *Women Intellectuals in Post-68 France: Petitions and Polemics.* London: Palgrave Macmillan, 2013.

Longone, Pierre. *53 millions de français: Qui sont-ils? Que font-ils?* Paris: Éditions de Claude Verrier, 1977.

Loos, Jocelyne, and Marie-Victoire Louis. "Femmes, travail, et temps partiel." Actes du colloque national. *Femmes, féminisme et recherches,* 283–84. Toulouse, December 1982. Toulouse: AFFER, 1984.

Lorwin, Val R. "Trade Unions and Women: 'The Most Difficult Revolution.'" In *Eurocommunism and Eurosocialism: The Left Confronts Modernity,* edited by Bernard E. Brown. New York: Cyrco, 1979.

Louis, Marie-Victoire. "Eléments pour une critique des rapports des féministes françaises au pouvoir." In *La démocratie à la française ou les femmes indésirables,* edited by Éliane Viennot, 91–107. Paris: Presses Universitaires de France, 1995.

——. "Féminisme et syndicalisme: Éloge de la diversité." *Pour* 108 (September–October 1986): 22–30.

——. "Recherches féministes et mouvements féministes, France, 1992." Paper presented at Colloque: "Le Féminisme en France, en Inde, en Russie," Paris, May 18, 1992.

Louis-Levy. *L'émancipation politique des femmes.* Paris: Éditions ouvrières, 1955.

Lowe, Keith. *Savage Continent: Europe in the Aftermath of WWII.* New York: Picador, 2013.

Macciocchi, Maria Antonietta. *De la France.* Paris: Éditions du Seuil, 1977.

——. "Quelque thèmes autour du marxisme et du feminism." In *Les femmes et leurs maîtres.* Séminaire Paris VIII, Vincennes. Textes rassemblés par Jacqueline Aubenas-Bastie. Paris: Éditions Christian Bourgeois, 1978.

Machard, Raymonde. *Les françaises: Ce qu'elles valent, ce qu'elles veulent.* Paris: Éditions Flammarion, 1945.

Mandel, Maud S. *Muslims and Jews in France.* Princeton NJ: Princeton University Press, 2014.

Mansker, Andrea. *Sex, Honor and Citizenship in Early Third Republic France.* New York: Palgrave Macmillian, 2011.

Marchais, Georges. "Discours: Femmes, pour changer votre vie." Paris, December 3, 1977. Palais de congrès. Paris: Parti communiste français, 1977.

——. "Le parti de la liberté pour les femmes." Paris: Parti communiste français, ca. 1975.

Marcilhacy, Charles, and S. Rollin. *Femmes face à vos responsabilités dans: La vie familiale, la vie sociale, la vie économique.* Paris: Éditions Marcel Dodeman, 1946.

Marks, Elaine, ed. *Critical Essays on Simone de Beauvoir.* Boston: G. K. Hall, 1987.

Marks, Elaine, and Isabelle de Courtivron, eds. *New French Feminisms: An Anthology.* Brighton UK: Harvester, 1986.

Marsh, Kate, and Nicola Frith, eds. *France's Lost Empires: Fragmentation, Nostalgia, and la Fracture Coloniale.* Lanham MD: Lexington Books, 2011.

Marso, Lori J. "Beauvoir on Mothers, Daughters, and Political Coalitions." In Marso and Moynagh, *Simone de Beauvoir's Political Thinking,* 72–92.

Marso, Lori J., and Patricia Moynagh, eds. "Introduction: A Radical Approach to Political Thinking." In Marso and Maynagh, *Simone de Beauvoir's Political Thinking,* 1–10.

———. *Simone de Beauvoir's Political Thinking.* Urbana: University of Illinois Press, 2006.

———. "Thinking Politically with Simone de Beauvoir in The Second Sex." *Theory & Event* 15, no. 2 (2012). http://muse.jhu.edu/article/478359.

Martel, Frédéric. *The Pink and the Black: Homosexuals in France since 1968.* Stanford CA: Stanford University Press, 1999.

Martin, Jacqueline. "L'epouse, partenaire à égalité." In Choisy et al., *Conscience de la féminité,* 269–81.

Martin, Yves. "Niveau de vie des familles suivant le nombre d'enfants." *Population* 11, no. 3 (July–September 1956): 407–28.

Maruani, Margaret. "Grèves de femmes, femmes en grève." *Economie et humanisme* 244 (November–December 1978): 25–35.

———. *Les syndicats à l'épreuve du féminisme.* Paris: Éditions Syros, 1979.

Marzellier, Françoise. "Une enquête sur le travail féminin." *Les temps modernes* 16, no. 180 (April 1961): 1393–1401.

Masse, Suzanne. "De la femme-esclave à la femme-vedette." *Perspectives socialistes* 55 (December 1962): 2–6.

Masson, Agnès. "Femmes, voici pourquoi je suis socialiste." *Problèmes d'aujourd'hui,* no. 28. Paris: Éditions de la liberté, 1947.

Mauduit, Jean. *La révolte des femmes: Après les états généraux de Elle.* Paris: Éditions Fayard, 1971.

Mauduit, Jean, and Anne-Marie Raimond, eds. *Elle: Ce que les femmes réclament.* Paris: Éditions Fayard, 1971.

Mauduit, Jean, and Service études et sondages. *Vous interroge sur la condition féminine.* Paris: Imp. M. Schiffer, 1970.

Mayer, Daniel. "Le droit à la maternité." *La nef* 17, no. 4 (October–December 1960): 115–19.

Mazelin, Lucienne. "Les femmes unies contre la misère et la guerre." *Cahiers de communisme* 32, no. 11 (November 1956): 1164–74.

———. "Pour une maternité et des familles vraiment heureuses." *Cahiers du communisme* 5 (May 1960): 872–77.

Mazur, Amy. *Gender Bias and the State: Symbolic Reform at Work in Fifth Republic France*. Pittsburgh: University of Pittsburgh Press, 1995.

———. "Strong State and Symbolic Reform: The Ministère des droits de la femme in France." In *Comparative State Feminism*, edited by Dorothy McBride Stetson and Amy Mazur, 76–94. London: Sage, 1995.

———. *Theorizing Feminist Policy*. Oxford: Oxford University Press, 2002.

McBride, Dorothy E., and Amy Mazur, eds. *Comparative State Feminism*. Thousand Oaks ca: Sage, 1995.

———, eds. *The Politics of State Feminism: Innovation in Comparative Research*. Philadelphia: Temple University Press, 2010.

McLaren, Angus. "Abortion in France: Women and the Regulation of Family Size, 1800–1914." *French Historical Studies* 10, no. 3 (1978): 461–85.

McMillan, James F. *Dreyfus to De Gaulle: Politics and Society in France 1898–1969*. London: Edward Arnold, 1985.

Mendras, Henri. *La sagesse et le désordre*. Paris: Éditions Gallimard, 1980.

Mendras, Henri, and Alistar Cole. *Social Change in Modern France: Towards a Cultural Anthropology of the Fifth Republic*. Cambridge: Cambridge University Press, 1988.

Michaut, Victor. "Le programme du psu et la lutte pour le socialisme." *Cahiers du communisme* 27, no. 2 (February 1950) 33–48.

Michel, Andrée. Activité professionnelle de la femme et vie conjugale. Paris: Centre national de la recherche scientifique, 1974.

———. "A propos du contrôle des naissances." *Les temps modernes* 16, no. 179 (March 1961): 1200–1218.

———. "Evaluation du rapport." In Muller et al., *Etre féministe en France*.

———. *Famille, industrialisation, logement*. Paris: Centre national de la recherche scientifique, 1959.

———. "Famille, société industrielle et démocratie." *Esprit* 28, no. 289 (November 1960):1754–72.

———, ed. *Family Issues of Employed Women in Europe and America*. Leiden: E. F. Brill, 1971.

———. "Ideologies, Pressure Groups and French Family Policy." Paper presented at the Third International Seminar of the ICOFA, Dubrovnik, December 7–9, 1972.

———. *Inégalités professionnelles et socialisation différentielle des sexes.* Paris: CORDES–Centre national de la recherche scientifique, 1975.

———. "La française et le démocrate." *La nef* 17, no. 4 (October–December 1960): 20–36.

———. "La personne, la femme, et le mythe." *Mouvement français pour le planning familial: Bulletin trimestriel d'information* 12 (March 1960): 1–12.

———. *Les travailleurs algérians en France.* Paris: Centre national de la recherche scientifique, 1956.

———. "Mouvements féministes en occident et projet de société." *Les temps modernes* 414, no. 37 (January 1981): 1270–84.

———. "Naissance du conscience féministe." *L'arc* 61 (1975): 31–38.

Michel, Andrée, and Geneviève Texier, eds. *Femmes, sexisme et sociétés.* Paris: Presses Universitaires de France, 1977.

———. *La condition de la française d'aujourd'hui: Mythes et réalités.* Paris: Éditions Gonthier, 1964.

Michel, Andrée, and le groupe des rôles des sexes, de la famille, et du développement humain. Prospective du travail féminin et aménagement du territoire. Paris: DATAR–Centre national de la recherche scientifique, 1974.

Michel, Andrée, Suzanne Béreaud, and Marguerite Lorée. *Inégalités professionnelles et socialisation différentielle des sexes.* Paris: CORDES–Centre national de la recherche scientifique, 1975.

Michel, Jacques. *Les nouveaux droits de la femme.* Paris: Éditions Dunod, 1970.

Michel, Hélène, and Micheline Pastre. *Aux urnes, citoyennes.* Paris: La Française libre, 1945.

Mignon, Jean. "Lutte contre l'avortement: Une erreur de méthode." *Concours médical* 7, no. 18 (February 1950): 489–90.

Ministère des droits de la femme. *Les femmes en France dans une société d'inégalités: Rapport au ministère des droits de la femme.* Paris: La Documentation française, 1982.

Mitterrand, François, and Parti socialiste. *Changer la vie: Programme du gouvernement du Parti socialiste.* Paris: Éditions Flammarion, 1972.

Moi, Toril. *Feminist Theory and Simone de Beauvoir.* Oxford: Basil Blackwell, 1990.

____, ed. *French Feminist Thought: A Reader.* Oxford: Basil Blackwell, 1987.

____, ed. *The Kristeva Reader.* New York: Columbia University Press, 1986.

———. *Sexual/Textual Politics: Feminist Literary Theory.* London: Methuen, 1985.

———. *Simone de Beauvoir: The Making of an Intellectual Woman.* Oxford/Cambridge: Blackwell, 1994.

Monestier, Claire. "Qui a peur d'Antoinette F?" *Politique hebdo.* (May 30, 1977): 33–34.

Moreau-Bourles, Marie-Ange, and Mariette Sineau. "Les femmes et le statut des travailleurs: Les discriminations au niveau de l'élaboration des normes." *Droit social* 12 (December 1983): 694–719.

Moreau, Gisèle. "Pour accéder à l'égalité." *Cahiers du communisme* 54, no.10 (October 1978): 62–72.

Morin, Edgar. "La promotion des valeurs féminines." *La nef* 17, no. 4 (October–December 1960): 83–88.

Morriandpre, Julliot de la. "The Reform of the French Civil Code." *University of Pennsylvania Law Review* 97, no. 1 (November 1948): 1–21.

Möser, Cornelia. *Féminismes en traduction: Théories voyageues et traductions culturelles.* Paris: Éditions des archives contemporain, 2013.

Moses, Claire Goldberg. *French Feminism in the Nineteenth Century.* Albany: State University of New York Press, 1984.

———. "Made in America: 'French Feminism' in Academia." *Feminist Studies* 24, no. 2 (Summer 1998): 241–74.

Mossuz-Lavau, Janine. "La loi et les mœurs: Politiques de la sexualité et comportements sexuels en France." *Cosmopoliques, ce sexe qui nous dépasse* 4 (July 2003): 145–56.

———. "La parité, de la France au monde." In *Les défis de la République*, edited by Bruno Perreau and Joan W. Scott, 169–87. Paris: Presses de Science Po, 2017.

———. "La parité en politique, histoire et premier bilan." *Travail, genre et sociétés* 7, no. 1 (2002): 41–57.

———. *Les clubs et la politique en France.* Paris: Librairie Armand Colin, 1970.

———. *Les françaises et la politique: Enquête sur une crise.* Paris: Éditions Odile Jacob, 1984.

———. *Les lois de l'amour: Les politiques de la sexualité en France, 1950–1990.* Paris: Éditions Payot, 1991.

———. "Le vote des femmes en France: 1945–1993." *Revue française de science politique* 43, no. 4 (1993): 673–89.

———. " Préface." In *L'égalité sous conditions: Genre, parité, diversité*, edited by Réjane Sénac-Slawinski, 13–18. Paris: Presses de Sciences Po (PFNSP), 2015.

Mossuz-Lavau, Janine, and Mariette Sineau. *Enquête sur les femmes et la politique en France.* Paris: Presses Universitaires de France, 1983.

———. "La parité, de la France au monde." *In Les défis de la République*, edited by Bruno Perreau and Joan W. Scott, 169–87. Paris: Presses de Science Po, 2017.

———. "Le vote des femmes en France (1944-1983)." Association française de science politique. Deuxième congrès national, Grenoble, January 25-28, 1984.

———. "Politics and Sexuality in France (1950-1991)." Symposium on "Sexual Cultures in Europe," Amsterdam, June 26, 1992.

Mounier, Emmanuel. "Faut-il refaire la déclaration des droits? *Esprit* 13, no. 105 (December 1944): 118-27; Suite 1, 13, no. 109 (April 1945): 696-708; Fin, 13, no. 110 (May 1945): 850-56.

———. *Le personnalisme.* Paris: Presses Universitaires de France, 1959.

———. "Situation du personnalisme." *Esprit* 14, no. 118 (January 1946): 4-25; Suite et Fin 14, no. 120 (March 1946): 432-57.

Mouvement de libération des femmes. *Génération MLF: 1968-2008.* Paris: des femmes/Antoinette Fouque, 2008.

Mouvement français pour le planning familial. D'une révolte à une lutte: 25 ans d'histoire du planning familial. Paris: Éditions Tierce, 1982.

Moyn, Samuel. "Personalism, Community, and the Origins of Human Rights." In *Human Rights in the Twentieth Century,* edited by Stefan-Ludwig Hoffmann, 85-106. New York: Cambridge University Press, 2011.

Moynagh, Patricia. "Beauvoir on Lived Reality, Exemplary Validity, and a Method for Political Thought." In Marso and Moynagh, *Simone de Beauvoir's Political Thinking,* 11-30.

MPMF. "Centre de documentation: Femmes mutilées, exploitées; Meeting samedi du mouvement de femmes noires." *Rouges* 787 (October 30, 1978), 4.

Muldworf, Bernard. "A propos de l'accouchement sans douleur: 'Mentalités' et 'psychologie' chez la femme enceinte." *La pensée* 105 (September-October 1962): 55-84.

Murphy, Julien. "Beauvoir and the Algerian War: Towards a Post-Colonial Ethics." In Simons, *Feminist Interpretations of Simone de Beauvoir,* 263-98.

Murray, Brittany, and Diane Perpich, eds. and trans. *Taking French Feminism to the Streets: Fadela Amara and the Rise of Ni Putes Ni Soumises.* Chicago: University of Illinois Press, 2011.

Myrdal, Alva. *L' UNESCO et les droits de la femme.* Paris: UNESCO, 1955.

Navarro, Elaine. "Questions d'une obscurantiste féministe à des savants éclairés." *La revue d'en face* 4 (November 1978): 30-36.

Netter, Yvonne. *La femme face à ses problèmes: Défense quotidienne de ses intérêts.* Introduction by Marie Bonaparte. Paris: Librairie générale de droit et de jurisprudence, 1962.

Nicollet, Albert. *Femmes d'Afrique Noire en France: La vie partagée.* Paris: Éditions L'Harmattan, 1992.

Niel, Mathilde. *Le drame de la libération de la femme*. Paris: Éditions le courrier du livre, 1968.

"Nous refusons les objectifs natalists." *Cahiers du féminisme* 9 (April–May 1979): 9.

Nouvion, Suzanne. "Fémininité et autonomie du jugement." In Choisy et al., *Conscience de la féminité*, 51–68.

Odette, "Lettre ouverte à Yvette Roudy, Ministre des droits de la femme." *Mignonnes, allons voir sous la rose . . .* 12 (June 1983), 14.

Offen, Karen. "Before Beauvoir, Before Butler: 'Genre' and 'Gender' in France and the Anglo-American World." In *"On ne naît pas femme: on le devient"*: *The Life of a Sentence*, edited by Bonnie Mann and Martina Ferrari, 11–36. Oxford: Oxford Univeristy Press, 2017.

———. "Body Politics: Women, Work and the Politics of Motherhood in France, 1920–1950." *In Maternity and Gender Policies: Women and the Rise of the European Welfare States, 1880s–1950*, edited by Gisela Bock and Pat Thane, 138–59. London: Routledge, 2012.

———. "Comment: Thoughts on 'Culture et pouvoir des femmes.'" *Journal of Women's History* 1, no. 1 (Spring 1989): 89–91.

———. "Contextualizing the Theory and Practice of Feminism in Nineteenth Century Europe (1789–1914)." In *Becoming Visible: Women in European History*, edited by Renate Bridenthal, Susan Mosher Stuard, and Merry E. Wiesner, 327–55. 3rd ed. Boston: Houghton Mifflin, 1998.

———. *Debating the Woman Question in the French Third Republic, 1870–1920*. Cambridge: Cambridge University Press, 2018.

———. "Defining Feminism: A Comparative Historical Approach." *Signs: Journal of Women in Culture and Society* 14 (Autumn 1988): 119–57.

———. "Depopulation, Nationalism, and Feminism Fin-de-Siècle France." *American Historical Review* 89 (June 1984): 648–76.

———. "Des modèls nationaux (1900–1945)." In Gubin et al., *Le siècle des féminismes*, 65–79.

———. "Ernest Legouvé and the Doctrine of 'Equality in Difference' for Women: A Case Study of Male Feminism in Nineteenth-Century French Thought." *Journal of Modern History* 58 (June 1986): 452–84.

———. *European Feminisms, 1700–1950: A Political History*. Stanford CA: Stanford University Press, 2000.

———. "The History of Feminism Is Political History." *Perspectives on History* (May 2011). https://www.historians.org/publications-and-directories /perspectives-on-history/may-2011/political-history-today/the-history -of-feminism-is-political-history.

———. *The Woman Question in France, 1400-1870.* Cambridge: Cambridge University Press, 2017.

———. "Women, Citizenship and Suffrage with a French Twist, 1789-1993." In *Suffrage and Beyond: International Feminist Perspectives,* edited by Caroline Daley and Melanie Nolan, 151-70. Auckland: Auckland University Press, 1994.

———. "Writing the History of Feminisms (Old and New): Impacts and Impatience." In *The Women's Liberation Movement: Impacts and Outcomes.* Edited by Kristina Schultz, 320-26. Berghahn Books, 2017.

Oliner, Marion Michel. *Cultivating Freud's Garden in France.* Northvale NJ: Jason Aranson, 1988.

Oliver, Kelly, and Lisa Walsh, eds. *Contemporary French Feminism.* Oxford: Oxford University Press, 2004.

Opello, Katherine A. R. *Gender Quotas, Parity Reform, and Political Parties in France.* Lanham MD: Lexington Books, 2006.

Organisation communiste gauche ouvrière et popularie. "Femmes exploitées, opprimées, ossons lutter." *Cahiers pour le communisme* 9 (October 1976): 1-104.

Ory, Pascal. *L'entre-deux-mai: Histoire culturelle de la France mai 1968-mai 1981.* Paris: Éditions du Seuil, 1983.

Ozouf, Mona. *Les mots des femmes: Essai sur la singularité française.* Paris: Éditions Fayard, 1995.

Parti communiste français. "La politique du Parti communiste français: Les femmes." *Dossiers du propagandiste,* no. 7. Paris: Parti communiste français, 1946.

———. *Semaine de la pensée marxiste de Lyon. La femme à la recherche d'elle-même.* France: Aubin Ligugé, 1965.

Parti socialiste, ed. *Femmes en lutte: Pour le droit à l'information sexuelle à la contraception et à l'interruption de grossesse.* Paris: Parti socialiste, 1979.

Pascal, George, and Henri Fabre. "Contraception et problèmes démographiques." *Partisans* 32-33 (October–November 1966-1967): 49-53.

Patience, Rose. "Psychanalyse et/ou politique." *L'alternative* 1 (June 1977): 76-79.

Patterson, Yolanda Astarita. *Simone de Beauvoir and the Demystification of Motherhood.* Ann Arbor MI: UMI Research Press, 1989.

Pavard, Bibia. *Les éditions des femmes: Histoire des premières années 1972-1979.* Paris: Éditions L'Harmattan, 2005.

Péchadre, Roudy. *La réussite de la femme.* Paris: Centre d'etude et de promotion de la lecture, 1970.

Pedersen, Susan. *Family, Dependence, and the Origins of the Welfare State: Britain and France 1914-1945.* Cambridge: Cambridge University Press, 1993.

Péquignot, Henri. "Simple remarques sur l'avortement." *Archives de médecine sociale* (March 1946): 175–81.

Perrot, Michelle. "Antoinette Fouque a un petit côté sectaire." *ProChoix* 46 (December 2008): 19–20.

———. "Écrire l'histoire des femmes: Récit dune expérience française." In *De l'égalité des sexes*, edited by Michel de Manassein, 48–59. Paris: Centre national de documentation pédagogique, 1995.

Philippon, Odette. *La jeunesse coupable vous accuse: Les causes familiales et sociales de la délinquance juvénile.* Paris: Librairie du Recueil Sirey, 1951.

———. *L'ésclavage de la femme dans le monde contemporain, ou la prostitution sans masque.* Paris: Librairie Pierre Téqui, 1954.

Picard, Jeanne. "L'indépendance économique de la femme." In Choisy et al., *Conscience de la féminité*, 153–61.

Picq, Françoise. "1970–1980 sauve qui peut, le MLF." *La revue d'en face* 11 (4th trimester 1981): 11–24.

———. "Du mouvement des femmes aux études feminists: 2001; Vingt-cinq ans d'études féministes." *Les cahiers du CEDREF* 10 (2001): 23–31. http://journals.openedition.org/cedref/430.

———. "'Le féminisme bourgeoise': Une théorie élaborée par les femmes socialistes avant la guerre de 14." In *Stratégies des femmes*, edited by Marie-Claire Pasquier, Marcelle Marini, Françoise Ducrocq, Geneviève Fraisse, and Anne-Marie Sohn, 391–406. Paris: Éditions Tierce, 1984.

———. "Le mouvement de libération des femmes et ses effets sociaux." Paris: ATP-GEF, 1987.

———. *Libération des femmes: Les années-mouvement.* Paris: Éditions du Seuil, 1993.

———. *Libération des femmes: Quarante ans de mouvement.* Brest: Éditions-dialogues, 2011.

———. "Parité, la nouvelle 'exception française." *Modern and Contemporary France* 10, no. 1 (February 2002): 13–23.

———. "Quelques réflexions à propos des études feminists." Actes du colloque national. *Femmes, féminisme et recherches*, 914–19, Toulouse, December 1982. Toulouse: AFFER, 1984.

———. "Simone de Beauvoir et 'la querelle du féminisme.'" *Les temps modernes* 647–648, no. 1 (2008): 169–85.

———. "Sur la théorie du droit maternel, discours anthropologiques et discours socialiste." PhD diss., Université de Paris IX, 1979.

———. "Two or Three Things about the Women's Movement in France since the 1970s." Paper presented at Colloque: Le féminisme en France, en Inde et en Russie, May 18–21, 1992, Paris.

Pingaud, Bernard. *L'avortement: Histoire d'un débat*. Paris: Éditions Flammarion, 1975.

Piton, Monique. *C'est possible*. Paris: Éditions des femmes, 1974.

Pivert, Marceau. *Correspondance socialiste: Réservé aux militants du Parti socialiste SFIO*. Paris: Section française de l'internationale ouvrière, 1947.

Pizan, Christine de. *Book of the City of Ladies*. New York: Persia Books, 1982.

Planté, Christine. "Questions de différences." *Futur antérieur*. Supplément: "Féminismes au présent." (March 1993): 111-31.

Plantey, Alain. *Prospective de l'etat*. Paris: Centre national de la recherche scientifique, 1975.

Plaza, Monique. "Pouvoir 'phalomorphique' et psychologie de 'la femme.'" *Questions féministes* 1 (November 1977): 91-119.

Pollard, Miranda. *Reign of Virtue: Mobilizing Gender in Vichy France*. Chicago: University of Chicago Press, 1998.

Popkin, Jeremy D. *A History of Modern France*. 4th ed. New York: Routledge, 2016.

"Pourquoi ce texte?" *Le torchon brûle* 5: 3-5.

"Pour une coordination horizontale des groups feminists autonomes." *L'information des femmes* 19 (October 1977): 19.

Pratique Politique et Psychanalyse. "C'est l'économie même de tout mouvement que d'être traversé, divisé par des contradictions." *des femmes en mouvements* 12 (December 1978-January 1979).

Praud, Jocelyne. "Gendering the Fifth Republic: The French Women's Movement at the Turn of the 21st Century." *Peace Research* 32, no. 4 (November 2000): 31-40.

"Préparation scolaire aux carrières féminine." *Avenirs* 93-95 (April-June 1958): 295-313.

Prigent, Robert, ed. *Renouveau des idées sur la famille*. Paris: Presses Universitaires de France, 1954.

Prudhomme, Madeleine. *Moi, une assistance sociale: Témoignes*. Paris: Éditions Stock, 1975.

Pulju, Rebecca. *Women and Mass Consumer Society in Postwar France*. Cambridge: Cambridge University Press, 2011.

Rabaut, Jean. *Histoire des féminismes françaises*. Paris: Éditions Stock, 1978.

Rameau, Pauline. "Pratiques illégales de l'avortement dans les années 68 à Dijon et à Saint-Étienne." *Vingtième siècle: Revue d'histoire* 3, no. 111 (2011): 133-46. https://www.cairn.info/revue-vingtieme-siecle-revue-d-histoire -2011-3-page-133.htm.

Ramsay, Raylene L. *French Women in Politics: Writing Power, Paternal Legitimization, and Maternal Legacies*. New York: Berghahn Books, 2000.

Rauch, William R. *Politics and Belief in Contemporary France: Emmanuel Mounier and Christian Democracy, 1932-1950*. The Hague: Martinis Hinjoff, 1970.

Rauze-Comignan, Marianne. *Pour la paix universelle*. Paris: Imprimerie moderne, 1949.

Ravelli, Catherine. "De l'intérêt de la féminitude pour le féminisme." *La revue d'en face* 4 (November 1978): 18-23.

Reader, Keith A. *Intellectuals and the Left in France since 1968*. London: Macmillan, 1987.

———. "Symbolic Violence in May 1968." Paper presented at the Annual Meeting for the Society for French Historical Studies, Atlanta, Georgia, 1995.

"Recruitment of Women Workers in France." *International Labour Review* 58, no. 2 (August 1948): 232-33.

Reineke, Sandra. *Beauvoir and Her Sisters: The Politics of Women's Bodies in France*. Urbana: University of Illinois Press, 2011.

Remy, Monique. *De l'utopie à l'intégration: Histoire des mouvements de femmes*. Paris: Éditions L'Harmattan, 1990.

———. "Le 'langage-femme': Naissance d'un concept, présupposés, implications." Actes du colloque national. *Femmes, féminisme et recherches*, 583-88. Toulouse, December 1982. Toulouse: AFFER, 1984.

Remy-Lallemand, Aude. "L'égalité dans le travail." CIDF *information* 13 (August 1983): 3-12.

Renard, Jean-Claude. "La vie comme une femme." *Esprit* 14, no. 118 (January 1946): 76-79.

Reynolds, Siân. *France between the Wars: Gender and Politics*. London: Routledge, 1996.

Ringart, Nadja. "La naissance d'une secte." In Association mouvement pour les luttes féministes, *Chroniques*, unpaginated.

Robcis, Camille. *The Law of Kinship: Anthropology, Psychoanalysis, and the Family in France*. Ithaca NY: Cornell University Press, 2013.

———. "Republicanism and the Critique of Human Rights." In Chabal, *France since the 1970s*, 225-44.

Roberts, Colin. "Secularization and the (Re)Formulation of French Catholic Identity." In Chadwick, *Catholicism, Politics and Society in Twentieth-Century France*, 260-79.

Roberts, Mary Louise. *Civilization without Sexes: Reconstructing Gender in Postwar France, 1917-1927*. Chicago: University of Chicago Press, 1994.

———. *What Soldiers Do: Sex and the American GI in World War II France*. Chicago: University of Chicago Press, 2013.

Robinson, Jean C. "Gendering the Abortion Debate: The French Case." In *Abortion Politics, Women's Movements, and the Democratic State: A Comparative Study of State Feminism*, edited by Dorothy McBride Stetson, 91–110. Oxford: Oxford University Press, 2005.

Rocard, Geneviève. *Sois belle et achète*. Paris: Éditions C. Gutman & Denoel-Gonthier, 1968.

———. "Sur le travail des femmes mariées." *Les temps modernes* 18, nos. 196–197 (September–October 1962): 459–508.

Rochefort, Christine (interview). "Le rôle laïcisateur." Translated by Carrie Noland. In Bard and Mossuz-Lavau, *Le planning familial*, 60–61.

Rolland, Gabrielle. *Seront-elles au rendez-vous? La nouvelle cause des femmes*. Paris: Éditions Flammarion, 1995.

Ross, George, and Laura Frader. "The May Generation: From Mao to Mitterrand." *Socialist Review* 4 (1988): 105–16.

Ross, Kristin. *Fast Cars, Clean Bodies: Decolonization and the Reordering of French Culture*. Cambridge MA: MIT Press, 1995.

———. *May '68 and its Afterlives*. Chicago: University of Chicago Press, 2002.

Rossiter, Margaret L. *Women in the Resistance*. New York: Praeger Special Studies, 1986.

Rouch, Hélène. "Recherches sur les femmes et recherches féministes: L'action thématique programmée du CNRS." *Les cahiers du CEDREF* 10 (2001): 103–12.

Roudinesco, Elisabeth. *Jacques Lacan: Esquisse d'une vie, histoire d'un système de pensée*. Paris: Éditions Fayard, 1993.

Roudy, Yvette. *A cause d'elles*. Paris: Éditions Albin Michel, 1985.

———. *La femme en marge*. Preface by François Mitterrand. Éditions Flammarion, 1975.

Roullet, Odile. "Les droits de la femme." *Revue de l'action populaire* 176 (March 1964): 293–301.

Rubellin-Devichi, Jacqueline. *L'evolution du statut civil de la famille depuis 1945*. Paris: CNRS, 1983.

Rudolph, Nicole C. *At Home in Postwar France: Modern Mass Housing and the Right to Comfort*. New York: Berghahn Books, 2015.

Salomon-Bayet, Claire. "La neutralité est impossible." *La nef* 17, no. 4 (October–December 1960): 12–19.

Salvaresi, Elisabeth. *Mai en héritage*. Paris: Éditions Syros Alternatives, 1988.

Sand, George. *Correspondance*. Vol. 20. Paris: Garnier, 1984.

Sanos, Sandrine. *Simone de Beauvoir: Creating a Feminist Existence in the World*. Oxford: Oxford University Press, 2016.

Sarazin, Michel. *Une femme: Simone Veil*. Paris: Éditions Robert Laffont, 1987.

Sartin, Pierrette. *La femme liberée?* Paris: Éditions Stock, 1968.

———. *La promotion des femmes.* Paris: Hachette, 1964.

———. "Le travail à temps partiel." *La nef* 26, no. 38 (October–December 1969): 37–43.

———. *Une femme à part entière.* Paris: Éditions Casterman, 1966.

Saumoneau, Louise. "Du droit au travail des femmes: Dans le monde ouvrier." *Propagande et documentation* 6 (2nd trimester 1947): 3–7.

———. "La femme et le socialisme." *Propagande et documentation* 5 (2nd trimester 1948): 3–7.

———. "Le devoir civique des femmes." *Propagande et documentation* 1 (2nd trimester 1947): 3–7.

Sauvy, Alfred. "Préface." In Prigent, *Renouveau des idées,* 9–18.

Sauvy, Alfred, and l'Institut national d'etudes démographiques. "The Housing Problem in France." *International Labour Review* 55, nos. 3–4 (March–April 1947): 225–46.

———. *Les travaux du haut comité consultatif de la population et de la famille en 1945.* Paris: Presses Universitaires de France, 1946.

Schnapp, Alain, and Pierre Vidal-Naquet. *The French Student Uprising November 1967–June 1968: An Analytical Record.* Translated by Maria Jolas. Boston: Beacon, 1971.

Schor, Naomi. "Cet essentialisme qui n'(en) est pas un: Irigaray à bras le corps." *Futur antérieur.* Supplément: Féminismes au présent. (1993): 85–109.

Schrift, Alan D. "Is There Such a Thing as 'French Philosophy'? Or Why Do We Read the French So Badly?" In Bourg, *After the Deluge,* 21–48.

Schwartz, Paula. "Redefining Resistance: Women's Activism in Wartime France." In Higonnet, *Behind the Lines,* 141–53.

Scioldo-Zürcher, Yann. "The Cost of Decolonization: Compensating the Pied Noirs." In Chabal, *France since the 1970s,* 99–114.

Scott, Joan W. *The Fantasy of Feminist History.* Durham NC: Duke University Press, 2011.

———. *Gender and the Politics of History.* New York: Columbia University Press, 1988.

———. *Only Paradoxes to Offer: French Feminists and the Rights of Man.* Cambridge: Cambridge University Press, 1996.

———. *Parité! Sexual Equality and the Crisis of French Universalism.* Chicago: University of Chicago Press, 1995.

———. *The Politics of the Veil.* Princeton NJ: Princeton University Press, 2007.

Section française de l'internationale ouvrière. *Sécurité sociale: Femme, connais tes droits.* Paris: SFIO, 1947.

Selous, Trista. *The Other Woman: Feminism and Femininity in the Work of Marguerite Duras*. New Haven CT: Yale University Press, 1988.

Sénac, Réjane. *L'égalité sous conditions: Genre, parité, diversité*. Paris: Presses de la Fondation nationale des science politiques, 2015.

Serre, Josiane. "Un instrument de promotion féminine: l'Ecole normale supérieure de jeunes filles (ex sèvres)." *Perspectives universitaires* 3, nos. 1-2 (1986): 50-58.

Servan-Schreiber, Claude. "Editorial." *F Magazine*, January 1978, 3.

Servan-Schreiber, J.-J. *The Spirit of May*. Translated by Ronald Steel. New York: McGraw-Hill, 1968.

Servin, Marcel. *Femmes de France! Vos difficultés et nos solutions: Un discours de Marcel Servin*. Paris: Parti communiste français, 1955.

———. *Le Parti communiste et la lutte des femmes de France pour la paix, l'indépendance nationale, et le progrès social: Rapport aux journées nationales des 2 et 3 février 1957 à Montreuil*. Paris: Parti communiste français, 1957.

Shepard, Todd. *The Invention of Decolonization: The Algerian War and the Remaking of France*. Ithaca NY: Cornell University Press, 2006.

———. "'Something Notably Erotic': Politics, 'Arab Men,' and Sexual Revolution in Post-Decolonization France, 1962-1974." *Journal of Modern History* 84 (March 2012): 80-115.

Sibalis, Michael. "And What Then About 'Our' Problem?—Gay Liberation in the Occupied Sorbonne in May 1968." In Jackson et al., *May '68*, 122-36.

———. "The Spirit of May '68 and the Origins of the Gay Liberation Movement in France." Frazier and Cohen, *Gender and Sexuality in 1968*, 235-53.

"Silence et émancipation des femmes entre privé et public." *Cahiers du CEDREF* 1 (1989).

Silverman, Debora. *Art Nouveau in Fin-de-Siècle France: Politics, Psychology, and Style*. Berkeley: University of California Press, 1989.

Simons, Margaret A. *Beauvoir and the Second Sex: Feminism, Race and the Origins of Existentialism*. Lanham MD: Rowman & Littlefield, 1999.

———, ed. *Feminist Interpretations of Simone de Beauvoir*. University Park: Pennsylvania State University Press, 1995.

Simons, Margaret A., and Marybeth Timmermann, eds. *Simone de Beauvoir: Feminist Writings*. Chicago: University of Illinois Press, 2015.

Sinclair, Barbara Deckland. *The Women's Movement: Political, Socioeconomic and Psychological Issues*. New York: Harper and Row, 1975.

Sineau Mariette. *Des femmes en politique*. Paris: Éditions Economica, 1988.

———. *La femme en marge*. Paris: Éditions Flammarion, 1975.

———. "Parité in Politics: From a Radical Idea to Consensual Reform." In Célestin et al., *Beyond French Feminisms*, 113–26.

Slama, Béatrice. "De la 'littérature féminine' à 'l'écrire-femme': Différence et institution." *Littérature* 44 (December 1981): 51–71.

Smith, Bonnie G. *Changing Lives: Women in European History since 1700*. Toronto: Heath, 1989.

"Social Security in France." *International Labour Review* 52, no. 5 (November 1945): 541–44.

Société française d'enquêt par sondages. *L'opinion française en 1977*. Paris: Presses de la FNSP, 1978.

Sohn, Anne-Marie. *Age tendre et tête de bois: Histoire des jeunes des années 1960*. Paris: Hachette, 2001.

Sorum, Paul Clay. *Intellectuals and Decolonization in France*. Chapel Hill: University of North Carolina Press, 1977.

Soubbotitch, Ivan. "Recent Important Reforms in the French Matrimonial Regime." *New York Law Forum* 12, no. 2 (Summer 1966): 245–56.

Sowerwine, Charles. *Sisters or Citizens? Women and Socialism in France since 1876*. Cambridge: Cambridge University Press, 1982.

Stavro, Elaine. "The Use and Abuse of Simone De Beauvoir: Re-Evaluating the French Poststructuralist Critique." *European Journal of Women's Studies* 6, no. 3 (1999): 263–80.

Steck, Philippe. "Les prestations familiales de 1946 à 1985: Ruptures ou constances?" *Extrait de la revue française des affaires sociales* 5 (July–September 1985): 1–38.

Stoetzel, Jean. "Les changements dans les fonctions familiales." In Prigent, *Renouveau des idées*, 343–69.

———. "L'étude du budget-temps de la femme dans les agglomérations urbaines." *Population* 3, no. 1 (1948): 47–62.

Storti, Martine. "Giscard: Le temps des électrices." *F Magazine*, December 1980, 58–59.

Stuart, Mary Lynn. *For Health and Beauty: Physical Culture for Frenchwomen, 1880s–1930s*. Baltimore MD: John Hopkins University Press, 2001.

Sullerot, Évelyne. *Demain les femmes: Inventaire de l'avenir*. Paris: Laffont-Gonthier, 1965.

———. *Droit de regard*. Paris: Éditions Denoël Gonthier, 1970.

———. *Le fait féminin*. Paris: Éditions Fayard, 1978.

Sullerot, Évelyne, Jacqueline Chabaud, and Claude Ulin. *L'amour . . . et, rien d'autre?* Paris: Éditions Fleurus, 1969.

Sullerot, Évelyne, with the journal Femmes d'aujourd'hui. *Les françaises au travail: Enquête*. Paris: Hachette, 1973.

Sweatman, Jennifer L. *The Risky Business of French Feminism: Publishing, Politics, and Artistry*. Lanham MD: Lexington Books, 2014.

"Syndiquées à la CGT." *Cahiers du féminisme 7* (December 1978–January 1979): 10–18.

Tapinos, George Photios. "Immigration féminine et statut des femmes étrangères en France." *Revue française des affaires sociale* 46 (December 1992): 29–60.

Texier, Geneviève. "Virilité et fémininité, pseudo-concepts." *La nef* 18, no. 5 (January–March 1961): 81–93.

Thébaud, Françoise. "Réflexions sur la nature du MFPF." In Bard and Mossuz-Lavau, *Le planning familial*, 93–108.

Thévenot, Isabelle. "La formation des femmes: Plus qu'une révolution un combat quotidien." *Des comités et entreprise et sciences sociaux* 264 (November 1984): 49–54.

Thiam, Awa. *La parole aux négresses*. Paris: Denoël, 1978.

Thibaut, Josy. "Entretien: Monique Witting raconte." *ProChoix* 46 (December 2008): 63–76.

Thompson, Paul. *The Voice of the Past: Oral History*. Oxford: Oxford University Press, 1978.

Thorez-Vermeersch, Jeannette. "Pour la défense des droits sociaux de la femme et de l'enfant: Rapport et conclusions de Jeannette Thorez-Vermeersch." In *Rapport et conclusions à la réunion des responsables du travail parmi les femmes*. Nanterre, October 24–25, 1964.

Tidd, Ursula. *Simone de Beauvoir*. London: Reaktion Books, 2012.

———. *Simone de Beauvoir, Gender and Testimony*. Cambridge: Cambridge University Press, 2004.

Tippett-Spirtou, Sandy. *French Catholicism: Church, State and Society in a Changing Era*. New York: Palgrave Macmillian, 2000.

Touraine, Alain. *The May Movement: Revolt and Reform—the Student Rebellion and Workers' Strikes—the Birth of a Social Movement*. Translated by Leonard F. X. Mayhew. New York: Random House, 1971.

Tranvouez, Yvon. "Left Catholicism and Christian Progressivism in France: 1944–1955." In *Catholicism 1945–1955: Catholics and Society in Western Europe at the Point of Liberation*, edited by Gerd-Rainer Horn and Emmanuel Gerard. Leuven: Leuven University Press, 2001.

Tristan, Anne, and Annie de Pisan. *Histoires du MLF*. Paris: Éditions Calman-Levy, 1977.

Turkle, Sherry. *Psychoanalytic Politics: Jacques Lacan and Freud's French Revolution*. 2nd ed. New York: Guilford Press, 1992.

"Une interview de Gisèle Halimi: 'Pourquoi le Programme commun des femmes; Pourquoi Choisir sera présent aux élections législatives?'" *Choisir: La cause des femmes* 29 (December 1977): 9.

Union nationale des caisses d'allocations familiales. *Eléments d'une politique de la famille:* Enquête. Paris: uncaf, 1948.

"Un groupe femmes sur un pré un beau Dimanche de mai." *Les femmes s'entêtent*, 349.

Vailland, Geneviève. *Le travail des femmes*. Paris: Centre des jeunes patrons, 1947.

Vaillant-Couturier, Marie-Claude. "Amies de la paix." *Femmes françaises* 92 (July 6, 1946): 1.

———. "Les femmes contre le fascisme." *Cahiers de communisme* 34, no. 9 (September 1958): 1343-51.

Valabrègue, Catherine. *Contrôle des naissances et planning familial*. Paris: La Table ronde, 1966.

———. *Eux, les hommes: Témoignes*. Paris: Éditions Stock, 1976.

van der Poel, Ieme. *Une révolution de la pensée: Maoïsme et féminisme à travers Tel Quel, Les Temps modernes et Esprit*. Amsterdam: Éditions Rodopi, 1992.

"Variations sur des themes communs: Une revue théorique féministe radicale." *Questions féministes* 1 (November 1977): 3-19.

Varikas, Eleni. "Féminisme, modernité, postmodernisme: Pour un dialogue des deux côtés de l'ocean." In *Futur antérieur*. Supplément: Féminismes au présent (1993): 59-84.

Vauthier, Germaine. "Famille et socialisme." *La revue socialiste* 142 (April 1961): 538-48.

———. "Famille responsable." *La revue socialiste* 129 (January 1960): 58-73.

Veil, Simone. *A Life*. London: Haus, 2009.

Vendeuil, Richard de. "La longue marche des femmes ingénieurs." *L'éxpress*, November 2-9, 1995, 2-3

Verdès-Leroux, Jeannine, and Odile Benoît-Guibot. "A propos de 'Travail féminin et revendications féministes.'" *Sociologie du travail* 3 (1974): 319-22.

Vermeersch, Jeannette. "Femmes: Rassemblez-vous pour vous défendre; Pour défendre vos enfants . . . vos foyers . . . la paix." Discours à l'l'assemblée de l'Alhambra, Paris, December 9, 1959.

———. "Les enseignements du 9 mars et l'activité des femmes communistes dans la lutte pour la paix." *Cahiers du communisme* 29, no. 5 (May 1952): 469-79.

———. "Les femmes dans la nation: Rapport." XIe Congrès national du Parti communiste français. Strasbourg, June 25-28, 1947. Paris: Éditions du Parti communiste français, 1947.

Vermeersch, Jeanette, and Jean Fréville. *La femme et le communisme: Anthologie des grands textes du marxisme*. Paris: Éditions sociales, 1950.

Vicky, "Harmonie ou si l'homosexualité m'était contée." In Beauvoir, *Les femmes s'entêtent*, 398–403.

Vieille-Michel, Andrée. "Famille, société industrielle et démocratie." *Esprit* 28, no. 289 (November 1960): 1754–72.

Viennot, Éliane. "Féminisme et partis politiques: Une greffe impossible." *Nouvelles questions féministes* 2 (October 1981): 35–46.

Viennot, Éliane, with Marie-Claire Boons. *C'est terrible, quand on y pense.* Paris: Galilée, 1983.

Viens, Yann. "Femmes, politique, Parti communiste français." In *La condition féminine*, edited by CERM Collective, 347–82. Paris: Éditions sociales, 1978.

Vilaine, Anne-Marie de, Laurence Gavarini, and Michèle Le Coadic, eds. *Maternité en mouvement: Les femmes, la re/production et les hommes de science*. Grenoble: Presses Universitaires de Grenoble, 1986.

Villeneuve, Bernard, and François-Henri de Virieu. *Le nouveau pouvoir: Les 1100 qui conduisent la France aujourd'hui*. Paris: Éditions Jean-Claude Lattès, 1981.

Vincendeau, Ginette. "The Old and the New: Brigitte Bardot in 1950s France." *Paragraph* 15, no. 1 (March 1992): 73–96. http://www.jstor.org /stable/43151735.

Vincent, Madeleine. *Femmes: Quelle libération?* Paris: Éditions sociales, 1976.

———. "Femmes: Un débat ouvert." *Cahiers du communisme* 9 (September 1970): 102–12.

———. "La restauration de la démocratie et le droit des femmes." *Cahiers du communisme* 1 (January 1960): 20–38.

———. "Pour changer la situation de la femme." *Cahiers du communisme* 49, nos. 1–2 (January–February 1973): 149–54.

———. "Pour la reduction du temps de travail des femmes." *Cahiers du communisme* 41, no. 2 (February 1965): 21–30.

Vincent, Madeleine, and Georges Marchais. *La femme aujourd'hui, demain: Que propose le Parti communiste français*. Paris: Le Parti communiste français, 1970.

———. "Pour la femme: Une vie heureuse, libre et responsable dans l'égalité." Rapport de Madeleine Vincent. Session du Comité central du PCF, November 9–10, 1976. Paris: PCF, 1976.

Vinteuil, Frédérique. "De psychanalyse et politique *à femmes en mouvement, hebdo*." *Cahiers du féminisme* 14 (Summer 1980): 5–9.

"Vocational Guidance and Training for Women." *International Labour Review* 66 (July–December 1952): 56–76.

Voldman, Danièle. "Mai '68 ou la féministe refusée." *La nouvelle revue social-*
iste (August–September 1985): 41–47.

Voldman, Danièle, and Sylvie Vandecasteele-Schweitzer. "The Oral Sources
for Women's History." In *Writing Women's History*, edited by Michelle Perrot, 41–50. Oxford: Blackwell, 1992.

Voreppe, Charlène. "Mères avant tout? L'image des femmes dans la Sec-
onde Guerre mondiale à travers la presse de la Libération." Master's
thesis, Université de Grenoble, 2012, http://journals.openedition.org
/genrehistoire/1744.

Wadia, Khursheed. "Women and the Events of May." In *The May 1968 Events*
in France: Reproductions and Interpretations, edited by Keith A. Reader and
Khursheed Wadia, 148–66. London: St. Martin's Press, 1993.

"Wage Increases in Liberated France." *International Labour Review* 51, no. 5
(May 1985): 589–612.

Webster, Paul, and Nicholas Powell. *Saint-Germain-des-Prés*. London: Con-
stable, 1984.

Weiner, Susan. *Enfants Terribles: Youth and Femininity in the Mass Media in*
France, 1945–1968. Baltimore MD: Johns Hopkins University Press, 2001.

Weitz, Eric D. "The Heroic Man and the Ever-Changing Woman: Gender and
Politics in European Communism, 1917–1950." In *Gender and Class in*
Modern Europe, edited by Laura L. Frader and Sonya O. Rose. Ithaca NY:
Cornell University Press, 1996.

Wilkinson, James D. *The Intellectual Resistance in Europe*. Cambridge MA: Harvard University Press, 1981.

Williams, Philip. *Politics in Post War France: Parties and the Constitution in the*
Fourth Republic. London: Longmans Green 1954.

Wittig, Monique. "La pensée straight." *Questions féministes* 7 (February
1980): 45–53.

———. *Les guérillères*. Translated by David Le Vay. Boston: Beacon, 1971.

———. "On ne naît pas femme." *Questions féministes* 8 (May 1980): 75–84.

Wittig, Monique, Giles Wittig, Marcia Rothenburg, and Margaret Stephenson. "Combat pour la libération de la femme." *L'idiot international* 6 (May
1970): 13–16.

Zakin, Emily. "Beauvoir's Unsettling of the Universal." In Marso, *Simone de*
Beauvoir's Political Thinking, 31–54.

Zancarini-Fournel, Michelle. *Le moment '68: Une histoire contestée*. Paris: Éditions du Seuil, 2008.

———. "Les feminismes: Des movements autonomes?" In Gubin et al., *Le siè-*
cle des féminismes, 227–38.

———. "Notre corps, nous mêmes." In Gubin et al., *Le siècle des féminismes*, 209-20.

Zancarini-Fournel, Michelle, Florence Rochefort, and Bibia Pavard. *Les lois Veil: Les événements fondateurs; Contraception 1974, IVG 1975*. Paris: Librairie Armand Colin, 2012.

Zarrouk, Claire. "Femmes: Un échec." *Politique hebdo*, March 18-24, 1978.

Zelensky (Tristan), Anne. *Histoire de vivre: Mémoires d'une féministe*. Paris: Éditions Calmann-Lévy, 2005.

Zelensky, Anne. "Projet de recherche sur femme-publicité-sexisme, proposé par une femme de la Ligue du droit des femmes au Ministère des droits de la femme et subventionné par celui-ci." Actes du colloque national. *Femmes, féminisme et recherches*, 595-99. Toulouse, December 1982. Toulouse: affer, 1984.

Zylberberg-Hocquard, Marie-Hélène. *Femmes et féminisme dans le mouvement ouvrière français*. Paris: Éditions ouvrières, 1981.

INDEX

Éditions *des femmes* (publishing house), 199, 200, 209, 218–23, 317n65, 320nn17–18

education: greater female presence in, 62–63; religious vs. secular, 5; tailored for women, 34–35, 284n26

Elle (magazine), 126–30

Elles voient rouges (journal), 195, 199

employment of women: arguments against, 35, 284–85n27; and child care, 36–37, 61, 112–13; full time, as essential for women's liberation, 104–5; increasing numbers of employed women, 298n35; inequality and discrimination, 60–61, 86–87, 109–10, 199; and maternity leave, 60, 190; occupations, 60, 97, 288n11; strikes, F3, 241–42; suggestions for reform of, 88–89; wages, 36, 59, 60, 240–41

Engels, Friedrich, 105, 115, 297n25

"L'ennemi principal" (The Main Enemy) (Delphy), 103, 135

equality: in 1946 Constitution, 42, 285n43; Beauvoir on, 50–51; in difference, 34–35, 45–46, 47–48, 52, 129–30, 141, 268–69; futility in fight for, 211; and parity, 188, 273–75, 278, 328n42; pretense of, 37, 44–45, 262, 273; radical, 113; between spouses, 64–71; through suffrage, 37–38. *See also* employment of women

essentialism, 50, 204, 205, 206, 275. *See also* particularism

États généraux de la femme (Estates-General of Women), 126–30

existentialism, 49, 197. *See also* individualism

Eyquem, Marie-Thérèse, 100, 240

Fabian, Françoise, 158

Fabre, Henri, 80

Le fait féminin (Sullerot), 199

familialism and natalism: fused with republicanism, 46–48; government policies supporting, 27–29, 36–37, 41, 61–62, 168, 285n30, 288–89nn15–16; importance of femininity for, 34; and patriarchal authority, 65, 68–70, 211. *See also* abortion; contraception

Fauré, Christine, 249

Fauret, Anne-Marie, 147

Feldman-Hogasen, Jacqueline, 101, 111–12, 116, 121, 136

feminine republicanism: ideology of, 37; importance of civic participation, 40–41, 43–45; upholding of femininity and gender roles, 45–46, 52–54

feminine writing: as concept, 195; criticism of, 196–98; ideologies in, 201–7

femininity and womanhood: and individualism, 95–96, 114, 116, 197–98; and natural order, 34–35, 47–48, 50–54, 141, 197–99; postwar, 26–27; and repression, 203–4; as social construct, 49, 50, 196–99; in state of flux, 89–90; as unfixed signifier, 203

Féminin-masculin-avenir. *See* FMA (Féminin-masculin-avenir)

feminism: definitions of, 11, 19–20; misconceptions of French, 12–13; scholarship on French, 15–16, 17; as term, 18–20; in United States,

Marzellier, Françoise, 89, 90, 295n86
materialist feminism, 10. *See also* radical feminism
Maternité heureuse (Happy Motherhood), 8, 77–78. *See also* MFPF (Mouvement français pour le planning familial)
maternity leave, 60, 190
Mauriac, François, 49
May 1968: broader context of, 94–99, 296n8; feminists' criticism of leftist politics, 110–16; women's social frustrations behind events of, 107–10, 116–19
Mazeaud, Henri, 67
Mazur, Amy, 204, 250–51, 260
McBride, Dorothy, 260
MDF (Mouvement démocratique féminin), 99–101, 114
Mendras, Henri, 327n23
Merleau-Ponty, Maurice, 49
Messmer, Pierre, 163
MFPF (Mouvement français pour le planning familial), 8, 77–78, 80, 166, 176–77
Michel, Andrée: cooperative approach of, 91; on family planning, 79; on feminist analysis, 255; influential role of, 9; as member of MDF, 100; on politics and political involvement, 63–64, 89; on prejudice, 88
Mignonnes, allons voir sous la rose . . . (journal), 195, 200–201, 315n28
Millett, Kate, 107
Ministry of Women (Ministre déléguée aux droits de la femme), 1–2, 246–48
Mitterrand, François, 83, 127, 164, 185, 200, 244–45, 247, 248, 249, 251, 312n8

MLAC (Mouvement pour la liberté de l'avortement et la contraception), 159, 163, 177–78, 246, 311n63
MLF (Mouvement de libération des femmes): conflicts in and shortcomings of, 150–52, 172, 174–76, 178, 179–81, 210–14, 259–68, 317n72; co-opted by Psych-et-Po, F6, 224–33; disinterest in, 260, 270–73; ideology of, vii, 93; loose organization of, 130–31; march at Arc de Triomphe, F1, 126, 142; relationship with MFPF and MLAC, 176–78; support for abortion legalization, 156–57, 158, 160–61, 165–66, 171, 306n10; as term, 19. *See also* feminine writing; feminist press; lesbianism and homosexuality; Marxist feminism; materialist feminism; politics and government; Psych-et-Po (Psychanalyse et Politique; Psychoanalysis and Politics); radical feminism
Monod, Jacques, 162
Montrelay, Michèle, 201
morality, and sexuality, 81, 167, 168–69
Moreau, Gisèle, 165, 322n50
Morgan, Robin, 106, 107
Mossuz-Lavau, Janine, 17, 278
Mother's Day protest, F5, 135, 175–76
Mounier, Emmanuel, 47, 284n23
Mouvement de libération des femmes. *See* MLF (Mouvement de libération des femmes)
Mouvement démocratique féminin (MDF) (Democratic Women's Movement), 99–101, 114

266–67; Fouque's criticism of, 141, 303n40; ideology of, 133–36; and political involvement, 189–94, 233–38, 244, 245. *See also* separatism

Ramsay, Raylene, 274

rape, 178–80, 191, 210. *See also* sexual assault

Rassemblement démocratique révolutionnaire (RDR) (Revolutionary Democratic Rally), 68, 290n27, 293n66

Rassemblement du peuple français (RPF), 30, 41

Rauze-Comignan, Marianne, 33, 43, 48

Reader, Keith, 95, 299n50

Rebes, Roger, 101

Réforme (magazine), 81

régime dotal (dowry regime), 65

reproductive rights. *See* abortion; contraception

republicanism. *See* feminine republicanism

Revolutionary Feminists (Féministes révolutionnaires), 133–35, 303n40

La revue d'en face (journal), 198–99, 316n57

Ringart, Nadja, 144–45, 151, 229

Rocard, Michel, 200

Rochefort, Christiane, 12, 103, 162

Rochefort, Florence, 4

Rogerat, Chantal, 110, 298n38

Rolland, Gabrielle, 268–69

Ross, George, 259–60

Rostand, Jean, 162

Roudy, Yvette, F9, 58; commitment to both socialism and feminism, 185–86; influenced by Beauvoir,

58, 106; involvement in politics, 155, 233, 240, 243, 245–46, 250–51, 301n6; involvement with Estates-General revision, 127; involvement with MDF, 100, 101

Roussel, Nelly, 7

Roussopoulos, Carole, 219, 220

Russier, Gabrielle, 118

Salomon-Bayet, Claire, 89–90

Salvaresi, Elisabeth, F4

Sarachild, Kathie, 121

Sartin, Pierrette, 57

Sartre, Jean-Paul, 255–56

Saumoneau, Louise, 39, 200

Sauvageot, Jacques, 96–97

Sauvy, Alfred, 25, 32, 34, 76, 84

Schwarzer, Alice, 135–36, 297n22

Scott, Joan, 275, 277

The Second Sex (Beauvoir), vii, 8, 18, 25, 49–51, 105–6; impact of, 50–53, 58, 88–89, 92, 251

Secrétariat d'etat à la condition féminine (Secretary of state for the "feminine condition"), 173–75, 310n51

Seé (Camille) law, 5

separatism: criticism of, 269–70; as essential to feminist movement, 114–16, 192, 265; lesbian, 212–13, 266–68, 318n76

Serre, Janine, F1

Servan-Schreiber, Claude, 206

sexage, 196

sexual assault, 151, 178–80, 191. *See also* rape

sexuality: demand for sexual liberation, 116–19, 146–50, 212–13, 297n23; FMA on, 105; and morality, 81, 167,

voting. *See* suffrage

Wadia, Khursheed, 295n1

Weiss, Louise, 9, 127, 301n6

Wittig, Monique, F4, 147, 149, 201, 202-3, 266

womanhood. *See* femininity and womanhood

Women's Common Program, 235-38

women's movement: support for employment reform, 88-89; support for legalization of abortion, 74-76, 80-81, 82-83, 292-93n63, 293n66; support for legalization of contraception, 74-80, 82-83, 291n49, 293n66; support for Civil Code reform, 64, 66-71, 289n22, 290n25; as term, 18-19. *See also* feminine republicanism

Zelensky, Anne: cooperative approach of, 155; criticism of Choisir, 323n53; experience of oppression, 111-12; on feminist factions, 131, 317n72; involvement with FMA, 101, 103, 119; publications of, 121; on separatism, 115-16